The Big Idea

The Big Idea

How Breakthroughs of the Past Shape the Future

Foreword by Timothy Ferris

NATIONAL GEOGRAPHIC

WASHINGTON, D.C.

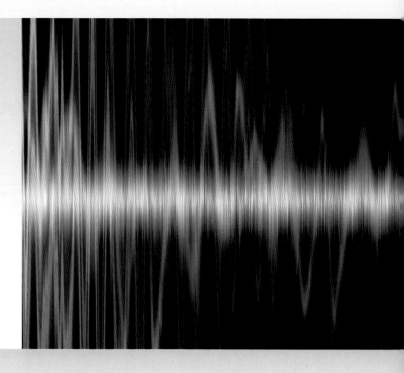

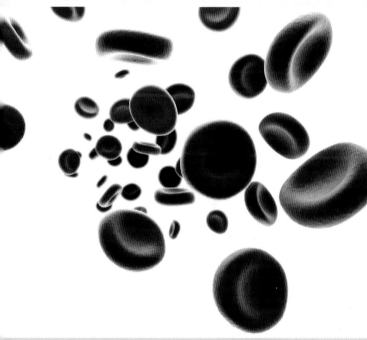

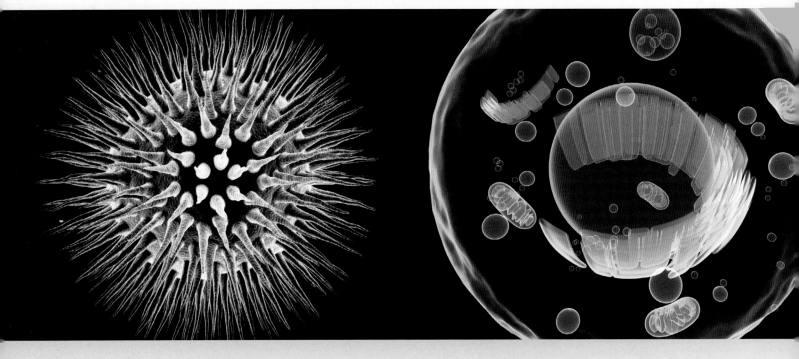

CHEMISTRY & MATERIALS   156

BIOLOGY & THE ENVIRONMENT   204

The original big ideas came from innovative men and women whose names are long lost. No monuments commemorate the inventors of the bowl, the dugout canoe, or the wheel, nor those who first planted crops, smelted copper, or etched marks into wet clay to inaugurate writing. Yet their legacies are all around us, in the foundations of the modern world.

With the advent of writing, big ideas came to be regarded as the providence of big thinkers. These intellectuals, as they were called, contributed valuable insights but seldom discovered or invented anything. Instead they analyzed and rearranged the relatively few facts that were then known, like jailhouse card sharks forever shuffling the same deck of cards.

Science and technology did not so much build on the intellectual tradition as react against it, returning to the habits of hands-on tinkering that characterized prehistoric innovation. Pioneering scientists like Galileo, Gilbert, Harvey, and Newton had little use for scholarly analysis of venerable opinions. They were more apt to agree with Francis Bacon, the great 17th-century prophet of science, who likened his Cambridge professors to "becalmed ships; they never move but by the wind of other men's breath."

The scientists preferred to find new facts, such as how gravity and magnetism work, how blood circulates through the human body, and how planets orbit the sun. Their points of reference came less from reading old books than from experimentation and observation—what Galileo called reading "the book of nature."

The result of their campaign was an unprecedented improvement in the lives of people around the world. Prior to the scientific and technological revolutions, the average human being was illiterate, earned a few hundred dollars a year, and was unlikely to survive to see age 30. Today, over 80 percent of all adults are literate, the global median annual income exceeds $7,000, and life expectancy at birth is approaching age 70. All this happened so quickly, measured against the long shadows of our history and prehistory, that many people don't yet realize that it has happened.

I keep on my desk a Neanderthal hand ax, chipped from a piece of obsidian some 34,000 years ago. It's a good ax; pick it up and you immediately start imagining all sorts of things you could do with it, from cutting meat to defending yourself to making another ax. That spirit, of learning and being inspired through direct physical interrogation of nature, is the real impetus behind science and technology alike.

Bacon, writing at the dawn of modern science, argued that experimenters "are like the ant; they only collect and use,"

whereas logicians "resemble spiders, who make cobwebs out of their own substance.

"But the bee takes a middle course," Bacon wrote. "It gathers its material from the flowers of the garden and of the field, but transforms and digests it by a power of its own."

Time proved Bacon right. Scientists today are so immersed in technology, and technologists in science, that it can be difficult to trace where one ends and the other begins. This messy process satisfies the neat prescriptions of neither scholars nor priests, but its results speak for themselves: More facts are now discovered in a decade than were once acquired in a century.

Were Bacon alive today he might compare global science and technology to fields of wildflowers fertilized by bees: astonishing in their variety, yet each part testifying to the nature of the whole. The volume you are holding is a way into that excitement and splendor. Welcome, in short, to a beehive of a book.

—Timothy Ferris

Idea Sourcing
A network of a hundred billion nerve cells composes the human brain, out of which big ideas, together with corollaries and contradictions, have been springing for many thousands of years.

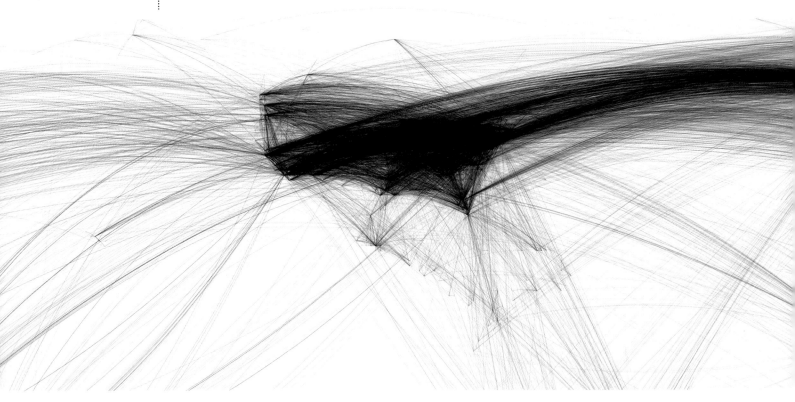

Most history books begin at what we customarily call the beginning—long ago, or not so long ago—and move through time in what we customarily call a forward motion—from the distant past to the more recent past, and ultimately to the present. Past to present: That's the way we are used to writing and reading history.

This book turns that convention on its head. Here, we begin with the present, or even the future, and track back, with each turn of the page stepping farther back into the past. It's as if you were asked to tell your own life story, and you began with what is happening now and then moved back in time to talk about your adolescence, and then your childhood, and then your birth.

You could say, in fact, that this book tells 24 such life stories: the fascinating and intertwining stories of 24 of the biggest ideas in science and technology today—24 life-changing innovations, destined to shape our future in ways that we can only begin to imagine.

Every one of these innovations builds on the ideas, experiments, observations, and constructions that preceded it. There would be no electric car were it not for the induction motor, or the generation and storage of electricity, or the smelting of iron, or the invention of the wheel. The point of this book is to make such connections, across all realms of experience and through the centuries.

ACROSS ALL REALMS
To guide our readers through this journey back in time, we have divided the world of big ideas into six realms of science and technology, which correspond to the chapters of this book:

- **Information & Communication,** which includes computing and broadcasting;
- **Health & Medicine,** with a focus on the human body;
- **Physics & the Cosmos,** which includes observations of outer space, principles governing the physical world on Earth, and lessons learned through their correspondences;
- **Chemistry & Materials,** the analysis, synthesis, and manipulation of matter;
- **Biology & the Environment,** the understanding of the world we live in;
- **Transportation & Space Exploration,** the many ways human beings have found to move and explore.

No such division into categories works perfectly, so we have kept an eye out for opportunities to show how influences and inventions cross these category lines. Cross-referencing notes indicate these connections throughout the book.

THROUGH THE CENTURIES
The baseline of every chapter is a reverse-chronological time line.

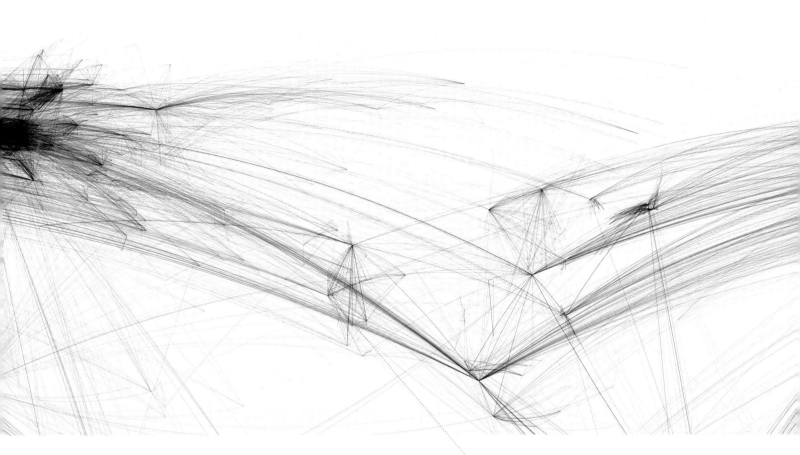

Idea Networking
With billions of potential nodes transmitting and receiving information around the world, conceptually mapped here, the Internet forms a constellation of connections along which ideas travel.

Each time line plots the important innovations, significant developments, or breakthrough events in that realm: the stepping stones of science and technology on which the big ideas of today and tomorrow build. The dates on each time line begin close to the present day and move back through time, sometimes by only a few years, or by decades, or even by centuries, backtracking through the flow of influence.

Labels identify each breakthrough on the time line as either "in use" or "in theory," since both form critical moments in the history of science and engineering. The pace of progress varies from one realm to another. Enlightenment thinkers of the 18th century made inroads essential to one field, while in another field, achievements cluster in the late 19th or early 20th century.

No flow of scientific and technological accomplishment happens independently of other fields. So while we divided that flow into six realms—the six chapters of this book—we bring all together in a concluding section that displays every landmark event, from today on back to prehistory, in a single time line (pages 302-309).

24 BIG IDEAS

Each of the six chapters in this book introduces four big ideas—innovations destined to change the shape of your world tomorrow and into the future. Appearing every ten pages or so, on facing pages, these introductions punctuate the chapter time lines. Were we to place them on the time lines, they would cluster at the very beginning—at the point that represents the present day; we decided instead to scatter them through each chapter as break-out features that remind you of the ways in which ideas of the future interact with ideas of the past.

Some of these big ideas are part of everyday life already—cloud computing, for example, on which many of us depend every day as we save, send, and share material through the Internet. Some ideas are very much a part of research science today but not so familiar to the everyday citizen—underwater exploration, for example, which continues to probe deeper and into unknown realms of our planet's oceans.

Still others reside as yet in the realm of ideas only—terraforming other planets, for example, a project that has drawn much engineering imagination but has yet to be put into actual practice. That it is a theory only, rather than something we use today, does not diminish the importance or influence of this big idea. As this book shows, theories from the past become the adopted realities of the future, and the big ideas of today will surely become the big accomplishments of tomorrow.

Two Kinds of Pages

Here we highlight all the features in this book. There are two kinds of pages: the time line pages with breakthroughs and the big idea pages. They differ in several ways, but they work together.

Time Line Spreads

Event Dates
Along the time line running through the center of every page, a tick mark indicates a key date for the landmark event described below it.

Kind of Event
Was it a theory proposed and proved? Or was it an innovation put to use in the real world? Labels specify each breakthrough as either "In Theory" or "In Use."

Profile
Meet the people behind the big ideas of today and yesterday in brief biographical profiles.

Connection or Backlash
Progress does not always travel in a straight line. Sometimes advancements from different realms converge: We label those "Connection." Sometimes social forces hinder progress: We label those "Backlash."

Building On
What ideas and innovations form the necessary groundwork for this landmark accomplishment? Whenever possible, cross-references here link backward and forward.

Big Idea Spreads

Big Idea Signal

Look for the yellow rectangle in the upper left-hand corner of the page. It signals a break in the time line with a big idea. Big ideas are numbered 1 to 24 through the book.

Mini Time Line

What landmark events paved the way to this big idea? Learn more about each big idea's precursors in the mini time line provided with every big idea.

Information & Communication

BIG IDEAS

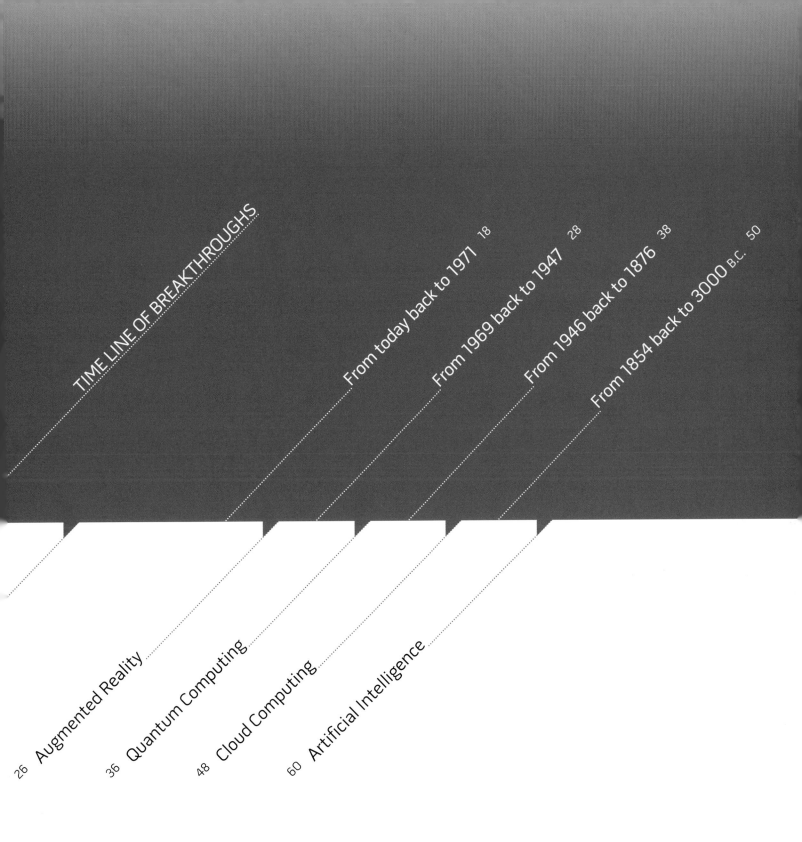

TIME LINE OF BREAKTHROUGHS

From today back to 1971 18

From 1969 back to 1947 28

From 1946 back to 1876 38

From 1854 back to 3000 B.C. 50

INTRODUCTION

Sending Signals

Electronic, wireless information and communication technologies are ubiquitous in today's world. However, just a generation ago, cell phones, the Internet, and personal computers were not a part of everyday life—although each had been invented. What were the key ideas behind these world-altering technologies? How did they evolve from earlier theories, discoveries, and inventions over the course of several centuries? What does the future of information technology look like in the 21st century?

Ideas never develop in isolation. Rather, they build on one another. Since the 17th century a sophisticated understanding of binary numbers has played a central role in both computer and telecommunications technologies. Computers are logic machines that operate on Boolean logic, which was invented in the 19th century. In the 1930s the theoretical idea known as a Turing machine revealed what it was possible to do with computers—although it preceded nearly all computing devices. The computer known as ENIAC—built in the 1940s, and which the U.S. Army used to calculate artillery-firing tables—was made of more than 17,000 vacuum tubes; it weighed more than 30 tons. The transistor, which replaced the vacuum tube, was invented not long after ENIAC, and the integrated circuit—the basis of today's microprocessor—a decade later, making the personal computer a possibility, although not a reality until the 1970s.

Where does the story go from there? Smaller, faster, cheaper—and the world is increasingly connected by way of the infrastructure known as the Internet. Now efforts are under way to exploit the laws of quantum mechanics to develop computers whose information-processing power could far exceed that of non-quantum computers; the Internet is being harnessed to create cloud-computing applications; and, with some success, computer programs are being created that have the ability to learn.

A continuous thread is evident in the history of communication technologies: the ability to send and receive electric signals in increasingly sophisticated ways. The telegraph, invented in the 1830s, was a breakthrough. For the first time, it was possible to communicate over long distances at an unimaginably fast speed. Radio waves were discovered in the second half of the 19th century—and they are the basis for wireless communications today. In the late 1940s—about a decade after the formulation of Turing theory—mathematician Claude Shannon developed a mathematical theory of communication now known as information theory, which forms the foundation of nearly all modern electronic communications. Making its way into peoples' lives today is augmented reality—a union of computer and communications technologies that exploits the global positioning system, wireless communication, and the ever smaller yet increasingly powerful computational devices.

Linux Operating System ....

Linus Torvalds was 21
when he developed the
Linux "kernel" in 1994.

From today back to 1971 >

1994 >

Linux Operating System

● IN USE

The Linux operating system revolutionized the world of software. Finnish software engineer Linus Torvalds created Linux, which was released to the public in 1994. The "kernel" is the heart of Linux and the center around which this operating system revolves. What makes Linux unique is the fact that the code is open source—it is freely available to anyone under a general public license such as GNU, a free license for software and other kinds of works. Users can manipulate it as they choose so that it suits their needs for both commercial and noncommercial purposes.

What was initially dismissed by critics as a "hobby" unsuitable for the general public's computing needs has been adopted throughout the world. Linux has proved to be a viable alternative to proprietary operating systems like Unix and Microsoft Windows because it is stable, robust, and can be adapted for use in a wide range of computing situations. IBM and Hewlett-Packard are two of the major organizations that have embraced Linux.

Typically Linux is packaged in a format known as a Linux distribution for desktop and server use. Commonly used applications with desktop Linux systems include the Mozilla Firefox Web browser, the OpenOffice.org office application suite, and the GIMP image editor.

Today, use of Linux in home and office desktop systems is increasing. In addition, Linux can be incorporated directly into microchips in a process called embedding; the system is increasingly being used this way in various appliances and devices—from mobile phones and tablet computers to mainframes and supercomputers.

Tux, penguin mascot of Linux

Building On >

Personal Computer *(p. 22)*

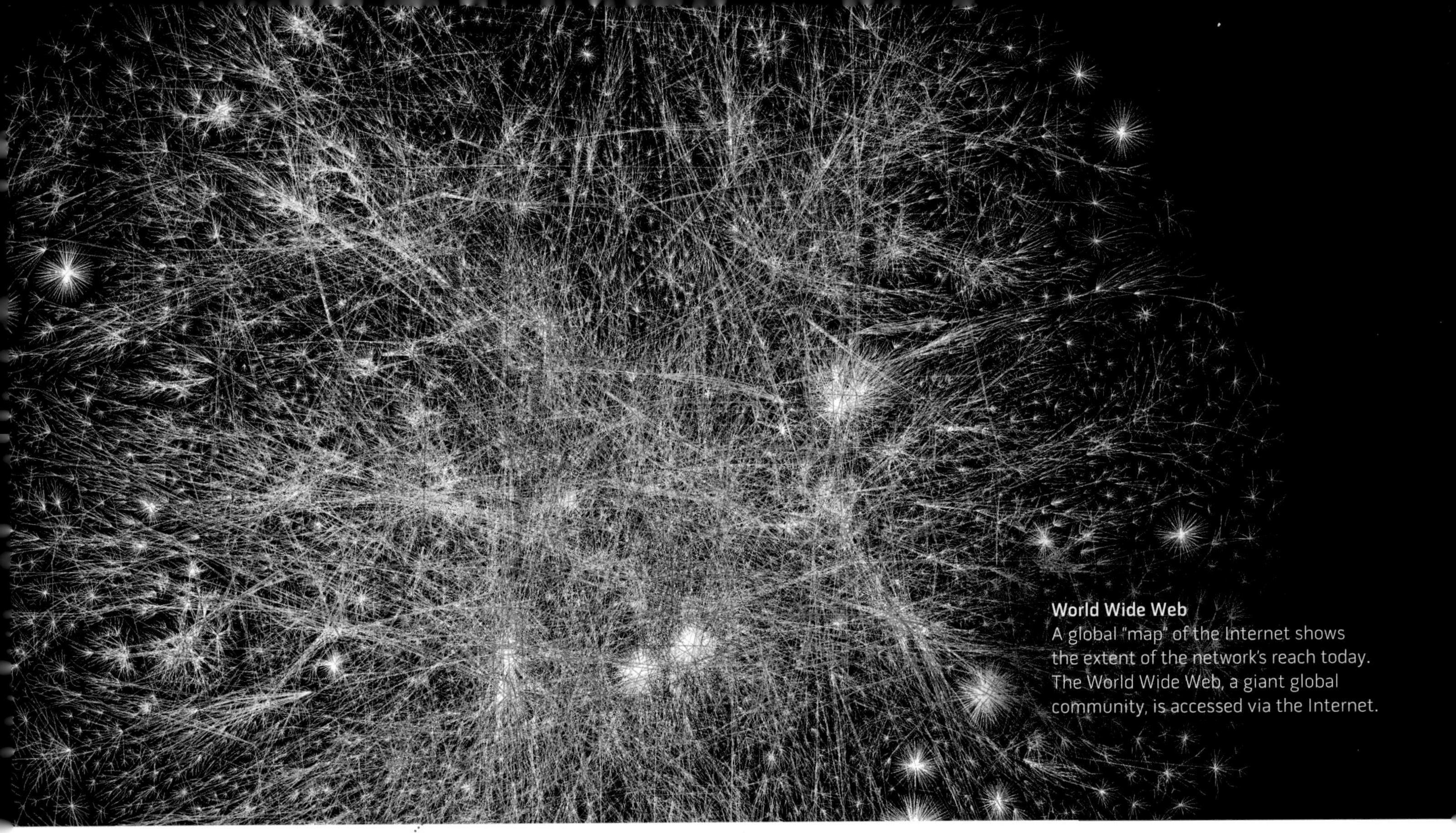

World Wide Web
A global "map" of the Internet shows the extent of the network's reach today. The World Wide Web, a giant global community, is accessed via the Internet.

1990 >

Open Source

→← CONNECTION

"Open source" refers to software that is freely available to anyone who wishes to view—and modify—it. According to the Open Source Initiative, the benefits are "better quality, higher reliability, more flexibility, lower cost, and an end to predatory vendor lock-in." While some cite the lack of a warranty and end-user support as distinct disadvantages, there is no denying the influence of open-source philosophy on the development of software. Consider the Linux operating system, for example, which held a server market share of 20 to 40 percent in 2009.

World Wide Web

● IN USE

The World Wide Web has changed lives forever by linking millions of computers throughout the world, making all the information they contain available to everyone. Although the terms World Wide Web and Internet are often used interchangeably, they are not the same thing. It is possible to have the Internet without the Web, but the Web cannot exist without the Internet. The Internet began as ARPANET in 1962, a network of two computers that was conceived of by the U.S. military. That network grew to more than a million computers by 1992.

In 1990 British computer scientist Tim Berners-Lee invented the Web—that is, he created the first Web browser and Web pages, which could be accessed via the Internet. Web pages incorporate hypertext—text displayed on a monitor that contains hyperlinks to other documents—a concept that dates back to the 1960s. And the rest, as the saying goes, is history. The most significant way in which the Web has affected economic and social life is the ease through which it makes communication possible. The Web is a giant global community.

People in Canada, South Africa, and Australia can share ideas with one another, or engage in a debate about current events. A woman in Moscow can purchase a collectible item from a man in Brazil who has the exact piece she is looking for.

▮ Public Key Cryptography (p. 23)
▮ Internet (p. 28)

Tim Berners-Lee

[PROFILE]

In 1989 the Internet had been around for about ten years. Oxford-educated British computer scientist Tim Berners-Lee (1955-) wanted to use the technology on which the Internet was based to provide a place where all kinds of information could be available to anyone, uncensored, in a user- and graphic-friendly environment. The result was the World Wide Web, which Berners-Lee invented while working at CERN, the European Particle Physics Laboratory. According to Berners-Lee, "[This] universality is essential . . . There was a second part of the dream, too, dependent on the Web being so generally used that it became a realistic mirror . . . of the ways in which we work and play and socialize."

Windows Operating System

Originally called Interface Manager, the operating system was released under the name of Windows since it best described the graphic nature of the system's computing "windows." Shown here are the system's 1985 logo (top) and the one in use today (below).

1985 >

Windows Operating System

● IN USE

An operating system is a software program that handles the communication and operation of various devices, including hardware and other software programs. A computer does not work without one. The operating system performs these various tasks by managing system resources, such as memory and processing power.

A key to the success of Windows was how Microsoft marketed the software in its early days, in the 1980s. Bill Gates made the software free to other developers just as personal computers were becoming affordable. Windows became the operating system of choice for most manufacturers, and has been dominant ever since.

Bill Gates, founder of Microsoft, in 1985

Personal Computer (p. 22)

Global Positioning System

Satellites
Twenty-four operational GPS satellites make up the GPS network. The satellites broadcast signals that contain data and the precise time the signals were transmitted.

Receiver
A receiver measures the time of the broadcast with the time of reception, thus estimating the amount of time the satellite's signal took to reach the receiver.

The device
When the receiver estimates the distance to at least four GPS satellites, it can calculate an individual's position in three dimensions.

1978 >

Global Positioning System

⮂ BACKLASH

The persistent dominance of the Windows operating system has caused some in the industry to deliberately choose other platforms—whether Linux, Mac OS, or something else. In spring 2007 Dell announced the release of three personal computers that would come preloaded with Ubuntu, a form of the Linux operating system. Since then, Linux has seen a slow but steady increase in its share of the operating system market. Whether this will be enough to topple Microsoft from its market supremacy, however, remains to be seen.

● IN USE

Located 12,000 miles above the Earth and traveling at a speed of 7,000 miles an hour, the satellite-based navigation system was launched in 1978 by the U.S. Department of Defense for military purposes. Shortly after, the manufacturers of GPS equipment recognized its mass-market potential and clamored for its use as a civilian application. The Defense Department complied with their request in the 1980s.

GPS, which is extremely accurate, works on the principle of triangulation in which the position of a given object (a person in a car, for example) is determined based on the distance of the object from four satellites in the network with which a device is communicating. The GPS network is composed of 24 satellites, with three on standby in case of failure, and each satellite makes two complete rotations around the planet every day.

So what does the future of GPS look like? To be sure, the network will continue to become more accurate and provide increasingly fine-grained information on a given location. Drivers still need to take their eyes off the road to look at the GPS device, but that may change. A company called Making Virtual Solid is working on a solution called Virtual Cable, which is designed to be built into a car's windshield. A red line that appears to follow the landscape guides the driver to his destination.

Cell Phone (p. 24)

Communication Satellites (p. 38)

John von Neumann

Regarded as one of the greatest mathematicians in history, John von Neumann (1903-1957) made major contributions to many fields, including mathematics, economics, quantum physics, and computer science. One of von Neumann's more significant contributions is the design for a stored-program digital computer that uses a central processing unit and memory to hold both instructions and data. A von Neumann architecture—a direct predecessor to the architecture of today's personal computers—has five parts: an arithmetic-logic unit, a control unit, a memory, some form of input/output, and a physical connection that provides a data path between these parts.

Personal Computer

Electronics company Commodore developed the personal computer PET, known for its "Chiclet" keyboard — the keys resembled the popular chewing gum. All consumers had to do was plug in the computer, and it was ready to use.

1977 >

Personal Computer

● IN USE

According to U.S. Census data, 62 million U.S. households, or 55 percent of American homes, had a Web-connected computer in 2003. Whether an early model—like the Commodore PET (very popular in schools in the late 1970s), the Apple II (one of the first highly successful mass-produced microcomputers), or the IBM-PC (designed to supplant the first two devices in homes)—or the latest and greatest in personal computers, they all have the same basic components. A computer is made up of a motherboard, processor, central processing unit, memory, drives, a fan, and cables. Attached to the computer are the peripherals: the mouse, keyboard, monitor, speakers, printer, scanner, and so on. These components work together to run software: the operating system and additional programs—such as a word-processing program, money management software, or photo-editing software.

With the personal computer, the technology became available to the general public. Computers were no longer large, highly expensive pieces of equipment that only major corporations or

Public Key Cryptography ....

The increasingly digital world and growing need for security motivated development of public key cryptography, a technology that ensures that data transmitted over the Internet remains protected.

Apple Computer

Apple logo, 1977

1976 >

Public Key Cryptography

● IN USE   →← CONNECTION

government agencies could afford or only computer scientists could operate. This significant development ultimately birthed new industries, changed how people communicate, and irrevocably altered their work and personal lives.

Invented in 1976 by Stanford University professor Martin Hellman and graduate student Whitfield Diffie, public key cryptography is a security technology that enables users, using an unsecured network (like the Internet), to transmit private data securely (like bank account numbers). Here is how it works: A public "key" and private "key" are created simultaneously by a certificate authority. Much like how a key unlocks a door, these keys are particular values that unlock encrypted data. The private key is given only to the person

requesting it, and the public key is made publicly available. The private key is used to decrypt information that has been encrypted with the public key. It is complex, but the end result is what matters: Whether buying a coveted collectible on eBay, paying bills, or renewing a driver's license online, public key cryptography protects personal data.

Public key cryptography, a milestone achievement of security, has also had a huge influence on common communication technologies. Data transmitted by mobile devices like phones and laptops must be kept secure. Public key cryptography has been more reliable in providing this security than Transmission Control Protocol/Internet Protocol, or TCP/IP. TCP/IP sessions can be interfered with in a variety of ways. Public key cryptography closes these loops, becoming a fundamental element of many wireless companies' infrastructures.

▼ Graphical User Interface *(p. 30)*

▼ ENIAC *(p. 38)*

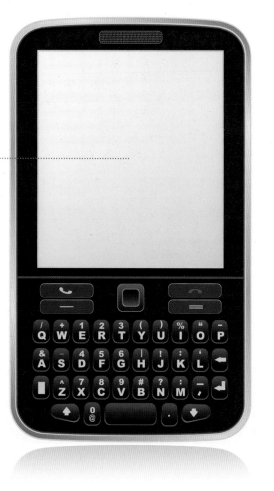

Cell Phone

"The C Programming Language," 19...

Cell Phone

● IN USE

It is hard to say what is more ubiquitous in today's world: the personal computer or the cell phone, which was invented by Martin Cooper in 1973 when he was the director of research and development at Motorola.

A cell phone is actually a radio, albeit a highly sophisticated one. It is a full-duplex device, which means that one frequency is used for talking and a separate frequency is used for listening. The communication occurs on channels, of which the average cell phone contains more than 1,650.

In a typical cell phone network, a carrier, which provides the cell phone service, is assigned 800 frequencies, which are divided into hexagonal units called cells; each cell contains about ten square miles. A base station and a tower are within each cell. Cell phones have low-power transmitters in them, as does the tower. The cell phone and the tower communicate with each other using a special frequency (if this frequency cannot be found, an "out of range" or "no service" message is displayed). As a caller uses the phone, moving from one cell to another, the frequency is "passed" from one cell to the next. The carrier maintains the frequency needed to communicate with the person on the other end and continually monitors the signal strength. If the caller moves from one carrier's network to that of another, the call will not be dropped, but the caller's jaw may drop when he sees the roaming charges on his bill.

C Language

● IN USE

A computer language consists of the vocabulary and syntax that is used to write a set of instructions—that is, a program—that tells a computer what to do. As a result of the control and efficiency it offers programmers, the C language, developed in 1972 by Dennis Ritchie at Bell Telephone Laboratories, is by far the most popular and widely used computer language in existence today, with applications in everything from microcontrollers to supercomputers.

Building On >

Communication Satellites *(p. 38)*

Radio Waves *(p. 44)*

Email

The "at" sign is a critical piece of every email address. According to Ray Tomlinson, founder of Internet-based email, the first electronic message sent was a test and forgettable. It may have read something like "QWERTYUIOP." Email is now a part of everyday life.

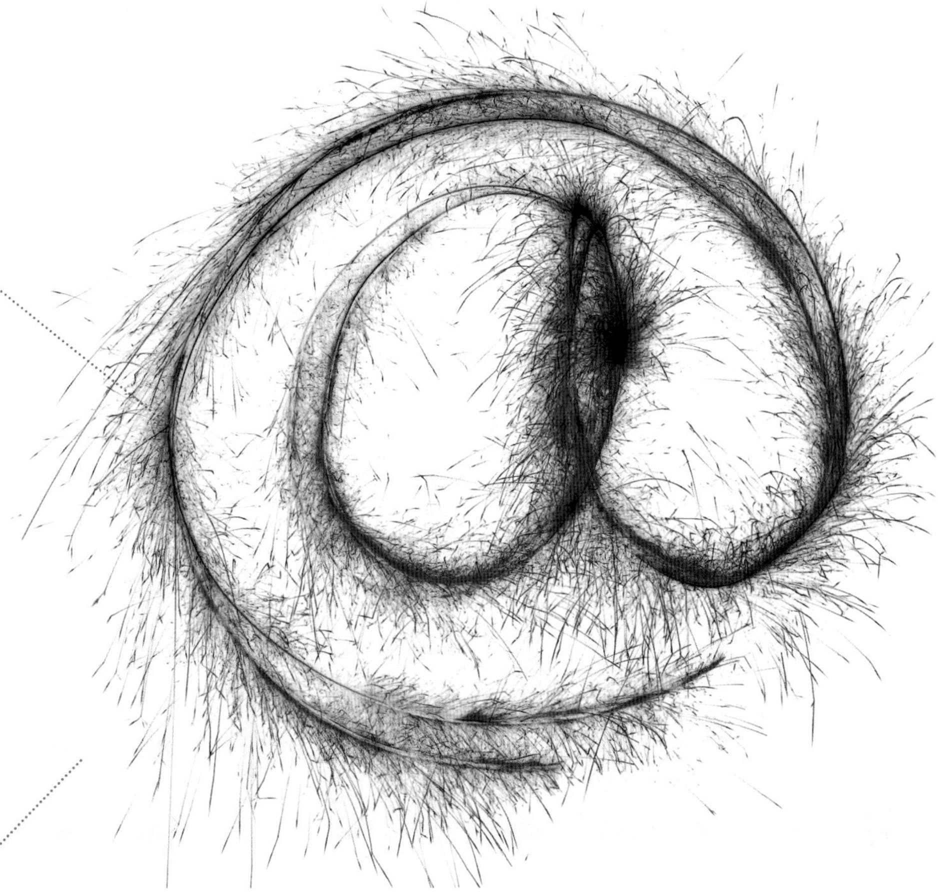

LAST; i++) {

, SUM);

1971 >

Breakthroughs continue on page 28

Email

● IN USE

Today, it is common to ask people for their email address, rather than their phone number. Ray Tomlinson invented this revolution in communication in 1971. Early emails contained only text and were used primarily by universities and research organizations. Throughout the 1970s and 1980s, various individuals and groups continued to expand upon the capabilities of email—adding, for example, the ability to send the same message to multiple addressees, the ability to sort email headers by subject or date, and the ability to forward messages. The year 1988 saw the first sanctioned commercial email use of the Internet with the introduction of the CompuServe email system.

→← CONNECTION

Packet switching—in which data are contained in special units called packets—is one of the primary means by which computer network protocols deliver data from one point to another. But packet switching is not just for computers. For example, VoIP (Voice over Internet Protocol), which is taking over the communications industry, uses packet switching instead of circuit switching, which is how the traditional telephone system transmits voice data. Circuit switching is more reliable, but packet switching is less expensive.

Email

Augmented Reality

Unlike virtual reality, which is based in a computer-generated environment, augmented reality is designed to enhance the real world by superimposing audio, visual, and other elements on your senses.

Boeing researcher Tom Caudell first coined the term in 1990 to describe the digital display used by airline electricians, which combines virtual graphics with physical reality. But the concept is even older than that. The 1988 movie *Who Framed Roger Rabbit?* is a good example of the technology—and before that, a more simplistic version is demonstrated in the yellow arrows announcers use on televised football games when analyzing a play.

Augmented reality is currently driving the development of consumer electronics because of the way it lends itself so readily to smart phone applications. Residents of the Netherlands, for example, can download an app called Layar that uses a cell phone's camera and GPS capabilities to gather information about the surrounding area. Layar then shows information about certain sites in the area, such as restaurants or movie theaters, overlaying this information on the phone's screen. Point the phone at a building, and Layar reports if any companies in that building are hiring, or Layar might locate the building's history in the online encyclopedia Wikipedia.

There are some limitations to augmented reality technology as it currently exists—the GPS system has a range of about 30 feet, the screens of cell phones are small, and understandable concerns about privacy exist, especially as the technology affects more aspects of our lives. Even so, the future of this technology is bright—with obvious, soon-to-be-tapped potential for gaming, education, security, medicine, and business, among other areas.

1978

The global positioning system is essential to augmented reality, which depends on GPS to pinpoint where someone is. *See page 21*

1973

Cell phones, or smart phones, are the devices on which most augmented reality technologies are currently implemented. *See page 24*

1948

Information theory prescribes how information is encoded to and from cell phones. *See page 34*

Learn More
Like captions on a page, augmented reality can provide background and explanations, such as a biography of architect Frank Gehry when visiting his signature buildings.

Orient and Navigate
Global positioning systems allow geographical tags that map a person's location at a moment's notice, then plot surrounding sites and pathways.

Make Choices
Consider options and make choices virtually. Here, galleries are represented by images of museum holdings, such as Richard Serra's *La Materia del Tiempo* (shown).

Guggenheim Museum / Bilbao

Frank Gehry, architect
The Guggenheim Museum Bilbao is a museum of modern and contemporary art designed by Canadian-American architect

Smartphones and Beyond
Today's handheld electronics portend the promise of tomorrow's augmented reality. View cues connected to an actual place, such as the Guggenheim Museum of Bilbao, through a smartphone, and you can layer information on to enrich the experience.

1945
Communication satellites made global positioning technology possible. *See page 38*

1888
Radio waves transmit information to and from cell phones. *See page 44*

Inform

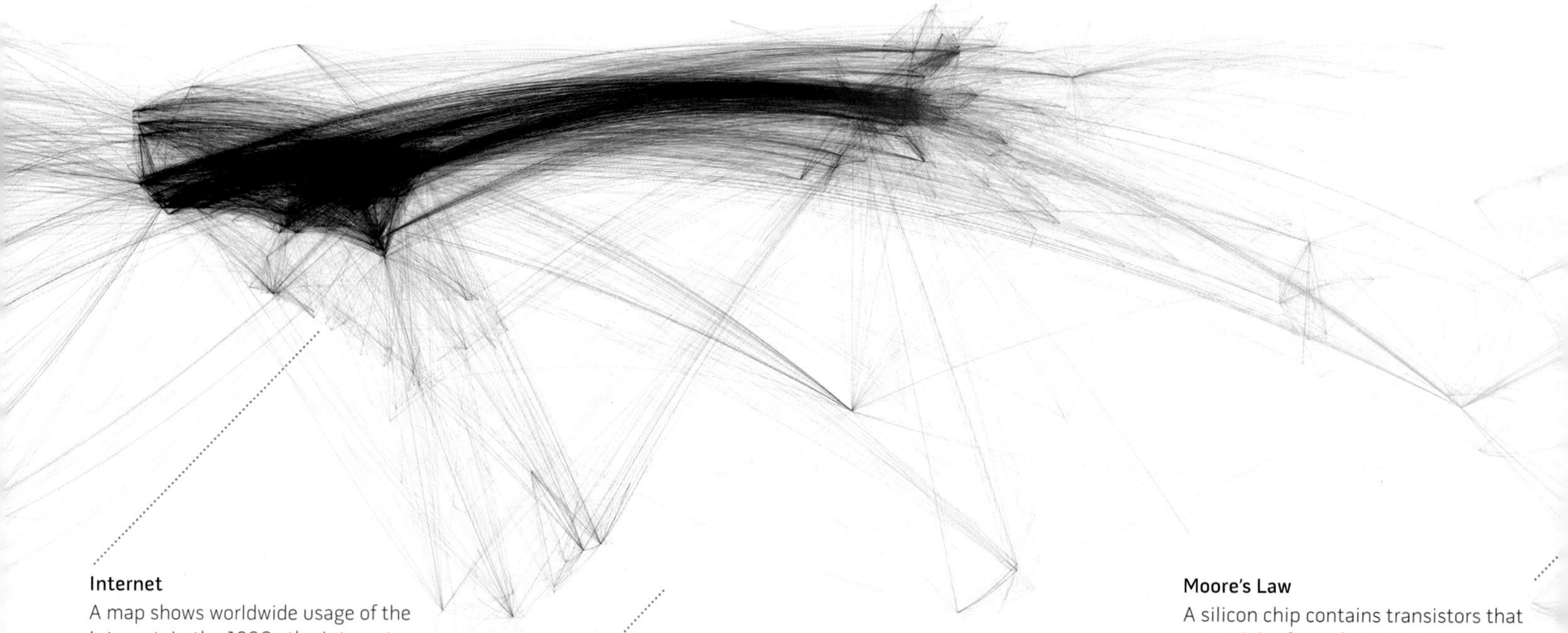

Internet
A map shows worldwide usage of the Internet. In the 1990s the Internet telecommunications network was often referred to as the information superhighway.

Moore's Law
A silicon chip contains transistors that control the flow of electricity. Gordon Moore predicted the increasing number of transistors on chips, thus establishing a yardstick for the progress of technology.

From 1969 back to 1947 >   1969 >

Internet

● IN USE

More aspects of life are moving online like never before, thanks to the Internet. What began as a collaboration among academia, government, and industry in the late 1960s and early 1970s has evolved into a vast information infrastructure.

The Internet works because of a few technologies, the first of which is packet switching, where data are contained in specially formatted units, or packets, that are routed from source to destination using network switches and routers. Each packet contains address information that identifies the sender and the recipient. Using these addresses, network switches and routers determine how best to transfer the packet between points on the path to its destination.

The Internet is also based on a key concept known as open architecture networking. In a sense, it is what makes the Internet the Internet. With this concept, different providers can use any individual network technology they want, and the networks work together through an internetworking architecture. Thus these networks act as peers for one another, offering seamless end-to-end service.

A third important technology is Transmission Control Protocol/ Internet Protocol, or TCP/IP. This is what makes an open architecture network possible. Think of it as the basic communication language of the Internet. TCP assembles a message or file into smaller packets that are transmitted over the Internet, and IP reads the address part of each packet so that it gets to the right destination. Each gateway computer on the network checks this address to see where to forward the message.

Building On >

Information Theory *(p. 34)*

Compact disc

1965 >

1965 >

Moore's Law

In 1965 Intel co-founder Gordon Moore predicted that the number of transistors on a chip would double every two years. Known today as Moore's law, this principle has driven the computer industry for nearly five decades, spearheading breakthroughs not only in dimensions and scaling, but also in integrated circuit materials and structure. Moore's law is not a law in the way that gravity is a law. It is simply an observation that has pushed the IT industry to do more, faster, than would have been possible in any other industry. In 2005 Moore made another prediction: "[Moore's law] can't continue forever. The nature of exponentials is that you push them out and eventually disaster happens . . . . [With regard to transistors,] we're approaching the size of atoms, which is a fundamental barrier . . . . We have another 10 to 20 years before we reach [that] fundamental limit. By then they'll be able to make bigger chips and have transistor budgets in the billions."

Silicon chip

Compact Disc

American James Russell first invented the compact disc in 1965, but it was the early 1980s before CDs began to surpass vinyl records and cassette tapes in popularity. Next came readable/writable CDs, then readable/writable DVDs, and then Blu-ray technology. The way in which these optical storage media work is simple: Data are encoded onto the disc in the form of pits, and when the disc is spun, the data can be read using a low-power laser beam. As the technology has continued to develop, there have been improvements in speed and capacity—for example, the first CD could hold about 700 megabytes, but today's latest discs can hold one terabyte of data, which is roughly a million megabytes.

▼ Laser (p. 31)

An early computer mouse

Graphical User Interface ···················
GUI is a program interface that makes computers
easier to use for the average consumer.
Components include a pointer, which allows the
user to move around the screen, and icons such
as a pointing finger (below), which let the user
select and click on hyperlinks.

1964 >

1962 >

Computer Mouse

● IN USE

The mouse, combined with
the graphical user interface,
transformed the computer from
a specialized piece of equipment
into a mass-market commodity
that all could use. The pointing
device works by detecting motion
in two dimensions relative to the
surface on which it sits. With it,
a computer user can manipulate
objects on a screen. The
invention is credited to Douglas
Engelbart, who created the first
prototype in 1964: a wooden
shell with two metal wheels.
Engelbart called it a "mouse"
because the wire coming out of

the device's end resembled the
tail of a mouse.

Graphical User Interface

● IN USE

A graphical user interface, or
GUI, is a means of interacting
with a computer by way of
pictures and symbols instead of
typing complicated commands
into a command-line interface.
Development of GUI cannot be
attributed to just one person,
although the genesis of the
idea is widely attributed to a
concept Douglas Engelbart came
up with in 1962. GUIs were no
doubt a major reason why the
personal computers designed
in the 1980s, first by Xerox and
then by Apple, became so widely
accessible. No longer did people

need a sophisticated knowledge of
programming to use a computer.

The most common form in
which the graphical user interface
is presented is known as the
WIMP style (window, icon, menu,
pointing device), which can be
encapsulated in three words:
point and click.

Building On >   ◤ **Personal Computer** *(p. 22)*

Virtual Reality

The concept of virtual reality draws on computer technology to create a simulated three-dimensional image. The viewer feels as if the re-created world is "real."

Laser

A stock-keeping unit, or SKU code, is an optical representation of data that reveals key information about a product, such as price, when read by a laser.

1962 >

1960 >

Virtual Reality

● IN USE

In the early 1960s American inventor Douglas Engelbart first came up with the concept of virtual reality, which is an immersive three-dimensional, computer-generated environment that is designed to replace the environment in which a person exists, as opposed to augmented reality, which is designed to enhance the environment in which a person moves rather than replace it.

Although just a concept in the 1960s, researchers have since expanded on Engelbart's visionary idea, and there are some interesting prospects for the future of virtual reality in science and medicine. For example, in the early 1990s, developers at the Electronic Visualization Laboratory, a graduate research center at the University of Illinois at Chicago, invented a virtual reality theater known as the CAVE (Cave Automatic Virtual Environment). CAVE lets researchers study pollution emission, design vehicle interiors and exteriors, simulate surgery, analyze architectural site plans, and test handling procedures for hazardous material.

Laser

● IN USE

German physicist Albert Einstein first suggested the laser, an acronym for "light amplification by stimulated emission of radiation," in 1916. However, the first working laser did not appear until 1960.

As improvements in design, chemical composition, and performance were made, it became obvious that communications in particular could benefit from the laser, which can carry more information than radio waves or microwaves. In 1962 American engineer Robert Hall invented the semiconductor injection laser, which is now found in all compact disc players and laser printers, laser pointers, supermarket bar-code readers, and most optical fiber communications systems.

Holography (p. 34)

Integrated Circuits ·····················

Integrated circuits are small electronic devices made from semiconductor materials. They are often mounted on computer circuit boards, as shown here.

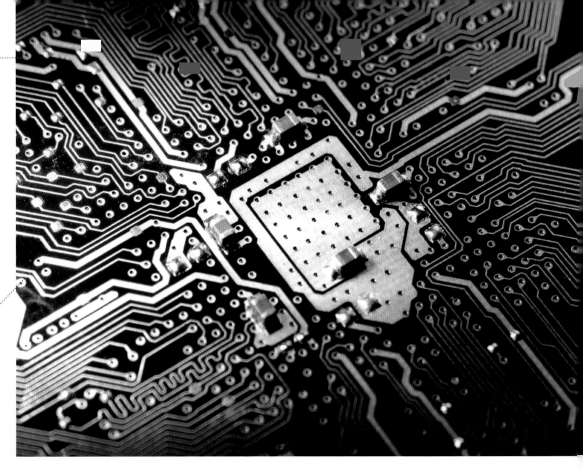

1958 >

Integrated Circuits

Integrated circuits are found in nearly every electronic device used today, from cell phones to television sets. A complex electronic circuit, each IC contains a diode, transistor, resistor, and capacitor. These components work together to regulate the flow of electricity through a device. But integrated circuits have disadvantages: All connections must remain intact or the device will not work, and speed is definitely a factor. If the components of the IC are too large or the wires connecting the components are too long, for

example, the device is slow and ineffective.

In 1958 Americans Jack Kilby and Robert Noyce individually solved this problem by constructing the integrated circuit and the chip it sat on out of the same material. Wires and components no longer had to be assembled manually. The circuits could be made smaller, and the manufacturing process could be automated. (To demonstrate just how small these circuits can be, consider this: The original IC had only one transistor, three resistors, and one capacitor, and

was the size of an adult's pinkie finger. Today, an IC smaller than a penny can hold 125 million transistors.)

In 1961 the first commercially available integrated circuits were introduced, and computer manufacturers immediately saw the advantage they offered. In 1968 Noyce founded Intel, the company that introduced the microprocessor, which took the IC one step further by placing the central processing unit, memory, and input and output controls for a computer on one small chip.

Early communication devices used vacuum tubes, which are inefficient and bulky. The advent of the semiconductor changed all that. Semiconductor devices harness the electronic properties of various organic materials. They can be used to create an individual device or a set of interconnected devices known as an integrated circuit. Their usefulness lies primarily in the ease with which their electrical conductivity can be manipulated through the application of heat, light, or pressure.

Building On >   ▼ Transistor *(p. 35)*

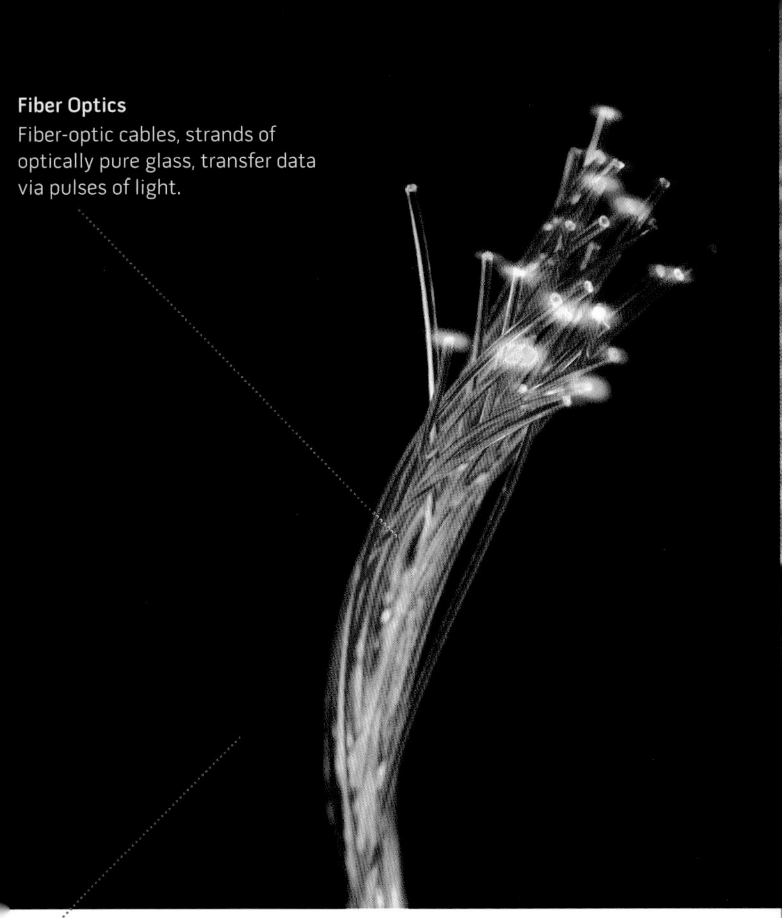

Fiber Optics

Fiber-optic cables, strands of optically pure glass, transfer data via pulses of light.

1952 >

Claude Shannon

Fiber Optics

 IN USE

When it comes to communications technology, fiber-optic cable has largely replaced electronic cable. Fiber-optic cable can provide a higher bandwidth and can cover longer distances without the signal becoming degraded. In addition, fiber-optic cable can be installed in areas with high electromagnetic interference, such as alongside utility lines, power lines, and railroad tracks.

The origin of the idea goes as far back as the 1790s; however, it was 1952 before British physicist Harold Hopkins took the concept and streamlined it, making it practical for everyday use. As opposed to electronic cable, which works by transferring data through pulses of electricity, fiber-optic cables transfer data via light pulses through thin strands of glass or plastic.

Modern electronic communications would not have been possible without the work of Claude Shannon (1916-2001)—a distant cousin of Thomas Edison. Shannon, a mathematical engineer, is considered the father of information theory, a mathematical model dictating how information can be transmitted from sender to receiver. Initially, however, Shannon was concerned with clearing up the "noise" that pervaded telephone connections at the time.

Shannon spent 31 years at Bell Laboratories, and while he is noteworthy for many accomplishments, it was his 1948 article, "The Mathematical Theory of Communication," that enabled those who followed to push the envelope of 20th-century science.

Information Theory

A music-mixing console uses information theory to electronically combine, route, and change the dynamics of audio signals. The modified signs produce the combined output signals.

Holography

Euro banknotes carry a holographic band or decal, depending on the note's denomination. Holograms are often used on money and other documents to prevent counterfeiting,

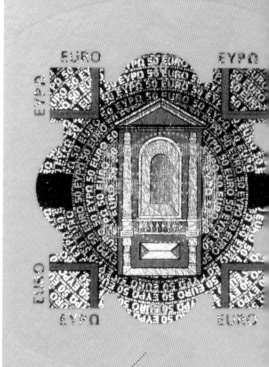

1948 >

1947 >

Information Theory

Information theory has its origins in a 1948 paper by American mathematical engineer Claude Shannon—"The Mathematical Theory of Communication." The theory allows the information in a message to be "quantified"— usually as bits of data that represent one of two states: on or off. It also dictates how to encode and transmit information in the presence of "noise," which can corrupt a message en route.

At the heart of Shannon's theory is the concept of uncertainty. The more uncertainty there is with regard to what the "signal" is, the more bits of information are required to make sure the essential information is transmitted. Shannon called this uncertainty-based measure of information "entropy"; he mathematically proved that a signal could be encoded—reducing it to its simplest form and eliminating interference or noise— to transmit a clear message, and only the message. Although there is always a possibility of errors in transmission, information theory vastly minimizes that possibility.

Coding theory, an important offshoot of information theory, studies the properties of codes for the purpose of designing efficient, reliable data by removing redundancy and errors in the transmitted data. It has two primary characteristics: Source encoding attempts to compress the data from a source in order to transmit the data more efficiently (if you have ever "zipped" a file to send it to someone, you have seen source encoding in action). Channel encoding adds extra data bits to make the transmission of data more able to resist disturbances present on the transmission channel.

Holography

Holography, invented in 1947 by Hungarian physicist Dennis Gabor, is a way of reproducing a recorded image so that it appears three-dimensional. First, light scattered from a subject is captured by a photographic plate. Then, another beam of light is reflected directly onto the plate, measuring the location of the object. When developed, a laser light is projected through the plate from the opposite direction, scattering the light to create a three-dimensional image of the original object.

This technology may change the way digital information is

Building On >

Transistor

Considered one of the most important inventions of the 20th century, the transistor was invented in 1947 to replace the bulky and expensive vacuum tube as a communication device

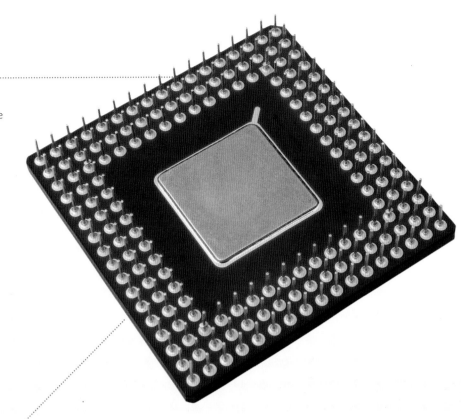

1947 >

Breakthroughs continue on page 38

Transistor

● IN USE

stored. Holographic storage can record and read millions of bits in tandem, enabling data transfer rates greater than those attained by optical storage.

A transistor is a type of semiconductor, without which modern electronic devices—including computers—could not function. Although there are several different types of transistors, all contain a solid piece of semiconductor material, with at least three terminals that can be connected to an external circuit. This technology transfers current across a material that normally has high resistance (in other words, a resistor); hence, it was a "transfer-resistor," or transistor.

Prior to the introduction of the transistor, computers operated by way of vacuum tubes, which were bulky and expensive to produce. The more powerful computers contained thousands of them, which is why early computers filled an entire room. In 1947 American physicists John Bardeen and Walter Brattain at Bell Labs observed that when electrical contacts were applied to a crystal of germanium, the power that was generated was larger than the power used. American William Shockley, also a physicist, saw the potential in this, and over the next few months the team worked to expand the knowledge of semiconductors. The three men won the Nobel Prize for physics in 1956 for inventing the transistor.

So why is the transistor so important to modern electronics? Among other things, it can be mass-produced using a highly automated process for a relatively cheap cost. In addition, transistors can be produced singly or more commonly packaged in integrated circuits with other components to produce complete electronic circuits. And transistors are flexible, which is why they are used in practically every electronic device known today.

▼ **Electron** (p. 180)

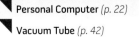

▼ **Personal Computer** (p. 22)

▼ **Vacuum Tube** (p. 42)

Quantum Capability

These images show a quantum gas held in a web of laser beams. As the particles repel each other, they move from a disordered phase (left) to an ordered phase (right). Researchers hope to use these organized sets of atoms to create quantum computers where each atom can store a small amount of information.

Particles Distributed

Here the atoms of an ultracold gas have distributed themselves into a distinctly peaked pattern.

Quantum Computing

Initially the brainchild of Paul Benioff, a physicist at Argonne National Laboratory in Illinois, a quantum computer is radically different from a traditional personal computer. With a traditional computer, data (in the form of bits) are stored and read in the grooves on a hard drive. With a quantum computer, the data (in the form of qubits) are stored in molecules and processed by being bombarded with pulses of radiation.

A traditional computer can solve only one calculation at time. Data are processed and categorized, as it were, as being in either one of two states. A quantum computer, on the other hand, can solve multiple calculations at once using a principle called superposition. Rather than looking at a segment of data as either 1 or 0, for example, it looks at the data as not only 1 and 0 but also all the states in between. The quantum computer can process these various states simultaneously, which is what gives it its processing power.

So how soon will it be before quantum computers can be found at the local computer retailer? Quite a while, as it turns out. Quantum computers must have at least several dozen qubits to be able to solve real-world problems, but the most advanced to date have not gone beyond 16.

Most of the current research in this field is still purely theoretical, but the potential quantum computers offer is undeniable, particularly for cryptography and database applications. Cryptographic problems often require many thousands of calculations, and a quantum computer can solve these in a fraction of the time it would take a traditional computer. A quantum computer could also be used to search large databases in a fraction of the time that it would take a conventional computer.

1936

Although the quantum computer represents a major break from traditional—that is, non-quantum—computers, the two share a crucial similarity: Both are Turing machines, and thus the same theoretical limits on computing power apply to both. *See page 40*

1927

Quantum mechanics made the theoretical break from classical computers possible. *See page 41*

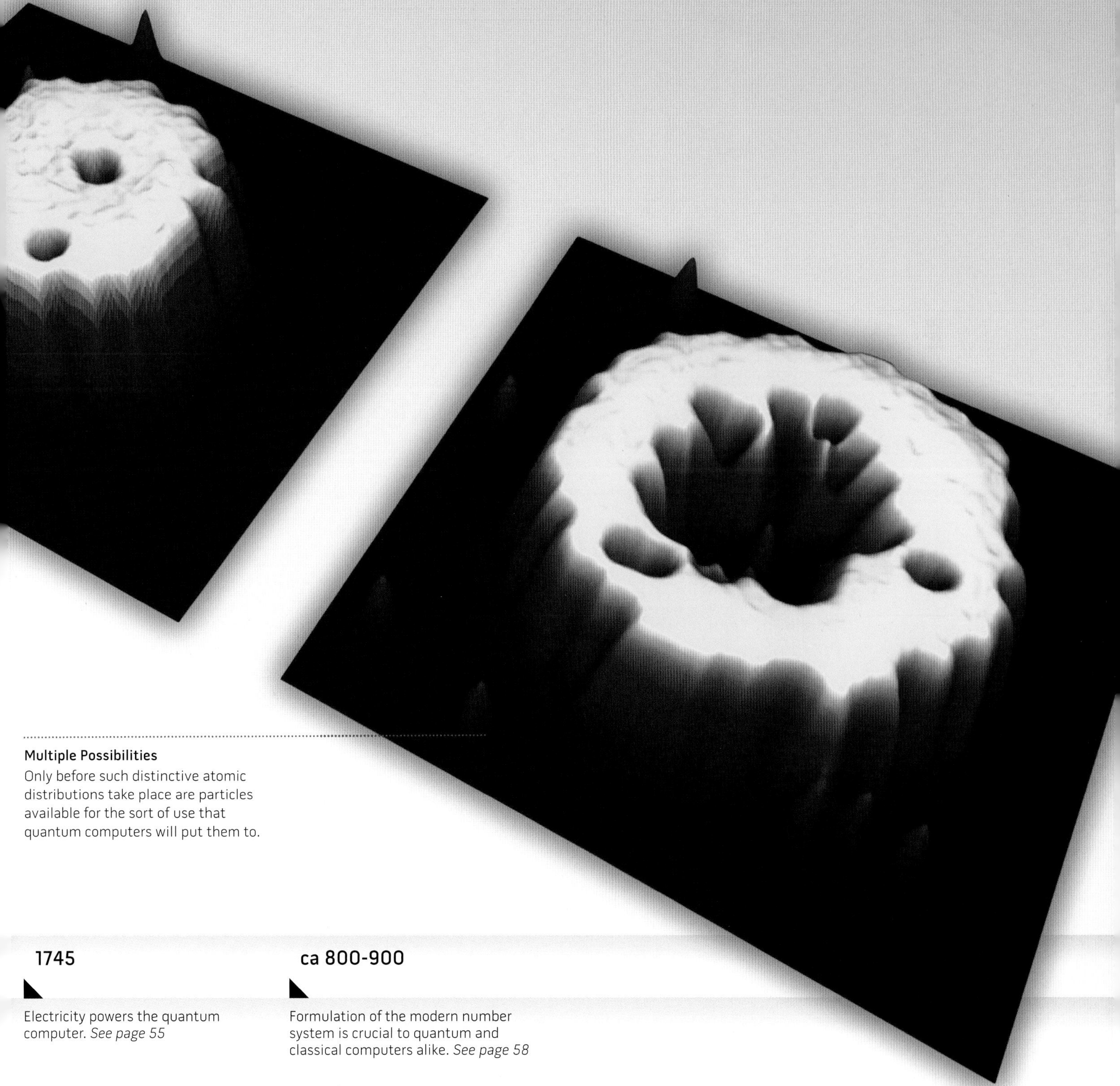

Multiple Possibilities
Only before such distinctive atomic distributions take place are particles available for the sort of use that quantum computers will put them to.

1745

Electricity powers the quantum computer. *See page 55*

ca 800-900

Formulation of the modern number system is crucial to quantum and classical computers alike. *See page 58*

ENIAC

A clerk registers information on the ENIAC at Aberdeen Proving Ground in Maryland. The gigantic machine, credited with initiating the modern computer age, was a product of World War II and financed by the U.S. Army.

From 1946 back to 1876 >

1946 >

1945 >

ENIAC

● IN USE

In 1946 Americans John Mauchly and John Presper Eckert developed the ENIAC (Electronic Numerical Integrator and Computer) for the U.S. Army, which needed a computer for calculating artillery-firing tables. The first electronic digital computer, it relied on both vacuum tubes and Turing theory to operate. In addition to its speed, its size and complexity were remarkable. Weighing 30 tons and occupying 680 square feet, ENIAC contained 17,468 vacuum tubes, 7,200 crystal diodes, 1,500 relays, 70,000 resistors, and 10,000 capacitors. Such a bulky, intricate design led many experts to predict that tube failures would cause the machine to break down frequently. This proved to be the case, as several tubes burned out each day, negatively affecting the functionality of the machine. Engineers adopted the practice of leaving ENIAC running constantly, reducing the amount of thermal stress on the tubes.

Communication Satellite

▲ IN THEORY

Although most know him as a prolific science fiction author, Arthur C. Clarke made a significant contribution to communications technology. In October 1945 he outlined his concept of geostationary communications satellites in a paper titled "Extra-Terrestrial Relays—Can Rocket Stations Give Worldwide Radio Coverage?" Although Clarke was not the first to come up with the theory, he was the first to popularize it.

The term "geostationary" refers to the position of the satellite's orbit around the Earth. The orbit

Building On >

Turing Machine (p. 40)

Boolean Logic (p. 50)

Abacus (p. 59)

Communication Satellites
Geostationary satellites orbit Earth.

Alan Turing

of a geosynchronous satellite repeats regularly over specific points. When that regular orbit lies over the Equator and is circular, it is called geostationary.

The advantages of geostationary satellites: Receiving and transmitting antennas on the ground do not need to track them as the satellites do not waver in their orbit. These antennas are cheaper than tracking antennas, so the costs of operating such a system are reduced. The disadvantages: Because the satellites are so high, radio signals take a little longer to be received and transmitted, resulting in a small but significant signal delay. In addition, these satellites have incomplete geographic coverage since ground stations at higher than roughly 60° latitude have difficulty reliably receiving signals at lower elevations.

Regardless of the disadvantages, there is no denying that communications satellites have revolutionized such areas as global communications, television broadcasting, and weather forecasting, and have important defense and intelligence applications.

▼ Global Positioning System (p. 21)

▼ Jet Engine (p. 267)

In addition to the Turing machine, Alan Turing (1912-1954)—a British mathematician, logician, and cryptanalyst—devised code-breaking techniques during World War II; created the Automated Computing Engine while working at the National Physical Laboratory; and later in life became interested in mathematical biology, which deals with the mathematical representation, treatment, and modeling of biological processes.

Turing, however, experienced personal challenges—his homosexuality resulted in a criminal conviction and chemical castration in 1952, and he took his life in 1954. In September 2009 British Prime Minister Gordon Brown made an official public apology for the way Turing was treated.

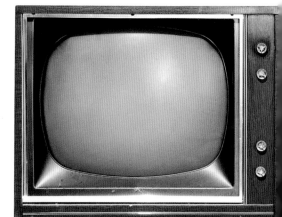

.... Detail of a Turing machine

An early model television

1936 >

1927 >

Turing Machine

▲ IN THEORY

In 1936 Englishman Alan Turing and American Alonzo Church, both mathematicians, formally introduced an algorithm that described what information can be computed and provided a model for computing. Known as the Church-Turing thesis, it essentially states that if a function is calculable, it is computable. The hypothesis addresses the nature of calculation devices, such as electronic computers, and claims that any calculation that is possible can be performed by an algorithm on a computer, provided that sufficient time and storage space are available.

The Turing machine, a theoretical device developed in tandem with the thesis, has an infinitely long strip of tape and a head that can move along the tape, reading the symbols on it and changing the values along the way based on a table of rules. Despite the theory's simplicity, a Turing machine can be adapted to simulate the logic of any computer algorithm; it is particularly useful in explaining the functions of a central processing unit inside a computer.

Computer scientists use Turing machines to understand the limits of mechanical computation.

There are limitations to the theory, however. For example, problems exist that not even a Turing machine can solve, and some models can perform calculations more quickly than a Turing machine can. In addition, Turing machines do not model concurrency well—a property in which several computations are executing simultaneously and potentially interacting with one another.

Television

● IN USE

The images on a television screen (and a computer screen, for that matter) are really nothing more than collections of small colored dots, called pixels, that the brain assembles into a recognizable image. How these images get to the screen is complicated, but basically involves a composite video signal being received and "painted" on the TV screen, line by line. It happens so quickly that all viewers see is the complete image.

The television is not really the invention of one single person so much as it is the end

Building On >

Personal Computer *(p. 22)*

Boolean Logic *(p. 50)*

Abacus *(p. 59)*

Vacuum Tube *(p. 42)*

Radio *(p. 43)*

Quantum Mechanics
A classic experiment of quantum mechanics shoots electrons through two slits (here, d) and tracks the pattern of interference.

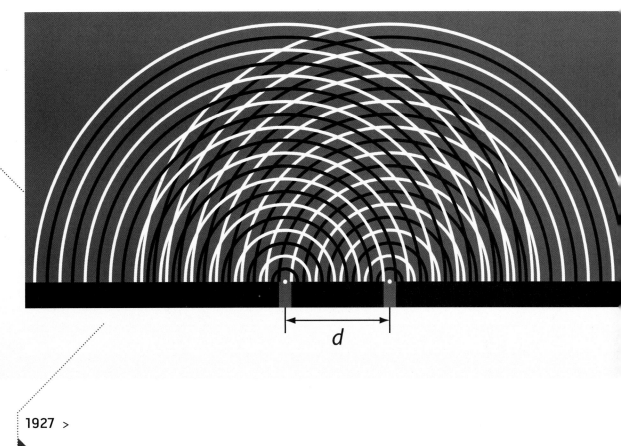

1927 >

Quantum Mechanics

▲ IN THEORY

result of various engineers and inventors working to make the concept a reality. However, 1927 is a significant year in TV's history because it marks Scottish inventor John Baird's broadcast of the first transatlantic television signal between London and New York, and the first shore-to-ship transmission.

The Howdy Doody Show,
1950s TV show

Quantum mechanics is a field of study dedicated to the behavior of matter on atomic and subatomic scales. It came about in the 1920s in response to the realization that classical physics could not explain certain phenomena, something first noted in physicist Albert Einstein's explanation of the photoelectric effect, also known as the general theory of relativity. The principles behind the theory can be hard to grasp, especially since scientists are used to viewing the world through the lens of classical physics.

A few of the main aspects of the theory that capture its "weirdness" are wave-particle duality, the uncertainty principle, and superposition—the last of which plays a major role in quantum computing. Wave-particle duality refers to the fact that on small scales light and matter have both wave- and particle-like properties. The uncertainty principle says that both a particle's position and its momentum cannot be known with certainty—the more accurately one of these quantities is measured, the less accurately the other is known. Superposition

is the quantum mechanical idea that a particle can be in all possible states at the same time. As odd as the theories of quantum mechanics seem, physicists have determined through experiments that the theories do accurately represent the nature of reality on very small scales.

Large-scale Electric Supply Network (p. 46)

Uncertainty Principle (p. 124)

General Theory of Relativity (p. 126)

Wave-particle Duality of Light (p. 129)

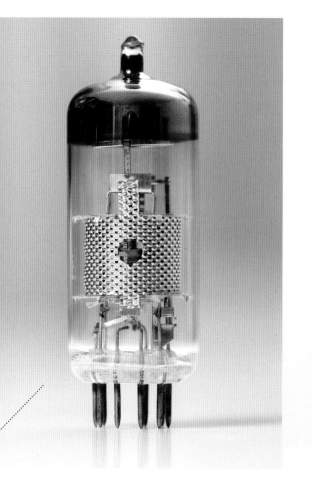

A vacuum tube, predecessor to the transistor

1906 >

Vacuum Tube
Loudspeakers are an example of the practical use of electromagnetism, one of the four fundamental interactions in nature. The other three are gravity, weak nuclear force, and strong nuclear force.

Vacuum Tube

⮌ BACKLASH

Since first introduced in 1927, quantum mechanics has engendered controversy with regard to its interpretation. Scientists Niels Bohr, Albert Einstein, and Hugh Everett all put forth different ways in which this theory could be viewed. Even today, it is not clear that anyone fully understands quantum mechanics or grasps its implications. It has been useful, however, in helping scientists better understand the world and the processes at work within it.

● IN USE

The vacuum tube was a milestone in the history of computing and communications. Prototypes were introduced in the late 19th century. Austrian physicist Robert von Lieben introduced the first practical vacuum in 1906.

Vacuum tubes—which allow the amplification, switching, or modifying of an electrical signal— are typically contained in a glass envelope that maintains a low pressure on its inside. Filaments within the vacuum are heated and release electrons, which are drawn to a small metal plate, establishing a flow of current. This seemingly simple device replaced the complicated relay-and-switch system that early computers used, which meant that computers could perform calculations at a faster rate.

→← CONNECTION

In 1865 Scottish physicist James Clerk Maxwell discovered electromagnetism, which deals with the interaction of electric and magnetic fields. This discovery has allowed for all sorts of developments in modern technology. The practical use of electromagnetism is vast, ranging from the magnetic strips in credit cards to loudspeakers, and MRI machines to mobile phones. More fascinating uses involve removing embedded magnetic metal particles from inside the eyes and harnessing electromagnetism to develop environmentally friendly energy systems.

Building On >

▼ Transistor (p. 35)

Magnetic Recorder

Most audio and video magnetic storage devices, such as this videocassette, use magnetic recording to store data on a magnetic medium.

1898 >

1897 >

Vintage radio

Magnetic Recorder

● IN USE

A magnetic recorder encodes data—electrical signals—as a pattern of magnetization on a magnetic material. This device reads data—that is, turns the data back into electrical signals—using a mechanism known as a head. Danish engineer Valdemar Poulsen first demonstrated publicly the magnetic recorder in 1898 at the Paris Exposition; the device recorded a signal on a wire wrapped around a drum.

Early magnetic recording devices were designed to record analog audio signals. However, computers, and now most audio and video magnetic storage devices, record digital data. These include floppy disks, magnetic recording tape, and magnetic strips on credit cards.

Radio

● IN USE

Although wireless devices are thought of as a "modern" development, the concept was first introduced in the 19th century. At the time, people were just beginning to understand electromagnetism and radio waves and their potential for transmitting information.

Several researchers conducted experiments in wireless telegraphy, including Michael Faraday, Heinrich Hertz, Thomas Edison, Nikola Tesla, and Guglielmo Marconi. The first radios consisted of a transmitter, a modulating system, and an antenna. One of the earliest wireless networks was established in 1897;

it transmitted communications between radio stations on the coast and ships at sea. The invention of amplitude-modulated, or AM, radio enabled more than one station to send signals. In 1933 Edwin H. Armstrong patented frequency modulation, or FM, radio. The frequency of a radio wave is modified to minimize static and interference from electrical equipment and the atmosphere.

Radio has been used for more than broadcasting. The technology has played a role in aircraft navigation systems and in color television transmission.

▼ Electromagnetic Induction *(p. 52)*

▼ Magnetic Needle Compass *(p. 145)*

▼ Fourier Analysis *(p. 54)*

Radio Waves
Artwork depicts radio waves, which are a type of electromagnetic radiation and travel at the speed of light.

Radio Waves
A satellite dish, so-called because of it dish-shaped antenna, receives radio waves from communications satellites, which send out transmissions and broadcasts.

1888 >

Radio Waves

▲ IN THEORY

Scottish physicist James Clerk Maxwell was one of the first to speculate on the nature of electromagnetism. The equations he formulated describe the behavior of electric and magnetic fields, as well as their interactions with matter. Maxwell theorized that electric and magnetic fields travel through empty space, in the form of waves, at a constant velocity. He also proposed that light waves and radio waves are two forms of electromagnetic radiation.

German physicist Heinrich Hertz was the first to demonstrate Maxwell's theory satisfactorily, proving the existence of radio waves in 1888. He did this by building a device that could detect very high frequency and ultrahigh frequency radio waves. Hertz published his work in a book titled *Electric Waves: Being Researches on the Propagation of Electric Action with Finite Velocity through Space*. These experiments greatly expanded the field of electromagnetic transmission, and the Hertz antenna receiver was developed further by others in the field.

Hertz also found that radio waves could be transmitted through different types of materials and were reflected by others, a discovery that ultimately led to the invention of radar. He even paved the way for wireless communication, although he never recognized that important aspect of his experiments.

In recognition of his contributions, since 1933 the hertz designation has been an official part of the international metric system—it is the term used for units of radio and electrical frequencies.

→← CONNECTION

Understanding radio waves has enabled scientists to make all sorts of devices wireless, from telephones to computer keyboards. German physicist Heinrich Hertz first demonstrated the phenomenon in 1888. Radio waves are a type of electromagnetic radiation, and like all electromagnetic waves, they travel at the speed of light. Artificially generating these waves has led to a wide range of developments in radio communications, broadcasting, radar and other navigation systems, satellite communications, and computer networks.

Building On >

◤ Cell Phone *(p. 24)*

◤ Maxwell's Equations *(p. 134)*

Nikola Tesla

[PROFILE]

Regarded as one of the greatest electrical engineers, Nikola Tesla (1856-1943) is perhaps best known for his revolutionary ideas in the field of electromagnetism, as well as for his famous "War of the Currents" with Thomas Edison, a heated competition in which each advocated a different kind of electric power distribution. Tesla also contributed to the fields of robotics, remote control, and computer science, and to the expansion of ballistics, nuclear physics, and theoretical physics. He was a man with an eccentric personality, which led to him being ostracized late in life. Tesla died at 86 in a hotel suite in New York City.

Alternating Current
Nikola Tesla's polyphase alternating current 500-horsepower generator was exhibited at the 1893 World's Columbian Exposition in Chicago. The exposition, or world's fair, was a gathering of ideas and the latest technologies from around the globe.

1887 >

Alternating Current

● IN USE

In 1887 Nikola Tesla worked with inventor George Westinghouse on the transmission of alternating current over long distances. (AC is the form of electricity you get when you plug something into an outlet.) The late 1880s saw the "War of the Currents": On one side was Thomas Edison, advocating direct current for electric power distribution. On the other side were Tesla and Westinghouse. In DC, electrons flow in a single direction. In AC, electrons periodically switch directions. Edison waged a fierce publicity campaign, but Tesla's AC eventually won out. Its advantages? AC can travel farther without losing energy, allowing for centralized power generation, and AC can transfer different amounts of power.

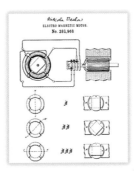

An alternating current motor invention

Ohm's Law *(p. 52)*

Electricity *(p. 55)*

Thomas Edison

Considered one of the most prolific inventors in history, Thomas Edison (1847-1931) built the world's first large-scale electrical supply network in 1882. Notable inventions include a stock ticker, a mechanical vote recorder, a battery for an electric car, the incandescent lightbulb, and recorded music and motion pictures. Dubbed "the wizard of Menlo Park" by a newspaper reporter, Edison applied the principles of mass production and large-scale teamwork to the process of invention, and is therefore often credited with creating the first industrial research laboratory.

Large-scale Electric Supply Network
In 1880 Thomas Edison produced a long-lasting source of light using a small filament and vacuum inside a glass globe. Many people had worked on creating electric lighting, but Edison was the first to achieve lighting that was practical for home use.

1880 >

Large-scale Electric Supply Network

● IN USE

Inventor Thomas Edison was the first to devise and implement electric power generation and distribution to homes, businesses, and factories, a key milestone in the development of the modern industrialized world. Edison patented this system in 1880 in order to capitalize on his invention of the electric lamp—Edison was nothing if not a shrewd businessman. On December 17, 1880, he founded the Edison Illuminating Company, headquartered at Pearl Street Station, in New York City. On September 4, 1882, Edison switched on his Pearl Street generating station's electrical power distribution system, which provided 110 volts direct current to about 60 customers in lower Manhattan.

Although Edison lost the "War of the Currents" that followed—with the consequence that alternating current became the system through which electrical power was distributed—his power distribution system is still significant for a few reasons. It established the commercial value of such a system, and it helped to stimulate advances in the

Telephone

The telephone—from early models to today's cordless phones—transformed business and personal communications worldwide.

1876 >

Breakthroughs continue on page 50

Telephone

● IN USE

field of electrical engineering; people began to see the field as a valuable occupation. For example, American electrical engineer Charles Proteus Steinmetz, through his work in alternating current, made possible the expansion of the electric power industry in the United States by formulating mathematical theories for engineers who were designing electric motors for use in industry.

Today, it is easy to take the telephone for granted; however, this was a significant development in terms of technology. While in pursuit of a multiple telegraph, or what he called a "harmonic telegraph," Alexander Graham Bell began playing with the idea of using the technology to transmit a human voice. Bell realized that different tones would vary the strength of an electric current in a wire. Thus, to transmit a voice successfully, he would need to build a transmitter capable of varying electronic currents and a receiver

that would reproduce these variations in audible frequencies.

On March 10, 1876, Bell was successful in this endeavor, transmitting the now famous words to his assistant Thomas Watson in another room: "Mr. Watson, come here, I want to see you." With that line, Bell effectively signaled the decline of the telegraph industry. The obvious communications potential contained in his demonstration of being able to "talk with electricity" far surpassed anything that the Morse code system—upon which

the telegraph system was based—could provide, no matter how that system was improved upon.

▼ Electricity (p. 55)

▼ Cell Phone (p. 24)

▼ Telegraph (p. 51)

Cloud Walking
Visit social media websites—such as Facebook, Twitter, Flickr, or National Geographic's Your Shot (shown here)—and you're entering the cloud.

Cloud Computing

In the past, computing relied on a physical infrastructure: routers, data pipes, hardware, and servers. These items have not gone away—nor are they likely to disappear altogether—but the process of delivering resources and services is moving to a model whereby the Internet is used to store the applications that are needed.

An immediate benefit of this model is cost. No longer does a company, for example, have to buy individual software licenses for every employee. With cloud computing, a single application gives multiple users access to the software, which they access remotely. Web-based email, such as Google's Gmail, is an example of cloud computing.

The concept of cloud computing can best be understood by thinking of it in terms of layers. The front-end layers are what users see and interact with—a Facebook account, for example. The back end consists of the hardware and software architecture that runs the interface on the front end. Because the computers are set up in a network, the applications can take advantage of all the combined computing power as if they were running on one particular machine. While there are advantages to this model, it is not without its drawbacks. Privacy and security are two of the biggest concerns. After all, a company is allowing important, potentially sensitive data to reside on the Internet, where, in theory, anyone could access it. The companies that provide cloud-computing services, however, are highly motivated to make sure that privacy and security are inherent in everything they do—their reputations are at stake. An authentication system that employs user names and passwords or other types of authorization helps to ensure privacy.

1990
Cloud-computing applications, by definition, reside in the World Wide Web. *See page 19*

1977
The personal computer is the means by which most people will access the cloud. *See page 22*

1976
Public key cryptography enables the encrypting of electronically transmitted private information. *See page 23*

Neither Here nor There
Cloud computing allows thousands, sometimes millions, of participants to access digital materials—images and text, encrypted into electronic pulses—without the data residing in the hardware of their computers.

1969

The Internet is the foundation of cloud computing and allows users to run applications on computers other than their own. *See page 28*

1880

A large-scale electrical supply network is necessary for the use of a cloud-computing infrastructure. *See page 46*

0 = OPEN
1 = CLOSED

Boolean Logic....................

The algebraic tradition in logic, developed by English mathematician George Boole, today finds application in computer construction. Zero indicates a "gate," or switch, is open; the number 1 indicates the gate is closed.

Doppler Effect
A sound wave builds and wanes, illustrating the Doppler effect.

From 1854 back to 3000 B.C. >

1854 >

1842 >

Boolean Logic

▲ IN THEORY

Computer operations are based on one thing: determining if a switch, or "gate," is open or closed—often signaled using the numbers 0 and 1. This is the essence of the Boolean logic that underlies all of modern computing. The concept was named after English mathematician George Boole, who defined an algebraic system of logic in 1854. Boole was motivated to create this theory because of his belief that the symbols of mathematical operation could be separated from those of quantity, and treated as distinct objects of calculation.

Nearly a century later, Claude Shannon would show how electric circuits with relays were a perfect model for Boolean logic, a fact that led to the development of the electronic computer. Computers use Boolean logic to decide if a statement is true or false (this has to do with a value, not veracity). There are three basic "gates": AND, OR, and NOT. The AND operation says if and only if *all* inputs are on, the output will be on. The OR operation says if *any* input is on, the output will be on. The NOT operation says that the output will have an opposite state from the input.

Doppler Effect

▲ IN THEORY

The Doppler effect, proposed by the Austrian physicist Christian Doppler in 1842, refers to a change in the frequency of a wave—whether composed of sound, light, or radio—when its source and observer are in motion with respect to each other. It is due to the nature of the wave's frequency and speed, which are directly correlated: As speed increases, frequency decreases; and as speed decreases, frequency increases. It is why a car horn, for example, changes pitch as a car drives by. Because sources and receivers of electromagnetic signals are

Building On >

Punch Card *(p. 54)*

Binary Numbers/Binary Code *(p. 55)*

Leibniz Calculator *(p. 56)*

1837 >

Telegraph

● IN USE

→← CONNECTION

often in motion with respect to one another, understanding the Doppler effect is crucial to modern information and communications technologies. Astronomers have been applying the principle behind the Doppler effect in an attempt to understand the universe better—in particular, what the observations of the electromagnetic force among stars and galaxies tell scientists about the expansion of the universe.

In 1837 American inventor Samuel Morse introduced the first working mechanical form of the telegraph. It was based on the principles of electromagnetism, and while Morse was not the only one to conceive of the idea, he was among the first to see its widespread commercial value. Here is how it worked: The circuit through which electricity flowed over a wire was broken by a human operator for a specific period. This resulted in an audible signal at the other end that was interpreted and transcribed by a human operator as either a dot or a dash, and the entire sequence

was put together to present the message.

In 1843 the U.S. Congress appropriated $30,000 to fund an experimental telegraph line from Washington, D.C., to Baltimore, Maryland. On May 24, 1844, Morse made the first public demonstration of his telegraph by sending the now famous message from the Supreme Court Chamber in Washington to the B & O Railroad: "What hath God wrought?"

The telegraph proved that electronic communication not only was possible, but also held enormous commercial potential.

Morse code is a means of transmitting information through a series of binary states—dots and dashes—that can be understood without the use of special equipment. The early telegraph system was based on a modified version of the Morse code. It encoded the Roman alphabet, Arabic numerals, and a small set of punctuation and procedural signals. Morse code can be seen as an early precursor to coding theory, an offshoot of information theory that prescribes how electrical signals can be encoded to maximize efficiency.

Hubble Telescope (p. 114)

Telephone (p. 47)

Electromagnetic Induction

English chemist Michael Faraday used a ring with two coils wound around it, like this replica, to discover the principles of electromagnetic induction in 1831.

Ohm's Law

A battery connected to a lightbulb illustrates the principle of Ohm's law, which defines the relationship between power, current, voltage, and resistance.

1831 >

1827 >

Electromagnetic Induction

▲ IN THEORY

In 1831 English chemist and physicist Michael Faraday discovered that an electric current is created in a conductor when it is moved through a magnetic field. This phenomenon—known as electromagnetic induction—remains true whether the field itself changes in strength or the conductor is moved through it.

Faraday later used this principle to create an electric dynamo, which made possible the operation of generators, electric motors, transformers, induction motors, synchronous motors, solenoids, and most other electrical machines.

Ohm's Law

▲ IN THEORY

Ohm's law defines the relationships between power, voltage, current, and resistance. One ohm is the resistance value through which one volt will maintain a current of one ampere. Ohm's law is one of the most basic, most useful equations in terms of electricity. And it can be applied to both AC and DC currents.

German physicist Georg Ohm first conceived of the equation as he experimented on how well metals conducted electricity, based on the work on resistance that others such as English scientist Henry Cavendish had done. Ohm realized that the current through a conductor between two points is directly proportional to the potential difference, or voltage, across the two points, and inversely proportional to the resistance between them. This was a key discovery in the history of electrical engineering; it represented the beginning of electrical circuit analysis.

At first Ohm's work was received with little enthusiasm, despite its undeniable influence on theory; however, his work was eventually recognized by the Royal Society, which awarded Ohm with the Copley Medal in 1841.

Building On >

Alternating Current (p. 45)

Electricity (p. 55)

First Permanent Photograph

The first permanent photo of nature depicts an 1826 courtyard scene at Saint-Loup-de-Varennes, France. The photo is on display at the University of Texas at Austin.

Difference Engine

English mathematician Charles Babbage had in mind to build a machine that could calculate without error and print the answers. The result: the mechanical calculator, a prototype he designed but never completed.

1826 >

1822 >

First Permanent Photograph

● IN USE

Photography is the result of several different discoveries made by various individuals, from the pinhole camera, first described in the fourth and fifth centuries B.C., to the chemicals used to develop the images, such as silver nitrate and silver chloride. In 1826 French inventor Joseph Nicéphore Niépce produced the first permanent photograph. He experimented with lithography (printing using a stone or metal plate), which led to an attempt to take a photograph using a camera obscura, an optical device that projects an image of its surroundings on a screen.

Niépce also experimented with silver chloride, which darkens when exposed to light, but found bitumen to be more successful at capturing images.

Difference Engine

● IN USE

Charles Babbage, an English mathematician, philosopher, inventor, and mechanical engineer, realized in 1822 that an "engine" of sorts could be programmed using paper cards that stored information in columns containing patterns of punched holes. Babbage saw that a person could program a set of instructions by way of punch cards, which could be carried out automatically by the machine. Although Babbage's difference engine—its intended use being the calculation of various mathematical functions, such as logarithms—was never completed, it is considered one of the first general-purpose digital computers.

Personal Computer (p. 22)

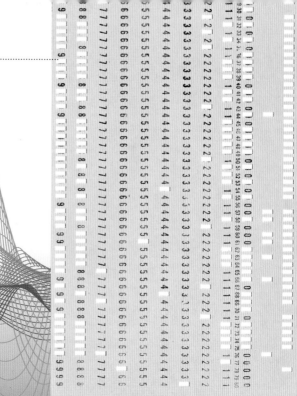

Punch Card
Joseph-Marie Jacquard first conceived of punch cards circa 1800. A stiff piece of paper containing information represented by the presence or absence of holes, the punch card was an early step in the development of computer programming.

Fourier Analysis
External sources of static add white noise on top of underlying sound waves. Fourier analysis provides mathematical models of complex waves as the sums of multiple simple waves.

1807 >

ca 1800 >

Fourier Analysis

▲ IN THEORY

Fourier analysis is named after French mathematician and physicist Joseph Fourier. In 1807 Fourier, who was working on heat propagation, showed that representing a heat source by a series of sine and cosine waves greatly simplified the problem. Fourier analysis, which grew out of the study of the so-called Fourier series, has widespread applications in mathematics. Many signal-processing techniques—such as those involving touch-tone signals, cell phones, radio scanners, and FM radio—consist of transforming a signal, manipulating the data it contains, and reversing the transformation using Fourier analysis.

Punch Card

● IN USE

During the late 1790s Joseph-Marie Jacquard was working on a mechanical loom that could weave complicated patterns described by holes in punched cards. The pattern could be changed simply by changing cards. Jacquard's loom was a significant early step in the development of computer programming. Charles Babbage used a similar concept in creating his difference engine in 1822, and during the 1880s American statistician Herman Hollerith devised a system that passed punched cards over electrical contacts. His machine enabled both the counting and sorting of data, a technology that has been deployed in a wide variety of contexts, from compiling statistical information for the 1890 U.S. Census to organizing mass deportations of Jews in the Nazi Holocaust.

Building On >

Benjamin Franklin tapped lightning to harness electricity.

1745 >

Binary Numbers / Binary Code
The binary code is a system where all information is expressed by the numbers 1 and 0. The system is used to convert verbal statements into mathematical ones.

ca 1679 >

Electricity

▲ IN THEORY

Some of the most important discoveries that paved the way for modern applications of electricity occurred in the 18th century.

In November 1745 German scientist Ewald Georg von Kleist invented a simple capacitor, which stored an electrical charge. Around the same time, Pieter van Musschenbroek, a Dutch professor at the University of Leyden, came up with a similar device in the form of the Leyden jar. The two men's work proved that static electricity could be transformed into an electric current.

German physicist Daniel Gralath combined several Leyden jars to increase the storage capacity. In 1747 American inventor Benjamin Franklin investigated this further and proved that the charge was stored on the glass, not in the water. In addition, Franklin established the link between lightning and electricity during his famous kite-in-a-thunderstorm experiment.

Other important figures during this time include Michael Faraday, Andre Ampere, Georg Ohm, Luigi Galvani, and Alessandro Volta—all of whom have their names attached to some measure of electricity.

Electrocardiogram (p. 86)

Hybrid Vehicle (p. 258)

Binary Numbers / Binary Code

▲ IN THEORY

In the 1670s German philosopher and mathematician Gottfried Wilhelm Leibniz—whose accomplishments include the invention of calculus and many important results in math, logic, and science—improved on French mathematician Blaise Pascal's "arithmetic machine" by inventing one that could multiply as well as add. Leibniz also saw how it could be altered to use a binary system of calculation—a concept that is at the heart of digital computing.

In Leibniz's system, the term binary refers to a number system whereby all values are expressed by using 1 and 0. The binary system can be best understood by contrasting it with the base 10 system in use today, which expresses numbers using zero through nine. In base 10, the number 367, for example, represents $3 \times 100 + 6 \times 10 + 7 \times 1$. Each position in the numeral 367 represents a power of ten, beginning with zero and increasing from right to left. In binary, or base 2, each position represents a power of two. So, 1101 in binary represents $1 \times 2^3 + 1 \times 2^2 + 0 \times 2^1 + 1 \times 2^0$, which is equal to $8 + 4 + 0 + 1$, or 13.

Modern Number System (p. 58)

Abacus (p. 59)

Gottfried Wilhelm Leibniz

[PROFILE]

Gottfried Wilhelm Leibniz (1646-1716), a 17th-century philosopher, mathematician, scientist, and prolific inventor, is perhaps most famous for his approach to calculus, his development of the binary number system, and the calculator that bears his name. In a sense, Leibniz can be considered the first computer scientist, since his contributions to mathematics, science, and even philosophy continued to resonate into the 1930s. Leibniz is also known for his approach to philosophy at a time when men like René Descartes asserted a highly rational view of the universe. Leibniz believed that the universe was the best possible universe God could have created and that God always chose the best for humans.

Leibniz Calculator

The first mechanical calculator, which used a cylinder with nine teeth of different lengths, performed the basic arithmetical calculations—addition, subtraction, division, and multiplication. The machine was used in the business marketplace of the day.

Slide Rule

First introduced in the early 1600s, slide rules were used primarily for multiplication and division, as well as other more advanced functions. Once standard tool used in mathematics and engineering, the slide rule has largely been replaced by today's calculators and computers.

1673 >

Leibniz Calculator

● IN USE

In addition to the binary number system and many other accomplishments, German mathematician Gottfried Wilhelm Leibniz invented a calculator that incorporated a stepped drum—a cylinder with nine teeth of different lengths that increased in equal amounts around the drum. Unlike Blaise Pascal's calculator, which could only be used for addition and subtraction, Leibniz's calculator could be used for multiplication and division as well.

This device was significant in that it reflected Leibniz's belief that logic could be described in mathematical symbols, rather than normal spoken and written language, which he found too ambiguous. According to Leibniz, complex ideas derive from simple ideas by combining them in a way similar to the logical operators of addition, subtraction, and multiplication.

Abacus (p. 59)

Castle Clock
The castle clock, developed by Al-Jazari in the early 1200s, is considered an early example of the programmable computer.

1624 >

1206 >

Slide Rule

● IN USE

In 1624 English mathematician Edmund Wingate published a description of a calculating device—an early slide rule, as it turns out. A slide rule is used primarily for multiplication and division, and also for functions such as roots, logarithms, and trigonometry. In its most basic form, the slide rule uses two logarithmic scales to allow rapid multiplication and division of numbers, which are operations that can be time-consuming and error-prone when done on paper. But it is not just a calculating tool. Because of its versatility, the slide rule can be seen as an early analog computer.

Slide rule

Castle Clock

● IN USE

The castle clock was a device invented by Al-Jazari, who in 1206 described it in his *Book of Knowledge of Ingenious Mechanical Devices*. The name derives from the fact that the device typically appears near the top of a castle or church tower.

Al-Jazari's mechanism was about 11 feet high, and could do more than just tell time. It included a display of the zodiac and the solar and lunar orbits, and could be reprogrammed to account for the changing lengths of day and night throughout the year. As a result of this feature, some consider this device an early example of a programmable analog computer.

▶ **Sundial** *(p. 153)*

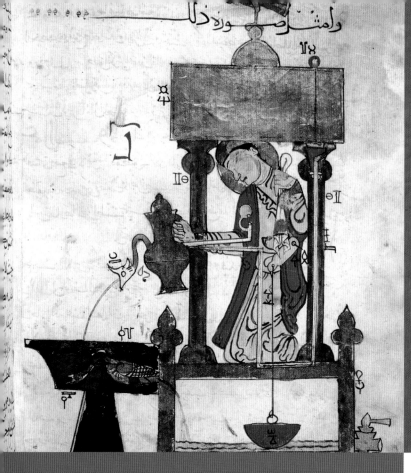

Al-Jazari

[PROFILE]

Al-Jazari (ca 1136-ca 1206) was many things: a scholar, inventor, mechanical engineer, craftsman, artist, mathematician, and astronomer. He is best known for his *Book of Knowledge of Ingenious Mechanical Devices* in 1206, in which he described 50 mechanical devices, along with instructions on how to construct them. These include the camshaft, crankshaft, segmental gear, water-raising machines, and even automatons. Not much is known about the man, other than what can be gleaned from the *Book of Knowledge*. He was named after the area in northern Mesopotamia in which he was born and was chief engineer at the Artuklu Palace, the residence of the Diyarbakır branch of the Turkish Artuqid dynasty.

ca 800-900 >

Modern Number System

● IN USE

The Hindu-Arabic numeral system upon which the modern number system is based was probably developed in the ninth century by Indian mathematicians, adopted by Persian mathematician Al-Khwarizmi and Arabic mathematician Al-Kindi, and spread to the Western world by the high Middle Ages.

The characteristics of the modern number system are the concepts of place values and decimal values. The place value system indicates that the value of each digit in a multi-digit number depends on its position. Take the number 279, for example. According to the place value system, the 2 represents hundreds, the 7 represents tens, and the 9 represents ones. Thus the number appears as 279. Meanwhile, the related decimal system presents numbers in increments of ten. In other words, each place value is ten times the value of the one before it. The decimal system allows mathematicians to perform arithmetic with high numbers that would otherwise be extremely cumbersome to manipulate.

Computers make use of the positional numbering system.

Binary Numbers/Binary Code *(p. 55)*

A wooden abacus

Modern Number System
A dial pad on an Egyptian public telephone features Western and Arabic numerals. The modern way of writing numbers evolved over centuries, eventually replacing the Roman system.

ca **3000** B.C. >

Abacus

↺ BACKLASH

● IN USE

Since a computer uses only a small amount of memory to store a number, some numbers are too large or too small to be represented. That is where floating-point numbers come in. The decimal point can "float" relative to the significant digits in a number. For example, a fixed-point representation that has seven decimal digits with two decimal places can represent the numbers 12345.67, 123.45, 1.23, and so on, whereas the same floating-point representation could also represent 1.234567, 123456.7, 0.00001234567, and so on.

Starting around the 13th century in Europe, the Roman number system was replaced with the Arabic number system, which uses positional and decimal notation. But the transition did not occur without a fight. In Florence, for example, Arabic numerals were outlawed because they were much easier to counterfeit and alter than Roman numerals, and thus posed a serious threat to commerce and banking. This distrust remains today: No check is acceptable unless it has the amount written as a word as well as a numeral.

The invention of the abacus is credited to the Chinese about 5,000 years ago, and its use quickly spread throughout the world. Whether counting flocks of sheep, decanters of wine, or sacks of grain, the abacus gave people the ability to keep track of numbers as they did their figuring. The abacus makes use of the place value system, in that each row of stones, beads, or marbles stands for a unit number—ones, fives, tens, and so on.

In a sense, the abacus can be considered one of the first "computers." While today's computers do the actual calculating, a truly proficient abacus user can perform simple calculations almost as fast.

▼ ENIAC (p. 38)

▼ Turing Machine (p. 40)

▼ Binary Numbers/Binary Code (p. 55)

▼ Leibniz Calculator (p. 56)

Identity Theft ....
Artificial intelligence raises fascinating questions of psychology and philosophy as well as technology. Can a robot develop an identity? Can computers understand themselves? Artificial intelligence verges on science fiction.

Artificial Intelligence

Artificial intelligence refers to the branch of computer science that is focused on giving computers human intelligence. Upon hearing the term, most people think of HAL 9000 from *2001: A Space Odyssey*, or maybe the character David from the movie *A.I. Artificial Intelligence*. The truth is that those forms of AI are still a long way off.

That is not to say that no forms of artificial intelligence exist. Consider, for example, the Deep Blue system, a chess-playing computer that defeated world champion Garry Kasparov in 1997. In February 2011 the Watson system, devised by IBM, competed on the game show *Jeopardy!* against the two best human contestants the show had ever hosted—Ken Jennings and Brad Ritter—and won. What was significant about Watson was its ability to process natural language. To win, of course, Watson had to figure out what the game show's questions—known for making use of wordplay and double entendres—were asking.

Many AI applications have already found their way into mainstream computer applications. Banks, medical clinics, telecommunications companies, and the U.S. Postal Service are a few examples of institutions that use AI systems to organize resources, manage schedules, process materials based on certain kinds of information, and carry out other tasks. The automotive industry has used robots for painting, welding, and assembly tasks for nearly 15 years.

So will there ever be a HAL or David? Despite Watson's significant achievement and what it means to human employment, another very important hurdle needs to be overcome. Humans, unlike computers, have common sense, learn from experiences, adapt to circumstances, and can make inferences about things. When contestant Ken Jennings made a joke on *Jeopardy!* Watson was unable to comprehend the humor. A computer may be able to think faster than a human and may be able to mimic one nearly perfectly, but for now a computer can only do what it is told and only knows what it is told. Because of these and other limitations, some critics believe that AI is inherently impossible. Time will tell who is right—the proponents or the critics.

1946

The first electronic digital computers inspired research into seemingly "smart" machines that could solve problems. *See page 38.*

1936

A Turing machine is a model for how computers can—and cannot—solve problems or perform tasks. *See page 40.*

1854

Artificial intelligence systems—as well as all computers—are essentially logic machines that operate on the principles of Boolean logic. *See page 50.*

1745

Electricity is necessary for all electronic digital computers on which current artificial intelligence systems are based. *See page 55*

02

Health & Medicine

BIG IDEAS

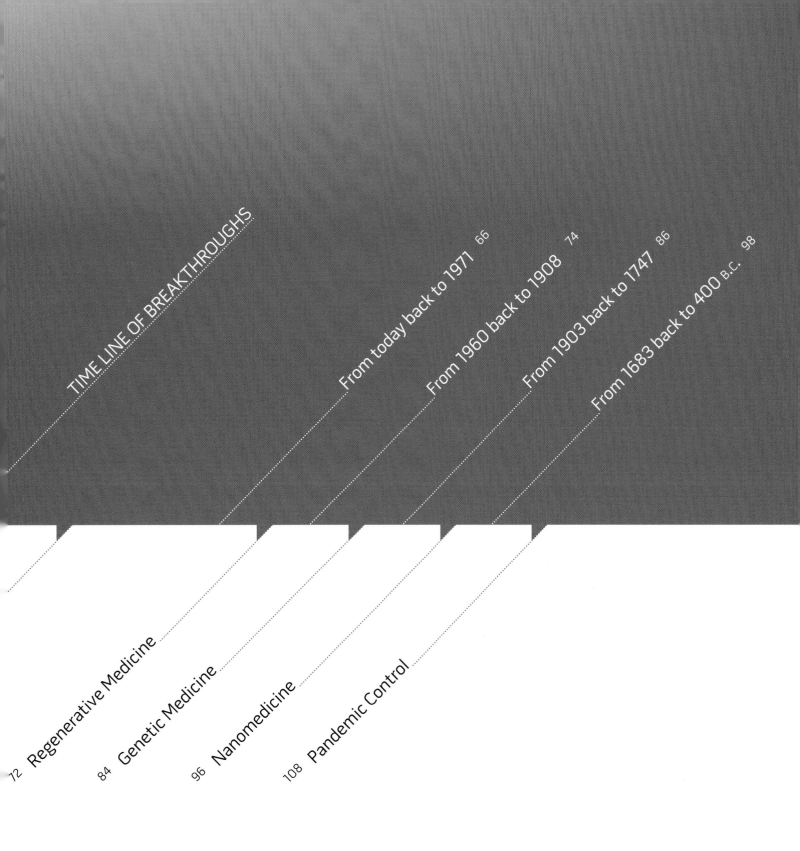

TIME LINE OF BREAKTHROUGHS

From today back to 1971 66

From 1960 back to 1908 74

From 1903 back to 1747 86

From 1683 back to 400 B.C. 98

INTRODUCTION

Understanding Ourselves

Afflictions of the body—sickness, injury, and disability—are a universal human concern stretching across boundaries of space and time. Against this dark backdrop, the history of medical science is inescapably a narrative of progress and hope.

Driven by a spirit of inquiry, medicine has radically transformed experience. For much of the human past, for example, the human body was a terra incognita, as much the object of fantasy as heaven or hell. Imagine the fascination with which early modern Europeans pored over the first accurate, detailed, full-color renderings of the stomach and bowels, or of the nervous system's delicate filigree. The first dissectionists, together with innovators in art and printing, had lifted a veil; today, every schoolchild understands basic anatomy.

This drive to explore the intricacies of biology led to the discovery of increasingly minute and finally invisible shapes—bacteria, viruses—whose discovery in turn reshaped the human life cycle. For most of the human career, death in childhood was a routine event; in the 20th century, thanks to the beating back of infectious disease, it became more of an anomaly.

The history of medicine is a story of pieces coming together, sometimes across cultures and great chasms of time, in an idea that suddenly quickens. The pus-pulling device of the ancient Greeks and the goose-quill needle of a Renaissance Englishman join in the hypodermic syringe of the mid-19th century. Medicine's history is built upon the invention of tools and methods, and the grasping and wielding of those implements in pursuit of further discovery. Encephalography made possible the study of brain waves; ultrasound opened the way for fetal medicine. Clinical trial design offered a way to exclude from medical research the inevitably biased perceptions of investigators, and the collection of vital statistics created databases revealing the warp and weft of a population's health.

If the challenges scientists face today—the quest to engineer replacement organs, or enlist stem cells to repair damaged hearts and brains—seem all but insurmountable, a backward glance at medicine's past accomplishments inspires confidence in its future.

Anthony Atala

1999 >

[PROFILE]

"A salamander can grow back its leg," Anthony Atala (1958-) said in a 2006 interview. "Why can't a human do the same?" The remark, a reference to work funded by the U.S. Department of Defense aiming to grow new limbs for wounded soldiers, captures the inventive spirit for which the Peruvian-born surgeon is known. Atala's research career, first at Harvard Medical School and later as director of North Carolina's Wake Forest Institute for Regenerative Medicine, is marked by a series of startling discoveries, from finding a way to correct weak ureters with injected cartilage cells to identifying a class of stem cells derived from placenta and amniotic fluid.

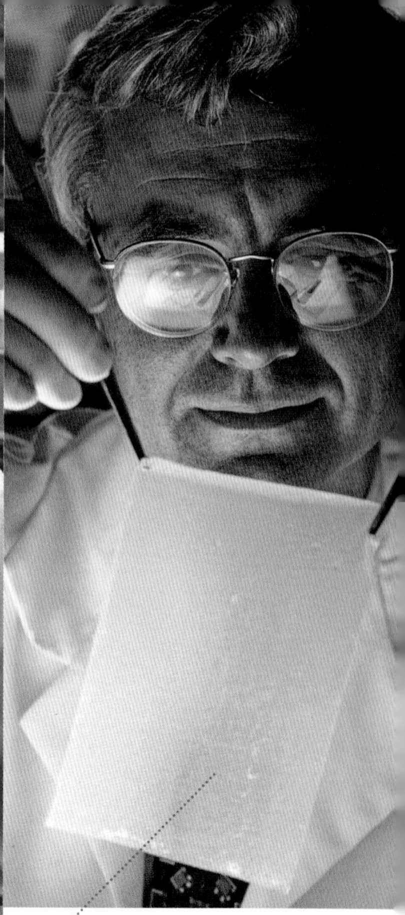

Transplantation of Engineered Tissue

● IN USE

Once the stage was set through years of basic science, the process of building the first functioning lab-grown human organ could seem deceptively simple. First researcher Anthony Atala and colleagues at the Wake Forest Institute for Regenerative Medicine collected muscle and bladder cells from their patient, and cultured them in the lab. The scientists formed a bladder-shaped "scaffold" of biodegradable material, covered this mold with the patient's own muscle cells, and lined it with bladder cells. Then they grafted their

Building On >

Bone-Marrow Transplant *(p. 76)*

Organ Transplant *(p. 78)*

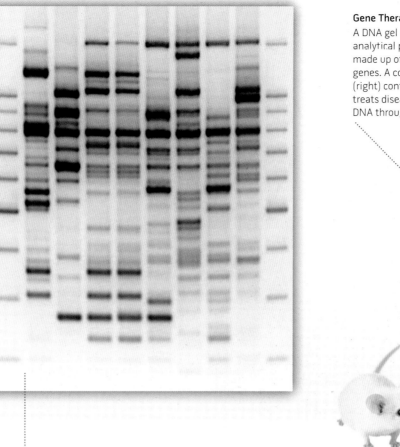

Transplantation of Engineered Tissue
A scientist holds a section of artificial skin in La Jolla, California. The field of tissue engineering uses a combination of cells, engineering methods, and materials to help repair or replace damaged tissue.

Gene Therapy
A DNA gel sequence (left) is used primarily for analytical purposes. Gene therapy inserts genes, made up of DNA, into cells to replace defective genes. A conceptual image shows a pill capsule (right) containing strands of DNA. Just as a pill treats disease, so can altering someone's DNA through gene therapy.

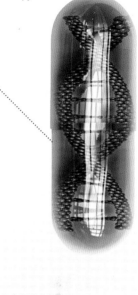

Laboratory mouse

1993 >

Gene Therapy

● IN USE

construction onto the patient's own dysfunctional bladder. More than six years later, in 2006, the group announced a triumph to the world: The first bladder they had implanted, as well as a handful of others, was working.

Devastating inherited diseases have played a key role in the nascent science of gene therapy, dealing researchers early triumphs—and painful setbacks.

In 1990 scientists at Maryland's National Institutes of Health launched gene therapy's first human trial, treating two girls with severe combined immunodeficiency, or SCID. They collected the children's defective white blood cells, inserted normal genes into them, then returned the cells to the patients. Though they required ongoing treatment, the girls developed normal immunity.

In 1999, though, the public learned of a gene therapy failure in the death of 18-year-old Jesse Gelsinger, whose inherited liver disease was being treated in a University of Pennsylvania clinical trial. A government investigation found a number of ethical lapses in the trial's conduct, including a failure to inform subjects fully about risks.

Then, in 2000 a team from Paris reported results of a gene-therapy trial in ten boys with a different form of SCID; the boys had received transplants of their own "corrected" bone-marrow cells. Tragically, two

years later the team reported that one boy, then another, developed a leukemia-like condition, apparently because the virus used to deliver the boys' corrected DNA had lodged near a gene that regulates cell growth. The alarming news led to the halting not only of the French trial but also of studies in Germany, Italy, and the United States.

More recently, though, small gene-therapy experiments have produced positive results. Reported in 2010, a University of Pennsylvania gene-therapy study showed activity against HIV, with seven of eight subjects improving.

◢ Cells (p. 247)

◢ Structure of DNA (p. 223)

Cord-Blood Transplant

A micrograph shows stem cells taken from umbilical cord blood. By extracting stem cells from the umbilical cord, scientists can culture blood cells of the immune system that are necessary to fight infection or cancer.

Artificial Heart

Dr. Robert Jarvik designed the first successful artificial heart, which was implanted in 61-year-old Barney Clark in 1982. Each section of the polyurethane heart was about the size of a fist.

1988 >

1982 >

Cord-Blood Transplant

● IN USE

At a Paris hospital in 1988 a six-year-old boy suffering from a hereditary blood disorder became the first person in the world to receive a transplant of stem-cell-rich blood from the human umbilical cord. In the two decades that followed, more than 12,000 cord-blood transplants were performed worldwide.

Capable of producing all the types of blood cells, cord-blood-derived stem cells are now used to replenish blood and immune systems damaged by cancer treatments and various other disorders. Often the procedure is an alternative to bone-marrow transplantation, the earliest form of stem-cell therapy. Cord blood is easier to collect and may provoke a less severe immune rejection in the recipient.

Petri dish

⮌ BACKLASH

In 1998 scientists at the University of Wisconsin isolated and cultured the world's first line of stem cells derived from human embryos. These cells are capable of multiplying prodigiously in the lab; they can differentiate into any of the body's more than 200 cell types. But because developing the cell lines involves destroying embryos, their potential role in research has been stymied by a thorny ethical debate. A critical juncture came in 2001, when President George W. Bush curtailed work on embryonic stem cells by limiting federal research funding.

Artificial Heart

● IN USE

The heart is a muscle, and the history of attempts to create a functioning synthetic version illustrates how complex a muscle it is. Barney Clark, who received the first permanent artificial heart in 1982, lived 112 days. The heart was designed by physician Robert Jarvik and implanted at the University of Utah Medical Center. Complications in subsequent cases led to government limits on the use of artificial hearts. In 2006 the U.S. Food and Drug Administration approved a new synthetic heart, the AbioCor, but only for heart-failure patients who had no other options.

Building On >

▼ Hospital Blood Bank *(p. 80)*

▼ Classification of Blood Types *(p. 86)*

▼ Blood Transfusion *(p. 93)*

▼ Blood Cells *(p. 99)*

▼ Organ Transplant *(p. 78)*

Eradication of Smallpox

In 1939 a doctor and nurse, both from the California Department of Public Health, immunize a family for smallpox and typhoid fever. The back of a station wagon served as a shelf on which to keep medical equipment.

Eradication of Smallpox
A microscopic view of the highly infectious smallpox virus, which was globally eradicated in 1980.

1980 >

Eradication of Smallpox

● IN USE

Bearer of that "speckled monster" otherwise known as smallpox, the variola virus probably emerged thousands of years ago in some of the first agricultural settlements of northeastern Africa, China, or the Indus River Valley. It left its pitted scars on the face of Egyptian Pharaoh Ramses V, and repeatedly scourged Europe during the Middle Ages. Variola sailed the Atlantic with Spanish and Portuguese conquistadors, laying waste to the Inca and Aztec. It harried the army of George Washington in the Revolutionary War, and, according to some scholars, racked President Abraham Lincoln with weakness and fever as he delivered his famous address at Gettysburg.

A country doctor from southwest England in 1796 set humanity on a path to vanquishing the disease by inoculating a young boy with material from a cowpox lesion on the arm of a local dairymaid. So was born the word "vaccination," which comes from the Latin *vacca*, meaning "cow."

Despite these efforts, 150 years later, smallpox continued to sweep the globe, producing some 50 million cases annually mostly in nonindustrialized countries. In 1966 the World Health Organization mounted an unprecedented and ambitious effort to wipe out the disease, spearheaded by American epidemiologist Donald A. Henderson. Public health workers went from village to village, zeroing in on cases and administering 100 million vaccinations in five years. In 1977 a hospital cook in Merka, Somalia, suffered the last naturally occurring case of smallpox. By 1980 the WHO declared the world and its people free of the disease.

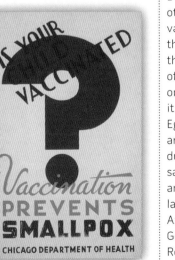

A poster encourages children to get the smallpox vaccine.

▼ Viruses *(p. 87)*

▼ Smallpox Vaccine *(p. 94)*

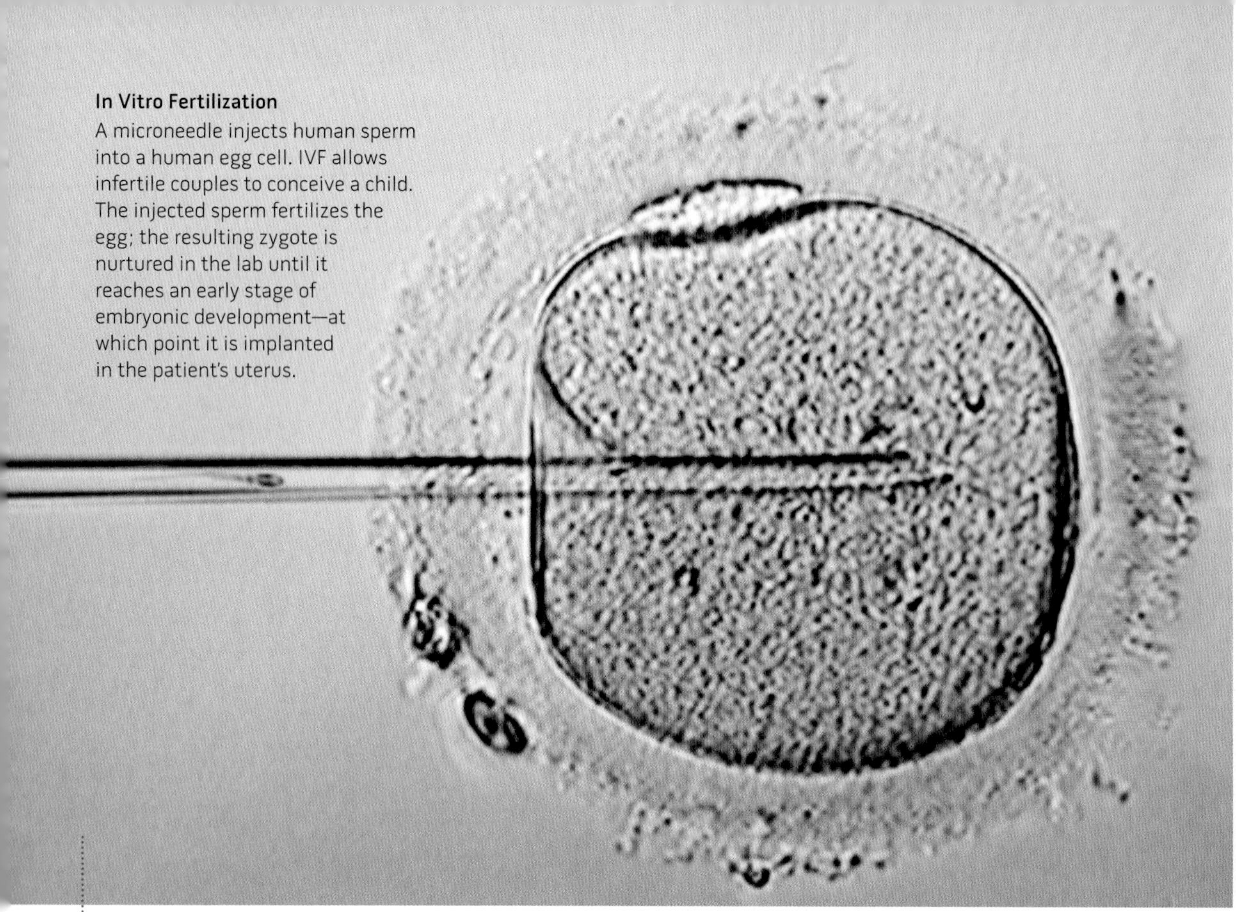

In Vitro Fertilization

A microneedle injects human sperm into a human egg cell. IVF allows infertile couples to conceive a child. The injected sperm fertilizes the egg; the resulting zygote is nurtured in the lab until it reaches an early stage of embryonic development—at which point it is implanted in the patient's uterus.

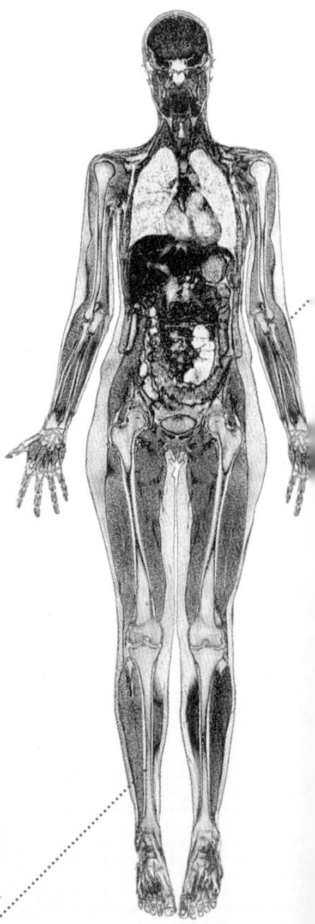

1978 >

1977 >

In Vitro Fertilization

● IN USE

It took British fertility researcher Robert Edwards decades to unlock the mysteries of conception, first working with animals, then struggling for years to create just the right hormonal conditions and achieve precisely the correct timing to fertilize and grow human eggs in a petri dish. When at last a successful implantation led to the 1978 birth of "test-tube baby" Louise Brown, the world all but gasped in astonishment.

By 2010, when Edwards won the Nobel Prize, the method he pioneered had become a common approach to infertility, and led directly to the births of more than four million human beings.

⮌ BACKLASH

Though in vitro fertilization has gained widespread acceptance, the procedure also has spawned considerable ethical quandaries. IVF clinics are the major source of discarded embryos used in highly controversial embryonic stem cell research. And although the American Society of Reproductive Medicine suggests no more than two embryos be implanted in women under 35, this limit has often been flouted—sometimes leading to risky high-multiple births or requiring selective reduction, in which one or more fetuses are eliminated.

Magnetic Resonance Imaging

● IN USE

What inspired Raymond Damadian, as a newly minted medical doctor in the 1960s, to begin his work developing the first magnetic resonance imaging machine? Sharp abdominal pains. At the time, because traditional x-rays could not produce detailed pictures of non-bony structures, the only way to examine soft tissues inside the body was to open the patient surgically.

Nearly a decade would pass before Damadian and his colleagues succeeded in producing the first grainy two-dimensional MRI image of a

Building On >   Meiosis *(p. 233)*

Magnetic Resonance Imaging
An MRI of the human body reveals
the internal organs and tissues
of a woman, including her bones,
muscles, and a layer of fat.

A computed tomography scanner

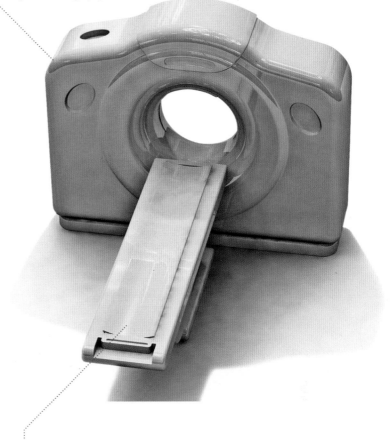

MRI of a human brain

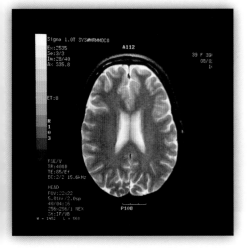

1971 >   Breakthroughs continue on page 74

Computed Tomography

● IN USE

graduate student's heart and
lungs. They dubbed their scanner
the "Indomitable."

Unlike x-rays or the more
complex computed tomography,
MRI does not use ionizing
radiation and so is considered
very safe. Instead it employs a
magnetic field (the patient lies
inside an enormous magnetic
tube), coupled with radio signals
sent to and received from the
body via temporary changes in
its water molecules. A computer
translates this information into
high-resolution pictures. MRI
has revolutionized diagnostic

medicine as a noninvasive way to
reveal pathologies of, for example,
the spinal column and nerves,
or of musculoskeletal structures
such as tendons and ligaments.
MRI scans are very useful in
examining the brain for evidence
of stroke, or looking at other
organs for signs of infection. One
disadvantage: The technology is
very costly.

Godfrey Hounsfield worked as an
engineer for the British record
company Electric and Musical
Industries in the late 1960s when
he hatched an ingenious idea.
A computer, he thought, could
turn hundreds of x-rays taken
from different angles into a three-
dimensional image. The company
produced the first successful
clinical trial of the technology in
1971, garnering worldwide sales of
some 450 scanners by the end of
1976. It was a time of rapid progress
in medical imaging, with computed
tomography, or CT, contributing a
quick, relatively simple, and cost-

effective way to image everything
from trauma-related internal
injuries to the precise size and
location of a tumor.

▼ Personal Computer *(p. 22)*

▼ X-ray Imaging *(p. 88)*

▼ Personal Computer *(p. 22)*

Regenerative Medicine

The burgeoning field of regenerative medicine seeks nothing less than to provide patients with replacement body parts. Here, the parts are not steel pins and such. They are the real thing: living cells, tissue, and even organs.

Regenerative medicine is still a mostly experimental enterprise, with clinical applications limited to such procedures as growing sheets of skin to graft onto burns and wounds. But the prospects go much further. As long ago as 1999, a research group at North Carolina's Wake Forest Institute for Regenerative Medicine implanted a patient with a laboratory-grown bladder. The team has continued to generate an array of other tissues and organs, from kidneys to salivary glands to ears.

In 2007 a team led by orthopedic surgeon Cato Laurencin, then at the University of Virginia, reported on a tissue-engineered ligament that could allow patients to recover more quickly and fully from one of the most common types of knee injury—the torn anterior cruciate ligament. Laurencin's ACL was made of braided synthetic microfibers "seeded" with actual ACL cells. Tested in rabbits, the "scaffold," a supporting framework, promoted new blood vessel and collagen growth within 12 weeks.

Also working in animal models, other researchers have made important strides testing therapies based on stem cells, which multiply rapidly and can differentiate into an array of cell types. These repair cells may eventually be deployed to regrow cardiac muscle damaged by heart attack, or replace nerve cells in victims of spinal-cord injury.

The genesis of this approach reaches back to the early 20th century and the first successful transplantations of donated human soft tissue, bone, and corneas. Much as transplant medicine has progressed, it suffers from an intractable problem regenerative medicine might one day sweep aside: There are not enough donor organs for those who need them. Many die while waiting for an organ. Another advantage of regenerative medicine is that tissues grown from a patient's own cells will not be rejected by the body's immune system.

1999

The transplantation of engineered tissue was an early step in the nascent field of regenerative medicine. *See page 66*

1988, 1956, 1954

Cord-blood transplants, bone-marrow transplants, and organ transplants are important precursors to—but fall short of—regenerative medicine. *See pages 68, 76, 78*

1025, 400 B.C.

Regenerative medicine would be impossible without medical research, which is founded on the ideas of experimental medicine and the scientific study of medicine. *See pages 103, 107*

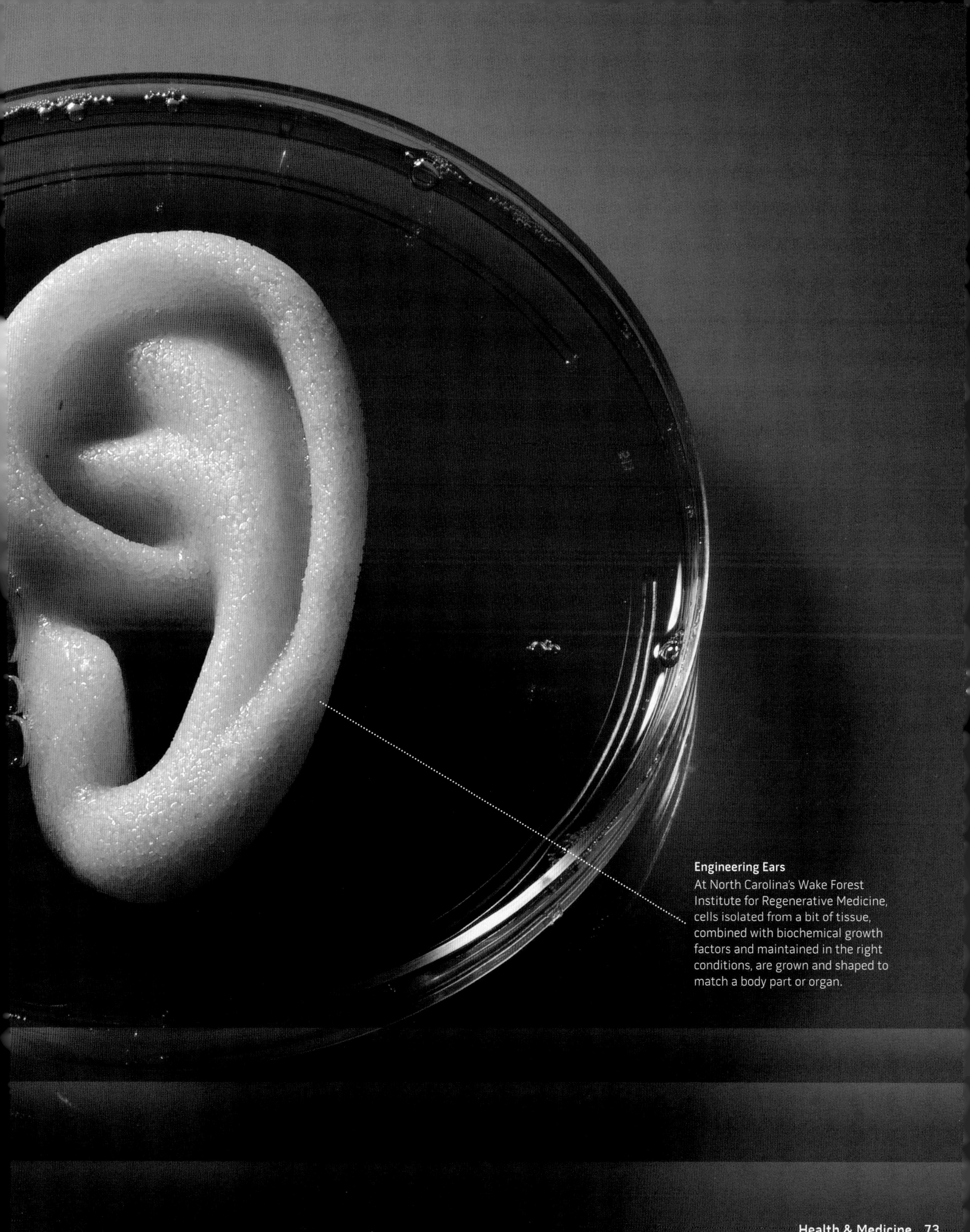

Engineering Ears
At North Carolina's Wake Forest Institute for Regenerative Medicine, cells isolated from a bit of tissue, combined with biochemical growth factors and maintained in the right conditions, are grown and shaped to match a body part or organ.

Birth Control Pill

The birth control pill, often referred to as the "pill," is widely used as a method to prevent pregnancy. Through a combination of estrogen and progestin, the pills inhibit fertility in women.

Birth Control Pill

The rosary is a traditional Catholic devotion. The Catholic Church has voiced strong objections to use of the pill to prevent pregnancy, stating that the rhythm method is the only appropriate method to control birth.

From 1960 back to 1908 >

1960 >

Birth Control Pill

● IN USE

Because of restrictions on contraceptive use in 1956 America, U.S. doctors launched the first large-scale human study of oral birth control in San Juan, Puerto Rico. Two years later G. D. Searle's Enovid was approved by the Food and Drug Administration to treat menstrual disorders—with an accompanying "warning" that the drug suppressed ovulation. Women flocked to Enovid. In 1960 Searle won approval to market the combination progesterone-and-estrogen pill as the simple and nearly fail-proof contraceptive that generations had awaited.

This medical breakthrough also proved a political and social watershed. In 1972 the Supreme Court struck down the last state laws limiting access to contraception.

A packet of birth control pills

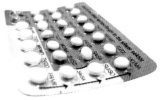

⊃ BACKLASH

Use of the pill provoked condemnation from two different quarters: religious traditionalists, most notably the Catholic Church, and feminist women's health advocates, led by journalist Barbara Seaman. Seaman's book, *The Doctors' Case Against the Pill*, exposed an increase in blood clots and strokes among pill users. In 1968 a papal encyclical reiterated the all-natural rhythm method as the only acceptable birth control. The following year Senate hearings on side effects resulted in new labeling for the pill, which listed the potential hazards.

Building On >

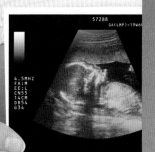

Ultrasound

A pregnancy ultrasound is an imaging test that uses sound waves to see how a baby is developing in the womb. The result: Parents get the first photo of their soon-to-be-born infant.

Bionics

Bionics—like this bionic hand—were popularized by the 1970s TV shows *The Six Million Dollar Man* and *The Bionic Woman,* which featured humans with superhuman powers derived from bionic implants.

1958 >

1958 >

Ultrasound

● IN USE

Around the same time the first ultrasound machine went on sale in the United States in 1963, Scottish physician Ian Donald was pioneering what would become ultrasound's best-known application: to "see" the fetus in the womb. In 1958 Donald had published a seminal paper in the *Lancet* documenting the use of ultrasound in more than 100 patients. Soon after, he noticed that the technology, which works by sending sound waves into tissue and measuring returning echoes, delivered a clear reading of the fetal head. During the 1960s, working at Glasgow's Queen Mother's Hospital, he and his colleagues refined techniques for monitoring fetal growth and detecting abnormalities.

Bionics

● IN USE

In 1958 doctors at Sweden's Karolinska Institute implanted the first pacemaker, regulating a patient's heartbeat by means of electrodes. That same year a U.S. Air Force doctor coined the term "bionics" to refer to engineering that mimics the design of nature. The word soon came to suggest prosthetic enhancements of the body itself—innovations like the first cochlear implant to restore hearing, approved for U.S. marketing in 1984; electronic retinal implants for blinding diseases, first implanted experimentally in 2002; and the high-performance "running blades," which permitted Pennsylvania native Amy Palmiero-Winters to become the first leg amputee accepted to the U.S. national track-and-field team in 2010.

▼ Stethoscope *(p. 94)*

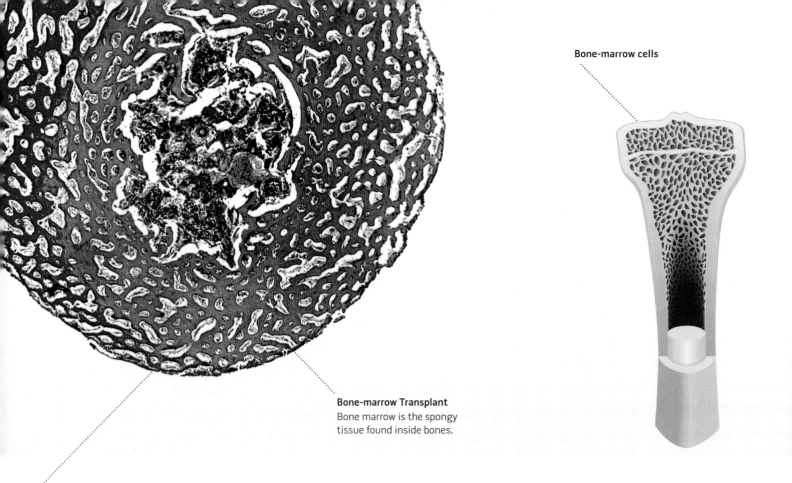

Bone-marrow cells

Bone-marrow Transplant
Bone marrow is the spongy
tissue found inside bones.

1956 >

Bone-marrow Transplant

● IN USE

The first successful bone-marrow transplant, performed in 1956 in Cooperstown, New York, on a three-year-old with end-stage leukemia, was a qualified success. The child's irradiated bone marrow was "rescued" by the stem-cell-laden marrow of her identical twin, but after six months her cancer returned and she died.

Even so, the procedure was an early demonstration that proliferative stem cells could be used as medicine to restore diseased constituents of the human body. And it helped spur the development of techniques and institutions that could one day prove vital to the success of other stem-cell-based therapies.

Early fatalities due to immune rejection of bone-marrow transplants motivated scientists to tackle this basic problem underlying use of donor cells or tissues, known as graft-versus-host disease. E. Donnall Thomas, the doctor who performed the 1956 bone-marrow transplant, went on to work on immune-suppressing drugs to control rejection. Around the same time, a French doctor named Jean Dausset was leading research that would describe human tissue types, allowing for closer genetic matching of donor and recipient.

In the late 1980s the nonprofit National Marrow Donor Registry began matching people willing to donate marrow with those who needed it. Twenty years later the registry included millions of marrow donors, as well as 160,000 available units of umbilical cord blood, another source of stem cells first identified in the 1970s.

➤◄ CONNECTION

Other early steps in the development of stem-cell therapies: In 1961 various animal experiments proved the existence of stem cells, and in 1978 blood-producing stem cells were discovered in human cord blood. Twenty years later scientists isolated the first line of human embryonic stem cells. In 1999 they succeeded in inducing stem cells to differentiate into specialized cartilage, fat, and bone cells. Using skin cells, investigators in 2007 engineered so-called induced pluripotent stem cells, with many of the capabilities of embryonic stem cells.

Building On >

Organ Transplant (p. 78)

Cell Nucleus (p. 238)

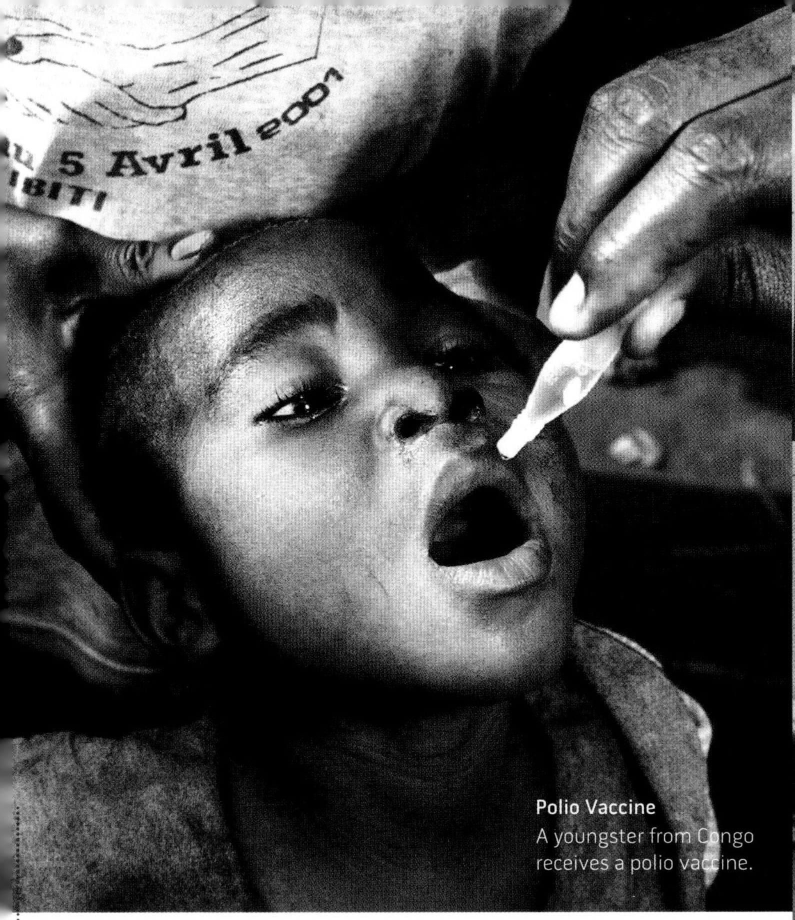

Polio Vaccine
A youngster from Congo receives a polio vaccine.

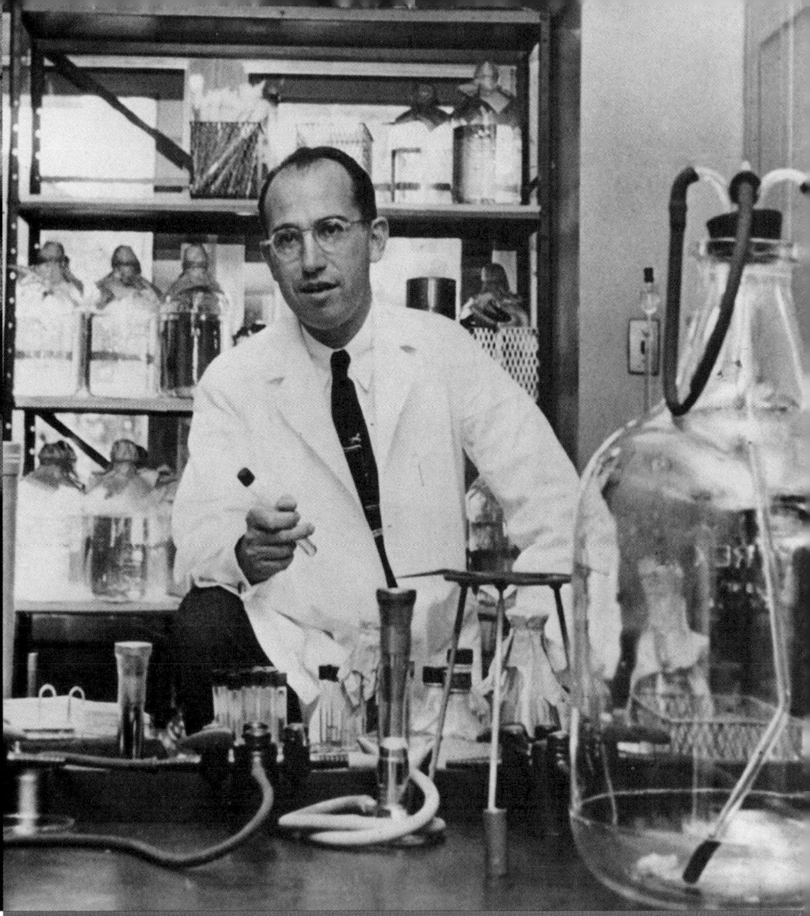

1955 >

Jonas Salk

Polio Vaccine

● IN USE

American doctor Jonas Salk studied influenza early in his career, when memories of its appalling lethality in a 1918 pandemic were fresh. His participation in developing a flu vaccine using killed, noninfectious virus—not the live virus thought necessary at the time—prepared Salk to develop a vaccine against an epidemic that peaked in the 1940s and 1950s, polio. Salk's vaccine was introduced in 1955; within several years, annual cases of the crippling scourge plunged from an average 45,000 to fewer than 1,000.

But many researchers at the time, including Russian-born Albert Sabin, believed Salk's dead-virus vaccine would not produce long-term immunity. While the Salk vaccine went into use in the United States, Sabin tested his oral vaccine made of live, weakened virus in millions of subjects in the Soviet Union and elsewhere. In 1962 the Sabin vaccine received U.S. licensure and became a mainstay in the fight to eradicate polio worldwide.

Jonas Salk (1914-1995), born to Russian-Jewish immigrants, grew up in the Bronx, a suburb of New York City. The oldest of three sons, he was the first in his family to attend college. "I think I was curious from an early age on," he said in an interview. "I tended to observe, and reflect, and wonder."

During medical school Salk fatefully questioned the then accepted notion that, while scientists could immunize against certain bacterial illnesses with chemically defanged bacterial toxins, only infection itself could induce immunity against viral diseases.

Viruses (p. 87)

Kidney Dialysis ....
In this archival photo a patient
undergoes kidney dialysis. The ma
purifies blood that flows from a tu
inserted into an artery in the patie
wrist and pumps it back into a vei

Organ Transplant
A surgeon holds a heart in his han
representing the importance of or
donation. According to experts in
the field, organs from one donor ca
help or save as many as 50 people

Organ Transplant
Mycophenolate is an
immunosuppressant that
helps prevent the rejection
of transplanted organs.

1954 >

Organ Transplant

● IN USE

At a Harvard-affiliated Boston hospital in 1954, doctors led by surgeon Joseph E. Murray performed the world's first successful organ transplant, removing a healthy kidney from one man and sewing it into his identical twin, a victim of severe renal disease.

The surgical challenges were considerable, and the procedure also raised a new ethical question: For the first time a patient (the donor) would submit to a highly invasive procedure solely to benefit another.

But the surgeons did not so much overcome as avoid the most substantial obstacle to success in that first transplant. The team understood from earlier work on skin grafts that the closer the relation between donor and recipient, the better the chances a graft would survive. Transplantation between genetically identical twins was a chance to demonstrate that if doctors could overcome immune rejection, they could save lives with organ transplantation.

The surgery's success encouraged a spate of attempts around the world to transplant organs and, perhaps even more important, a period of intensive experimentation in immunology. Researchers tried a number of approaches, including bombarding the recipient's immune system with radiation and suppressing it with experimental drugs. Murray's own lab worked with Imuran, the first drug approved in 1963 for immunosuppression in transplant surgery. The first two patients to receive Imuran under his care died from its toxicity, but the third represented the first successful organ transplant from an unrelated donor.

➡◄ CONNECTION

Mortality was very high among the first transplant patients of the 1950s and 1960s. However, improvements in the heart-lung machine, the advent of tissue typing to match donor and recipient, and the discovery of new immunosuppressive drugs to prevent rejection set the stage for much better survival odds as the 20th century waned. The first successful transplants of a cornea, kidney, lung, liver, and heart-lung came in 1905, 1954, 1964, 1967, and 1981, respectively.

Building On >

Classification of Blood Types (p. 86)

Blood Transfusion (p. 93)

Antibiotics

An antibiotic is introduced into a bacteria-laden petri dish to test the bacteria's sensitivity to the drug. Effective antibiotics destroy the surrounding bacteria.

1943 >

1943 >

Kidney Dialysis

● IN USE

The anguish of watching a young man die slowly of kidney failure moved Dutch physician Willem Kolff to throw himself into designing a kind of washing machine for the blood, the first dialysis machine. This was in the early 1940s, when Nazis occupied Kolff's homeland; he had to scrounge parts for his construction, which pulled blood through tubing into a bath of purifying fluid and returned it into the patient's body. His initial test of the prototype came in 1943; the first several patients died, but in 1945 the machine revived a comatose patient. By keeping kidney-failure patients alive, dialysis paved the way for the first successful kidney transplantations.

Antibiotics

● IN USE

"Thanks to PENICILLIN . . . He Will Come Home!" Thus proclaimed a World War II–era ad featuring the image of a medic crouched beside a fallen soldier, injecting him with a new bacteria-killing wonder drug. It was an entirely reasonable claim for the world's first potent antibiotic, capable of clearing away diseases that had plagued humanity for generations—from pneumonia and gonorrhea to wound infections.

A British bacteriologist first noted the antibacterial properties of the blue mold *Penicillium notatum* in 1928, but it was more than a decade later that pathologists at Oxford University managed to purify it and demonstrate its effectiveness against infection. They were keenly aware of the need for such a medication to stem mortality in the war. With the British chemical industry fully engaged in that effort, the scientists called on the United States to mount large-scale clinical trials, then ramp up production.

Thanks to this unprecedented collaboration, by June 1944 there was enough penicillin to treat casualties among Allied troops who landed on the beaches at Normandy.

▼ Classification of Blood Types *(p. 86)*

▼ Penicillin *(p. 81)*

▼ Germ Theory of Disease *(p. 90)*

Nuclear Medicine ·······················
A bone scan image of a patient
injected with a radioactive isotope
shows areas of uneven radiation; these
areas might indicate medical problems.

Hospital Blood Bank
In 1967 potential donors gather at the
entrance of a blood bank in New York
City. The "bank" stores donated blood
for later use in blood transfusions.
Today, blood banks are most commonly
kept in hospital laboratories.

1937 >

1934 >

Hospital Blood Bank

● IN USE

By 1937, when physician Bernard
Fantus established the first
permanent blood-storage
facility at Cook County Hospital
in Chicago, Illinois, the basics
of blood transfusion were well
understood. The trouble was,
performing the process at the
bedside of a bleeding trauma
patient—taking blood from friends
and relatives, typing and testing
it for infection, adding sodium
citrate to prevent clotting—
often meant the patient died
before receiving the transfusion.
Fantus's great contribution was
in systematizing the institution

he dubbed a blood "bank."
Community members would make
deposits on which they all could
draw in future emergencies.

Blood preserved in bags

Nuclear Medicine

● IN USE

In the late 19th century, while
examining the effects of passing
electrical discharges through a
vacuum tube, German physicist
Wilhelm Conrad Röntgen noticed
the tube seemed to be emitting an
"invisible" light that cast a greenish
glow on a nearby object—a light
that could pass through objects,
including human flesh. He named
the mysterious beams x-rays.

Their energy would have
important applications in
medicine—chiefly to destroy
diseased (particularly cancerous)
tissue via external beams or
injected materials, and to "mark"

various biochemical carrier
substances whose behavior in the
body can then be carefully observed
with external imaging devices.

Nuclear medicine took a vigorous
step forward in 1934, when Irène
Joliot-Curie and her husband,
Frédéric, discovered it was possible
to produce artificial radioactivity
from generally stable elements
such as nitrogen and phosphorous.
This meant the field would not be
dependent on the relatively scarce,
naturally occurring radioactive
elements first described decades
before by Irène's mother, Marie
Curie.

Building On >

Classification of Blood Types (p. 86)

Hospitals (p. 105)

Cyclotron (p. 121)

X-ray Imaging (p. 88)

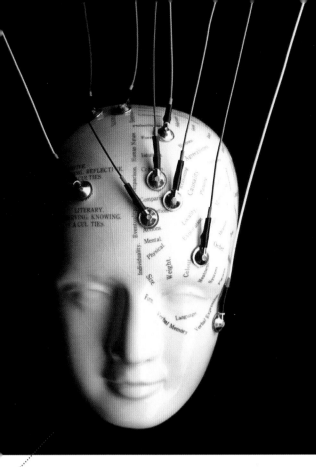

Electroencephalogram
An EEG detects abnormalities in brain waves by using sensors to measure and record the organ's electrical activity.

Penicillin
The fungus *Penicillium notatum,* a mold widely distributed in nature, is the source of the antibiotic penicillin.

1924 >

1928 >

Electroencephalogram

● IN USE

In summer 1924 German psychiatrist Hans Berger became the first to record the electrical activity of a human brain with electrodes attached to the subject's head. Five years later Berger published a trailblazing paper based on 73 electroencephalograph, or EEG, readings from his son, Klaus.

The first empirical technique for observing brain function, electroencephalography is used today in the diagnosis of seizure disorders, to monitor anesthesia, and to confirm brain death. Researchers often rely on EEG to measure responses in studies of psychology and cognition.

Penicillin

● IN USE

When Scottish biologist Alexander Fleming returned from his 1928 summer vacation, he noticed a mold growing in one of his dishes of cultured bacteria. Surrounding the mold was a bacteria-free nimbus, as if its juice were toxic to the pathogenic *Staphylococcus* bug.

Fleming understood the potential of the agent he named penicillin. He tested it against an array of disease-causing organisms, with promising results. But the mold was hard to grow, its active ingredient hard to isolate—difficulties that would be overcome a decade later when, in the context of World War II, Allied governments mounted an intensive effort to produce a potent weapon against infection.

Amoxicillin capsule

▼ **Electricity** *(p. 55)*

▼ **Germ Theory of Disease** *(p. 90)*

Laparoscopic Surgery

A team of surgeons performs laparoscopic surgery on a patient. They insert a fiber-optic viewing tube, or laparoscope, through the patient's abdominal wall to view the organs on a monitor. Laparoscopic surgery is considered to be minimally invasive; it avoids major surgical incisions.

Insulin Therapy

A student nurse instructs a patient how to measure a dose of insulin. The discovery of insulin as a treatment for diabetes was considered a miracle for those who had suffered from the debilitating disease.

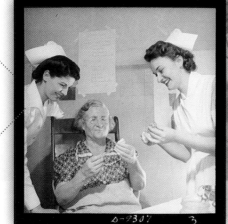

1922 >

1910 >

Insulin Therapy for Diabetes

● IN USE

It was a miraculous moment: A 14-year-old Canadian boy, suffering from the late stages of a disease considered invariably fatal, received injections of a biological extract called insulin and became well.

The 1922 victory emerged from an insight by surgeon Frederick Banting. He guessed that in order to isolate a critical pancreatic hormone missing in diabetes, he would have to neutralize the pancreas's digestive juices, which might be destroying the hormone. Repeated experiments in dogs proved successful. By 1923 Eli Lilly and Company was producing commercial quantities of insulin. It would save millions of lives, a success that inspired generations of medical researchers and helped spawn the modern pharmaceutical industry.

Pen used to inject insulin

Laparoscopic Surgery

● IN USE

In 1910 Hans Christian Jacobaeus published a report describing a diagnostic procedure he had performed on 17 patients with fluid in the abdomen. The Swedish internist had inserted into these patients a special trocar, or port, through which he passed an endoscope featuring a light and a lens system; with this scope he examined their abdominal and chest cavities. Jacobaeus called the procedure "laparothorakoskopie."

The idea of peering inside the human body without a large surgical incision had circulated since the early 19th century.

The advent of minimally invasive surgery came with major technological advances that allowed doctors not only to see inside body cavities but also to operate there with accuracy. The 1950s saw the invention of a system of flexible glass rods for transmitting light into the body from an external source, coupled with a TV camera for projecting the images onto a screen. The watershed technology was the charge-coupled device system, a tiny digital camera that by the mid-1980s could provide surgeons with video from within the body.

Building On >

Hypodermic Needle *(p. 92)*

German bacteriologist Paul Ehrlich

Breast cancer drug Herceptin

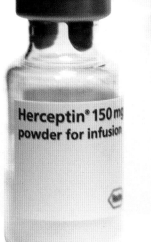

Chemotherapy
A magnified blood smear from a patient with acute granulocytic leukemia, a cancer of the white blood cells

Breakthroughs continue on page 86

1908 >

Chemotherapy

● IN USE

German immunologist Paul Ehrlich was fascinated by the notion of a lock-and-key relationship between certain chemicals and particular living cells. He spent much of his research career testing chemicals from his enormous collection for their ability to target disease-causing microorganisms, while sparing other cells and tissues. "We must search for magic bullets," he said. "We must strike the parasites, and the parasites only, if possible."

In 1909 Ehrlich and student Sahachiro Hata hit pay dirt with compound number 606, a derivative of arsenic that proved a formidable match for the spirochete that causes syphilis, then a widespread, debilitating, and even fatal disease shrouded in secrecy and stigma. Injections of 606 cured experimental rabbits and other animals of their syphilitic lesions. The next year German drug company Hoechst AG began marketing the compound under the trade name Salvarsan; it became a worldwide sensation and is considered the first chemotherapy agent.

Ehrlich's methodical screening of chemical compounds inspired Scottish bacteriologist Alexander Fleming, who discovered the mold-based penicillin in the late 1920s, thereby inaugurating the era of antibiotics—and displacing Salvarsan as a cure for syphilis.

Meanwhile, Ehrlich's insight about targeting parasitic cells also branched off into the development of cell-destroying drugs for cancer. This kind of chemotherapy attacks fast-dividing cells, thus arresting or slowing tumor growth, and is the basis for much of today's cancer treatment.

→← CONNECTION

Here are a few milestones in the development of chemotherapy: In 1942, after noticing dramatically reduced white blood cells in victims of mustard-gas attacks, U.S. Department of Defense scientists used the agent to reduce tumor size in a cancer involving these cells. In 1948 a Harvard pathologist enlisted a drug that blocks folate, a vitamin important for the production of new cells, to treat leukemia successfully. In the 1960s and 1970s multiple-drug therapies and treatment regimens combining drugs with surgery were studied and introduced.

Diabetic Genetics
Gene-testing identifies those with special susceptibility to various forms of diabetes, which can cause retina damage (shown). In the future gene therapy will allow doctors to replace diabetes-prone genes with others free of the disease.

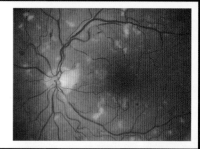

Genetic Medicine

Some three billion DNA base pairs make up the human genome. Just as mere letters spell out the profoundest of sacred texts, the order of these basic chemical components along the DNA strand expresses a complete set of instructions for building the human body.

Completed in 2003, the Human Genome Project for the first time documented a generic human DNA sequence, determining that unrelated individuals are typically 99.9 percent alike genetically. Two years later an international group of scientific collaborators finished the HapMap Project, a database describing common genetic "variations"—the 0.1 percent of the genome that may help explain why one person gets cancer, for example, and another does not.

Using HapMap and new, more efficient technology for sequencing DNA, researchers are now conducting so-called whole-genome association studies, which link risk for complex diseases like diabetes or schizophrenia with specific patterns of genetic variation. Such work introduces a wealth of prospects for both research and medical care.

Doctors can use newly developed gene tests as part of a personalized risk assessment for such conditions as breast, colon, and lung cancers. One day doctors may be able to predict risk with greater precision and for a much broader range of health problems. Positive genetic findings might suggest an individual should be screened for a disease earlier or more often.

Researchers are using associations between disease and DNA changes as clues to disease "pathways" that may in turn suggest ways to correct pathology. For example, genetic variations now linked to inflammatory bowel disease are thought to be involved in immunity and autophagy, a process by which cells degrade or self-digest.

Genetic variation also helps explain individual reactions to medications, and may eventually be used to fine-tune prescriptions. One example: Research has identified genetic patterns that seem associated with a failure to respond to antidepressants.

2000

Sequencing of the human genome was a crucial step along the way to understanding the gene-level causes of human disease and illness. *See page 208*

1976

The Human Genome Project was made possible by DNA sequencing technology. *See page 272*

1961, 1953

Prior to DNA sequencing, the genetic code was cracked and the structure of DNA discovered. *See pages 221, 223*

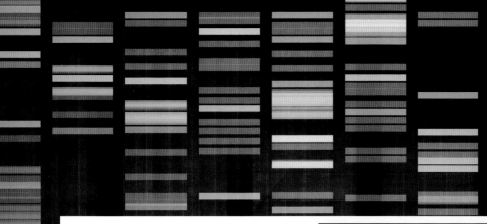

MS Susceptibility

Scientists are studying gene combinations that occur more often in those who suffer from multiple sclerosis, which affects nerve sheaths in the brain (shown). Such knowledge could underpin early detection, treatment, and cure of the disease.

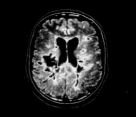

Mutation Effects

Bladder cancer, revealed in a pelvic x-ray (shown), has been linked to genetic mutations experienced during an individual lifetime. Genetic medicine holds the key to detecting and preventing the disease.

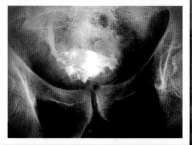

400 B.C.

The incorporation of the knowledge of biology into the practice of medicine goes as far back as the origins of the scientific study of medicine. *See page 107*

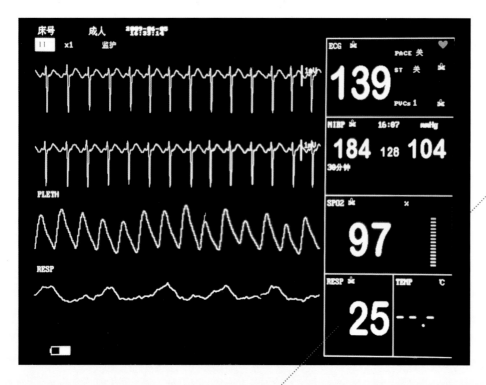

床号　成人　监护
Ⅱ　x1

ECG
139　PACE 关
ST 关
PVCs 1

NIBP　16:07　mmHg
184　128　104
30分钟

SPO2　%
97

RESP　TEMP ℃
25　-・-

Electrocardiogram
A heart and blood pressure monitor is standard fare in any hospital room. The device interprets the electrical activity of the heart over time.

From 1903 back to 1747 >

1903 >

1901 >

Electrocardiogram

● IN USE

More than a hundred years ago Dutch physiologist Willem Einthoven devised an apparatus that could record the heart's tiny electrical impulses accurately enough to serve as a diagnostic tool—an early form of the electrocardiograph, which even today is used to help identify abnormalities like arrhythmia and heart attack.

In Einthoven's device, a very thin wire conducted electrical currents from the heart. This filament was suspended between the poles of an electromagnet. The electromagnet's constant force, interacting with the changing current running along the filament from heart impulses, bent the string. The string's movements were recorded by a system of lenses that essentially photographed it at regular intervals.

Classification of Blood T

▲ IN THEORY

By the turn of the 20th century, blood transfusions had been performed for centuries—sometimes, but not always, with catastrophic effect. Why the inconsistency? In 1901 Austrian pathologist Karl Landsteiner reported on simple experiments in which he exposed red blood cells to the blood serum of other individuals. In some cases it was as if the person's blood cells had been mixed with his own serum; in other cases the red blood cells clumped in the way they do when the blood of different species is mixed. Landsteiner went on to

Building On >

Electricity (p. 55)

Classification of Blood Types

A blood group test shows reactions between blood types and antibody serums. There are four human blood types: A, B, AB, and O. The test shows the agglutination reaction, which results in the clumping of suspended particles in some of the blood types.

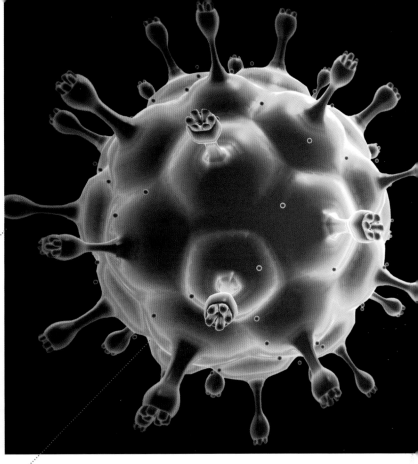

Viruses

A scanning electron microscope reveals a microscopic image of HIV, the virus that often develops into AIDS.

1898 >

Viruses

describe blood types and their patterns of compatibility.

Landsteiner discovered blood types A, B, and O. In 1902 his colleagues Alfred von Decastello and Adriano Sturli identified the fourth basic blood type, called AB.

When, in 1910, scientists discovered the heritability of blood types—one of the first human traits to be identified as such—blood typing became a fertile area for research in hereditary transmission.

→← CONNECTION

Pathologist Karl Landsteiner's categorization of blood types into different groups allowed doctors to match blood before transfusion, avoiding a potentially fatal immune reaction that clumps and destroys the donated red blood cells. His theories found a large-scale proving ground in World War I, when blood typing proved a critical element of safe transfusions. This period also saw the first use of the anticlotting agent sodium citrate and of chilled storage methods for keeping blood fresh longer when outside the body.

▲ IN THEORY

In 1898, the idea that bacteria cause infectious diseases firmly established, a Dutch scientist introduced the world to an even tinier foe: the virus. Working with the mottled leaves of an infected tobacco plant, Martinus Beijerinck pressed their juice through a filter known to exclude bacteria, then introduced the supposedly purified juice to new plants. They became infected; yet unlike bacteria the infectious agent could not be cultured.

As is often the case in scientific discovery, Beijerinck built his case using the insights of others.

The work of French chemist Louis Pasteur had proved the existence of pathogens too small to see. German bacteriologist Robert Koch had set forth a method for connecting a disease with a causative bacterial agent. Beijerinck's experiments replicated similar experiments by a Russian scientist who had supposed the tobacco-plant disease might be caused by a bacterial toxin. But it was Beijerinck who put the pieces together, positing a tiny pathogen he called a virus could reproduce only "with and through cell-multiplication of the plant."

▼ Blood Cells (p. 99)

▼ Theory of Humors (p. 106)

◢ Microscope (p. 101)

◣ Cell Theory (p. 237)

X-ray Imaging

A colored x-ray of an American bullfrog reveals the skeleton of the aquatic frog. A form of electromagnetic radiation, x-rays are useful for detecting disease in the skeletal system as well as in some soft tissue.

A dental x-ray

1895 >

X-ray Imaging

● IN USE

German physicist Wilhelm Conrad Röntgen, intent on studying beams of charged particles emitted from a cathode-ray tube, instead discovered beams of ionizing radiation—beams carrying enough energy to dislodge electrons from their atoms.

Röntgen asked his wife, Anna, to place her hand between the source of the beams he called x-rays and some unexposed film. The rays passed easily through her flesh, but her bones and rings cast shadows, resulting in a picture of her skeleton. "I have seen my death!" she remarked.

After centuries in which autopsy had been the only way to examine the skeleton and internal organs, x-ray represented the first in a long line of technologies for glimpsing inside the living body. The medical community put it to use with surprising alacrity. Within several years some U.S. hospitals boasted x-ray equipment, used mainly for imaging bones for evidence of fractures or to identify foreign objects. Meanwhile, many doctors sent patients to x-ray laboratories, and certain entrepreneurs offered x-rays to the public as a curiosity. Especially popular was the use of x-ray technology to remove unwanted hair painlessly. Physicians using the technology in diagnosis in the early 20th century began to notice the ameliorative effects of x-ray in such conditions as cancer and skin lesions as well as the burns and swelling that could result from overexposure. A quarter century after x-ray's discovery, it had spawned a medical specialty in safely conducting and interpreting the tests: radiology.

→← CONNECTION

The 20th century was a golden age of medical imaging. The groundbreaking x-ray took off early in the century, followed by the first ultrasounds in the 1950s and 1960s, and x-ray-based computed tomography and magnetic resonance imaging in the 1970s. First introduced for research in the 1970s, positron emission tomography, or PET, entered into more widespread use, especially in oncology, in the 1990s. PET creates three-dimensional images that reflect functional processes such as sugar metabolism by means of injected radioactive dyes or tracers.

Building On >

Radioactivity (p. 130)

Antiseptic Surgery

A 1902 illustration depicts English surgeon Joseph Lister using carbolic spray during surgery. Lister discovered that use of the spray killed organisms that had previously killed patients in the Glasgow hospital where he worked.

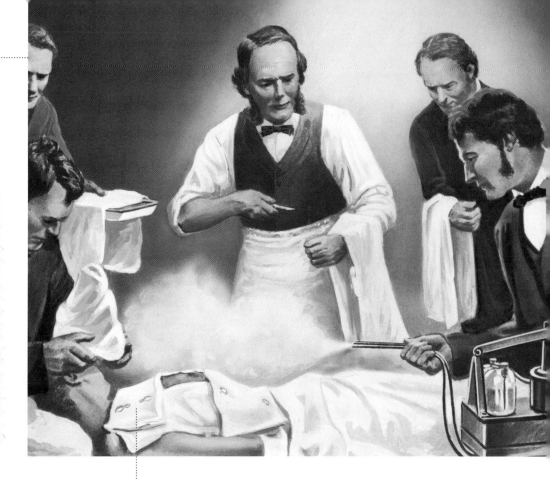

Koch's Postulates

A Russian stamp depicts German scientist Robert Koch.

1884 >

1867 >

Koch's Postulates

▲ IN THEORY

With the advent of the germ theory, which theorized that microorganisms were the cause of disease, came a fervor to isolate the specific microbes responsible for various diseases afflicting humanity. German bacteriologist Robert Koch developed steps for establishing this causal link that, while subject to exceptions, remains influential today: (1) The germ must be present in all animals with the disease, but not in healthy animals. (2) It must be isolated from the host and grown in vitro. (3) The cultured microbes should produce disease when reintroduced to the animal. (4) The microbe—re-isolated from the inoculated, sick host—must prove identical to the original pathogen.

Antiseptic Surgery

▲ IN THEORY

When English surgeon Joseph Lister read about Louis Pasteur's theory blaming microorganisms for the decay of matter, Lister thought of the suppurating wounds seen all too often in the wards of the Glasgow hospital where he worked. Surgery was a gruesome affair with some half of patients dying in its aftermath. The surgeon surmised that perhaps it was not contact with the air itself but with "minute organisms suspended in it" that caused wound infection. He seized on the idea of applying carbolic acid to kill these organisms. It was an outlandish proposition to many of Lister's peers, but he soon had a vivid set of facts on his side. Limbs were saved. Patients lived. Lister disseminated his technique in a classic 1867 paper, "On the Antiseptic Principle of the Practice of Surgery."

Joseph Lister, 1902

Clinical Trials *(p. 95)*

Germ Theory of Disease *(p. 90)*

Health & Medicine   89

Louis Pasteur

Louis Pasteur (1822-1895), a French chemist and biologist, was born in 1822 to humble circumstances, the son of a tanner. His simple but elegant experiments would deal a terminal blow to the idea that air or spontaneously generated microbes cause infection, and replace it with the germ theory of disease. This and subsequent discoveries brought incalculable benefits to humanity; indeed Pasteur believed deeply in the redemptive virtues of science. He was also ambitious and quite competitive. "Let me tell you the secret that has led me to my goal," he once said. "My strength lies solely in my tenacity."

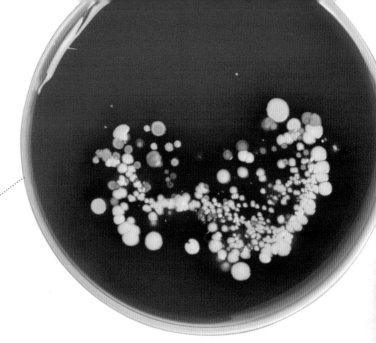

Germ Theory of Disease
A petri dish grows a harmful bacteria found around the home or office: *Enterococcus,* which can cause urinary tract infections and meningitis, and *Staphylococcus aureus,* the most common cause of staph infections. Hand washing is critical in reducing the spread of germs and illness.

1859 >

Germ Theory of Disease

▲ IN THEORY

Puzzling out the true nature of infectious disease was perhaps the most important scientific project of the 19th century. Observation over many generations had led to various erroneous but persistent theories. At mid-century a belief prevailed that microbes could simply spring to life out of inanimate matter (spontaneous generation), and that disease, if transmitted at all, was not spread from host to human host on droplets of sputum and the like, but carried on a "miasma" of noxious, foul-smelling air.

Scientists overturned these ideas in fits and starts. Dutch amateur lens grinder Anton van Leeuwenhoek first spied various bacteria in the 1670s. It was not until Hungarian physician Ignaz Semmelweis developed, tested, and proved his theory that a much dreaded childbed fever was being transmitted on the hands of physicians, who, fresh from their work at the autopsy table, attended women giving birth in Semmelweis's Vienna hospital in the 1840s. Unfortunately, his urging that doctors clean their hands before treating patients

Epidemiology

An 1855 map shows a devastating cholera outbreak in London. Physician John Snow created the map to show how cases of cholera cluster, thus disproving the theory that the disease was caused by a noxious form of "bad air." His historical treatise, published in 1855, helped establish the field of epidemiology.

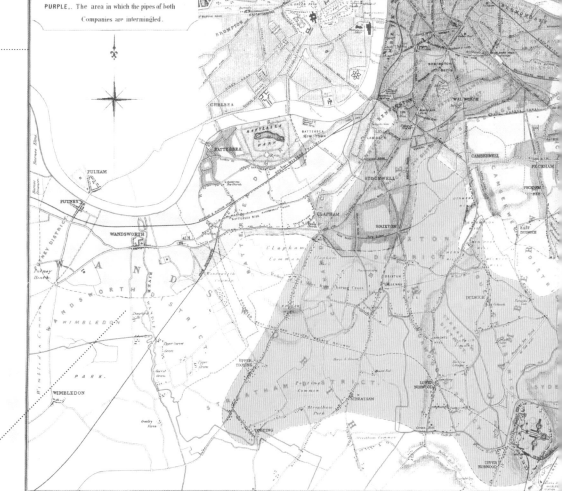

Hungarian physician Ignaz Semmelweis, 1860

1854 >

Epidemiology

▲ IN THEORY

was met with indifference and outright hostility.

By the time Louis Pasteur conducted his famous experiment in 1859, the idea that germs could infect and sicken a person was familiar, but locked in a pitched battle with competing theories. Pasteur's work all but decided the contest. His flasks of broth covered with filters or fitted with narrow, downward-curving stems admitted air, but excluded the tiniest particles—and remained free of growth. The enemy, though invisible to the naked eye, lay in medicine's sights.

The science of epidemiology attempts to uncover risk factors for disease through the careful study of patterns across populations. Where does the illness strike hardest? Who gets sick and who stays well? John Snow, a surgeon and anesthesiologist in Victorian London, was a founding practitioner of the discipline.

In Snow's day, the world's great cities were essentially helpless against the epidemics that tore again and again through their teeming streets; those with means simply fled to the countryside. Popular explanations for these

waves of disease included the damp, miasmic atmosphere and divine judgment. But by meticulously recording cases, interviewing survivors, and plotting deaths on a city map during a terrifying 1854 outbreak of cholera, Snow was able to trace infections in the Soho neighborhood to a particular well on Broad Street. He convinced authorities to remove the well's pump handle, which helped bring the Soho outbreak to a speedy close. Snow's theory—that cholera spreads by contaminated water—was vindicated.

But it was only gradually over

the decades that colleagues built on Snow's ideas in addressing disease outbreaks. Today, epidemiologists use similar systematic methods not only to track infectious disease— whether the 2009 global influenza pandemic or a 2010 cholera outbreak in earthquake-ravaged Haiti—but also to explore associations between lifestyle and risk for chronic disease. For example, population studies first uncovered the link between smoking and lung cancer, and implicated dietary saturated fats in heart disease.

Microbiology *(p. 246)*

Viruses *(p. 87)*

Eradication of Smallpox *(p. 69)*

Hypodermic Needle
The discovery of the hypodermic needle made it possible to inject a substance into the body without having to make an incision.

Anesthesia
William Morton's inhaler for ether anesthesia was first used in 1846. The discovery of anesthesia allowed surgeons more time for operations as patients were no longer in pain.

An anesthesia face mask, early 1900s

1853 >

1846 >

Hypodermic Needle

● IN USE

A sharp, hollow needle connected to a pump seems a simple enough device, but it took centuries for these components to come together in the hypodermic syringe of today. The ancient Greeks used a syringe to draw pus from boils and infected wounds. During the 1650s English scientist (later architect) Christopher Wren injected a dog with aqueous opium using a goose quill (passed through a small incision) and a frog bladder. Injecting medicines became practical only after the 1850s, when Charles-Gabriel Pravaz, of France, and Alexander Wood, of Scotland, independently introduced the needle-and-syringe combination.

Anesthesia

● IN USE

It is difficult to imagine how anyone endured a tooth extraction—much less a limb amputation—before the age of anesthesia. A key qualification for surgeons of the day was speed; attendants had to be strong enough to restrain the patient's agonized writhing. By the early 1840s physicians had no better methods for dulling surgical pain than to stupefy the patient with a kind of hypnosis known as mesmerism—or, indeed, with whiskey.

A turning point came in 1844 when Connecticut dentist Horace Wells attended a demonstration of nitrous oxide's intoxicating effects. Wells thought of using the so-called laughing gas during invasive procedures when he noticed one participant had scraped his leg badly but suffered no pain. Like others before him— the anesthetic properties of nitrous oxide had been recognized for decades—Wells failed to develop the idea beyond a demonstration at Massachusetts General Hospital, which went poorly. The patient cried out as his tooth was pulled.

The eureka moment would be left to Wells's associate, dentist

Building On >

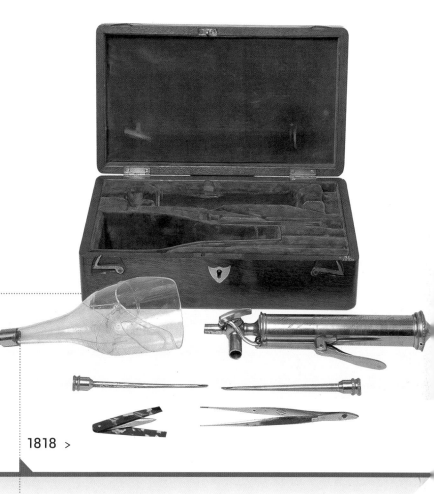

Blood Transfusion ....

A blood-transfusion apparatus, designed by physician James Blundell, was first used in the early 1800s to treat patients suffering from severe hemorrhaging. Blood group test shows the reaction between a blood type and an antibody serum.

1818 >

Blood Transfusion

William Morton. In 1846, while working with ether, Morton seized the opportunity to work on a patient with an infected tooth; he etherized the man, extracted his bicuspid, and when the patient awakened a few minutes later, announced to his astonishment that the procedure was done. Morton ventured another demonstration at Massachusetts General, anesthetizing a patient undergoing surgery on a neck tumor. After the procedure the initially skeptical surgeon turned to the audience and announced, "Gentlemen, this is no humbug."

→← CONNECTION

Modern anesthesia rests on more than 150 years of incremental developments. In the 1840s came the first use of the inhalation anesthetics nitrous oxide and ether. A decade later England's Queen Victoria delivered her eighth and ninth children with chloroform for pain relief. The first uses of tracheal intubation to maintain airways during anesthesia occurred in the 1870s and 1880s; later in the century cocaine was introduced as a local anesthetic. In the 1930s the first barbiturates were used in sedation and anesthesia.

● IN USE

British obstetrician James Blundell received a medical education in anatomy, physiology, midwifery, and surgery, and went on to make contributions in all these fields. He advocated restraint in obstetrical interventions during pregnancy and defended the practice of experimenting on animals, which helped prepare him to perform the first documented successful human-to-human blood transfusion.

In 1818 Blundell reported his experiments transfusing dogs, discussing the importance of performing the procedure quickly to prevent clotting, of admitting no air into the vein, and of using related donors. Around the same time, he transfused a patient in the throes of postpartum hemorrhage, using her husband's blood.

Blood group test

▼ Organ Transplant *(p. 78)*

◥ Cord-Blood Transplant *(p. 68)*

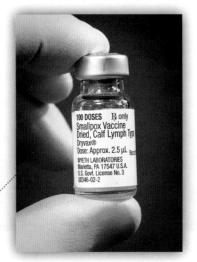

Clinical Trials ....
A lime slice contains vitamin C, which today is known to prevent scurvy. Scottish physician James Lind found the link between the vitamin and disease in 18th-century trials.

Stethoscope
In a 1950s photo a woman uses a replica of René Laënnec's stethoscope to listen to her friend's heartbeat at the Smithsonian Institution. Laennec designed this, his third model, between 1816 and 1819.

A vial of the smallpox vaccine

1816 >

1796 >

Stethoscope

● IN USE

The stethoscope was born in an awkward moment in 1816. Paris doctor René Laënnec, faced with a young woman likely suffering heart trouble, was reluctant to assess her heart sounds in the usual manner—by pressing his ear to her chest. Laënnec improvised the first stethoscope with a rolled-up sheet of paper, but soon developed a more permanent model, a wooden tube. To this day, primary care doctors use a similar tool to listen to patients' hearts and lungs. Laënnec went on to correlate particular stethoscopic sounds with specific disease states found during autopsies, setting guidelines for the diagnosis of ailments like pneumonia and tuberculosis.

A monaural, or single-channel, stethoscope similar to Laënnec's design

Smallpox Vaccine

● IN USE

It was during his apprenticeship that English country physician Edward Jenner overheard a local girl pass on a folk belief. She would never suffer the ugly scars of smallpox, she exulted, because she had already had cowpox—a minor affliction common to dairymaids.

Years later, in 1796, Jenner collected material from a cowpox lesion on the arm of a local milker and rubbed it into a small scoring in the skin of an eight-year-old boy. Eight weeks later Jenner exposed the boy to smallpox. The child remained well. Cowpox was similar enough to smallpox to induce immunity.

Over the next several years, Jenner published further experiments, supplying cowpox material and promoting his techniques to physicians around the world. Bavaria, Denmark, Prussia, and finally Britain, in 1853, made vaccination with cowpox mandatory. American states also began to require the vaccine at mid-century.

Jenner's innovation was a critical step toward reducing the threat of infectious disease, making early childhood, in particular, vastly safer.

Building On >

▼ Ultrasound *(p. 75)*

▼ Viruses *(p. 87)*

▼ Eradication of Smallpox *(p. 69)*

Clinical Trials

James Lind discovered that the men who had citrus in their diet recovered from scurvy, which plagued sailors of the time. He published his finding in his *Treatise on the Scurvy* in 1757.

A

TREATISE

ON THE

SCURVY.

IN THREE PARTS.

CONTAINING

An Inquiry into the Nature, Causes, and Cure, of that Disease.

Together with

A Critical and Chronological View of what has been published on the Subject.

By JAMES LIND, M.D.

Fellow of the Royal College of Physicians in *Edinburgh*.

The SECOND EDITION corrected, with Additions and Improvements.

LONDON:

Printed for A. MILLAR in the *Strand*.

MDCCLVII.

1747 >

Breakthroughs continue on page 98

Clinical Trials

▲ IN THEORY

Scurvy among mariners in the 18th century provided the context for a simple but foundational clinical trial testing remedies for this puzzling disease. The problem of scurvy at sea also offers an excellent illustration for why experimental trials are indispensable.

As early as the Middle Ages, seaman had struck upon citrus juice as a cure for scurvy, which causes victims to bleed from the mucous membranes, lose teeth, succumb to lethargy, and eventually die. But citrus was only one of a host of recommended therapies. Men suffered numerous privations while at sea for many weeks, often remedying them at a stroke in ports of call. So it was no easy task to pin down just what was causing the problem and which intervention was restoring its victims to health.

In 1747, on a ten-week journey aboard the warship H.M.S. *Salisbury*, Scottish naval doctor James Lind chose 12 men with comparable symptoms of scurvy and assigned each of six pairs a different dietary supplement in addition to standard fare: a mixture of horseradish, garlic, and mustard seed; cider; vinegar; seawater; a tonic called elixir vitriol; or lemons and oranges. The sailors getting citrus fruits recovered fully within days. The others remained ill.

Of course, the difficulty of acquiring fresh fruit at sea still existed. Lind recommended "rob," a concoction of citrus condensed by boiling; however, the cooking destroyed its protective value. It was not until the 1930s that scientists definitively solved the cause of scurvy—a deficiency in vitamin C.

➡⬅ CONNECTION

In 1863 the first use of a placebo, or dummy medication, occurred in a clinical trial of treatments for rheumatic fever. In 1926 and 1927 a Detroit sanatorium used the flip of a coin to assign randomly one set of patients to a treatment arm and another to serve as controls in a trial of tuberculosis treatments. Some 15 years later the British Medical Research Council tested a mold toxin against the common cold in a placebo-controlled trial that was also "double blind" (when neither subjects nor investigators know which patients are receiving active treatment).

Poking Around ....

Using the stylus of an atomic force microscope, the operator can probe, single out, and separate atoms from their bonds as if they were billiard balls, creating new nanometric rearrangements.

Nanomedicine

The prefix "nano" means one billionth. Thus a nanometer is a billionth of a meter, about half the diameter of DNA's famous double helix. This is the scale at which the field of nanotechnology aspires to manipulate matter, made possible—or at least imaginable—by the emergence in the 1980s of high-powered microscopes that for the first time permit scientist to see such tiny particles.

The ultimate medical application of nanotechnology would be to engineer minuscule "machines" capable of repairing cells. In the meantime, scientists are working to develop novel drug-delivery systems in which active ingredients ride straight to their target cells on nanoparticles; scientists are also working to develop diagnostic tools featuring nanoparticles that bind to or otherwise mark disease-indicating molecules. Other applications use the tiny particles to attack viruses or inflammation-causing free radicals preferentially.

One nanotech drug candidate now being tested in humans, Maryland-based CytImmune's Aurimune, is designed to overcome a notorious problem in cancer treatment: Drugs that kill cancer cells often are toxic to the entire body. Aurimune is a 27-nanometer particle of gold carrying a tumor-killing molecule as well as one designed to hide the particle from the immune system. The idea—and early studies suggest it just might work—is that the drug flows freely through the bloodstream; small enough to escape through the leaky blood vessels in and around tumors, it deposits its cargo there, sparing healthy tissue.

In another intriguing example, researchers at 11 sites across Europe and Australia are working on a wound dressing coated with nanocapsules, which contain both an antibiotic and a dye. These exquisitely tiny capsules are designed to burst when exposed to a toxin secreted by pathogenic bacteria; the dressing immediately begins to treat the wound infection while changing color to alert doctors. The project is scheduled to wind up in 2014, by which time scientists hope to have a prototype ready for industrial production.

For all its promise, nanomedicine also raises new controversies. Perhaps chief among these is a concern that particles so tiny that they readily enter cells and cross the blood-brain barrier may carry long-term risks that are not well understood.

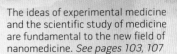

1991	**1985**	**1959**	**1025, 400** B.C.
Carbon nanotubes will form the foundation of some of the technologies of nanomedicine. *See page 161*	The properties of nanoparticles called fullerene make them a great candidate for use in nanomedical technologies. *See page 163*	The existence of nanotechnology was predicted more than 50 years ago by physicist Richard Feynman. *See page 165*	The ideas of experimental medicine and the scientific study of medicine are fundamental to the new field of nanomedicine. *See pages 103, 107*

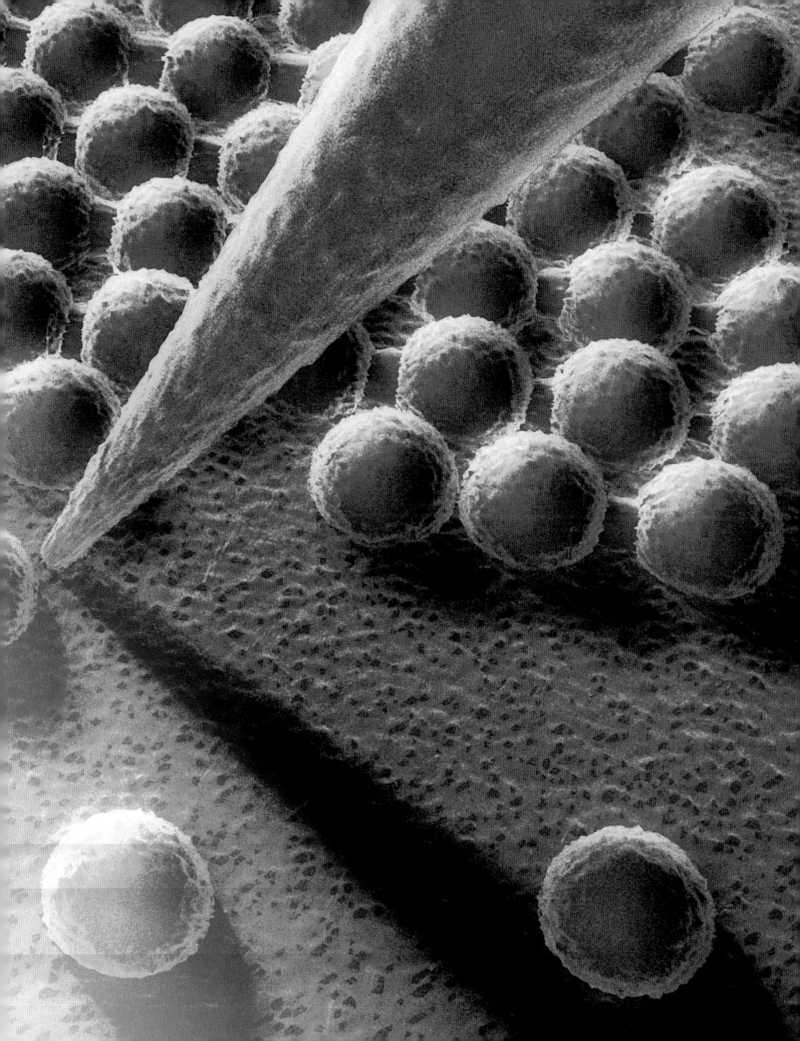

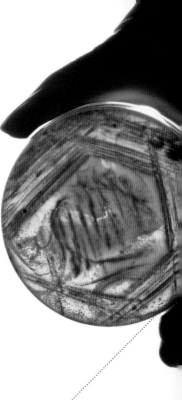

Anton van Leeuwenhoek

[PROFILE]

Born to a family of basketmakers and brewers in 17th-century Delft, Anton van Leeuwenhoek (1632-1723) showed considerable skill as a lens grinder and diligence in recording what he saw through his magnifying glasses. But it was Leeuwenhoek's "great wonder," as he himself put it, that drove him to examine the contents of everything from lake water to his own feces—and that exploration earned him the privilege of being the first human being to perceive a world teeming with microscopic life.

Bacteria

▲ IN THEORY

Anton van Leeuwenhoek, the tradesman and civil servant who would become known as the father of microbiology, wrote hundreds of letters in his native Low Dutch to the Royal Society in London. Leeuwenhoek described in the letters incredible varieties of life, theretofore wholly unknown, glimpsed through his handmade magnifying glasses. In 1683 he wrote of "many very little living animalcules, very prettily a-moving" in a sample of dental plaque. These, of course, were bacteria.

Leeuwenhoek spied any number of minuscule entities, living and

Building On >

Bacteria
A microbiologist holds a petri dish containing a culture of *Escherichia coli* bacteria. *E. coli* bacteria are normal intestinal inhabitants. However, some strains produce a toxin that can lead to serious and potentially fatal food poisoning.

Bacteria
Using a microscope of his own design, Anton van Leeuwenhoek was the first to observe bacteria and published his findings in a 1695 series of letters to the Royal Society.

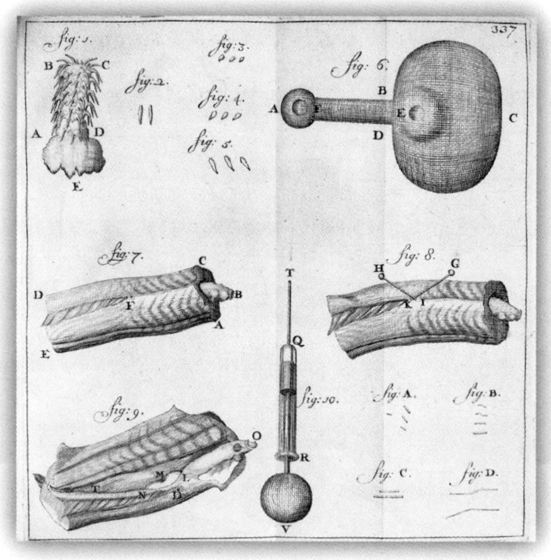

Blood Cells
Artwork depicting red blood cells, first described in detail by Anton van Leeuwenhoek

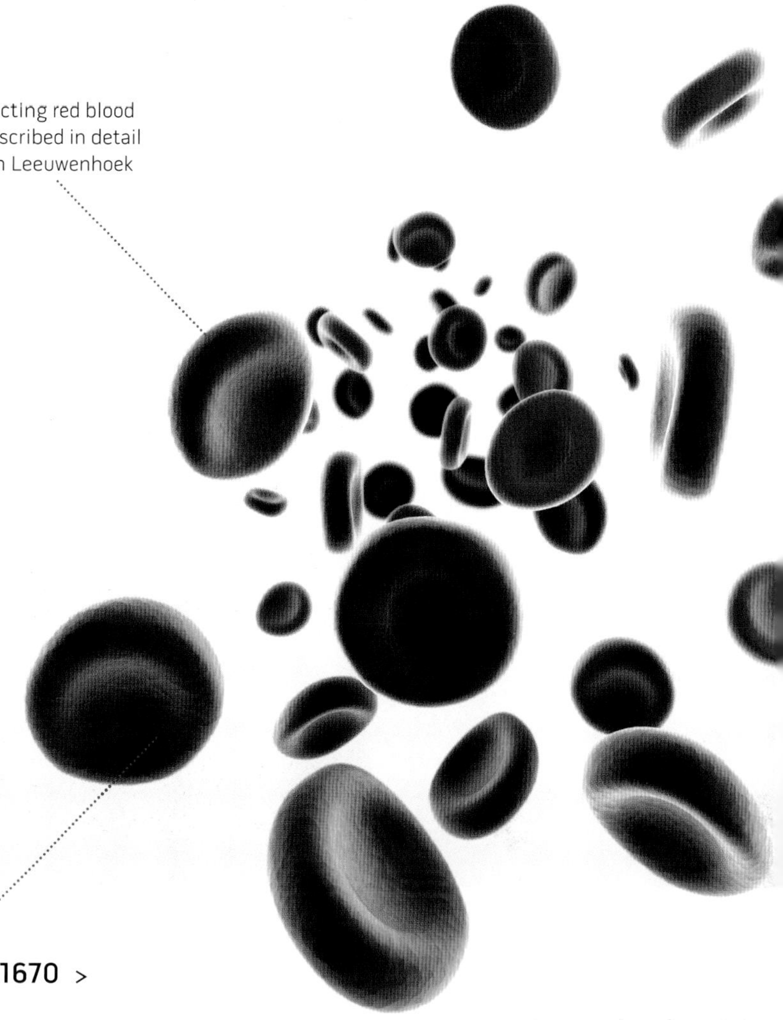

ca 1670 >

nonliving, through his scope—including protozoa, spermatozoa, muscle fibers, algae, and yeast cells. For generations, however, these observations were regarded as a fascinating curiosity, but hardly relevant to human health. Though his descriptions and intricate drawings were so precise as to be recognizable by modern microbiologists, 200 years would pass before his animalcules were identified as agents of specific diseases.

Meanwhile, the enormous cache of new information unlocked by this brilliant polymath informed a host of other scientific disciplines, from microscopy to botany, zoology to embryology.

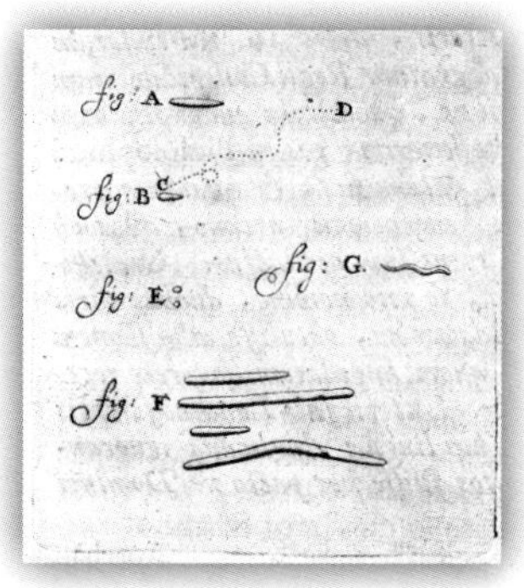

1695 sketch of bacteria by Anton van Leeuwenhoek

Blood Cells

▲ IN THEORY

Although Dutchman Jan Swammerdam first described red blood cells in 1658, another Dutchman, Anton van Leeuwenhoek, detailed with uncanny accuracy their size and oval shape around a clear center in the 1670s. Specimens he sent to the Royal Society in England survived more than three centuries in society archives, to be rediscovered in 1981 by independent scientist Brian J. Ford.

In 1843, more than 150 years after red blood cells were identified, French physician Gabriel Andral and English country doctor William Addison separately reported on another key component of blood: leukocytes, or white blood cells. They make up only about one percent of blood volume, but are a critical part of the body's system for fending off invasion by germs and other foreign materials.

Microscope *(p. 101)*
Microbiology *(p. 246)*
Classification of Blood Types *(p. 86)*
Cells *(p. 247)*
Theory of Humors *(p. 106)*

n the Walls, Total of the Funerals 15207 ; Died of the Plague 9887.

03	St. Botolph Aldgate,—	4926	4051	St. Saviours Southwark ——	4235	3446
44	St. Botolph Bishopsgate —	3464	2500	St. Sepulchres ——	4509	2746
39	St. Dunstans in the West —	958	665	St. Thomas Southwark —	475	371
27	St. George Southwark ——	1613	1260	Trinity Minories ——	168	123
79	St. Giles Cripplegate —	8069	4838	At the Pesthouse ——	159	156
755	St. Olaves Southwark ——	4793	2785			

t the Walls, Total of the Funerals 41351 ; Died of the Plague 28888.

216	Lambeth Parish ——	798	537	St. Mary Islington ——	696	593
132	St. Leonards Shoreditch —	2669	1949	St. Mary Whitechappel ---	4766	3855
377	St. Magdalens Bermondsey	1943	1363	Rotherhith Parish ——	304	210
501	St. Mary Newington.——	1272	1004	Stepney Parish ——	8598	6583

outer Parts, Total of the Funerals 28554 ; Died of the Plague 21420.

319	St. Martins in the Fields —	4804	2883	St. Margarets Westminster	4710	3742
261	St. Mary Savoy ——	303	198	Whereof at the Pesthouse—		156

iberties of Westminster, Total of the Funerals 12194 ; Died of the Plague 8403:

Total of the Funerals --- 97306.

Died of the Plague ---- 68596.

Account was given by the Parish-Clerks, and who were privately Buried;

Public Health Statistics and the Life Table

Records from 1662 list the deaths and burials of Londoners, many of whom died from the plague that devastated the English city. In the 1600s merchant John Graunt compiled many of these death records, looking for patterns and insights to help track the disease.

Theory of Circulation

The heart is the central component of the cardiovascular system, which pumps blood to all chambers of the body. For hundreds of years scientists considered the liver to be the central organ of the body; that thinking changed in the early 1600s when physician William Harvey published his treatise on the subject.

1662 >

1628 >

Public Health Statistics and the Life Table

● IN USE

Is a city's population growing or dwindling? What is the life expectancy of a child born there? How likely is a woman to die in childbirth?

Today, thanks to a highly developed apparatus for collecting and analyzing vital statistics, these questions have ready answers.

It was John Graunt, a prosperous merchant of small wares in 17th-century London, who demonstrated for the first time how such statistics could shed a clarifying light on everyday life, and provide an empirical basis for public policy. Since the early 1600s

London parishes had recorded each week's deaths and christenings, an effort first requested by local merchants intent on tracking the depredations of the plague. The statistics were of limited value until Graunt compiled them and plumbed the numbers for patterns and insights.

In 1662 he published his *Natural and Political Observations Made Upon the Bills of Mortality*. It included the first life table, showing the rates of death in each age interval and the overall likelihood of surviving to each.

Graunt's analysis also laid

bare certain facts that might not have been clear to Londoners, but greatly impacted them. For example, the most dangerous period of life by far was early childhood, with more than a third of children dying before the age of six. In certain plague years, a fifth of the population had perished. Autumn was the most unhealthful season, Graunt observed, and only "hated persons" had been reported as having died from the "French pox," or syphilis, with other such deaths discreetly put down to tuberculosis, or simply "ulcers."

Theory of Circulation

▲ IN THEORY

Much as Copernicus broke the news that the sun, not the Earth, is the center of the universe, English physician William Harvey had the task of convincing his colleagues that the beating heart—not the liver—is the fulcrum of blood circulation.

In so doing he overturned understandings that had persisted for more than a millennium. The prevailing belief at the dawn of the 17th century was that the liver converted food into "natural" blood, which circulated through veins to all the body's tissues (including through the

Building On >

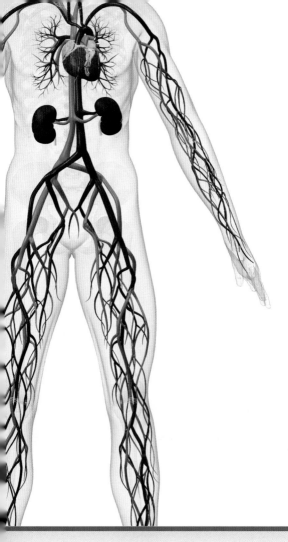

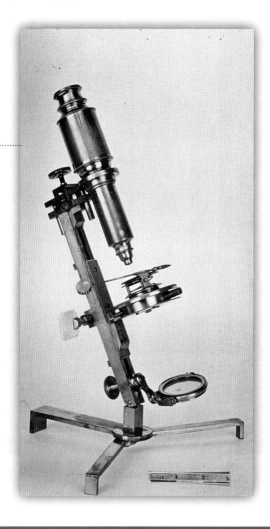

Microscope ....
An undated image shows a Beck international microscope, which had dividing eyepieces. In the late 19th century the British optical company helped popularize the use of microscopes by offering reasonably priced models.

1590 >

Microscope

● IN USE

heart), where it was consumed. The arterial system on the other hand carried air—breath—and was separate from the venous circulation, though supplied with a small amount of blood via holes in the septum separating the heart's chambers.

Harvey's careful deductions and experiments proved this could not be so. A cut artery spurted blood in concert with the heartbeat. In a live dissection of a snake, a pinched artery seemed to engorge the heart, whereas a pinched vein made it shrink and go pale. Harvey furthermore calculated that the

amount of blood entering the arterial system from the heart in a single hour equaled a multiple of the person's entire blood volume—far more than could plausibly be synthesized in the liver.

In 1628 Harvey published his famous treatise on the subject, saying the movement of blood through the body is circular, its perpetual motion driven by the pulsing heart.

Perhaps science owes the invention of the compound microscope in late 16th-century Holland to another innovation developed in medieval Italy: eyeglasses. It was eyeglass makers Zacharias Janssen and his father, Hans, who around 1590 discovered that magnification could be enhanced by using two lenses. Soon after, Galileo would explore the heavens with newly developed telescopes, but it would be more than a half century before microscopes would reveal a secret terrain closer at hand. In the late 1600s Dutchman Anton van

Leeuwenhoek made improvements to the technology, creating a scope capable of magnifying objects nearly 270 times.

Portrait of surgeon William Harvey

▶ Telescope *(p. 139)*

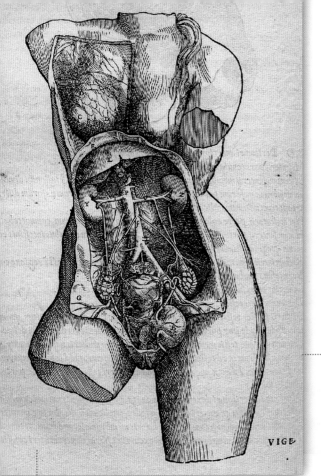

VIGE

Anatomy Text

The 1543 text *On the Fabric of the Human Body* by Andreas Vesalius is considered a groundbreaking work on human anatomy. The illustrations were based on human dissections performed by the author.

1543 >

1343 >

Anatomy Text

▲ IN THEORY

Andreas Vesalius's study of anatomy began with a determination to recover the ancient wisdom of Hippocrates and Galen, an ethnic Greek born in A.D. 129, from medieval vulgarizations. But before long the humanist approach of anatomist Vesalius led him to correct some of Galen's errors by the evidence of his own senses. Like his forerunner Leonardo da Vinci, who performed human dissections in the service of science and art, Vesalius took every opportunity as a professor in Padua and later Bologna to work with cadavers, often filched from graveyard or gallows. Vesalius was only 30 years old at the first publication of his book *On the Fabric of the Human Body*, a text in seven volumes based on his lectures in Padua.

Richly illustrated with engravings from the workshop of celebrated Italian painter Titian, the book is an exemplar of Renaissance flowering in scientific learning, artistic technique, and printing acumen. It contains intricate and often accurate renderings of the bones (with labels in Latin, Greek, and Hebrew), as well as of the musculature, vasculature, nervous system, and urinary and reproductive tracts. The book is as much an artistic work as a clinical text. Drawings show cadavers or skeletons posed in front of pastoral or village landscapes, often in postures of considerable pathos; one skeleton is shown with its face turned toward the heavens, leaning on a shovel and gesturing toward a freshly dug grave.

Quarantine

● IN USE

Both the Book of Leviticus in the Bible and the Koran prescribed isolation for victims of leprosy. However, a more formal policy of quarantine was first conceived in the context of Europe's Black Death. Beginning in 1343, ships arriving in Venice were required to remain offshore for 40 days before landing. The word "quarantine" comes from *quaranta*, Italian for "40." The cosmopolitan Adriatic Sea port of Ragusa, today's Dubrovnik, followed in 1377—establishing a rule that ships from places suspected of harboring infection stay offshore for 30 days.

Building On >

Classification of Animals *(p. 249)*

Experimental Medicine ⋯⋯⋯⋯⋯⋯⋯

The Canon of Medicine, a 14-volume Arabic medical encyclopedia written by Persian scientist and physician Ibn Sina, was completed in 1025. The work covers basic subjects such as anatomy and hygiene, describes a vast range of diseases, and lists hundreds of medicines.

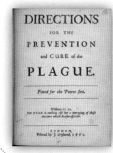

DIRECTIONS
FOR THE
PREVENTION
and CURE of the
PLAGUE.

Quarantine

A light micrograph shows the female rat flea (left), a common parasite of the rat. This tiny insect played a leading role in the spread of the bubonic plague. A 1665 book (above) provided directions for the prevention and cure of the plague. At the time the plague was thought to be contagious. Thus policies of quarantine were put in place to try to contain it.

1025 >

Experimental Medicine

▲ IN THEORY

For centuries American and European governments implemented isolation policies for the sick or those thought to be sick in order to check the spread of such diseases as yellow fever, cholera, smallpox, and tuberculosis. But quarantine has become a far less important weapon against epidemics since the advent of antibiotics, vaccination, and better public-health infrastructure in the 20th century.

Ibn Sina, often called by his Latinized name Avicenna, was a Persian philosopher-physician who penned perhaps the most famous medical work of medieval Islamic societies, *The Canon of Medicine.* The second book of this five-volume series presents some 760 drugs Ibn Sina judged useful, along with standards for determining efficacy that laid out the basic tenets of experimental medicine: Each drug, unadulterated and unspoiled, should be tested in patients with a single condition. The investigator should begin with the smallest dose. Efficacious drugs, according to Ibn Sina, should have a consistent effect.

Persian scientist Ibn Sina

→← CONNECTION

The medieval Islamic world, centered by the middle of the eighth century around Baghdad, produced abundant works on medicine, a field that took on subjects from diet to divination. This tradition's impact on the development of Western medicine stems in part from the fact that its physicians tended also to be students, teachers, and writers—in short, communicators. They systematized and made consistent much of Greco-Roman medical knowledge, but also were at pains to record their own findings.

Clinical Trials *(p. 95)*

Scientific Study of Medicine *(p. 107)*

Abu al-Zahrawi

Abu al-Zahrawi (ca 926-1013), known as Abulcasis in the West, was born around 936 in the palace city of El-Zahra, built by the Iberian peninsula's most powerful Muslim prince, who ruled from nearby Córdoba. It was in Córdoba that al-Zahrawi spent the greater part of his extraordinarily fruitful medical career. He has been described as the father of modern surgery; he also was a chemist, a designer of surgical tools, and an innovator of doctoring techniques—from cauterizing injured tissue to repositioning the fetus in obstructed birth.

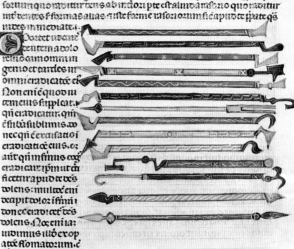

1000 >

The Method of Medicine

▲ **IN THEORY**

During his decades-long career as a surgeon and instructor in medieval Andalusia, Abu al-Zahrawi, also known as Abulcasis, amassed encyclopedic medical knowledge based on existing texts and his own experience. He recorded this knowledge in 30 volumes known as *The Method of Medicine*. Its 28th treatise dealing with medicines, translated into Latin from its original Arabic, was printed in Venice in 1471. Gerard of Cremona translated the final volume, which appeared in 1497, also in Venice. This last treatise, on surgery, is the longest, with sections describing cauterizations, operations, and treatment of dislocated or broken bones. For centuries this book served as a central medical text in Europe as well as in the Islamic world.

Magisterial in scope, *The Method of Medicine* captured essentially all there was to know about medicine at the time. It opens with general concepts, including the Hippocratic notion of the four humors and principles of anatomy and pathology, then goes on to describe hundreds of diseases. The collection deals with food and nutrition, hygiene, skin

A blue sign with a large H indicates a hospital is nearby.

Hospitals

The Bimaristan Al-Nouri in old Damascus, Syria, treated patients and served as a medical school. Bimaristans were the first hospitals to treat patients based on medical approaches not spiritual concerns.

The Method of Medicine

A page from Abu al-Zahrawi's multivolume treatise on medical practices displays an array of surgical instruments.

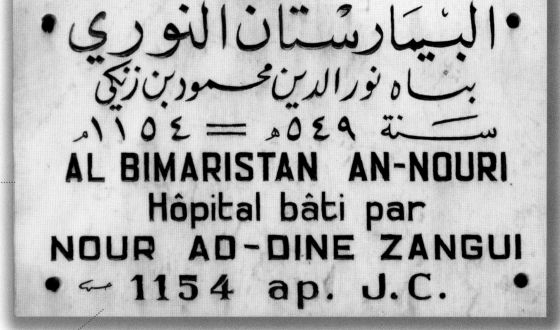

البيمارستان النوري

بناه نور الدين محمود بن زنكي

سنة ٥٤٩ هـ = ١١٥٤ م

AL BIMARISTAN AN-NOURI
Hôpital bâti par
NOUR AD-DINE ZANGUI
↙ 1154 ap. J.C.

800 >

Hospitals

● IN USE

diseases, poisons and antidotes, pediatrics and geriatrics, dentistry (including cauterization to the root of an infected tooth and placement of cow-bone false teeth), ophthalmology, pharmacology (including instructions for compounding and dosing), midwifery, and surgical technique. In the latter category, al-Zahrawi's great work describes how to treat head and spinal injuries, remove kidney stones, and amputate limbs. It includes drawings of various surgical probes, cauterizing irons, knives, scissors, forceps, and hooks.

Early hospitals with trained doctors developed in the Byzantine Empire, beginning in the fourth century and continuing into the Middle Ages. Whether founded by the church, the imperial government, or well-to-do patrons, these institutions hearkened to early Christian houses for the sick and destitute, and focused on the condition of the soul as the root of physical and mental health.

In the ninth century, hospitals began to flourish in the Islamic world—in cities like Baghdad, Damascus, and Cairo. Perhaps influenced by the Byzantine

model, they were more elaborate establishments, with specialized areas for treating everything from diarrheal diseases to mental illness. Some had libraries and pharmacies. They were largely secular, basing their medical approach on classical examples that looked at disease as a material and not primarily a spiritual problem. Reflecting an Islamic cultural tradition of hospitality and charity, the *bimaristans* (the word joins the Persian *bimar*, or sick person, and *stan*, place) admitted patients of different faiths and economic

strata. Christian and Jewish doctors worked alongside their Muslim colleagues.

These hospitals created a model for care of the sick that went beyond isolating patients from society or overseeing their inevitable demise. These forerunners of the modern hospital also helped nurture and develop a tradition of medical learning that lay fallow for centuries in Latin Europe. Western doctors, in their quest to take up the advancement of medicine during the 12th century and later, often looked to Arabic sources.

▼ Theory of Humors (p. 106)

▼ Bone-marrow Transplant (p. 76)

▼ Organ Transplant (p. 78)

▼ Hospital Blood Bank (p. 80)

والأخرى من بعض
وبعضها أيضا

Regarding Medical Materials

De Materia Medica was the basis for herbal and pharmaceutical writing until the late 16th century. An illustration from an Arabic translation is shown here.

Theory of Humors

The theory of humors held that human moods, emotions, and behaviors were caused by four body fluids, called humors: blood, yellow bile, black bile, and phlegm.

100 >

400 B.C. >

Regarding Medical Materials

▲ IN THEORY

Pedanius Dioscorides was a Greek doctor who, like Galen, rose to prominence in the Roman world. He traveled throughout the empire with Emperor Nero's army, gathering material by direct observation for his five-volume encyclopedia of medicinal plants and other substances, *Regarding Medical Materials*.

Though Dioscorides' work would serve as a template for all subsequent pharmacopeias, no other compendium supplanted it for more than a thousand years. In the Middle Ages physicians could consult *Regarding Medical Materials* in its original Greek, or in a Latin and Arabic translation.

Dioscorides originally organized his work according to the pharmaceutical properties of plants and other substances, though entries were later alphabetized in some editions. He included some 500 medicinal plants, explaining where each grows, how to collect and prepare it, and how to apply it for the relief of illness. He prescribed rhubarb for diarrhea, autumn crocus and opium from poppy heads as painkillers, and willow bark for gout.

Theory of Humors

▲ IN THEORY

The theory of humors held that the human body is made up of four substances—blood, yellow bile, black bile, and phlegm—which correspond to cosmic elements and whose proper balance is the basis of good health. Medicine's goal was simply to counteract a surfeit or shortage of a particular humor. Although thinkers in the time of Hippocrates first systematized this idea, it was Galen whose writings ensured its survival for hundreds of years, across a vast territory stretching from India to Spain.

The humors were thought to affect not only the body but also the mind and general character. A surfeit of blood was thought to yield a sanguine personality type, too much phlegm a phlegmatic one. An excess of yellow bile or "choler" led to a choleric character, and an overabundance of black bile or "melan-choler" produced a melancholic type. The words' basic meanings survive today.

Building On >

▼ Classification of Blood Types (p. 86)

Hippocrates is generally regarded as the father of medicine. The Hippocratic oath, attributed to the Greek physician, serves as the foundation for good medical practice and morals.

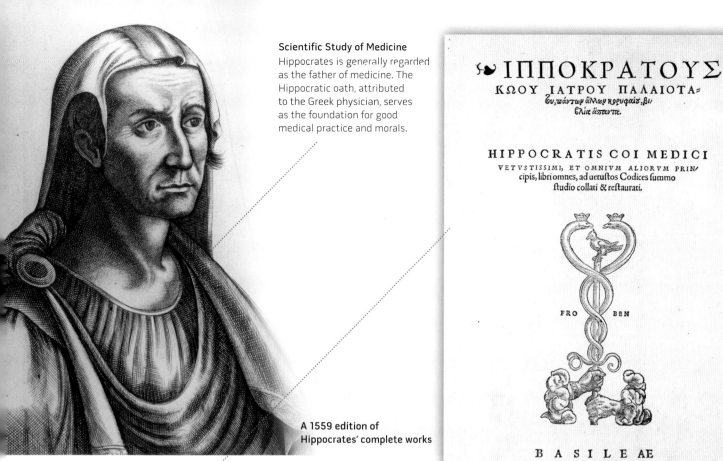

A 1559 edition of Hippocrates' complete works

400 B.C. >

Scientific Study of Medicine

▲ IN THEORY

The rod of Asclepius, the universal medical symbol

Many scholars trace the origins of Western medicine to a radical moment in ancient Greek society, when Hippocrates and his followers first sundered the art of doctoring from that of the magician or priest.

Hippocrates, born on the Greek island of Kos about 460 B.C., may or may not have authored the early Greek writings of the Hippocratic Corpus. But it is clear from these texts that some physicians of the period were beginning to insist that disease be attributed to natural or material causes—to a patient's environment, diet, or daily habits, for example—and not to divine intervention. One text, *On the Sacred Disease*, specifically excludes mystical influence in epilepsy (which the Greeks had set apart as a strange affliction certain to reflect some divine curse or power), calling it instead a disease of the brain. The Hippocratic physicians for the first time located all thoughts and feelings in the brain. They counseled careful and close observation of individual patients, and a gentle, conservative approach to treatment that strove to assist the body's own restorative powers—probably a blessing in an era of few bona fide cures.

This movement also espoused a scrupulous professionalism on the part of doctors, a value encoded in the famous Hippocratic oath, and in other texts. Doctors, according to Hippocratic writings, should seek to benefit and never to harm their patients. They should be honest and well kept, protect the privacy of houses they enter, and avoid any form of corruption, including sexual relations with clients.

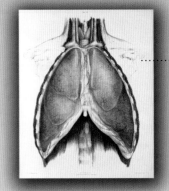

Tiny Intruders
Influenza virus cells, measuring as small as 0.0001 millimeter across, invade the lungs, causing inflammation and damaging tissue.

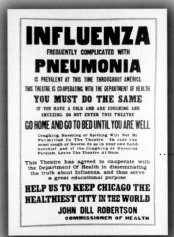

Wanted Poster
In 1918 a new influenza arose, killing tens of millions around the world. Posters in Chicago described the symptoms and advised people to stay in bed until they were well.

Treacherous Spikes
A computer-generated image of an influenza particle, or virion, shows the protein spikes with which it finds and clings to its host—the longer hemagglutinin and the shorter neuraminidase give the virus its name: H1N1.

Pandemic Control

A virus is a kind of vampire. The tiny package of genetic material must enlist the life functions of a host organism's own cells to survive and reproduce.

Unfortunately this process is an exceptionally effective way for viruses to perpetuate themselves, often at great cost to hosts. Vaccines, which stimulate immunity against specific viruses or viral strains, and antiviral drugs, which attack specific viruses directly, are only partially effective weapons—largely because viruses are such protean shape-shifters. Their quick and profuse proliferation via host cells allows them to continually tweak their own genetic makeup, developing resistance to medications and storming the barricades of vaccine-induced immunity.

Recently, however, researchers have seized upon a promising third approach: What if they could find a drug that knocked out some function of the host cell, making it impossible for a virus—perhaps a whole range of viruses—to engage its services? The result would be a broad-spectrum antiviral, and, potentially at least, one far less likely to promote drug-resistant new strains.

One such drug candidate is DAS181, or Fludase, made by U.S. biopharmaceutical startup NexBio. It works by disabling flu-virus receptors on the surfaces of cells lining a host's respiratory tract. Evidence in animal models suggests the drug may effectively gird host cells against any influenza strain—including the highly virulent avian flu, and the highly transmissible pandemic strain of 2009.

In fact, the drug and others like it could be of critical value in any future pandemic. The spread of a pandemic flu strain can easily outpace the manufacture of a targeted vaccine. Witness 2009, when a vaccine became widely available only after so-called swine flu infections had peaked. And, although not the case in 2009, there could come along a pandemic strain resistant to existing antivirals like Tamiflu; some strains of seasonal influenza have already proved impervious to these potentially lifesaving medications.

1955
The creation and dissemination of the polio vaccine is an example of controlling a viral disease on a population-wide scale. *See page 77*

1898
The discovery of viruses was crucial in understanding viral diseases and epidemics. *See page 87*

1857
The germ theory of disease gave a theoretical framework for understanding illness as caused by microorganisms. *See page 90*

1854

The field of epidemiology seeks to control an outbreak of a disease on the scale of a population. *See page 91*

03

Physics & the Cosmos

BIG IDEAS

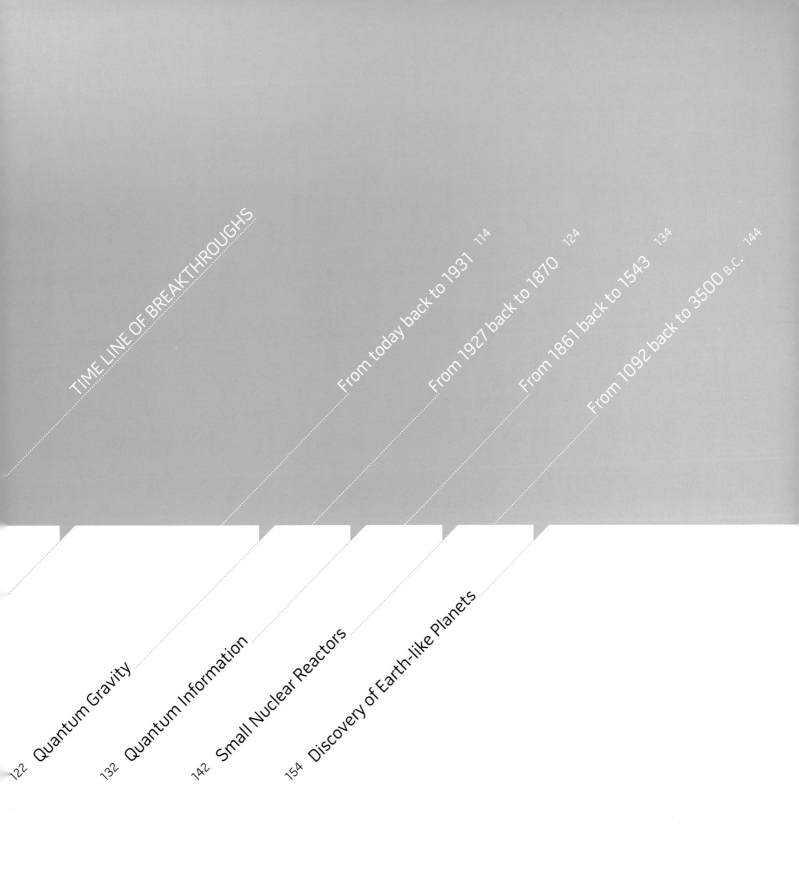

TIME LINE OF BREAKTHROUGHS

INTRODUCTION

Exploring the Heavens

Since time began, humans have looked to the heavens and wondered: Are we alone? What is the nature of time? Of space? What more is there to discover about the universe than what is known? How can the natural phenomena in the world be explained?

The quest to understand the universe scientifically—and human beings' place within in it—goes as far back as 600 B.C., when Greek philosopher Thales first attempted to explain natural phenomena in rational rather than supernatural terms. In the years between the fall of the Roman Empire and the European Renaissance, much ancient knowledge was preserved and advanced in the medieval Islamic world of the Byzantine Empire, including the invention of algebra in the ninth century. Then, thanks to European scientists and mathematicians of the 16th through 19th centuries—such as Copernicus, Galileo, René Descartes, Gottfried Leibniz, Isaac Newton, James Clerk Maxwell, and Francis Bacon—it became increasingly apparent that the universe is governed by physical laws that can be described by mathematical equations. Newton formulated the laws of motion and universal gravitation in the 17th century, for example, and Maxwell derived the equations that describe electromagnetism in the 19th century.

Just as it seemed that researchers were closing in on a complete scientific understanding of nature, however, theories of 20th-century physics—most notably Einstein's theories of relativity, which deal with the nature of space and time on large scales, and the theories of quantum mechanics, which apply to the fabric of reality on the smallest scales—overturned much of what scientists thought they knew about the fundamental workings of the universe. These theories have formed much of the basis of today's theories of space, time, matter, and the forces of nature. The Schrödinger equation, for example, gives a description of the evolution of a system of matter and forces on the smallest scales—much in the way Newton's law of motion describes how things move and affect one another on a larger scale. General relativity, the big bang theory, and the inflationary theory provide a framework for understanding the evolution of the universe as a whole from its earliest moments. The standard model of particle physics unites the fundamental forces of nature—with the significant exception of gravity—into a single model.

Today, efforts are under way to unite quantum mechanics and general relativity into a theory of quantum gravity, and scientists are exploiting their knowledge of quantum physics to devise new ways to transmit information. Astronomers are searching for Earth-like planets that exist outside of the Milky Way, in other parts of the galaxy—a quest made possible by the Arecibo radio telescope and the Hubble telescope. And the knowledge of nuclear physics is being employed to create small nuclear reactors that will be able to power remote locations not only efficiently but also safely.

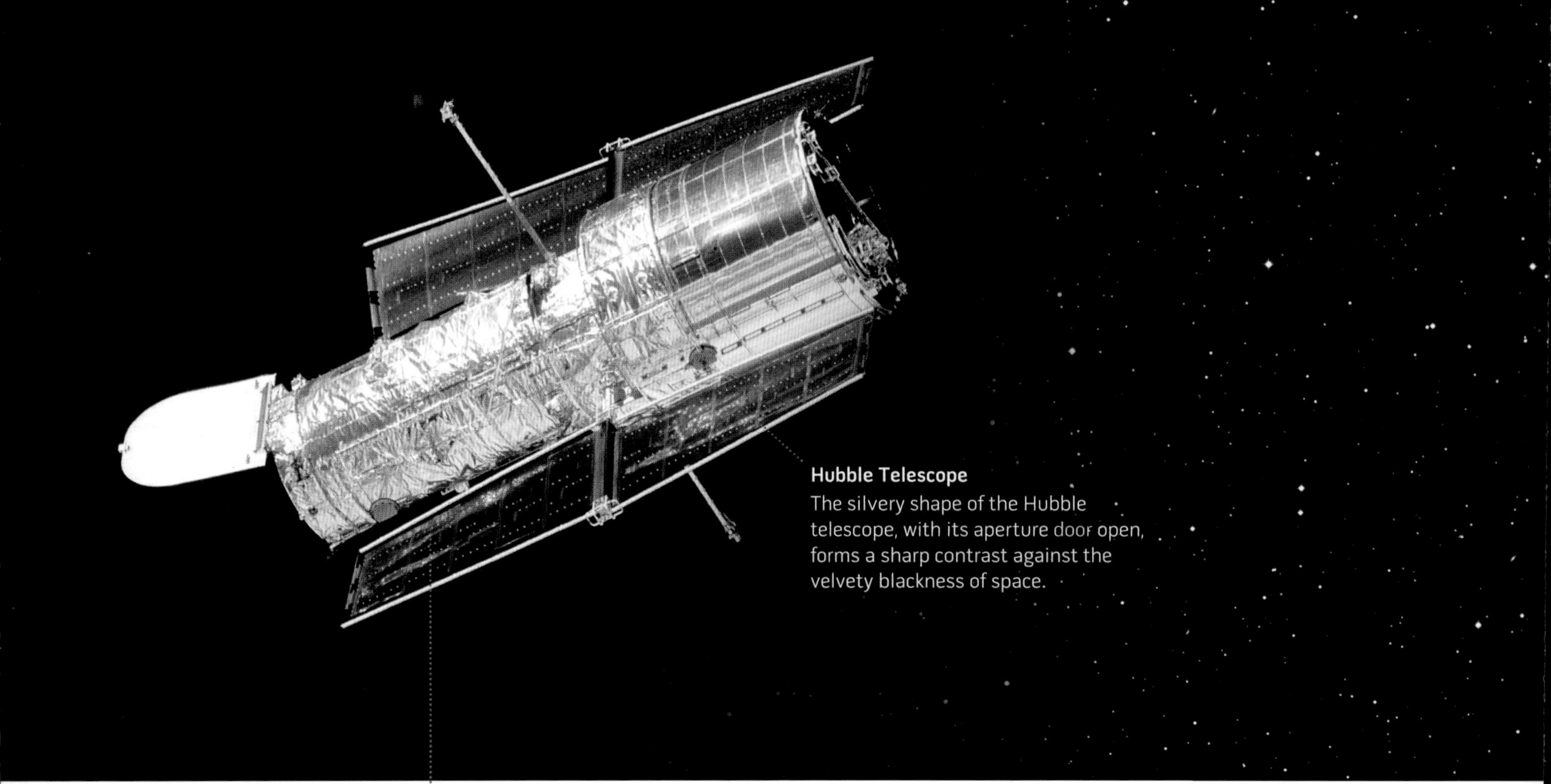

Hubble Telescope
The silvery shape of the Hubble telescope, with its aperture door open, forms a sharp contrast against the velvety blackness of space.

From today back to 1931 >

1990 >

Hubble Telescope

● IN USE

The Hubble telescope, launched in 1990, is both a spacecraft and a telescope. Located 370 miles above the Earth's surface, it orbits the planet once every 97 minutes. Its distance above the Earth is significant—Earth's atmosphere distorts and blocks the light that reaches the surface of the planet. Thus, placing Hubble beyond the atmosphere gives astronomers a view of the universe that far surpasses that of ground-based telescopes.

As a result of Hubble's launch, astronomers hope to answer important questions about the age and size of the universe; how planets, stars, and galaxies form; and how stars are born and die.

American astronomer
Edwin Powell Hubble

→← CONNECTION

Since the Hubble telescope was launched in 1990, it has discovered some amazing information about the universe. It has sent back pictures of the birth of stars, enabled astronomers to observe black holes, and aided scientists' understanding of how galaxies evolve.

Hubble has also given astronomers a better understanding of the planets in the Milky Way. For example, from July 16 to July 22, 1994, Comet Shoemaker 9 crashed into Jupiter. Hubble sent back pictures during and after the collision.

Building On >

Sputnik I *(p. 261)*

Telescope *(p. 139)*

Standard Model of Particle Physics
Quarks, whose existence was confirmed in the mid-1970s, are elementary particles that help make up all the matter in the universe.

1980 >

1973 >

Inflationary Theory of the Universe

▲ IN THEORY

Inflationary theory was developed by Alan Guth in 1980 to explain observable features of the universe. According to the theory, the universe is the result of an extremely rapid but short-lived expansion—known as the inflationary epoch—during its early history.

Precursors to inflationary theory include thinking by Albert Einstein, several Soviet cosmologists, and others who attempted to explain why the universe appears flat, homogeneous, and uniform in all directions—rather than highly curved and heterogeneous.

The big bang, the prevailing theory of the development of the universe, is a classic example of inflationary theory at work. Astronomers have made precise measurements of the cosmic radiation left over from the big bang and have determined that the radiation arrives at Earth from all directions with the same intensity. Tracing the development of this radiation backward, cosmologists conclude that the temperature and density of matter in the universe must have been uniform when the cosmic background radiation was released.

Standard Model of Particle Physics

▲ IN THEORY

The standard model of particle physics describes the universe in terms of matter, which is made up of particles called fermions, and force, which is made up of particles called bosons. There are four known forces of nature, each mediated by a fundamental boson particle: strong nuclear force, weak nuclear force, electromagnetic force, and gravity.

The standard model as it currently exists was finalized in the mid-1970s with the confirmation of the existence of quarks. Discoveries of the bottom quark, the top quark, and the tau neutrino have given this model even more credibility. Because scientists can use it to explain a wide range of experimental results, the standard model is sometimes called the "theory of everything." However, this model is not without its limitations. For example, it does not take the physics of general relativity, such as gravitation and dark energy, into account.

Despite these limitations, the standard model of particle physics is one of the best explanations scientists have for how the universe works.

Big Bang Theory *(p. 121)*

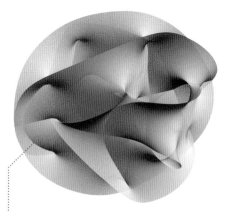

String Theory
An illustration that conceptualizes the extra dimension as theorized by string theory and other physics models

Cosmic Microwave Background Radiation
A time-lapse view of a radio telescope's moving dish at Owens Valley in California shows star trails in the sky. Cosmic microwave telescopes are used to detect radiation left over from early stages in the universe's development.

1969 >

1964 >

String Theory

▲ IN THEORY

String theory, which was first explored by physicists who were studying the dual resonance model—a physical theory of the strong nuclear force—attempts to bring together quantum mechanics and general relativity by removing the discrepancies between the two theories. According to string theory, electrons and quarks within an atom are not zero-dimensional objects. Instead they are one-dimensional, oscillating lines called strings. How a string vibrates will determine the amount of energy that is produced—resulting in a specific type of subatomic particle.

Five major string theories have been formulated since the theory's beginnings in the late 1960s. In the mid-1990s they were unified into what is called M-theory, which asserts that strings are really one-dimensional slices of a two-dimensional membrane vibrating in 11-dimensional space.

String theory is difficult to test; particle accelerators could be on the verge of finding evidence for high-energy supersymmetry—a key prediction of string theory—in the next decade.

Cosmic Microwave Background Radiation

▲ IN THEORY

According to standard cosmology, the cooling and expansion of the universe resulted in the release of radiation some 400,000 years after the big bang. This radiation—a remnant of the big bang that still can be observed today—is known as cosmic microwave background. Precise measurements of CMB—which was first observed by radio astronomers Arno Penzias and Robert Wilson in 1964—are critical to cosmology, since any proposed model of the universe must explain this radiation. The CMB has a temperature of 2.725 kelvins—very close to absolute zero. Its glow is almost—but not quite—uniform in all directions, showing a pattern that supports ideas about the origin of the universe that are crucial to the big bang theory and inflationary theory.

Cosmic microwave radiation, thermal radiation that fills the universe

Building On >

◢ Quantum Mechanics *(p. 41)*
◤ General Theory of Relativity *(p. 126)*

Arecibo Observatory

The Arecibo radio observatory in Puerto Rico is the world's largest and most sensitive radio telescope. Its new Gregorian sub-reflector system helps illuminate the main reflector.

Laser

A laser burns data onto a DVD. Lasers are ubiquitous today, finding use in many areas—from consumer electronics and home entertainment to law enforcement and the military.

1963 >

1960 >

Arecibo Observatory

● IN USE

The world's largest and most sensitive radio telescope is located in Arecibo, Puerto Rico. Part of the National Astronomy and Ionosphere Center, this observatory operates 24 hours a day, seven days a week, and has been recognized as one of the most important national centers for research in radio astronomy, planetary radar, and terrestrial aeronomy (the science of the upper atmosphere) since it was completed in 1963.

The location of the observatory is no accident. It had to be near the Equator, where a radar capable of studying the ionosphere—a part of the upper atmosphere—could also be used to study nearby planets that pass overhead. In addition, the large limestone sinkholes of the terrain provided a natural geometry for the construction of the giant reflector.

The Arecibo telescope has led to many significant scientific discoveries—among them, the first solid evidence that neutron stars actually exist. In 1970 scientists discovered the first extrasolar planets using the telescope, and in August 1989 the observatory directly imaged an asteroid for the first time in history.

Laser

● IN USE

The term laser is actually an acronym for "light amplification by stimulated emission of radiation." The significance of the device lies in the fact that laser light has a high degree of a property called coherence, which allows laser light to be focused very narrowly and to be effective over long distances— feats that are unattainable with other technologies.

Albert Einstein established the foundation for the laser in 1917. From that came the maser, which used microwave radiation rather than infrared or visible radiation. The maser, however, was incapable of continuous output. In 1957 scientists at Bell Laboratories abandoned infrared radiation altogether, concentrating upon visible light. However, Theodore H. Maiman, a researcher at Hughes Research Laboratories in California, beat the team at Bell Labs to the punch, making the first functioning laser in 1960.

Several different types of lasers are in use today in thousands of applications, including consumer electronics, science, medicine, law enforcement, entertainment, and the military.

▼ Radio Waves (p. 44)

▼ Holography (p. 34)

Atomic Clock

Archival photo shows a scientist repairing an atomic clock, the most accurate type of clock known to date. The time scale is derived from the vibrations of atoms or molecules.

Atomic Bomb

A sequence of six images illustrates the detonation of the world's first atomic bomb on July 16, 1945. The explosion illuminated the night sky, shattered windows 125 miles away, and produced a mushroom cloud more than 50,000 feet high.

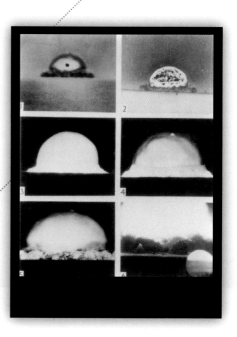

1949 >

1945 >

Atomic Clock

● IN USE

Despite the name, atomic clocks are not radioactive. While nearly all clocks measure time by way of some kind of oscillation, the big difference between a standard clock and an atomic clock is that in an atomic clock the oscillation takes place within an atom itself. Through the theories of quantum physics, scientists were able to understand and predict these oscillations and ultimately use them to construct extremely accurate timekeeping devices.

The first atomic clock was built in 1949 at the National Bureau of Standards. Although not as accurate as existing quartz clocks, it proved that the device was possible. The first accurate atomic clock was built in 1955 at the National Physical Laboratory in the United Kingdom. Today, these clocks are manufactured on a chip-level scale and make GPS navigation, the Internet, and even the space program possible.

Atomic Bomb

● IN USE

Atomic bombs involve harnessing forces that hold the nucleus of an atom together. Nuclear energy can be released from an atom in two ways: fission and fusion.

In direct warfare, atomic bombs have been detonated only twice, near the end of World War II by the United States against Japan. These bombs were the result of work conducted on the Manhattan Project, which was led by the United States, and included the United Kingdom and Canada. The scientific research portion was directed by American physicist J. Robert Oppenheimer; the first successful detonation of an atomic bomb was in July 1945 at what is now the White Sands Missile Range in New Mexico.

Hiroshima clock stopped at 8:15 a.m., when the bomb dropped on August 6, 1945

Building On >

▼ Global Positioning System *(p. 21)*

▼ Internet *(p. 28)*

▼ Existence of Atoms *(p. 128)*

Nuclear Reactor
The world's first nuclear reactor, Chicago Pile-1, sits on a racquet court at the University of Chicago. The work on this project led to production of the fuel for the first atom bombs as part of the Manhattan Project.

Nuclear Fission
A diagram shows a nuclear fission chain reaction, a series of reactions in which the particles released by one nucleus trigger the fission of other nuclei.

1942 >

1940 >

Nuclear Reactor

● IN USE

A nuclear reactor is a device used to initiate and control a sustained nuclear chain reaction. Today, the most common use of these devices is to generate electrical power and to provide power in some ships.

A chain reaction is used to produce nuclear fission from a fissile material at a controlled rate, releasing both energy and free neutrons. All nuclear reactors have a core that is usually surrounded by graphite or what is called heavy water. This is used to moderate the neutrons. Control rods or a similar mechanism is used to control the rate of the reaction.

The concept of a nuclear chain reaction was first developed by Hungarian scientist Leo Szilard in 1933. He filed a patent for his idea in 1934. Physicist Enrico Fermi and his team at the University of Chicago constructed the first artificial nuclear reactor in 1942, which they called Chicago Pile-1, or CP-1. The Fermi team initiated the first artificial self-sustaining nuclear chain reaction at CP-1.

In 1943 the U.S. military developed nuclear reactors for the Manhattan Project.

Nuclear Fission

▲ IN THEORY

When certain substances called nuclear fuels are struck by free neutrons, they undergo fission and generate neutrons when they break apart. This results in a self-sustaining chain reaction that releases energy at either a controlled or uncontrolled rate.

In 1932 English physicist James Chadwick discovered the neutron. In 1934 Enrico Fermi and his colleagues in Rome bombarded uranium with neutrons and examined the results. Fermi called the new element that his experiments created "hesperium." However, Lise Meitner, Otto Hahn, and Fritz Strassmann began performing similar experiments in Berlin, and in 1938 realized that Fermi's hesperium was actually a sample containing barium, krypton, and other elements.

Finally, in 1940 a team at the University of California, Berkeley, isolated the element known as plutonium by a similar procedure. Researchers soon discovered an isotope of plutonium that could, under certain circumstances, release energy in a chain reaction with potentially awesome destructive force.

Cyclotron *(p. 121)*

Quantum Entanglement
Physicists in Geneva, Switzerland, employ lasers to test the theory of quantum entanglement, whereby subatomic particles appear to be linked across space and time, with one particle's changes simultaneously affecting the other.

1935 >

Physicist John Bell

Quantum Entanglement

▲ IN THEORY

Quantum entanglement is a property of certain states of quantum systems containing two or more distinct objects, in which the information describing the objects is so thoroughly intertwined that observing one object instantaneously changes the other. No matter how far apart these objects are—whether on opposite sides of the galaxy, or universe—a change in one is instantly reflected in the other.

Quantum entanglement—a concept introduced by physicists working on quantum mechanics in the 1930s—presented a serious challenge to physicists like Einstein because it seemed to be in direct opposition to the generally accepted idea that nothing could travel faster than the speed of light. Quantum entanglement, however, has since been verified through a series of experiments beginning in 1972 and ending with definitive proof in the 1980s.

So now that scientists know quantum entanglement exists, what can they do with it? Perhaps the most exciting use for entanglement is quantum teleportation. Not exactly the teleportation depicted in *Star Trek*, quantum teleportation refers to the transfer of information through pairs of entangled photons. In 2010 Chinese scientists successfully teleported information over a distance of ten miles—a significant feat that presages the use of entanglement in future information and communication technologies.

⇄ BACKLASH

Albert Einstein, Boris Podolsky, and Nathan Rosen formulated a thought experiment that involved the measurement of two spatially separated systems, concluding that quantum mechanics must be an incomplete representation of the physical world. Einstein believed that mathematicians would discover that quantum entanglement was a result of "hidden variables"—aspects of reality that were not accounted for in the theories of quantum physics. Physicist John Bell proved in 1964, however, that the predictions of quantum mechanics are not the result of hidden variables.

Building On >   Quantum Mechanics *(p. 41)*

Cyclotron

Ernest Lawrence manufactured the first cyclotron in the 1930s. Cyclotrons work by accelerating charged particles using a high-frequency, alternating voltage.

Big Bang Theory

The big bang, which describes the evolution of the universe since it came into being, emitted energy in such powerful amounts that scientists continue to measure it today.

1932 >

1931 >

Breakthroughs continue on page 124

Cyclotron

 IN USE

Cyclotrons accelerate charged particles using a high-frequency, alternating voltage. A magnetic field causes the particles to spin so that they repeatedly encounter the accelerating voltage over and over again. As the process continues, the particles gain energy and move toward the edge of the accelerator until they gain enough energy to exit it. The first cyclotron was built by Ernest Lawrence at the University of California, Berkeley, in 1932, and became key equipment for experiments in nuclear physics on that campus.

In addition to the cyclotron, other types of particle accelerators include linear accelerators, betatrons, synchrotrons, and storage ring colliders. According to William Barletta, director of the U.S. Particle Accelerator School, there are about 26,000 accelerators worldwide. They are used in research, radiotherapy, ion implantation, industrial processing and research, and biomedical research.

Big Bang Theory

 IN THEORY

According to the big bang theory, the universe was initially in an extremely hot, dense state that expanded rapidly; it has since cooled by expanding to its present diluted state, and it continues to expand. Belgian physicist Georges Lemaître first proposed this theory in 1931. The theory is often put forth as explaining *how* the universe came into being. Rather, it describes the general evolution of the universe *since* it came into being.

The kernel of this theory lies in the observations of spiral galaxies in 1912, which American astronomer Vesto Slipher showed to be receding from the Earth. In 1929 Edwin Hubble discovered that all remote galaxies and clusters are moving directly away from Earth's vantage point. Two years earlier, in 1927, Lemaître had proposed that the universe was expanding in order to take into account some astronomical observations. In 1931 he took this a step further, suggesting that the universe began as the explosion of a single point—bringing time and space into existence.

▼ Nuclear Medicine *(p. 80)*

▼ General Theory of Relativity *(p. 126)*

Grave Influences
The theories of quantum gravity propose that the space-time continuum warps—that is, what was pictured as a flat sheet is shaped more like a funnel—in the presence of a massive gravitational object such as planet Earth.

Quantum Gravity

Quantum gravity is an area of research in physics that is attempting to unify Albert Einstein's theory of relativity with quantum mechanics, also known as quantum theory. The difficulty with this task lies in the two very different, contradictory approaches these theories present on how the universe works. There are four fundamental forces of nature: gravity, electromagnetism, strong nuclear force, and weak nuclear force. These are the ways in which individual particles interact with one another. According to classical physics, these forces have definite and specific strengths, directions, velocities, and masses, which can be used to determine the curvature of space-time. According to quantum mechanics, however, the forces do not have definite values and are affected by subatomic particles such as photons, W and Z bosons, gluons, and the graviton. Thus, whereas scientists might expect an atom of matter to behave in a certain way when looked at through the lens of classical physics, this same atom could behave in quite different ways when seen through the lens of quantum physics.

Quantum gravity is a theory that is unconfirmed—and is likely to remain so for the foreseeable future. For one thing, the energy levels required to observe the phenomena that are predicted by the theory cannot be achieved in current laboratory experiments. In addition, Einstein's theory of general relativity makes certain assumptions about the universe at the macroscopic scale that are quite different from the assumptions made by quantum mechanics, which works at the microscopic scale.

Several different lines of research into quantum gravity are being conducted. But many researchers believe that even more radical concepts of space-time must be formulated before quantum gravity can be properly studied. Researchers and scientists also disagree whether quantum gravity is an entirely new field, with new concepts, or whether it is putting a new face on old mathematical differences and contradictions between general relativity and quantum mechanics.

1973
The standard model incorporated the forces of nature, with the exception of gravity, into a single theory of particle physics. *See page 115*

1969
String theory is a significant—yet unverified—theory of quantum gravity. *See page 116*

1915
The general theory of relativity gives scientists a mathematical description of the force of gravity and how it affects time and space. *See page 126*

ca 1830

Non-Euclidean geometries provide new ways to mathematically model space and time. *See page 135*

Uncertainty Principle

Heisenberg's translation into plain language of his formula—written in mathematical symbols here—was: "The more precisely the position is determined, the less precisely the momentum is known in this instant, and vice versa."

$$\Delta x \, \Delta p \geq \frac{\hbar}{2}$$

Austrian physicist Erwin Schrödinger, circa 1933

From 1927 back to 1870 >

1927 >

1926 >

Uncertainty Principle

▲ IN THEORY

The uncertainty principle, which was first published by German theoretical physicist Werner Heisenberg in 1927, states that given a pair of properties, the more precisely one property is measured, the less precisely the other property can be measured. This is not a defect in the research; rather, it is a fundamental statement about the nature of the system itself.

The mathematics behind this theory concentrates on particle and wave mechanics. With Danish physicist Niels Bohr, Heisenberg put forth what became known as the Copenhagen interpretation of quantum mechanics, in which the wave and particle representations of an atom are mutually exclusive, yet both are necessary to understand quantum events. However, an atom cannot be both a wave and a particle at once. The observer has to choose which state to focus on, which then affects the reality he sees.

This principle is a key way in which quantum physics differs from classical physics. The notion of the observer becoming part of the observed system shook the world of physics to its core, marking the end of neutrality on the part of the experimenter.

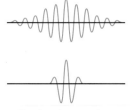

Graphs of uncertainty

Schrödinger Equation

▲ IN THEORY

In classical physics, Newton's laws of motion describe how any system of physical objects—a baseball thrown by a pitcher and then hit by a batter, for example—will evolve over time. That is, given sufficient initial data—the speed of the baseball, the speed and angle of the bat swing—scientists can theoretically calculate the state of the system—the location of the ball—at any time in the future.

The Schrödinger equation, formulated in 1926 by Austrian physicist Erwin Schrödinger, does the same thing for a quantum system. One crucial difference is

Building On >

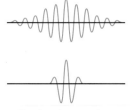

▼ Quantum Mechanics *(p. 41)*

$$E\Psi = \hat{H}\Psi$$

Formula showing the time-independent Schrödinger equation

Schrödinger Equation
Hugh Everett's "many worlds" interpretation of quantum mechanics pushed physics deeper into the realm of philosophy.

Quartz Crystal
A quartz crystal oscillator, mounted on a circuit board, creates an electrical signal with a very precise frequency. The frequency is used to provide a stable clock signal to the rest of the circuit.

1921 >

Quartz Crystal Oscillator

→← CONNECTION

● IN USE

that unlike the laws of Newtonian mechanics, which make deterministic predictions about the future state of a system, the laws of quantum mechanics make probabilistic predictions—that is, given initial data, there are different possible future states of the quantum system that occur with certain probabilities. Thus an inescapable element of randomness exists that is central to the Schrödinger equation. Schrödinger's formulation of this equation was a milestone in 20th-century physics, for which he received the Nobel Prize in 1933.

The "many worlds" interpretation of quantum mechanics was conceived of by American physicist Hugh Everett in 1957. This original approach to quantum physics claims to resolve the paradoxes that are intrinsic to quantum theory. Whenever a quantum event occurs, researchers see but one of the possible outcomes that are prescribed by the Schrödinger equation. However, according to the many worlds interpretation, each of the other possible outcomes does occur—it just takes place in a parallel universe that branches off from the known universe.

American physicist and electrical engineer Walter Cady developed the first crystal oscillator in 1921, which was driven by the work on arc and wave energy he had done during World War I in the support of submarine detection. This invention replaced the mechanical oscillator in timepieces, relying instead on the natural vibrations that occur in a quartz crystal in response to an electric current—a phenomenon known as piezoelectricity. (Cady would use this knowledge again during World War II, applying piezoelectricity to various military applications.)

The quartz crystal is the most common type of piezoelectric resonator used; oscillator circuits designed around the crystal became known as crystal oscillators. The use of crystal oscillators improved timing accuracies immensely. Most are small and used in devices such as clocks, radios, and cell phones.

Piece of raw quartz crystal

▶ Cell Phone *(p. 24)*

▶ Radio *(p. 43)*

General Theory of Relativity
Images of a 1919 total solar eclipse helped confirm Einstein's theory of general relativity. The photos showed that nearby stars had shifted slightly because their light was curved by the sun's gravitational field.

General Theory of Relativity
Hubble Space Telescope data reveal the presence of a black hole in the Messler 84, or M84, galaxy. Einstein's general theory of relativity allowed astronomers to predict and prove the existence of black holes.

1915 >

1915 >

General Theory of Relativity

▲ IN THEORY

When Albert Einstein introduced his general theory of relativity in 1915, it showed that Newton's law of universal gravitation—which had been accepted for more than 200 years, and which formed the foundation for how scientists understood the universe—was only partially correct. It no longer applied when the gravitational force became too strong. While Newton's laws of motion are very accurate at explaining most kinds of motion, they could not predict movements like the slight anomalies in planetary orbits.

With Einstein's earlier special theory of relativity, time was no longer objective and absolute, and moreover, space and time could be considered to be united in a single four-dimensional continuum, space-time. General relativity was a completely new, astounding mathematical theory that interpreted the force of gravity as a curvature in space-time. Einstein's formulation of this theory began with a simple thought experiment: What happens when, he wondered, someone falls out of his chair? Starting from the key insight that a person in free fall will not feel his own weight, he constructed a theory that models gravity as curved space-time.

General relativity provided not only a new way to interpret gravity but also a new framework within which to understand the evolution of the universe. The mathematical aspects of the big bang theory are based on general relativity, for example. Also, using the general theory of relativity, cosmologists and astronomers were able to predict accurately and subsequently prove the existence of neutron stars, black holes, and gravitational waves.

Noether's Theorem

▲ IN THEORY

The mathematical theorem known as Noether's theorem—which was proved by German mathematician Emmy Noether in 1915—has become a fundamental tool in the study of theoretical physics and the calculus of variations. Author W. J. Thompson describes it in layman's terms: "If a system has a continuous symmetry property, then there are corresponding quantities whose values are conserved in time." In other words, each mathematical symmetry of a system leads to a physically conserved quantity.

Noether's theorem has allowed physicists to delve deeper into

Building On >

Big Bang Theory *(p. 121)*

Newton's Laws of Motion and Universal Gravitation *(p. 136)*

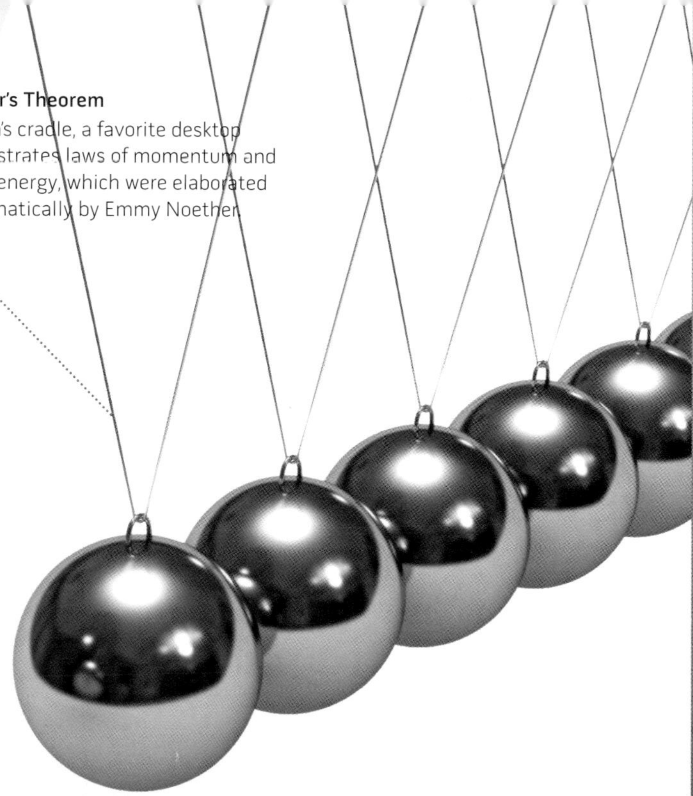

Noether's Theorem
Newton's cradle, a favorite desktop toy, illustrates laws of momentum and kinetic energy, which were elaborated mathematically by Emmy Noether.

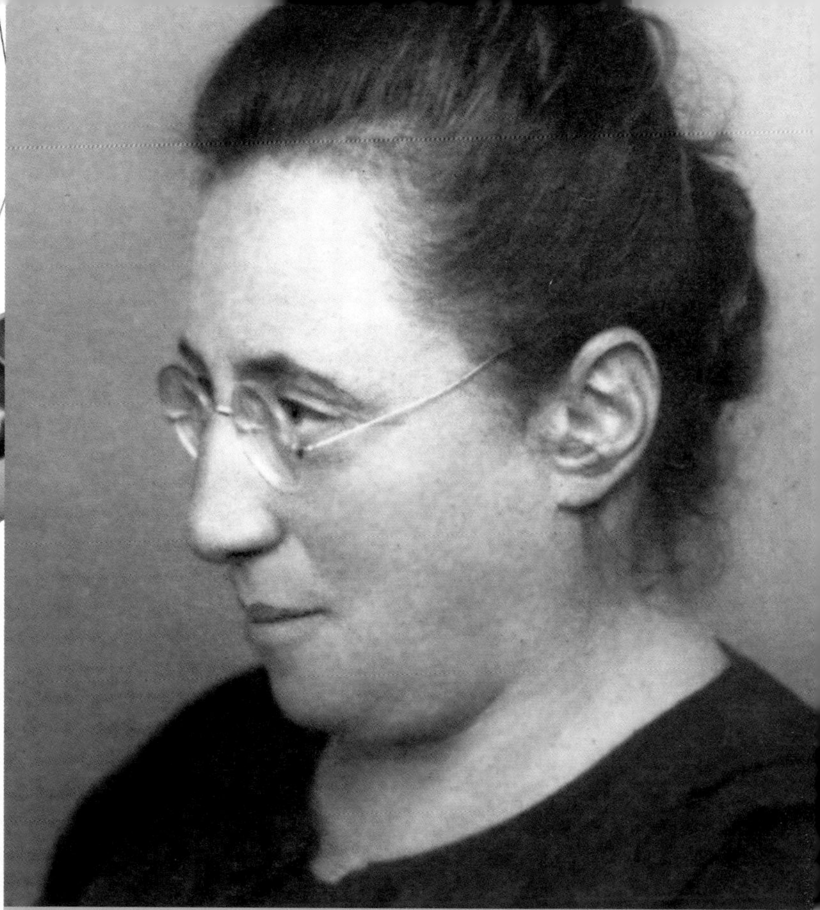

Emmy Noether

German mathematician Emmy Noether (1882-1935) is undoubtedly one of the most important women in the history of mathematics. Her work revolutionized the field of mathematics now known as abstract algebra. She is most famous for her theorem that explains the fundamental connection between symmetry and conservation laws.

In 1915 Noether joined the Mathematical Institute in Göttingen, Germany, and started working with Felix Klein and David Hilbert on Einstein's general theory of relativity. In 1918 she proved two theorems that provided the foundation for both general relativity and elementary particle physics. In 1933 she left Germany and took a position at Bryn Mawr College in Pennsylvania, where she taught until her death in 1935.

many general theories of physics, simply by studying certain transformations that would make the laws of these theories invariant—in other words, which transformations would leave these laws unchanged. For example, the fact that the laws of physics are invariant with respect to locations in space leads to the law of conservation of linear momentum; invariance with respect to rotation provides the basis for the law of conservation of angular momentum; and invariance with respect to time translation is the foundation for the law of conservation of energy. Noether's theorem is also used in calculating the entropy of stationary black holes.

The plot shows the positions of microscopic pollen grains suspended in water, as observed at 30-second intervals. Named Brownian motion, the concept helped Albert Einstein prove the existence of atoms.

Scottish botanist Robert Brown

1905 >

1905 >

Existence of Atoms

Special Theory of Relat

▲ IN THEORY

In 1827 Scottish botanist Robert Brown—who first described the cell nucleus—looked at pollen grains in water through a microscope and observed that the pollen particles were randomly moving, but he could not figure out why. In 1905 Albert Einstein used this concept of Brownian motion to prove the existence of atoms. He predicted that the pollen grains were moving because molecules of water were hitting them. The pollen grains could be seen; the water molecules could not; thus it looked like the pollen grains were moving randomly.

Einstein's paper made predictions about the properties of atoms, which others tested and confirmed. French physicist Jean Perrin, for example, used Einstein's predictions to calculate the size of atoms, which effectively did away with any residual doubts the scientific community had as to their existence.

→← CONNECTION

The phrase "annus mirabilis" has been applied to different periods in history, but is generally used today to refer to the year 1905, when Einstein published four groundbreaking papers on physics. These works were published in the *Annals of Physics*, one of the best-known and oldest physics journals worldwide.

The discoveries that Einstein made in his "year of miracles" had to do with the photoelectric effect, Brownian motion, and the special theory of relativity—all of which ultimately provided much of the foundation of modern physics.

▲ IN THEORY

In 1905 Albert Einstein published the special theory of relativity, which made use of two key physical ideas that were previously known—the principle of relativity and the constant speed of light.

Prior to this theory, physicists believed that electromagnetic waves moved through a medium called ether—much like ocean waves move through water. The ether was seen as a background against which all movement took place; all objects in motion moved relative to the ether. Einstein felt that it was a mistake to assume

Building On >

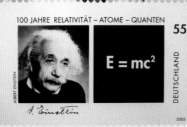

100 JAHRE RELATIVITÄT – ATOME – QUANTEN

55

E = mc²

ALBERT EINSTEIN

DEUTSCHLAND

2005

Physicist Albert Einstein
and his famous equation

1905 >

Wave-particle Duality of Light

▲ IN THEORY

the existence of the ether, which had not been experimentally verified. In special relativity, he did away with the ether altogether, assuming only that the laws of physics, including the speed of light, worked the same no matter how an observer was moving.

The mathematical consequences of the theory were stunning, but they have been experimentally verified. For example, as an object moves with a velocity relative to an observer, the object's mass increases and its length contracts. Perhaps the most famous consequence of the

theory is the equivalence of mass and energy that is captured in the equation $E=mc^2$. The special theory of relativity also created a fundamental link between space and time, a four-dimensional space called the space-time continuum. This continuum consists of three dimensions representing space—up/down, left/right, forward/backward—and one dimension representing time.

The theory is called "special" because it applies the principle of relativity only to the special case where the motion of objects is uniform.

In the 17th century the scientific world debated whether light was a wave or a particle. The answer is a paradox: All particles, whether light or matter, also have a wave-like aspect, and all waves have a particle-like aspect. This duality applies not only to light but also to all objects, regardless of size.

The photoelectric effect refers to the phenomenon that shining a light on certain metals generates an electric current. Physicists of the late 19th and early 20th centuries thought that the light was knocking electrons out of the metal, causing current to flow. According to the

classical theories of light and matter, the strength or amplitude of a light wave is in proportion to its brightness: the brighter the light, the larger the amplitude of the light wave. However, scientists observed that the color of the light—a result of the frequency of a light wave—determined the strength of the current.

In 1905 Albert Einstein—owing much to the work of physicist Max Planck—published an explanation of the photoelectric effect proposing that light traveled as discrete particles of energy. The frequency of the light determined the energy of the bundles.

Wave-particle Duality

Louis de Broglie was instrumental in showing that waves and particles can behave like each other at a quantum level. This double-slit experiment demonstrates the inseparability of the wave and particle natures of light.

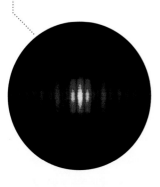

Radioactivity

Radioactive phosphorus is absorbed by the leaf of a coleus plant, which leaves its imprint on photographic paper.

Speed of Light

An engraving from a book published in 1858 shows the apparatus used by 19th-century French physicist Hippolyte Fizeau to measure the speed of light.

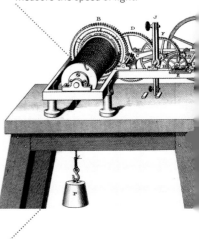

1896 >

1887 >

Radioactivity

→← CONNECTION

In 1924 French physicist Louis de Broglie theorized that light was not the only substance that exhibits wave-particle duality. He proposed that ordinary particles and objects also exhibited wave characteristics under certain circumstances. De Broglie came up with a mathematical equation in which the wavelength of a particle was associated with its mass and speed. That is, as the momentum of a particle changes, the wavelength decreases, and as the particle's kinetic energy increases, the wavelength's frequency increases.

▲ IN THEORY

In 1896 French physicist Henri Becquerel discovered that uranium salts emitted penetrating rays similar to x-rays that seemed to arise spontaneously from the uranium itself. He published seven seminal papers on the subject. Marie Curie, a Polish-born French scientist, was intrigued by Becquerel's findings and decided to investigate. Using the Curie electrometer, a device that her husband and brother-in-law had invented to measure electrical charge, she showed that the activity she measured was dependent solely on the amount of uranium, and that it was not the result of the interaction of molecules—as in a chemical reaction. Rather, it was coming from the uranium atom itself. Curie coined the term "radioactivity" to describe this finding. Her work with radioactivity and her discovery of new, radioactive chemical elements earned her two Nobel Prizes, one in physics and one in chemistry.

The hazard symbol indicates the presence of radiation.

Speed of Light

▲ IN THEORY

In the late 19th century physicists believed that just as sound and other substances must have a medium to move through—such as water or air—so, too, must light. This medium was called ether, and several scientists undertook the task of proving its existence.

The most famous experiment was performed by American scientists Albert Michelson and Edward Morley in 1887. They constructed an elaborate apparatus—known as an interferometer—that would allow them to detect the ether. Basically, they would measure the speed of

Building On >

Laws of Thermodynamics ·················
A melting ice cube illustrates the second law of thermodynamics. Energy in the ice changes from being localized to spreading out.

Physicist Albert Abraham Michelson

ca 1870 >

Breakthroughs continue on page 134

Laws of Thermodynamics

light in two directions, one the same as the Earth's motion, the other perpendicular to the Earth's motion. If the ether existed, the beam of light traveling parallel to the Earth's motion should be slower—that is, it should take longer to travel an equal distance—than the beam traveling perpendicular to the Earth's motion. This would establish the existence of the ether.

Michelson and Morley expected to find different speeds of light in each direction; however, they found no discernible changes in speed: The ether did not exist.

▲ IN THEORY

The laws of thermodynamics were developed in the 1800s to explain the absence of perpetual motion in nature. They are expressed in three basic tenets. The first law has to do with the conservation of energy. It states that energy in a system can be transformed, but it cannot be created or destroyed.

The second law of thermodynamics states that heat cannot spontaneously flow from a colder location to a hotter location. Over time, differences in temperature, pressure, and chemical potential tend to even out in an isolated physical system, and this evening-out can be measured in terms of what is called entropy.

The third law of thermodynamics states that entropy is dependent on temperature, which provides an absolute reference point for its determination. In other words, as temperature approaches absolute zero, a system's entropy approaches a constant minimum and all processes end.

Together these laws have become some of the most important fundamental laws in physics.

➡◀ CONNECTION

The second law of thermodynamics states that heat cannot flow from a colder location to a hotter location. When this law is applied to the universe, the implications are something to think about. According to the second law, the universe will eventually reach a state of "heat death," in which all energy is evenly distributed. While this has an egalitarian ring to it, it is a decidedly negative fate for the universe: Just like a weight on the end of a spring will eventually cease oscillating, in this state the universe will not be able to sustain any movement—let alone any life.

Analytic Geometry (p. 138)

Newton's Laws of Motion and Universal Gravitation (p. 136)

Quantum Information

In physics, "information," sometimes thought of as nebulous and virtual, is in fact physical. Thus the laws of physics apply to it, which means that the theories of quantum physics can be applied to information. In fact, the laws of quantum mechanics provide researchers with new ways of transmitting and processing information—such as the unconditionally secure transmission of a message by way of quantum cryptography—that are not possible under the laws of classical physics alone.

Most often, information is represented by bits, which can take on one of two well-defined, mutually exclusive values, usually represented as 0 and 1, where 0 represents "off" and 1 represents "on." This is called a two-state system and is necessary to represent a bit physically, whether in a classical system or a quantum system. What makes quantum information unique, however, is that a quantum bit (called a qubit) can be both 0 and 1 at the same time—a result of the quantum mechanical phenomenon known as superposition. The amount of information that a single qubit can store is still equal to one bit. However, it is in the processing of information that the difference lies—and this is the area of most interest to current researchers. Quantum computing appears to be the area that shows the most promise as far as actually implementing the quantum information theory.

The components of computers are growing smaller and smaller, and will likely consist of single atoms at some point. Thus quantum technology simply has to move from theory to application. For example, quantum algorithms can aid in the factoring of large numbers, turning mathematically difficult problems into easier ones. Another potential use is in code-breaking, which is something that cryptologists and those in the data security industry find extremely interesting.

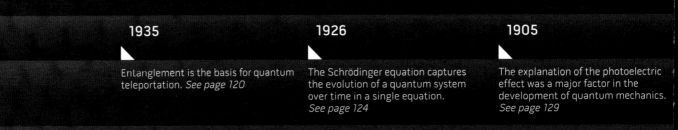

1935

Entanglement is the basis for quantum teleportation. *See page 120*

1926

The Schrödinger equation captures the evolution of a quantum system over time in a single equation. *See page 124*

1905

The explanation of the photoelectric effect was a major factor in the development of quantum mechanics. *See page 129*

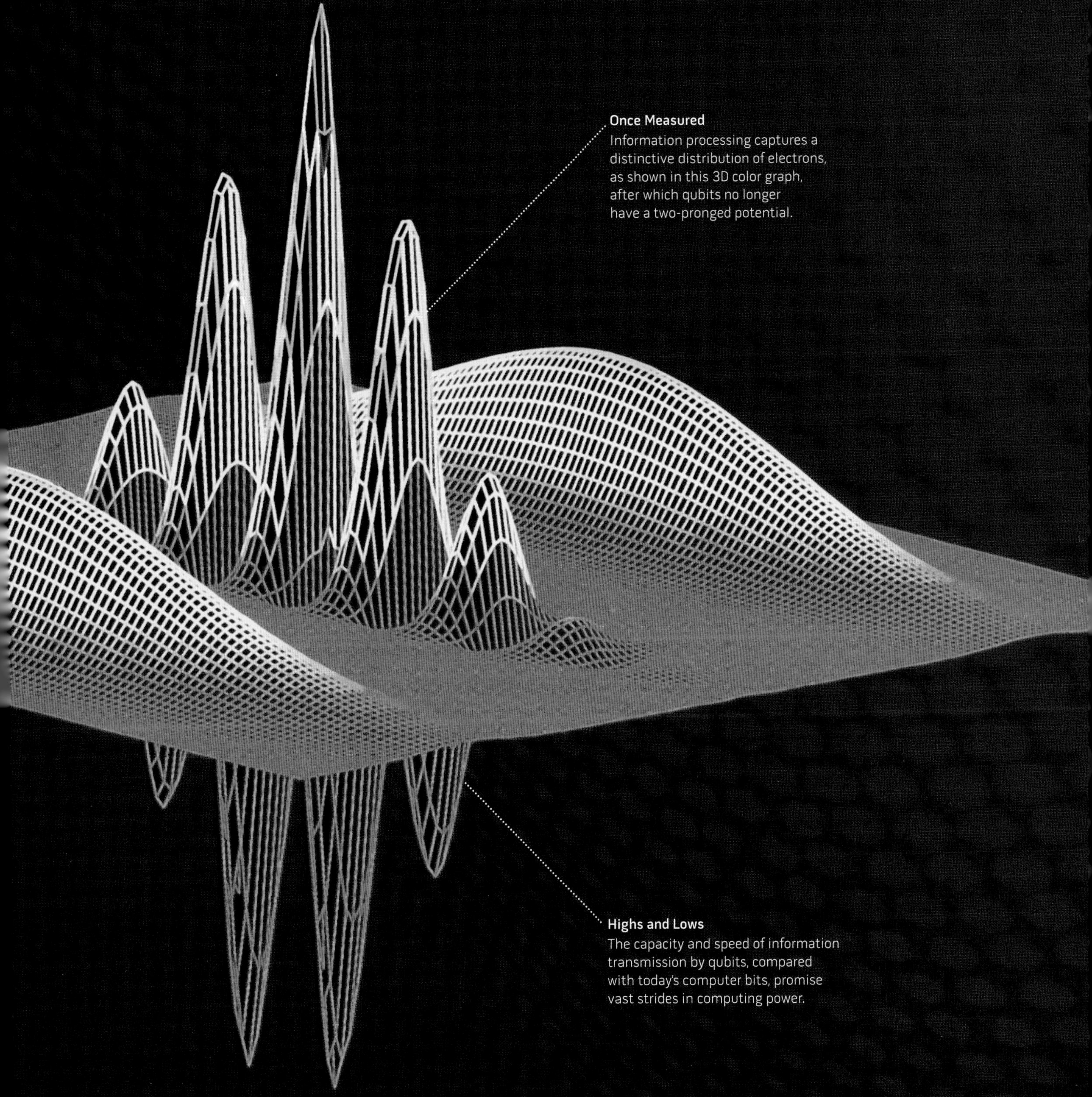

Once Measured
Information processing captures a
distinctive distribution of electrons,
as shown in this 3D color graph,
after which qubits no longer
have a two-pronged potential.

Highs and Lows
The capacity and speed of information
transmission by qubits, compared
with today's computer bits, promise
vast strides in computing power.

From 1861 back to 1543 >

Maxwell's Equations

A magnetic field near the end of a horseshoe magnet is visible in the lines of the iron filings. Interactions between the filings cause them to accumulate in arcing lines in the continuous field. Magnetic fields are one aspect of electromagnetism; electric fields are the other.

1861 >

Maxwell's Equations

▲ IN THEORY

In 1861, while working on his paper "On Physical Lines of Force," Scottish physicist and mathematician James Clerk Maxwell formulated what are known today as Maxwell's equations—a set of four equations describing how electric and magnetic fields are two aspects of a single source: electromagnetism. These equations form the foundation of electrodynamics, optics, and electric circuits. Maxwell's own achievement lies largely in the elegance and concision of his equations, which brought together theories of electricity, magnetism, and light in a unified, usable form. His correction to the last equation is known as the displacement current and was an essential piece of the puzzle.

Two of the equations, Gauss's law for electric fields and Gauss's law for magnetism, describe how the electromagnetic fields emanate from charges. The other two equations, Faraday's law and Ampère's law with Maxwell's correction, describe how the magnetic field "circulates" around electric currents and the time-varying electric field, while the electric field "circulates" around time-varying magnetic fields. These equations demonstrated that electric and magnetic fields could feed off each other indefinitely through space, due to Maxwell's displacement current. This current, in turn, could be used to predict the speed of the electromagnetic fields (i.e., the speed of light). Because they predict the existence of a fixed speed of light, regardless of the speed of the observer, Maxwell's equations were the starting point for Einstein's special theory of relativity.

James Clerk Maxwell

Building On >

Special Theory of Relativity *(p. 128)*

Non-Euclidean Geometries

A sphere, a curving plane, and a Möbius strip—a three-dimensional object with one surface and one edge, shown here—are all examples of non-Euclidean geometry.

Marine Chronometer

Marine chronometers are highly accurate clocks kept aboard ships to aid in navigation. They can determine longitude and latitude by comparing Greenwich time with the local time at sea.

ca 1830 >

1761 >

Non-Euclidean Geometries

▲ IN THEORY

Euclidean geometry, which dates back to 300 B.C., makes use of five axioms, or postulates—statements that are taken as true. These postulates are used to prove many theorems about geometric figures and other mathematical objects. Euclid's fifth postulate, also known as the parallel postulate, is as follows: Given a straight line and a point *p* that is not on that line, there is exactly one straight line through *p* that never intersects the original line.

In the 1800s mathematicians discovered that they could modify the fifth postulate and thus create very different—yet mathematically consistent—geometries. The discovery of non-Euclidean geometry had wide-reaching consequences, especially in physics, because it showed that conceptions of space and time other than the familiar Euclidean one were possible.

The two primary types of non-Euclidean geometry are hyperbolic geometry and elliptical geometry. In elliptical geometry—given a line, one cannot find a line that is parallel to that line. In hyperbolic geometry—the Euclidean parallel postulate also does not hold.

Euclidean Geometry (p. 149)

Marine Chronometer

● IN USE

Until the mid-1750s accurate navigation at sea, out of sight of land, was practically impossible. Latitude, which measures distance from the Equator, could be measured by the position of the sun at noon or the North Star; measuring longitude was much trickier because the Earth rotates to the east, constantly shifting the ship along that axis in relation to heavenly bodies.

The solution: the marine chronometer. The device, which was developed in 1761 by English clockmaker John Harrison, was precise enough to be used as a portable time standard; thus it could be used to determine longitude by means of celestial navigation.

Portrait of John Harrison, 1768

Pendulum Clock (p. 138)
Water-driven Clock (p. 144)
Magnetic Needle Compass (p. 145)
Astrolabe (p. 146)

Newton's Laws of Motion and Universal Gravitation
With artwork from his 1687 *Principia*, Sir Isaac Newton showed that a projectile fired from a very high peak on Earth would never hit ground if launched from high in the Earth's atmosphere with enough initial speed. Instead it would remain in orbit around the Earth.

Sir Isaac Newton

1687 >

Calculus
A curve illustrates integral calculus.

1684 >

Newton's Laws of Motion and Universal Gravitation

▲ IN THEORY

According to Newton's law of universal gravitation, every massive particle in the universe is attracted to every other massive particle with a force that is directly related to the sum of their masses and is inversely related to the square of the distance between them. Proportionality is held constant in this theory at all places and all times; thus it is known as the universal gravitational constant.

Newton's laws of motion consist of three physical laws that describe the relationship between forces acting on a body and its motion due to these forces. They can be summarized as follows: (1) A body remains at rest or in uniform motion in a straight line unless acted upon by a force. (2) The acceleration of a body is proportional to the force causing the acceleration and is inversely proportional to its mass. (3) When a force acts on a body due to another body, an equal and opposite force acts simultaneously on that body.

Taken as a whole, these laws are significant in that they established the notion of a "clockwork universe," which permeated science for the next 200 years. In this view the universe is akin to a clock wound up by God and set in motion, with everything running as a perfect machine. Deists embraced this idea, delighting in the concept that God simply set the wheels of the universe in motion and then sat back, content to let the laws of science govern any and all events. Newton was dismayed by this interpretation, fearing it would lead to atheism.

Calculus

▲ IN THEORY

Calculus is an area of mathematics that deals with, among other things, how things change. There are two major branches of calculus, differential calculus and integral calculus—the modern versions of which both rest on the concept of limit, which was introduced in the 19th century. Roughly speaking, limits are a way of incorporating the concept of infinity into mathematics—they deal with what happens when one quantity gets infinitely close to another, or when a quantity gets infinitely large or small. Differential calculus is

Building On >

Newton's Laws of Motion and Universal Gravitation (p. 287)

Kepler's Laws of Planetary Motion (p. 140)

Anchor Escapement
Just as gears move the hands that tell the hour and minute of the day, the anchor escapement controls the swing of the pendulum, making timekeeping more precise.

Gottfried Wilhelm Leibniz

1657 >

Anchor Escapement

→← CONNECTION   ● IN USE

used to solve problems involving velocity and acceleration, the slope of a curve, and the process of determining the best element from among a series known as optimization. Integral calculus is used to solve problems involving area, volume, arc length, center of mass, and pressure as it is applied to the surfaces of objects. Calculus also enables mathematicians to understand more precisely (and possibly determine) the nature of space, time, and motion in situations where algebraic calculations are insufficient and limiting.

Both Isaac Newton and Gottfried Wilhelm Leibniz are credited with inventing calculus independently of each other in the late 17th century; however, Leibniz, of Germany, published his theories before Newton did, so he sometimes gets the credit.

The basic concepts of calculus, however, were worked out long before Newton and Leibniz by mathematicians in Egypt, Greece, Japan, India, China, and Persia. Arabic and Indian mathematicians played a role as well, including Ibn al-Haytham and Bhaskara II.

In horology—the science of measuring time—the anchor escapement, also called a recoil, is a device used in mechanical pendulum clocks. It maintains the swing of the pendulum and allows the clock's wheels to advance with each swing. Most people credit British scientist Robert Hooke with inventing it in 1657, although some attribute the discovery to clockmaker William Clement.

The anchor escapement was significant because it supported the ability to keep time more accurately than had been possible prior to its invention.

Coupled with the invention of the pendulum, minute and eventually second hands were added to the clock face for even more precise timekeeping.

▼ Leibniz Calculator (p. 56)

▼ Wheel (p. 299)

An antique wall clock with a pendulum

French philosopher and
mathematician René Descartes

1656 >

1637 >

Pendulum Clock

● IN USE

The pendulum clock, with its swinging weight, was invented in 1656 by Dutch scientist and mathematician Christian Huygens, who was inspired by Galileo's work on isochronism. Isochronism refers to something that occurs for the same amount of time at regular intervals. Galileo made note of this observation in his study of pendulums, remarking on the fact that the swing of a pendulum is constant, regardless of its angle.

This, however, was not quite true. Huygens showed that if the swing of the pendulum was too wide, the isochronism would deteriorate and the pendulum would be useless as a timekeeping device. Only pendulums with small swings of a few degrees (between three and five degrees) are truly isochronous. Huygens's discovery led to the invention of the anchor escapement, which reduced the pendulum's swing appropriately.

Pendulum clocks were advantageous in that they kept highly accurate time, to about 15 seconds a day. They remained the standard throughout the world for accurate timekeeping for 270 years, until the invention of the quartz crystal oscillator clock in 1927.

Analytic Geometry

▲ IN THEORY

When French mathematician René Descartes invented Cartesian coordinates in the 17th century, it changed the face of mathematics forever because it allowed geometric shapes to be described in algebraic terms—the study of this is called analytic geometry.

In analytic geometry, each point in a Cartesian coordinate system is determined by taking a pair of numerical coordinates and calculating the specific distances from the point to two fixed axes—often called the x-axis and y-axis. This can be calculated, regardless of the dimensions, number of coordinates, and planes.

Stamp with portrait of René Descartes

Building On >

Water-driven Clock *(p. 144)*

Sundial *(p. 153)*

Analytic Geometry
Cartesian coordinates provide a method of indicating the positions of points on a two-dimensional surface or in three-dimensional space. René Descartes introduced the use of these coordinates in 1637.

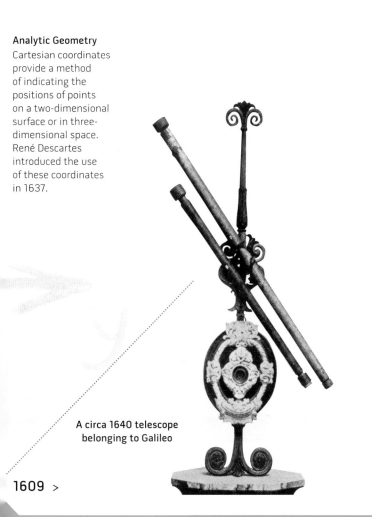

A circa 1640 telescope belonging to Galileo

1609 >

Galileo Galilei

Galileo Galilei (1564-1642), born in Pisa, has been called the father of modern observational astronomy, the father of modern physics, the father of science, and the father of modern science. His achievements are vast and widespread. Galileo discovered Jupiter's four largest moons; he was unafraid to embrace Copernicanism, the belief that the sun, not the Earth, was the center of the universe—even when it meant spending the rest of his life under house arrest. One of his most famous contributions to science, however, involves his equation of falling bodies, which he formulated after dropping objects from the Leaning Tower of Pisa in order to prove that all objects fall at the same rate, regardless of mass.

Telescope

● IN USE

Although Galileo was not the first to invent the telescope, he made significant improvements to its design in 1609 and was undoubtedly the first to make such amazing use of it. His telescope was unique in that it produced upright images. Although the images it produced were blurry and distorted, it was still good enough for Galileo to explore the sky. He was the first to document the phases of Venus, craters on the moon, and the four largest moons orbiting Jupiter, for example. Galileo's observations confirmed for him that the Earth was definitely not the center of the universe, as the Aristotelian view of cosmology claimed; rather, Galileo began to see that the Copernican view was correct: The sun was the center of the universe.

Microscope *(p. 101)*

Kepler's Laws of Planetary Motion
Orbits of our solar system's four outer planets—Jupiter, Saturn, Uranus, and Neptune, shown here in green, along with dwarf planet orbits—roughly conform to physical laws articulated 400 years ago.

1609 >

1572 >

Kepler's Laws of Planetary Motion

Changing Nature of the Universe

▲ IN THEORY

German astronomer and mathematician Johannes Kepler formulated his first two laws of planetary motion in 1609, and his third law around 1619. His work was largely based on the previous work of his mentor, Tycho Brahe. The laws are as follows: (1) Each planet moves in an elliptical orbit, with the sun at one focus of the ellipse. (2) A line from the sun to each planet sweeps out equal areas in equal time; this law implies that a planet will move faster when it is closer to the sun. (3) The square of a planet's orbital period is proportional to the cube

of the distance from the sun; in other words, the time it takes a planet to orbit the sun is related to its distance from the sun.

Although these laws seemed to be true based on observation, it would be nearly a century before anyone could prove that they were correct. Newton's law of universal gravitation proved that Kepler's laws actually do describe the motion of the planets in orbit. Today, scientists know that Kepler's laws apply only approximately to motions in the solar system; however, they are close enough for most purposes.

→← CONNECTION

The Scientific Revolution that took place in Europe during the 16th and 17th centuries was a time when scientists began to reject doctrines that had held sway since ancient Greece— instead using special tools to discover the laws of nature. These tools included the microscope, thermometer, sextant, telescope, and slide rule, among others. Some of the most famous thinkers of this time were men like Johannes Kepler, Isaac Newton, Nicolaus Copernicus, Francis Bacon, and René Descartes.

▲ IN THEORY

In 1572 Danish nobleman and astronomer Tycho Brahe observed a previously unknown bright star in the constellation Cassiopeia. He was able to prove through precise measurements that this was a new star (now known as a nova or supernova). His work upended the centuries-old belief that the world beyond the moon's orbit was fixed and unchanging. Brahe's critics at the time claimed that the phenomenon he had observed was in the terrestrial sphere below the moon and could not possibly be a part of the celestial sphere. But Brahe's observations showed that

Building On >

Newton's Laws of Motion and Universal Gravitation (p. 136)

Copernican System

Diagrams of the systems of Ptolemy and Tycho Brahe surround a cosmological illustration detailing Copernicus's astronomical vision; astronomical figures line the circle. Copernicus believed the sun, not the Earth, was the center of the solar system.

1543 >

Breakthroughs continue on page 144

Copernican System

over time the object did not change its position relative to the known fixed stars. Thus, he concluded, this was a fixed star in the sphere beyond the moon—and a new one at that.

Tycho Brahe's celestial sphere

▲ IN THEORY

Published in 1543 by Polish astronomer Nicolaus Copernicus, the Copernican system, which places the sun at the center of the universe, overturned preconceived notions not only about the cosmos, but also about humankind's place within it. Prior to Copernicus, the prevailing theory was the Ptolemaic system. In this view of the universe, Earth was at the center, stars were embedded in a large celestial sphere, and the other planets were in smaller spheres in between. Ptolemy's system included epicycles—smaller circles in which the planets moved while they orbited the Earth—in order to explain the apparent backward motion that the planets sometimes exhibited.

Copernicus described his system as follows: The motions of heavenly bodies are uniform, eternal, and circular or made up of several circles, or epicycles; the center of the universe is near the sun; around the sun, in order, are Mercury, Venus, Earth and its moon, Mars, Jupiter, Saturn, and the fixed stars. It would take 200 years for the Copernican model to replace the Ptolemaic model.

↻ BACKLASH

When Polish astronomer Copernicus published his *On the Revolutions of the Celestial Spheres*, few astronomers of the time were convinced by his argument that the sun, not the Earth, was the center of the universe. Some, in fact, found it heretical. For a thousand years, the Catholic Church had dictated not only dogma, but also political and scientific beliefs. The Copernican system challenged the church's views of the way the universe worked, which was unsettling to church leaders and to the uneducated masses.

Planisphere (p. 146)

Neighborhood Nukes.....................
Designed for safety, small underground nuclear reactors currently in development could generate ten megawatts of power for 30 years, enough to power 8,000 households.

Small Nuclear Reactors

In the never ending quest for inexpensive, efficient, and environmentally friendly sources of power, interest has turned once again to the nuclear reactor, albeit on a smaller scale than before. Its advantages: It produces no greenhouse gases (and thus makes no contribution to global warming) and exposes the environment to fewer contaminants than traditional fossil fuel–based sources of power. Also, nuclear power-generating units can be located underground.

A company called Hyperion Power Generation aspires to become one of the first to provide this power to small factories or towns too remote to be connected to traditional electricity grids. A 25-megawatt reactor would cost an estimated $50 million, could be transported by truck, and would require less maintenance than a fossil fuel plant. These reactors could be independent, stand-alone units—one module could theoretically provide enough electricity for 20,000 average-size homes—or they could be chained together in a modular fashion, with more added as needed.

Besides costing less to build than traditional reactors, some small reactors also could be inherently safer. For example, NuScale, in Corvallis, Oregon, has designed a small nuclear power system that requires no reactor cooling pumps. Toshiba has a design that employs electromagnetic pumps with no moving parts—which minimizes the possibility of disaster. In China researchers are developing a small reactor in which the nuclear reaction burns itself out after a certain period of time.

Critics claim that these mini-reactors pose a dual threat, noting that a risk still exists of radioactive materials leaking or terrorists hijacking a unit and using it as a weapon. John Deal, CEO of Hyperion, rejects these fears, stating that "the power-producing core [of the reactor] ships in multiple sealed chambers, containing any leak and the entire unit would be installed in an underground vault to protect it from tampering and natural threats."

1942
The first nuclear reactor is an obvious predecessor to the small nuclear reactors in development today. *See page 119*

1938
The idea of nuclear fission gave scientists the theory behind the nuclear reactor. *See page 119*

1905
The special theory of relativity showed how much energy could be released from the change in mass that takes place in a nuclear reaction. *See page 128*

1898

The discovery of radioactivity and radioactive elements was an essential step toward a nuclear reactor.
See page 130

Shen Kuo

[PROFILE]

One of the greatest scientific minds in Chinese history, Shen Kuo (1031-1095) studied fields ranging from mathematics to astronomy, biology to geology, engineering to finance, and diplomacy to music. Living in the 11th century, during the Song dynasty, Shen is noteworthy for first describing the magnetic needle compass. He improved upon the designs of the gnomon, the part of a sundial that casts a shadow, and invented a new kind of inflow water clock, which used the flow of water to tell time. Shen was also the first climatologist in that he hypothesized that the Earth's climate changed gradually, based on his discovery of ancient petrified bamboos in an area that was too dry and cool to support bamboo in his time.

Building On >

Water-driven Clock
This clock tower featured a power-driven sphere for observations, a rotating celestial globe, and panels with doors, through which mannequins rang bells and held tablets indicating the hour.

1092 >

Water-driven Clock

● IN USE

In the late 11th century polymathic engineer Su Song designed a water-driven astronomical clock tower in Kaifeng, China. The timekeeping device was significant in that it employed the use of an early escapement mechanism—a component of a clock that regularly advances its internal wheels, in this case the result of a container periodically filling up with water. Mechanical escapements—as opposed to the water-driven escapement of Su Song's clock—would later become crucial in the design of

Magnetic Needle Compass

A Chinese magnetic compass and calendar has a magnetized needle at its center. The needle is attracted by a magnetic force to indicate north or south direction. Chinese characters surround the needle, representing the names of a year and assigning astrological characters to them.

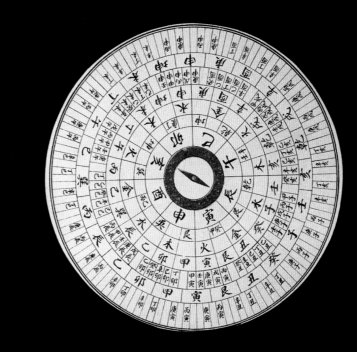

Chinese polymath Su Song

1088 >

pendulum clocks. The tower was 40 feet tall and weighed between 10 and 20 tons. Mechanically timed, rotating figures dressed in miniature Chinese clothes would come through small doors and announce the time of day by displaying small plaques, ringing bells and gongs, or beating drums.

Magnetic Needle Compass

● IN USE

Most notable of Chinese polymath Shen Kuo's many achievements is perhaps the magnetic needle compass, which he described in a 1088 book called *Dream Pool Essays*. Shen discovered that steel needles became magnetized once they were rubbed with lodestone, and when suspended in some way, the magnetic needles pointed either south or north. He also discovered the concept of true north based on this study.

These discoveries were significant in that they made compasses more useful for seafaring navigation. However,

the initial impetus for the compass was probably not for this purpose. Instead some scholars believe that early compasses were used to order and harmonize environments and buildings in accordance with the geomantic principles of feng shui, an ancient Chinese system of aesthetics.

Magnetic lodestone

Pendulum Clock *(p. 138)*

Sundial *(p. 153)*

Marine Chronometer *(p. 135)*

Planisphere
The 1540 atlas *Astronomicum Caesareum* was noted for its highly intricate wheel charts, such as this planisphere. Layers of paper were placed on top of one another and rotated to produce the desired result. In this case, the chart shows the night sky for a given latitude, time, and date.

Astrolabe
A 1493 illustration depicts an astronomer holding an astrolabe, a primitive instrument used to measure the altitude of stars.

1050 >

996 >

Planisphere

● IN USE

The planisphere—a chart used to calculate the location of visible stars and constellations for any time and date—was first described in the 11th century by Persian astronomer Abu Rayhan al-Biruni. The chart was circular and attached to an opaque overlay with a clear window in it so that only a portion of the chart was visible at any given time. Planispheres only showed the stars visible from the observer's latitude; stars below the horizon were not included. It also pinpointed the determination of the Milky Way.

Today, amateur and professional astronomers use planispheres to help determine the best places in the night sky to point a powerful telescope, especially when viewing an area of the sky they may not be familiar with.

→← CONNECTION

The Islamic golden age is traditionally dated from the mid-8th century to the mid-13th century. During this time, artists, engineers, scholars, poets, philosophers, and geographers contributed to the arts, economics, law, navigation, philosophy, sciences, and technology.

Early scientific methods were developed in the Islamic world, such as an empirical, experimental, and quantitative approach to scientific inquiry. The planisphere dates back to this period, as do astrolabes, and the beginnings of astrophysics.

Astrolabe

● IN USE

The astrolabe is a device used to locate and predict the positions of the sun, moon, planets, and stars; to determine local time given local latitude; to aid in surveying; and even to cast horoscopes. Although it dates back to the Greek and Byzantine periods, it was in the Islamic world that the modern astrolabe began to take shape. Mathematician Muhammad al-Fazari is credited with first introducing the astrolabe in the eighth century. Later, Muslim astronomers added angular scales to the astrolabe, with circles indicating arcs on the horizon

Building On >

Telescope *(p. 139)*

Copernican System *(p. 141)*

Astrolabe

The astrolabe was an early time-telling instrument that calculated the positions of the sun and stars in the sky at a given moment and location. Developed in the Islamic world, the astrolabe was used to determine prayer times as well as the direction to Mecca.

A Soviet stamp issued in 1983 depicts Al-Khwarizmi.

ca 820 >

Algebra

▲ IN THEORY

based on fixed positions. In 996 scholar Abu Rayhan al-Biruni—who has been honored by having a crater on the moon named after him—created an astrolabe with eight geared wheels, a device suited to making astronomical predictions, as well as one that had influence on the later development of mechanical clocks.

The roots of algebra began with the ancient Babylonians, who developed an advanced arithmetical system with which they were able to do calculations in an algorithmic fashion. The Greeks provided the foundation, whereby the solutions of individual problems could be gathered and applied in a more general fashion. Indian mathematicians continued to build on the traditions laid down by the Babylonians, Egyptians, and Greeks. However, it is in the Islamic world where modern algebra began to take form.

Although several cultures helped shape algebra, one man is credited with writing down many of the rules known today. Al-Khwarizmi, known as the father of algebra, was a Muslim mathematician who, around 820, compiled these rules in a book called *The Compendious Book on Calculation by Completion and Balancing*. The word "algebra" is derived from *al-jabr*, one of the two operations Al-Khwarizmi used to solve quadratic equations. The word "algorithm" stems from the Latin form of his name.

Al-Khwarizmi's book established algebra as a mathematical discipline independent of geometry and arithmetic. The volume presented the various ways polynomial equations could be solved, and demonstrated how transferring subtracted terms to the other side of an equation and cancelling similar terms on opposite sides of an equation could result in its being solved. *The Compendious Book* was also noteworthy because it was written in ordinary language, which meant the average person could potentially understand the mathematical concepts.

Copernican System *(p. 141)*

Modern Number System *(p. 58)*

Principles of Leverage and Hydrostatics

Pliers, used today to hold, cut, or bend objects, are an example of the principle of leverage, which allows a person to accomplish a task using less force.

ca 250 B.C. >

Principles of Leverage and Hydrostatics

▲ IN THEORY

Although Archimedes—who lived in the Greek city of Syracuse, in Sicily, in the third century B.C.—did not invent the lever, he did explain the principle behind its action, which has to do with the amount of force in relation to the length of the lever arm and the pivot point. His principle of hydrostatics states that when a body is partially or fully immersed in a fluid, an upward force acts upon it that is equal to the weight of the fluid that the object is displacing. Archimedes' principles of leverage and hydrostatics led to the study of hydraulics and fluid dynamics, which are important concepts in physics.

Building On >

Archimedes

[PROFILE]

Archimedes (ca 287 B.C.-ca 212 B.C.), a Greek mathematician, physicist, engineer, and astronomer, made significant contributions to physics with his foundations of hydrostatics and an explanation of the principle of the lever. His technological achievements include siege engines and the screw pump. But he made his greatest contributions in mathematics. Archimedes used the method of exhaustion to calculate a remarkably accurate approximation of pi, a mathematical constant. He also defined the spiral that bears his name, formulas for the volumes of surfaces of revolution, and a system for expressing very large numbers.

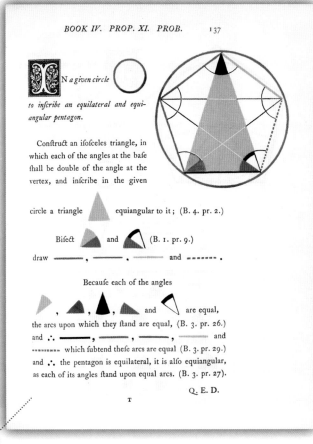

ca 300 B.C. >

Euclidean Geometry
A diagram illustrating the method of drawing a pentagon within a circle uses Euclid's theorems to complete the formula. Euclid's contribution to mathematics has been a major influence for more than 2,000 years.

Theories of Motion and Causation
The seasons, shown in this 18th-century diagram, exemplified the Aristotelian principles of causation, whereby all things in nature have a proper place in which they rest or to which they are tending.

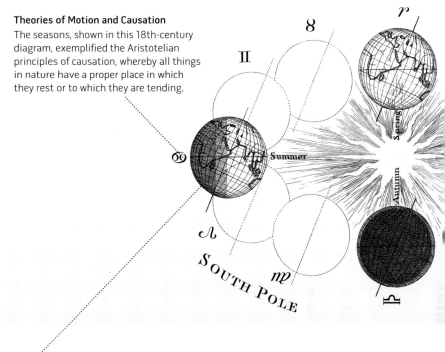

ca 330 B.C. >

Euclidean Geometry

▲ IN THEORY

Prior to Euclid, geometry was utilitarian in nature, improvised to meet a particular need in surveying or astronomy. The ancient Egyptians knew how to calculate the area of a circle. The Babylonians knew how to measure areas and volumes. It was in the Hellenistic period, around 300 B.C., that the state of geometry changed forever with a mathematician named Euclid.

Euclid published his revolutionary approach to geometry in a series of books called *The Elements of Geometry*. The series presents a set of axioms and from these, deduces propositions and theorems. Although Euclid's work was not necessarily new, he was the first to show how these theorems could fit into a comprehensive, deductive, and logical system.

According to Euclid's axioms, any two points can be connected by a straight line; any straight line whose length can be determined can be extended in a straight line; a circle can contain any center and any radius; and all right angles are equal to each other. The fifth axiom has to do with the intersections of lines in a plane.

Theories of Motion and Causation

▲ IN THEORY

Greek philosopher Aristotle, who lived in the fourth century B.C., theorized that everything in the natural world was composed of four elements that are constantly striving to move toward their natural place. Objects resist this natural motion only when forced to do so and only for as long as that force is applied.

Aristotle's theory of causation comprised material cause, formal cause, efficient cause, and final cause—each of which attempts to answer a question in four different ways. These theories were influential (and have remained so) because they ascribed a natural order to things. Everything had its place and was striving either to stay in that place or get back to it.

Athenian philosopher Aristotle

Non-Euclidean Geometries *(p. 135)*

Newton's Laws of Motion and Universal Gravitation *(p. 136)*

First Theory of Atoms

A model of a helium atom—the second simplest atom, after hydrogen. Greek philosopher Leucippus devised the idea that everything is composed of indivisible elements called "atoms," which translates to "unable to cut" in Greek.

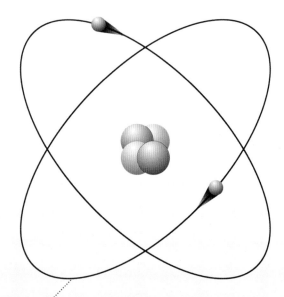

400 B.C. >

Will a runner ever catch up with a tortoise? Not if the tortoise has a head start, proposed Zeno—with every human advance, the tortoise moves ahead a little farther. The paradoxes still puzzle.

ca 450 B.C. >

First Theory of Atoms

▲ IN THEORY

Although some might think the atom is a relatively modern discovery, its existence was speculated upon as far back as 400 B.C., first by Greek philosopher Leucippus and then by his student Democritus. Leucippus believed that everything is composed of various imperishable, indivisible elements called atoms (the word comes from the Greek words meaning "unable to cut"). Democritus took his mentor's work a step further, theorizing that the solidness, or lack thereof, of a given material was directly related to the shape of its atoms. Iron atoms were solid and strong, for example, whereas air molecules were light and whirling.

A carbon 60 molecule structure, in the form of a hollow sphere, is a fullerene.

Zeno's Paradoxes

▲ IN THEORY

Zeno's paradoxes are perhaps the first examples of reductio ad absurdum, or proof by showing the absurd consequences of a proposition. Zeno, an ancient Greek philosopher of the fifth century B.C., devised his paradoxes to support his belief that "all is one," and despite what the senses reveal, plurality, change, and motion are nothing but illusions.

Two of the more famous paradoxes are the paradox of motion and the dichotomy paradox. The paradox of motion involves a footrace between Achilles and a tortoise. Achilles allows the tortoise a head start. However, if Achilles and the tortoise are assumed to be running at constant speeds (one fast and one slow), whenever Achilles reaches somewhere the tortoise has been, the tortoise has advanced, and Achilles still has some distance to go to catch up. This process continues indefinitely, and thus Achilles can never overtake the tortoise.

The dichotomy paradox can be demonstrated with the example of a man and a mountain. The man wants to reach the mountain; however, before he can reach the

Building On >   **Existence of Atoms** (p. 128)

Pythagorean Theorem
A triangular wooden ruler can be used to compute the Pythagorean theorem, one of the earliest known theorems to ancient civilizations. It is named for Greek mathematician Pythagoras.

Pythagorean Theorem
An Arabic textbook discusses the Pythagorean theorem, which is a statement about triangles containing a right angle. Algebraically, it reads: $a^2 + b^2 = c^2$.

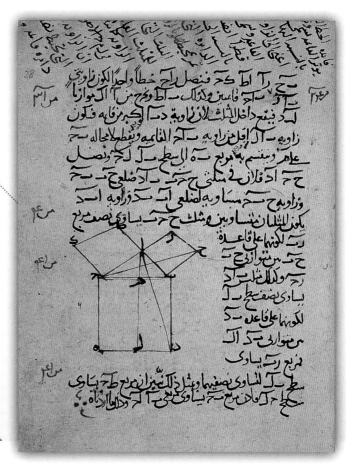

ca 530 B.C. >

Pythagorean Theorem

▲ IN THEORY

⤳ BACKLASH

mountain, he must get halfway to it; before he can get halfway to it, he must get a quarter of the way to it; and so on. The journey can neither be completed nor begun; thus all motion must be an illusion.

Zeno's three other paradoxes are the paradox of place, the paradox of the grain millet, and the moving rows. Debate still exists over whether or not the paradoxes have been resolved mathematically. What is not in dispute is how their subtlety has influenced scientists' thinking about the nature of time and space.

The Pythagorean theorem states the now well-known relationship among the three sides of a right triangle: The area of the square of the side opposite the right angle (the hypotenuse) is equal to the sum of the areas of the squares of the two sides that meet at a right angle—better known as $a^2 + b^2 = c^2$.

This theorem has greatly aided the understanding of the physical world through its application in many areas of mathematics. For example, the Pythagorean theorem is commonly used to derive the formula for the distance between any two points—and knowing

how to compute distance is a fundamental concept that is crucial for many types of mathematics.

The theorem is named after Pythagoras, although evidence indicates that the Babylonians and Egyptians understood this formula prior to the Greeks. Pythagoras was an Ionian Greek philosopher, mathematician, and founder of a religious movement. Mathematics dominated the belief system of the Pythagoreans, and one of the movement's most famous tenets states that it is only through the notion of the "limit" that the "boundless" takes form.

The development of the Pythagorean theorem led to a shocking discovery—that of irrational numbers, originally called *alogon*, which means "unutterable" in Greek. The culprit was the square root of two, which is the measure of the hypotenuse if the other sides of the isosceles triangle each measure one. The square root of two cannot be expressed by a fraction and thus cannot be measured on a ruler. With all the resistance to this concept, it would take 200 years before Greek mathematician Eudoxus developed a way of working with these numbers.

Thales

ca 600 B.C. >

Greek philosopher Thales (ca 624 B.C.-546 B.C.) of Miletus was one of the Seven Sages of Greece, a title given by ancient Greek tradition to seven early sixth-century B.C. philosophers, statesmen, and lawgivers who were renowned for their wisdom. Among his many accomplishments, Thales is credited with applying deductive reasoning to mathematics in the form of five geometric propositions for which he wrote proofs. He is also noteworthy for ushering in the birth of science by attempting to explain natural phenomena without invoking the supernatural. Thales' most famous belief, however, was his cosmological thesis, which held that the world started from water.

Beginning of Natural Philosophy

 IN THEORY

In the sixth and seventh centuries B.C., Greek philosopher Thales attempted to explain natural phenomena without reference to mythology, instead defining general principles and setting forth hypotheses. As such, he was laying the foundation for natural philosophy that others like Francis Bacon and René Descartes would build upon 2,000 years in the future. For example, Thales explained earthquakes not by attributing them to the capricious nature of the gods, but by hypothesizing that the Earth is not solid, but rather floats on water; when the Earth is rocked by waves, earthquakes are the result. Water actually formed the basis of much of Thales' natural philosophy. He considered the substance to be at the base of all phenomena in one way or another.

Thales' interests were not restricted to the natural world. He was also passionately interested in mathematics, astronomy, politics, and engineering. Interestingly enough, nearly all other philosophers of his day, rather than feeling threatened by Thales' potentially heretical practice,

Beginning of Natural Philosophy
The Seven Sages of Greece hold a discussion in a banqueting area. The philosophers and statesmen from the seventh and sixth centuries B.C. were seen as the wisest of men, according to ancient Greek tradition.

Sundial
A 16th-century woodcut shows a vertical sundial and how it works. The sun casts two shadows, one for the vertical slab and one for the horizontal rod. The combination of the shadows as the sun moves through the sky is used to determine the time.

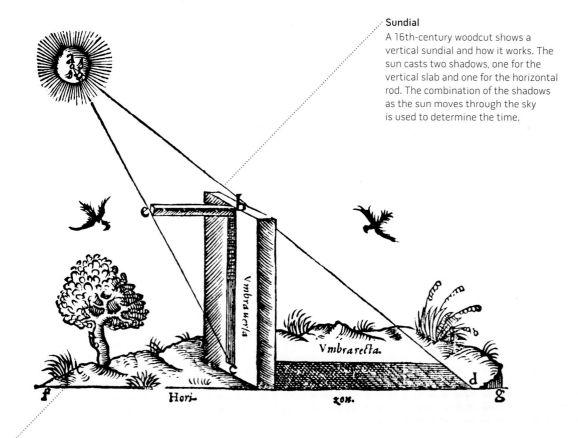

ca **3500** B.C. >

Sundial

● IN USE

followed his example, employing scientific hypotheses instead of supernatural explanations to explain the world around them. Thales and his contemporaries were quite successful in this endeavor, and their rejection of mythological explanations for natural phenomena formed the foundation of modern science. In fact, then and now, Thales and his peers were considered to be the wisest men in ancient Greece and were called the Seven Sages (also in this list are Bias, Pittacus, Solon, Chilon, Cleobulus, and Periander).

A sundial is a device that measures time based on the position of the sun as it moves from east to west during the day. The Babylonians and Egyptians were among the first to build sundials in the form of obelisks. As the shadows of the obelisks moved, they formed a rudimentary sundial, dividing the day into two parts by indicating noon. Later sundials employed a gnomon—the thin rod or sharp, straight edge of the sundial—inserted into a hollowed-out bowl. The gnomon specified the time of day, and the size of the shadow indicated

the time of year. When the shadow at noon was the longest or shortest, this indicated the year's longest and shortest days, respectively, which was important for everything—from the timing of religious ceremonies to the planting and harvesting of crops. Eventually, marks were added around the base of the monument to indicate even more specific time divisions.

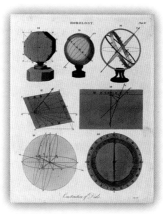

An 1809 diagram illustrates how to set a sundial.

Atomic Clock (p. 118)

Pendulum Clock (p. 138)

Water-driven Clock (p. 144)

Hello Out There
Astronomers hedge their bets, hypothesizing that life-supporting conditions may exist on planets outside our solar system. Artists can only imagine, as in this view from orbit of a planet and, beyond it, two moons and its distant star-sun.

Discovery of Earth-like Planets

To date, about 490 alien planets have been discovered. Could any of them be similar to Earth? Projects like SETI (Search for Extraterrestrial Intelligence) have tried to determine this by scanning the heavens using radio telescopes, but this has its limitations. (What if life on other planets has not developed the means to transmit radio signals yet?) Scientists from NASA think they have come up with a way to find Earth-like planets based on color alone. When planets are looked at through a set of filters—red, green, and blue—Earth, in particular, stands out among the others, appearing much bluer. This is because the Earth's atmosphere is low in infrared-absorbing gases like methane and ammonia, compared to planets like Jupiter and Saturn.

Various projects are exploring this new approach. The Keck Interferometer, for example, combines the light of the world's largest optical telescopes, using a technique known as interferometry, to study dust clouds around stars where Earth-like planets may be forming. In March 2006 the first mission to look for Earth-like planets in the Milky Way was launched, and the Kepler spacecraft, with its giant telescope, was sent into space.

SIM PlanetQuest, which will follow Kepler, will measure the distances and positions of stars with unprecedented accuracy, allowing scientists to locate planets in the zones around nearby stars that look like they could be conducive to life.

So far, astronomers have only discovered huge planets that likely do not contain life. However, given the vastness of the universe and the billions of planets that the Milky Way contains, it is surely only a matter of time before planets are discovered like Earth—perhaps ones that support life-forms. Finally, the holy grail of astronomy would be achieved: indisputable proof that we humans are not alone.

1990
The Hubble telescope is one of the main tools for the discovery of extrasolar planets. *See page 114*

1963
The Arecibo radio telescope made the first discovery of an extrasolar planet. *See page 117*

1609
The telescope is an important precursor to the tools used today to scan the galaxy for planets that might have Earth-like qualities. *See page 139*

1543

The Copernican system changed humanity's place in the cosmos; without it scientists would not be searching for other planets like Earth. *See page 141*

04

Chemistry & Materials

BIG IDEAS

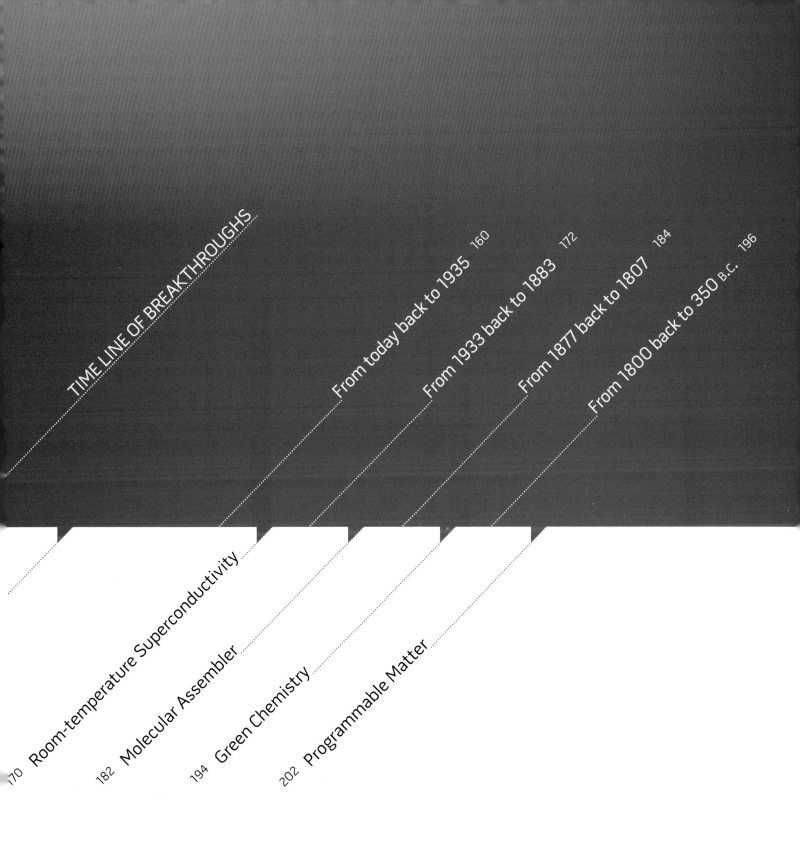

TIME LINE OF BREAKTHROUGHS.

INTRODUCTION

Manipulating Matter

For more than two millennia, philosophers and scientists have asked: What are the basic constituents of matter? How do elements combine to form new chemical compounds? Can this process be controlled to create substances and materials with special properties? The quest to understand and manipulate matter on the most basic level has profoundly shaped today's world.

Building on an earlier theory of four elements, Greek philosopher Aristotle proposed a theory of five elements in the fourth century B.C., variations of which persisted for more than 1,000 years. In the 17th century Irish philosopher and chemist Robert Boyle put chemistry on a firm scientific foundation. Boyle's emphasis on carefully performed experiments in addition to theory was crucial in the transition from alchemy to the science of chemistry.

Breakthrough ideas in the history of chemistry—Englishman John Dalton's 1808 atomic theory, German chemist Friedrich Kekulé's unraveling of the structure of chemical bonds in his 1865 work with benzene, and Russian Dmitri Mendeleev's creation of the periodic table of elements in 1869, for example—led not only to an increasing understanding of the natural world, but also to the discovery and engineering of new materials with desirable properties.

In 1911 Dutch physicist Heike Kamerlingh Onnes discovered the phenomenon of superconductivity when he cooled mercury to a temperature near absolute zero, the point at which no more heat can be removed from a system. Onnes's discovery ignited the continuing quest for high-temperature superconductors and even for the so-called holy grail—a material that is superconductive at room temperature. Concerns about humanity's impact on the environment, together with the knowledge of chemical compounds and the laws of chemistry, have inspired another big idea on the horizon—green chemistry, the engineering of chemicals and materials that do not have a negative impact on the environment. Researchers are also striving to incorporate a hallmark of the 21st century—information technology—into materials to make programmable matter.

A major advance in the science and engineering of the 20th century was the ability to manipulate matter down to the scale of single atoms. English chemist and physicist Michael Faraday's 19th-century work with colloidal gold, or particles of gold suspended in a solution, is a precursor to developments in 20th-century nanotechnology. In fact, research on gold nanoparticles continues today—they hold potential for applications in electron microscopes and drug delivery systems. In 1917 chemist Irving Langmuir discovered monolayers—layers of substances that are only a single molecule thick—allowing scientists to isolate single molecules before the invention of electron microscopes. In the last decades of the 20th century, researchers synthesized nanomaterials such as buckyballs, carbon nanotubes, and quantum dots, and invented methods for working with nanomaterials such as nanolithography. But the ultimate nanotechnology on the horizon is the molecular assembler, a molecule-size, computer-programmable machine that would be capable of precision manufacturing by mechanically positioning individual molecules that chemically react with another.

Nanolithography

Computer artwork depicts a nanotube, bent to form a ring. Nanolithography is a method used to create circuit boards, and the atom-size nanotubes are arranged into these structures by an atomic force microscope.

A graphic shows successive snapshots in which rubidium atoms were cooled to near absolute zero, causing the atoms to condense and behave as a single entity—thus creating a new state of matter as described decades ago by physicists Albert Einstein and Satyendra Nath Bose.

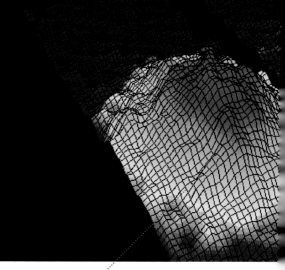

From today back to 1935 >

1999 >

1995 >

Nanolithography

● IN USE

It would not be an overstatement to say that scientists and researchers are looking for answers to hundreds of problems with the use of nanotechnology, including one very important segment of the science—nanolithography.

Nanolithography is a method used to create circuit boards for a variety of electronic devices, such as computers, cell phones, and GPS systems. Atom-size nanomaterials such as nanocrystals, nanolayers, and nanotubes are arranged into structures with the use of an atomic force microscope.

Dip pen nanotechnology, developed in 1999 by Chad Mirkin of Northwestern University, has allowed circuit boards to become much smaller. This, in turn, has led to the development of computers so tiny that they could be used in other nanoscale technologies, such as programmable matter.

Bose-Einstein Condensa

● IN USE

A Bose-Einstein condensate is a state of matter created when a certain kind of gas is cooled to near absolute zero. Subatomic particles in this cooled gas merge and overlap until they lose their identity—leading to a state of superfluidity, when fluid flows without energy loss or resistance. Since Albert Einstein and Satyendra Nath Bose first proposed their existence in 1925, scientists have sought to create Bose-Einstein condensates. It took 70 years, but in 1995 Wolfgang Ketterle of MIT and Eric Cornell and Carl Wieman of the

Building On >

Nanotechnology (p. 165)

Microscope (p. 101)

Superfluid (p. 168)

Quantum Mechanics (p. 41)

Carbon Nanotubes

Carbon nanotubes comprise rolled sheets of carbon atoms. Structurally related to fullerenes, the tiny size of the tubes has raised hope that they may find uses in electrical components far smaller than those available today.

1991 >

Carbon Nanotubes

University of Colorado, Boulder, accomplished this goal.

The importance of this discovery is that it allows researchers to "see" the quantum-mechanical behavior of subatomic particles—the ones that merge in the cooled gas—in macroscopic form. This new form of matter has played an important role in physics research. Cornell, Wieman, and Ketterle say, for example, that Bose-Einstein condensates could lead to the precise control of atoms, which could mean more exact timekeeping and improved transistors.

● IN USE

Considered one of the most important discoveries in physics, carbon nanotubes were discovered in 1991 by Japanese physicist Sumio Iijima. Nanotubes can be constructed by an arc evaporation method, in which a 50-amp current is passed between two graphite electrodes in helium. The results are nanotubes that measure 3 to 30 nanometers in diameter.

One of the amazing properties of carbon nanotubes is their strength. Their resistance to stress is five times that of steel, and their tensile strength is up to 50 times that of steel. Carbon nanotubes can also be used as semiconductors. Some nanotubes' conductivity is greater than that of copper, for example.

Scientists and engineers are looking for ways to use nanotubes in the construction industry, as well as in aerospace applications. Today, flat panel displays and some microscopes and sensing devices incorporate carbon nanotubes. In the future many everyday items—from homes, to computer chips, to car batteries—might be made of carbon nanotubes.

⊃ BACKLASH

Since the discovery of carbon nanotubes, some conservationist groups have called for further studies to determine their safety. For example, in April 2010 the League for the Environment and Nature Conservation, Germany, voiced concerns over pharmaceutical company Bayer's plans to build a carbon nanotube production plant in Germany, until the potential environmental impacts of the production process were studied. So far, though, no regulatory body has stepped forward to propose special guidelines or regulations for the use of carbon nanotubes.

◢ Absolute Zero *(p. 190)*

◢ Scanning Tunneling Microscope *(p. 164)*

Quantum Dots

Quantum dots are nano-size semiconductor crystals. New generations of quantum dots have potential for the study of intracellular processes at the single-molecule level, tumor targeting, and cellular labeling.

High-temperature Superconductor

A demonstration shows magnetic levitation at work using a high-temperature superconductor. Superconductors are materials that conduct electricity with no loss or resistance when heated or cooled. Since the levitating currents in the superconductor meet no resistance, they adjust to maintain the levitation.

1988 >

1986 >

Quantum Dots

● IN USE

In the continual search for faster and smaller semiconductors, scientists created quantum dots—nano-size particles that have found use in a variety of industries and applications— in the early 1980s. The term "quantum dots" was first applied to these particles in 1988 by American physicist Mark A. Reed of Yale University. He used it to describe the matter first created (through independent efforts) by Russian physicist Alexey Ekimov and American Louis E. Brus. Quantum dots are semiconducting nanocrystals created with materials such as lead sulfide.

There are many potential applications for quantum dots. Because they are water soluble, the medical community is particularly excited by the possibility of using them for cellular labeling, deep-tissue imaging, and assay labeling.

They can also be used as quantum dust and applied as security tags, or mixed with ink and used as a deterrent to counterfeiting. Many scientists are researching their potential use in creating more efficient solar panels.

High-temperature Superconductor

● IN USE

Scientists for a century have been working to discover superconductors—materials that conduct electricity with no loss or resistance when heated or cooled—that work at relatively high temperatures. In 1911 Dutch physicists Heike Kamerlingh Onnes and Gilles Holst discovered superconductivity after noting that mercury's conducting resistance dropped to zero at temperatures below 4.2 on the kelvin scale—a low-temperature scale named for British physicist Lord Kelvin—or a frigid minus 452.1°F.

In 1986 Karl Alexander Müller and Johannes Georg Bednorz were able to achieve superconductivity in lanthanum barium copper oxide at a temperature of 35K (-396.67°F). Prior to that, the highest temperature achieved had been 23K (-418.27°F). Müller, a Swiss physicist, and Bednorz, a German physicist, received the Nobel Prize in physics in 1987 for this achievement. Despite thousands of studies, scientists have no clear theory of how high-temperature superconductors work. However, continued work has led to important milestones in recent years. In 2005 researchers at the University of

Building On >   ◥ Superconductivity *(p. 176)*

◥ **Scanning Tunneling Microscope** *(p. 164)*

◥ **Superconductivity** *(p. 176)*

Buckyball

A fullerene is a molecule composed of carbon. The first fullerene was named buckminsterfullerene for architect Richard Buckminster Fuller, the inventor of the geodesic domes it resembles. It is called buckyball for short.

1985 >

Buckyball

● IN USE

Aberdeen in the United Kingdom, led by Abbie McLaughlin, studied a crystal structure of a new chemical compound containing the combination of copper and ruthenium. Their findings showed for the first time that the mechanism of high-temperature superconductivity is actually coupled to the crystal lattice, a three-dimensional structure that is repeated at regular intervals. As scientists gain more knowledge of what causes a material to be superconductive, it will help them develop superconductors at a much faster rate.

The theoretical existence of a molecule made of multiple carbon atoms and shaped as a sphere or a cylinder was predicted as early as 1965. But not until 20 years later did Richard Smalley and Robert Curl, both professors at Rice University in Houston, Texas, U.S., and Harry Kroto, a professor at the University of Sussex, U.K., discover one. By focusing lasers on graphite rods, they generated molecules shaped symmetrically, somewhat like geometrically regular cages. Seeing in these remarkable molecules a similarity to the geodesic dome—a construction made of a lattice of triangles and designed by visionary architect R. Buckminster Fuller—they named the newfound molecule buckminsterfullerene, or fullerene—buckyballs for short. The three researchers received the Nobel Prize for Chemistry in 1996.

The discovery of fullerene has both scientific and technological implications and uses. Analysis of buckyballs has advanced understanding of the behavior and manipulability of sheet metals. A material that is an excellent conductor of heat and electricity, fullerene materials may replace silicon-based devices in computers, cell phones, and similar electronics. The material also exhibits incredible tensile strength, thus promising new possibilities in architecture, engineering, and aircraft design.

The discovery of an oblong version of the buckyball by Japanese researcher Iijima Sumio in 1991, ultimately called the nanotube, spurred the nanotechnology revolution of the early 21st century.

Existence of Atoms (p. 128)   First Theory of Atoms (p. 150)

Bohr Model of the Atom (p. 174)

Scanning Tunneling Microscope

A scanning tunneling microscope (STM) image reveals a section of a double-stranded DNA molecule, with coils of the helix appearing as peaks.

Scanning Tunneling Microscope

A physicist looks at the head of a scanning tunneling microscope. The STM allows scientists to visualize regions of high electron density and infer the position of individual atoms and molecules on the specimen's surface.

1981 >

Scanning Tunneling Microscope

● IN USE

Before the world's scientists could begin to manipulate atoms, they had to be able to see them. Gerd Binnig and Heinrich Rohrer, researchers at IBM's Zurich facility, created the first microscope that allowed scientists to do just that. The two scientists announced the development of the scanning tunneling microscope, or STM, in 1981, and received the Nobel Prize in physics for their work in 1986.

The tunneling microscope uses a stylus that scans a sample and records its surfaces at the atomic level, providing a three-dimensional profile at nanoscale resolution—that is, it can image individual atoms and render distances as small as a billionth of a meter. The STM, in turn, led to the creation of other microscopes—the photon scanning microscope, the spin polarized scanning tunneling microscope, and the atomic force microscope—that have propelled the science of nanotechnology. Along with the STM, these powerful microscopes have allowed researchers to manipulate and create nanomaterials such as fullerenes, buckyballs, and carbon nanotubes.

Magnified image of a scanning tunneling microscope's atom-scale needle

→← CONNECTION

The significance of the scanning tunneling microscope, or STM, to scientific and industrial communities cannot be overstated. From a research perspective, it has allowed scientists all over the world to study surfaces at the atomic level. It has also become a precursor to other microscopes that are used in nanolithography, and has resulted in significant improvements in the semiconductor industry. Along with cutting-edge manipulation techniques, the STM has opened completely new fields in nanoscale engineering.

Building On >   ▼ Microscope (p. 101)

Molecular Electronics

Gold metal has been deposited on a wafer to form electronic circuitry for micro-electro-mechanical (MEM) devices, which are constructed on a microscopic scale. MEM applications include sensors and optical displays.

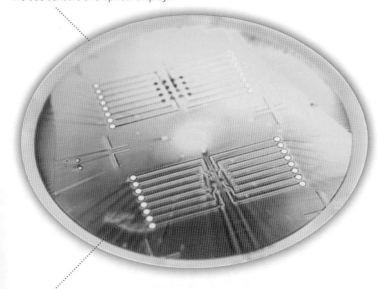

1974 >

Nanotechnology

Graphene is an atomic scale lattice made of carbon atoms arranged in a hexagonal pattern. Stacked graphene sheets form the material graphite, which is used in pencils. Graphene is strong and flexible; one day it may replace silicon in computer chips.

1959 >

Molecular Electronics

▲ IN THEORY

Like its name implies, molecular electronics refers to the use of molecular components to build electronic devices. Since chemists Mark Ratner and Ari Aviram created the first molecular electronic device in 1974—a rectifier, which converts alternating current to direct current—scientists have continued to advance their understanding and potential applications of the science.

Many researchers are working to replace semiconductors in all of their applications with molecular electronic switches.

Some companies are poised to deliver such switches to computer and electronic device manufacturers. One example is a Huntsville, Alabama–based company called CALMEC, which has created a molecular-size switch. This device can be used in electronic semiconductors, enabling electronic technology to be miniaturized even more than it is today.

◤ Alternating Current (p. 45)

Nanotechnology

▲ IN THEORY

By late 1959 the goal of creating smaller and smaller devices had already been on the minds of scientists and researchers, and some progress had been made. For example, small motors had been developed that were about the size of a fingertip.

Richard Feynman, a California Institute of Technology physics professor, envisioned far greater advances. On the evening of December 29, 1959, he gave his now famous speech on nanotechnology at an event for the American Physical Society. Titled "There's Plenty of Room at the Bottom," it described the ability to write the entire *Encyclopedia Britannica* on the head of a pin using atom-size tools or machines.

Feynman's vision of nanotechnology considered the many practical applications it could provide. He based his then revolutionary ideas on the fact that each living cell of an organism contains all of the genetic information needed to create that organism. This showed that storing vast amounts of data in minute objects was possible.

◤ Nanolithography (p. 160)

◤ Chromosomes Carry Genes (p. 230)

A crushed plastic container

Karl Ziegler

[PROFILE]

Even as a child Karl Ziegler (1898-1973) loved being a chemist, performing experiments in a home laboratory. Born in Germany, Ziegler's passion for chemistry became a lifelong career. He received his doctorate in 1920 from the University of Marburg, where he worked for six years.

Ziegler's experiments focused on free radicals and the creation of carbon chains for more than 20 years. In 1953 an accidental discovery led to the creation of polyethylene. He licensed his process to many companies and became a wealthy man. Ziegler, along with Italian chemist Giulio Natta, received the Nobel Prize in chemistry in 1963 for advances in plastics. Ziegler started the Ziegler Fund for Research in 1970.

1953 >

Polyethylene

● IN USE

It is hard to imagine daily life without polyethylene. From plastic grocery bags to laundry baskets and gallon milk containers, polyethylene products are everywhere. The production of polyethylene is now a $7 billion industry, but it all started by accident in 1953.

German chemist Karl Ziegler was working at the Kaiser Wilhelm Institute (later named the Max Planck Institute), analyzing free radicals—molecules that have an uneven number of electrons, and so look to bond with other molecules—and the reactions of ethylene. While conducting an experiment, a trace amount of nickel was accidentally left in the chamber of his apparatus. The result was a long chain of carbon atoms that had not been seen before. Ziegler conducted similar experiments with other metals and found that aluminum produced the best results: a plastic structure that was not only strong but also bendable. Although plastics had been created before this, Ziegler's process was considered a breakthrough because it could be done at close to room

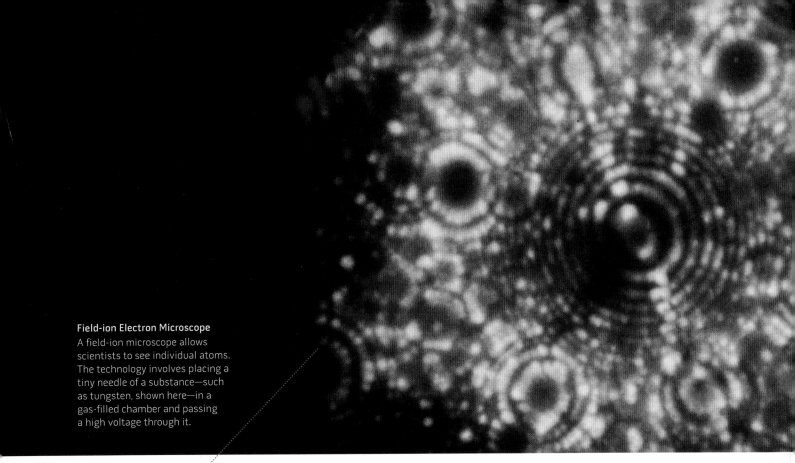

Field-ion Electron Microscope
A field-ion microscope allows scientists to see individual atoms. The technology involves placing a tiny needle of a substance—such as tungsten, shown here—in a gas-filled chamber and passing a high voltage through it.

1951 >

Field-ion Electron Microscope

● IN USE

temperature and atmospheric pressures, rather than the very high pressures and temperatures needed for other methods.

Giulio Natta, an Italian chemist, expanded on Ziegler's work and used his process to develop polypropylene, a material that is used in products such as food containers and carpet fibers. Natta and Ziegler were jointly awarded the Nobel Prize for chemistry in 1963.

Today, concern has been voiced about plastic's lack of biodegradability, leading to research into biodegradable forms of plastic.

Although scientists had theorized about the existence of atoms for centuries, it was not until the 1950s that anyone actually saw one. Based on his work at Berlin's Kaiser Wilhelm Institute, in 1951 physicist Erwin W. Müller published images of atoms that he captured with the field ion electron microscope he had invented. The field ion microscope allowed researchers to discover that changes in a material's properties could be related to its atomic structure and makeup. Scientists were also able to gain a more accurate understanding

of atoms and their properties, leading to the development of nanotechnology.

In 1967, Müller and his colleagues improved upon their design of the field ion microscope by adding a device called a mass spectrometer. This device allowed scientists to analyze the mass-to-charge ratio of various particles, thus helping them discern the masses, structures, and compositions of molecules and other chemical compounds. The field ion microscope became known as an atom probe field ion microscope (or simply

atom probe), and previously unidentifiable atoms could now be observed for further study at high levels of resolution. This observation led to discoveries about the microscopic world, such as the link between changes in chemical properties and changes in molecular structure—for example, when small amounts of certain elements lodge between crystalline grains of a material.

Technetium-97

The first technetium-99m generator was developed by scientists Walter Tucker and Margaret Greene in the 1950s. A radioactive isotope of technetium-97—the first man-made chemical element—technetium-99m is widely used in nuclear medicine.

Emilio Gino Segre, 1954

1937 >

1937 >

Technetium-97

● IN USE

In the 1920s scientists across the globe worked to find elements to fill the empty boxes in the periodic table. One of them was the element with atomic number 43. It was not until 1937 that physicist Emilio Segrè and mineralogist Carlo Perrier, both then at the University of Palermo in Sicily, were able to fill in that box.

Using a particle accelerator—a machine that accelerates particles to very high speeds—these researchers created technetium-97. It was the first man-made element, although some scientists say it exists naturally in the Earth's crust. Technetium is radioactive, but it can be used to create a steel alloy that is highly resistant to corrosion. An isotope of technetium (an isotope of an element has the same number of protons as the element but a different number of neutrons), technetium-99m, is used for medical imaging.

→← CONNECTION

After technetium was created in 1937, other artificial elements followed. Among them were promethium, plutonium, fermium, lawrencium, rutherfordium, and dubnium. Traces of plutonium are still found in the Earth, but the remaining elements must be created in laboratories. They are all radioactive. Some have found uses in weapon making, such as plutonium, while most are useful in experiments only. Some of these elements are thought to exist naturally on other planets.

Superfluid

● IN USE

Similar to a superconductor, a superfluid has some amazing properties that have inspired a great deal of research by scientists in the past 40 years. Superfluidity was first discovered in 1937 by Russian scientist Pyotr Leonidovich Kapitsa and John F. Allen and Don Misener of the Royal Society's Mond Laboratory at Cambridge. These scientists were able to cool an isotope of helium, helium-4, to -455.67°F. At this extreme temperature, they found that it would flow without energy loss and lose all resistance or friction. Kapitsa

Building On >

Periodic Table (p. 185)

Superfluid
Liquid helium in its superfluid phase fills a small cup. At extreme temperatures, scientists found that liquid helium would flow without energy loss and loses all resistance or friction.

Spools of nylon thread

1935 >

Breakthroughs continue on page 172

Nylon

● IN USE

received the Nobel Prize in physics for the discovery.

Since the first superfluidity experiments with helium, scientists have discovered that other elements can be cooled to become superfluids, including isotopes of rubidium and lithium. It also appears that there may be some solids that can achieve these amazing properties—in fact, many scientists expect that other elements and states of matter will be discovered to have superfluid-like properties.

The future applications of superfluids are still being determined. One branch of science where they have begun to find use is that of spectroscopy, or the study of the interaction between matter and radiated energy. While such developments are still in their nascent stages, at this point the best application of superfluids may be educational, in that they can demonstrate properties of matter that would be otherwise unobservable.

During the Great Depression, a chemist working at DuPont Manufacturing named Wallace Carothers wanted to create a man-made fiber that could replace silk in stockings, which had become too expensive for most women. Before working for DuPont, Carothers had taught organic chemistry at Harvard and specialized in polymerization— that is, creating long chains of molecules that would form new materials.

In 1935 he was successful in creating nylon, which quickly became a substitute for silk in stockings. In fact, many women referred to stockings as "nylons" for years. Today, the material is used in a wide range of materials for clothing as well as parachutes, sails, sleeping bags, and tents. Another of Carothers's projects resulted in neoprene, a form of rubber used today in tires.

▶ **Bose-Einstein Condensate** *(p. 160)*

▶ **Superconductivity** *(p. 176)*

Room-temperature Superconductivity

The potential applications of room-temperature superconductivity have captured the imaginations of scientists, resulting in an abundance of research in the last 100 years. Superconductors are materials that conduct electricity with zero loss of energy or resistance. Most superconductive materials discovered to date must be cooled to hundreds of degrees below freezing in order to attain superconductivity. If scientists could discover a material and method for creating room-temperature superconductivity, it would be a world-changing breakthrough.

Because using superconductive materials in everyday life would mean transmitting power with zero loss of energy, tremendous amounts of energy could be saved. The realization of room-temperature superconductivity could also lead to superfast elevated trains, super-efficient magnetic resonance imaging, powerful supercomputers, superconducting magnetic energy storage, and many other potentially life-altering inventions. In fact, many have called room-temperature superconductivity the holy grail because of the vast number of important applications that could result from its discovery.

Superconductivity was accidentally discovered in 1911 when Dutch physicist Heike Kamerlingh Onnes and his assistant Gilles Holst noted that mercury's conductivity resistance dropped to zero at temperatures below 4.2K (-452.1°F). In the last 30 years researchers have worked to create superconductors at higher temperatures. In 1986 physicists Karl Alexander Müller and Johannes Georg Bednorz were able to achieve superconductivity in lanthanum barium copper oxide at a temperature of 35K (-396.67°F)—considered the first high-temperature superconductor. In 2001 Japanese scientists Jun Nagamatsu, Norimasa Nakagawa, Takahiro Muranaka, Yuji Zenitani, and Jun Akimitsu discovered that magnesium diboride becomes a superconductor at 39K (-389.47°F). In 2006 researchers discovered pnictides, a group of iron-based compounds that become superconductive at 50K (-369.67°F). Scientists have yet to identify a material that is superconductive at room temperature—but the quest continues.

1986

The discovery of high-temperature superconductors was a major step toward room-temperature superconductivity. *See page 162*

1937

Substances in a state of superfluidity exhibit unusual properties when they reach critically low temperatures. *See page 168*

1911

The discovery of superconductivity in 1911 is a watershed moment on the way to room-temperature superconductivity. *See page 176*

Laboratory Levitation
Current moves through superconductive metals with little to no resistance, increasing the power of an electromagnetic field significantly. So far, only in lab settings (shown) can superconductors generate enough magnetic force to levitate objects at room temperatures.

Maglowering Cost
High-speed trains in Germany (shown), Japan, and China use maglev—magnetic levitation—to transcend friction and increase speed. Room-temperature superconductivity will bring the cost of this technology down.

1848

Lord Kelvin's formulation of the concept of absolute zero paved the way for low-temperature technologies like superconductors. *See page 190*

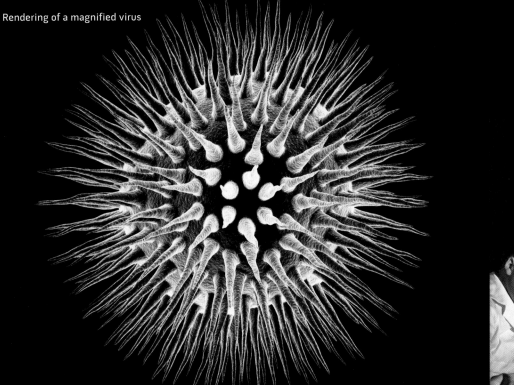

Rendering of a magnified virus

From 1933 back to 1883 >

1933 >

Electron Microscope

In Australia a scientist studies wool through an electron microscope, a type of microscope that uses a beam of electrons to illuminate a specimen and produce a magnified image.

Electron Microscope

● IN USE

By the early 1930s scientists had become frustrated by the limitations of optical light microscopes, which could not exceed a magnification of 2,000 times due to the wavelength of visible light. A new kind of microscope was needed, and by 1931 a prototype of an electron microscope was developed by German engineers Max Knoll and Ernst Ruska in Germany. Using electrons instead of light, this prototype was able to magnify its specimen 400 times. Building on this discovery, Knoll and Ruska

completed work two years later on an electron microscope that exceeded the 2,000-times magnification of the best optical microscope.

Today, several types of electron microscopes exist, but all use electrons as the basis for magnification. Transmission electron microscopes focus electrons on a specimen; some of these electrons go through the specimen while others bounce off, resulting in a two-dimensional image. Very high-resolution electron microscopes have allowed nanotechnology

researchers to view single atoms within an object.

The scanning electron microscope, or SEM, behaves as its name implies: The electrons are scanned across the surface of the image. Data are then sent to a computer, which creates an image of the scanned object. SEM microscopes can produce good three-dimensional images of a sample.

Building On >

Nanotechnology *(p. 165)*

Microscope *(p. 101)*

Irving Langmuir

Irving Langmuir (1881-1957) was an American chemist and physicist who focused on refining lightbulbs for general use early in his career. However, his research led him to other important discoveries. Langmuir's 1917 paper on monolayers garnered him the 1932 Nobel Prize in chemistry. His work led to significant improvements of the incandescent lightbulb, and the discovery of atomic hydrogen and an atomic hydrogen welding process. Later in his career he studied weather and the atmosphere, and defined a wind-driven circulation in the sea that bears his name—the Langmuir circulation.

Monolayer
A graphene carbon monolayer is an atomic scale framework made of carbon atoms arranged in a hexagonal pattern.

1917 >

Monolayer

● IN USE

In the early 1900s American chemist Irving Langmuir was trying to build more effective and efficient lightbulbs. During his research he inserted molecular hydrogen into tungsten—resulting in the creation of a monolayer, a layer of a substance that is only one molecule thick.

The discovery of monolayers allowed scientists to isolate molecules before the invention of the field ion electron microscope. Monolayers are also a precursor to the engineering of atom-size materials, which is at the core of nanotechnology and the development of nanomaterials.

Nanotechnology (p. 165)

Field-ion Electron Microscope (p. 167)

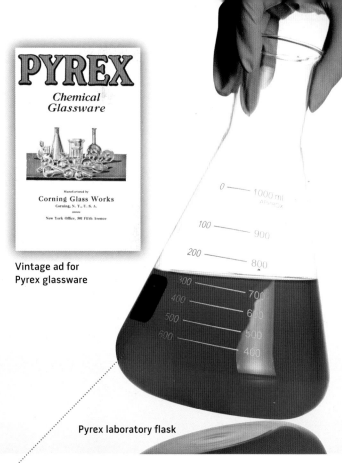

Vintage ad for
Pyrex glassware

Pyrex laboratory flask

1915 >

1913 >

Pyrex

● IN USE

German glassmaker Otto Schott first created borosilicate glass in 1893. However, it was not until U.S. manufacturer Corning Incorporated marketed it under the Pyrex name that it became a household product used widely across the country. Eugene Cornelius Sullivan, a scientist at Corning, and his assistant J. T. Littleton are given the credit for inventing Pyrex bakeware. The story is that Littleton's wife suggested the company create a longer-lasting type of glass cookware when hers broke. Today, Pyrex is made of tempered soda lime glass, which is cheaper to manufacture, but Pyrex borosilicate glass is still sold in Europe.

Bohr Model of the Atom

▲ IN THEORY

When Danish physicist Niels Bohr joined forces with British physicist Ernest Rutherford at Manchester University, his primary goal was to improve on Rutherford's model of the atom, which had been introduced in 1911. Rutherford's model depicted the atom with electrons orbiting the nucleus, much the way the planets orbit the sun. However, the model was flawed: The atom would have much too short a life span because the electrons would lose energy, emit electromagnetic radiation, and spiral inward in an unstable fashion.

While analyzing a hydrogen atom, Bohr quickly found the solution to Rutherford's problem and created his own model of the atom in 1913. Bohr's model was the first to use quantum mechanics to describe the behavior of an atom. In it, when an electron absorbs electromagnetic radiation, the electron jumps into a different—but very specific—orbit. That is, the electrons can only occupy the orbits prescribed by Bohr's theory: They cannot be in between orbits. Because there is an innermost allowed orbit, the electrons will not spiral into the

Building On >

Bohr Model of the Atom

Niels Bohr's model of a hydrogen atom depicts it as a positively charged nucleus surrounded by electrons, which travel in orbits. His model advanced the study of atoms, and he was awarded the Nobel Prize in physics in 1922 for his work.

X-ray Crystallography

A crystal of beryl fragments a beam of x-rays. X-ray crystallography lets scientists use the beam's diffractions off of the crystal to see its electron density.

Danish physicist Niels Bohr

1912 >

X-ray Crystallography

● IN USE

nucleus. Using his model, Bohr was able to calculate the energies of the orbits of hydrogen and other similar atoms. Bohr's model advanced the study of atoms, and he was awarded the Nobel Prize in physics in 1922 for his work.

While Bohr's model is still used to introduce the topic of atomic structure and behavior to new physics students, it is not considered the best model. The model used today is called the electron cloud model, which depicts electrons in a random cloud pattern around the nucleus, rather than orbiting it.

Researchers have found continuing value in x-ray crystallography, a technique created in 1912 that focuses an x-ray beam on a crystal. Scientists can use the beam's diffractions off of the crystal to see the density of its electrons. German scientist Max von Laue was the first to use x-ray crystallography to depict the electron density of a copper sulfate crystal, and he was awarded the 1914 Nobel Prize in physics for his work.

Since numerous materials, both organic and inorganic, form crystals, x-ray crystallography has been a key technology in the advance of many branches of science. Metallurgists, for instance, have used it to locate atomic-scale differences between materials such as alloys, while biologists have used it to map the structures and functions of nucleic acids such as DNA. Other examples of researchers who have successfully used this technique include 2009 Nobel Prize winners Venkatraman Ramakrishnan of the MRC Laboratory of Molecular Biology, Cambridge; Thomas A. Steitz of Yale University; and Ada E. Yonath of the Weizmann Institute of Science in Rehovot,

Israel. All three scientists used x-ray crystallography to create the first model of a human ribosome, a very complex structure. Today x-ray crystallography remains the foremost means of describing the atomic structures, tracking nuances in electronic or elastic properties, and illuminating chemical processes of new materials.

Existence of Atoms (p. 128)

First Theory of Atoms (p. 150)

Radioactivity (p. 130)

X-ray Imaging (p. 88)

Stainless steel pots and pans

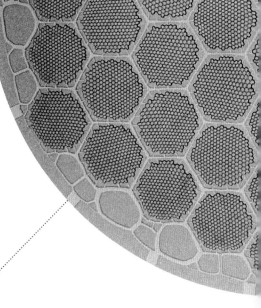

Superconductivity
Image of a transverse section of a superconductor, which is a material that conducts electricity with zero loss of energy or resistance.

1912 >

1911 >

Stainless Steel

● IN USE

From its use in rifle barrels to expensive refrigerators, stainless steel has come a long way since its accidental invention in 1912. Harry Brearley, a steelworker in Sheffield, England, was given the task of improving a rifle barrel. His work led him to add chromium to steel. He noticed that the chromium steel was corrosion resistant and difficult to etch. The first products to be made with stainless steel were knives.

Today, there are many grades of stainless steel with varying applications. They are highly desirable in appliances because they are durable and need little maintenance. Other applications include cookware, hardware, surgical instruments, jewelry, watches, and construction material. More than 20 million tons of stainless steel are produced annually.

Superconductivity

● IN USE

Scientists including Heike Kamerlingh Onnes were studying low-temperature refrigeration in the early 1900s. Onnes wanted to investigate the effects of low temperatures on the properties of metals. There were several theories about what would happen to electrical current passed through a metal cooled to absolute zero (-459.67°F). Some scientists thought the resistance to electricity would diminish, while others thought it would increase.

Onnes discovered that when mercury was cooled to a temperature close to absolute zero its resistance to electricity disappeared altogether. That is, the electrical current that he passed through the mercury did not diminish or dissipate. He called this phenomenon superconductivity.

In the years that followed Onnes' discovery, other materials—including tin, aluminum, and lead—were found to be superconductors when cooled to very low temperatures. In 1986 physicists Karl Alexander Müller and Johannes Georg Bednorz discovered a ceramic composite that superconducted

Building On >

▼ Magnetic Levitation Transportation (p. 260)

▼ Absolute Zero (p. 190)

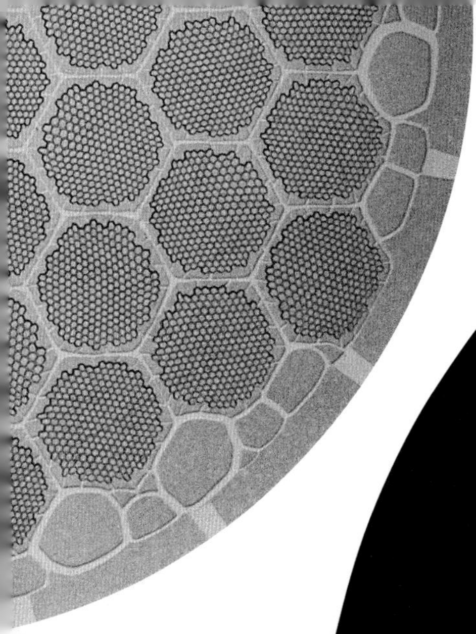

Bakelite
Vintage 78 rpm records, unlike the vinyl ones most people know today, were made from Bakelite. Scientist Leo Baekeland developed Bakelite as a substitute for shellac.

1909 >

Bakelite

● IN USE

at a higher temperature, 90K (-297.67°F). If scientists could create a superconductor at room temperature, it could mean the ability to create electricity that would flow unceasingly.

Potential applications of superconductors have already begun. In Japan a prototype of a levitated train has been constructed using superconducting magnets. Magnetic resonance imaging, or MRI, a technology that also uses superconducting magnets, continues to play a very important role in diagnostic medicine.

Belgian scientist Leo Baekeland made a fortune by selling his invention of photographic paper—paper that could be developed in artificial light—to George Eastman in 1898 for one million dollars. Next, Baekeland turned his attention to creating a substitute for shellac, a thick waxy substance used to insulate electrical coils, among other coating applications. Since the building of electrical lines and stations was booming across the nation at the time, Baekeland stood to increase his fortune if he succeeded.

Using the money he had made on the photographic paper, Baekeland started his own company. After three years of experiments he was successful in creating a material he called Bakelite, securing a patent on the discovery in 1909. Bakelite was the first completely man-made plastic material to be used widely in a large number of industries. It was a combination of carbolic acid and formaldehyde that, when melted, formed a liquid that could coat surfaces. Baekeland then melted it further in a heavy iron boiler until the material

was resistant to heat and water, moldable yet sturdy. Called "the material of a thousand uses," Bakelite gave birth to the plastics industry. It has been used to manufacture products such as telephone handsets, costume jewelry, engine parts, insulation for electronics, televisions, radios, records, pipe stems, billiard balls, knobs, buttons, and knife handles.

Electricity *(p. 55)*

Polyethylene *(p. 166)*

Haber Process

An ammonia molecule is made up of one nitrogen atom and three hydrogen atoms. German scientists Fritz Haber and Carl Bosch created the Haber process, the method for producing ammonia from nitrogen and hydrogen.

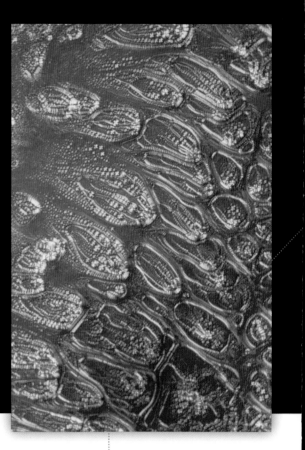

1905 >

1904 >

Haber Process

Liquid Crystals

⮐ BACKLASH

It is difficult for most people to imagine life without plastic in some form. From shampoo bottles to milk containers, trash bags, and appliances, plastic is everywhere.

Plastic began to be mass-produced in the 1940s, but it was not until the mid-1980s that its potentially harmful effects on the environment were researched and made public by scientists across the globe. At that time, it was reported that plastic in landfills could take centuries to decompose and bits of plastic in the environment were being consumed by wildlife.

● IN USE

The world owes much of its fertilizers to Fritz Haber and Carl Bosch, German scientists who created the process for making the ammonia used in fertilizers from nitrogen and hydrogen. Although the process was in development since 1905, Haber did not introduce it until World War I. His system, however, was slow—producing ammonia drop by drop. Bosch was able to improve it to produce ammonia on an industrial scale.

The Haber process—also known as the Haber-Bosch process—has proved to be indispensable to the field of chemistry. Until it was developed, there had been no method for adequately creating nitrogen, an important element in many applications such as fertilizers and explosives.

● IN USE

Austrian botanist Friedrich Reinitzer first researched liquid crystals in 1888, discovering that when he boiled cholesteryl benzoate—an organic compound consisting of cholesterol and benzoic acid—it appeared to become cloudy first, then clear.

German physicist Otto Lehmann continued this work using a microscope with a heating element. It was Lehmann who discovered that some molecules (before they melted) formed crystals that flowed like a liquid while retaining the properties of a crystal. He coined the phrase

Building On >

11:59

A digital clock, which uses liquid crystal technology, displays the time of day.

Liquid Crystals
A polarized light micrograph reveals liquid crystals. German physicist Otto Lehmann discovered that some molecules form crystals that flow like a liquid while retaining the properties of a crystal.

The neon lights of the Flamingo Hotel in Las Vegas

1902 >

Neon Lamp

→← CONNECTION

● IN USE

"liquid crystals" in 1889, and in 1904 published "Liquid Crystals," expanding on his work. It was not until 1969, however, that scientist Hans Keller found a way to synthesize stable liquid crystals, and by the 1990s liquid crystal displays were in watches, computers, dashboards, and flat-screen displays all over the world.

Liquid crystal displays, or LCDs, are a component of many digital electronic devices today, from televisions, watches, and microwaves to signs, calculators, and telephones. In 1969 Hans Keller found a way to synthesize stable liquid crystals. Swiss company Hoffmann-LaRoche invented one of the first LCD digital quartz watches in 1970. The following year inventor James Fergason filed the first U.S. patent related to liquid crystal displays. Japanese company Hitachi created the first LCD television 26 years later, in 1997.

In 1898 in London, chemists William Ramsay and Morris W. Travers discovered neon, a gas that is present in air in very small amounts. Georges Claude, a French engineer, began producing it as a by-product of air liquefaction.

In 1902 Claude discovered that passing an electrical charge through neon in a tube produced a bright, glowing light. He was able to twist the tubes into many different shapes. By introducing other gases into the tube, he could create different colors. He introduced the first neon light

sign in Paris in December 1910. Claude owned the U.S. patent on neon signs through the 1930s.

▼ Microscope *(p. 101)*

▼ Electricity *(p. 55)*

J. J. Thomson

Sir Joseph John "J. J." Thomson (1856-1940) was a physicist whose aptitude for science and math was clear early in his life. Thomson was just 14 years old when he enrolled in Manchester College in England in 1870, and by 1880 he was a fellow of Trinity College. It was while he was the Cavendish Professor of Experimental Physics at Cambridge that he proposed his theory of the existence of electrons. Thomson was awarded the Nobel Prize in physics in 1906 and knighted in 1908.

A notable achievement is the fact that six of his research assistants, including British physicist Ernest Rutherford, went on to win the Nobel Prize. His son, Sir George Paget Thomson, also received the Nobel Prize in physics.

Electron

An electron cloud surrounds a helium atom. In 1897 scientist J. J. Thomson was the first to propose the theory of the existence of electrons.

1897 >

Electron

▲ IN THEORY

English scientist John Dalton introduced the theory of the existence of atoms in the early 1800s. Sir Joseph John "J. J." Thomson, a physicist, wanted to expand on Dalton's theory. Most of Thomson's work consisted of conducting electricity through gases, including the study of cathode rays (streams of electrons in vacuum tubes). In 1897 Thomson realized that the cathode ray was actually a stream of electrons given off by an atom, which led him to formulate the theory that because an atom is neutral, it consists of an equal number of negatively and positively charged particles. This was later called the plum pudding theory of the atom, because when drawn as a diagram, the atom resembled a bowl of plum pudding—the atom is the bowl and the "plums" are the charged particles.

Just over a decade later, physicists Ernest Rutherford and Niels Bohr's work furthered the development of atomic theory. Rutherford proposed that the atom had a nucleus with electrons "orbiting" it, much the way the planets orbit the sun, but this

Solar Cell
Dr. Charles Alexander Escoffery poses with the solar-powered car he invented. The 1912 Baker Electric Mode was adapted to run from energy obtained from the sun's rays.

A photovoltaic cell

1883 >

Breakthroughs continue on page 184

Solar Cell

● IN USE

theory was flawed because the atom was not stable. Bohr solved this problem by using quantum mechanics to describe the behavior of an atom.

The idea of creating a solar cell was sparked by the research of Antoine-César Becquerel, a French physicist. In 1839 he discovered the photovoltaic effect when he realized that voltage was produced when light fell onto an electrode. More than 40 years later, Charles Fritts, an American inventor, created the first solar cell. Fritts's solar cell used the semiconductor material selenium, which he covered with a thin layer of gold. It was only one percent efficient—that is, its electrical output was only one percent of the potential energy it could

derive from the sunlight that fell on it—and expensive to use. Selenium cells were subsequently used to time light exposure in cameras.

→← CONNECTION

Since 1883, when American inventor Charles Fritts created the first solar cell, scientists and engineers have improved their efficiency and lowered manufacturing costs, leading to more widespread use. The first big advancement after Fritts occurred in 1941 when American engineer Russell Ohl developed the silicon solar cell. Throughout the 1950s the efficiency of solar cells rose to around 5 percent. Today, some solar cells achieve efficiency as high as 37 percent and are used to produce energy to heat and light homes and businesses.

BIG IDEA | NO. 14

Let's Stick Together
In a Northwestern University lab, gold nanorods—sticks of gold ten nanometers across, smaller than the eye can see—self-assemble into an ultratiny sphere, potentially useful in electronics or drug delivery.

Tiny Helpers
Nanoscale robots, or nanobots—microscopic flying machines—are envisioned as programmable mechanisms for delivering drugs, repairing cells, or performing other functions at the microscopic level.

Molecular Assembler

In 1986 K. Eric Drexler, a pioneer of nanotechnology, first presented the controversial idea of the possibility of a molecular assembler—a molecule-size, computer-programmable machine capable of precision manufacturing by mechanically positioning molecules that trigger a chemical reaction. To date, the molecular assembler is still only theory, although scientists are working on technologies that may ultimately lead to it becoming a reality.

While Drexler embraces the idea of creating a molecular assembler, he also cautions scientists about its potentially destructive aspects. Drexler's vision includes devices that can manufacture products with no pollution. Molecular assemblers could also lead to faster computers, stronger materials, and more efficient and effective medications. The potential applications are far reaching. Drexler is concerned, however, that if molecular assemblers become reality they could self-replicate so rigorously they would become ecological disasters. As a result he has called for government regulation of the technology, which is not yet in place.

There is no current method for creating an assembler that fulfills

Drexler's ideal. Indeed some scientists dispute the possibility of building a molecular assembler in the first place—Nobel Prize winner Richard Smalley has said that the only molecular assembler that is possible is the one currently found in nature, the ribosome, which works in conjunction with transfer RNA. Ribosomes are components of cells that "read" information on RNA and use the information to synthesize proteins from amino acids. Smalley argues that computer-controlled "fingers" would be too large or too sticky to allow for precision placement.

If scientists could make molecular assemblers, their significance would be without equal. Thus far, none of the calls for regulation have prevented scientists and organizations from exploring this arm of nanotechnology. Researchers continue to take steps that could ultimately lead to the reality of a molecular assembler. For example, the National Nanotechnology Initiative has developed "molecular machines" that are made of interlocking parts and assemble themselves by ensuring that the parts come in contact with another.

1999

Nanolithography is a technology that deals with how nanomaterials are arranged into structures. *See page 160*

1991, 1988, 1985

Nanomaterials such as carbon nanotubes, quantum dots, and buckyballs have paved the way for a molecular assembler. *See pages 161, 162, 163*

1959

Physicist Richard Feynman predicted the possibility of nanotechnology in 1959. *See page 165*

On the Head of a Pin
This artist's conception of a nanobot mirrors a fly. Others in development mirror cell structures. Their shapes depend on molecular self-assembly: combined correctly, these molecules twist, bind, and build predictable structures.

1917, 1857

Monolayers and gold colloids are early precursors to nanotechnology. *See pages 173, 187*

Dioxygen cooled to a very low temperature, causing it to solidify

American mathematical physicist Josiah Willard Gibbs

From 1877 back to 1807 >

1877 >

1876 >

Liquefaction of Gases

● IN USE

As with many scientific advancements, the liquefaction of gases developed over many decades. After the experiments of Englishman Michael Faraday, who liquefied chlorine by heating chlorine hydrate in a closed glass tube in the 1820s, scientists wanted to liquefy gases so they could better study their properties.

With inventor Jacob Perkins's fabrication of the first practical refrigeration machine, scientists were able to liquefy heavier gases using ultralow temperatures. Louis Paul Cailletet, a French physicist, and Raoul-Pierre Pictet, a Swiss scientist, were the first to liquefy oxygen in 1877. Scottish scientist James Dewar successfully liquefied hydrogen in 1898, and Dutch physicist Heike Kamerlingh Onnes liquefied helium in 1908. Today, these gases find uses as refrigerants and are used for medical and scientific purposes. For example, liquid nitrogen is used to store cells and tissue samples at low temperatures for laboratory work, and as a coolant for computers.

Physical Chemistry

▲ IN THEORY

Chemistry and physics seemed destined to remain two separate disciplines until scientists began studying thermodynamics in the mid- to late 1800s. Chemistry was seen as the science of changes to the molecular structure of an object, while physics focused on changes that occurred to an entire object or system.

Some Europeans were making progress bridging the divide between chemistry and physics. However, it was not until American Josiah Willard Gibbs published a milestone theory in 1876 that the foundation for

Building On >

Transplantation of Engineered Tissues *(p. 66)*

Periodic Table
Russian chemist Dmitri Mendeleev's periodic table of 1869. He left gaps in the table for new elements, which were added later.

A contemporary periodic table

1869 >

Periodic Table

physical chemistry was truly laid.

Gibbs's paper, *On the Equilibrium of Heterogeneous Substances,* did not cause much stir when it was first published through Yale University, where he was professor of mathematical physics—a position he held without pay for nine years. In the following years researchers slowly began to understand the significance of his discoveries, which applied the laws of thermodynamics to chemistry, creating mathematical equations that explained and predicted the laws of chemical reactions.

▲ IN THEORY

Dmitri Mendeleev, a Russian chemist, created the first periodic table by using individual cards that he laid out like a game of solitaire. He made a card for each of the 63 elements known at the time; the cards included the elements' atomic weight and inherent properties. He placed each card on a table in order by ascending weight, creating columns and rows that indicated relationships and similarities in properties. Mendeleev's periodic table was included in his 1869 work *On the Relationship of the Properties of the Elements to Their Atomic Weights.*

While Mendeleev was the first to create a table this extensive, the work of several other scientists had preceded his periodic table. In 1864 John Newlands, a chemist in England, created a table that grouped the 56 known elements at the time. Lothar Meyer, of Germany, created a table similar to Mendeleev's around the same time, which included only 28 elements.

Mendeleev's table was considered most significant because he left spaces for elements that had not been discovered yet.

➤◄ CONNECTION

There were 63 known elements when Russian chemist Dmitri Mendeleev created the first periodic table. Today, that number has nearly doubled—there are now 118 elements in the table, with others still to be discovered. Of the 118 elements, 94 are naturally occurring elements on the Earth. The remaining elements are the result of nuclear reactions or are man-made, such as technetium. Some of the most recently discovered elements include bohrium, ununnilium, and ununbium.

Laws of Thermodynamics (p. 131)

Atomic Spectra (p. 190)

Existence of Atoms (p. 128)

Chemical Structure

The compound benzene, a six-sided ring of carbon attachments, was first visualized by chemists Friedrich August Kekulé and Archibald Scott Couper.

1865 >

1862 >

Chemical Structure

▲ IN THEORY

Chemists Friedrich August Kekulé, of Germany, and Archibald Scott Couper, of Scotland, arrived independently at a similar idea about the structure of a compound called benzene. Originally created by Englishman Michael Faraday in 1825, benzene is a flammable solvent used in the production of plastic, oil, and rubber. Kekulé and Couper proposed that benzene's structure could be visualized as a six-sided ring of carbon attachments or chains. Kekulé's work was published before Couper's, so he is given the bulk of the credit for this first attempt at the theory of chemical structure.

Kekulé's work is considered the beginning of an explosive time of discovery in organic chemistry, as other scientists, following his lead, began to explore the structure of chemicals. His work is even more impressive considering the fact that there were no tools at the time that could be used to observe the structure of chemical compounds.

In 1890, when the German Chemical Society held a celebration in Kekulé's honor, he said that the inspiration for his discovery had come in a dream he had of a snake grabbing its tail in its mouth and forming a six-sided shape. Scholars debate whether Kekulé was serious when he said this. They feel it was his earlier education as an architect—his field of study prior to switching to chemistry—that provided the inspiration for his discovery of the structure of benzene.

Parkesine

● IN USE

When Alexander Parkes, an English inventor, introduced Parkesine at the Great International Exhibition in London in 1862, it was heralded as the next great material for manufacturing. Parkesine was designed to replace Charles Goodyear's Vulcanite, a material that was a combination of natural rubber and sulfur.

Parkesine was the first plastic material created. Parkes made it by melting cellulose nitrate and forming it into shapes that would harden when cooled. Unfortunately, Parkesine was

Building On >

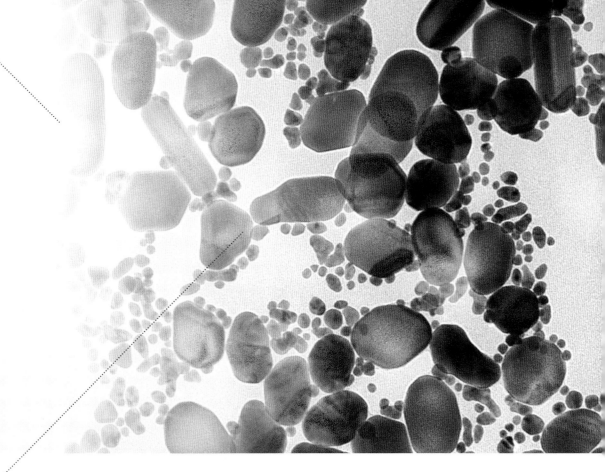

Gold Colloids

Gold colloids are very fine particles of gold suspended in a liquid. Also called nanogold, gold colloid can be used to detect and trap biological toxins; it is also used in cancer treatment research.

Alexander Parkes, who discovered Parkesine

Commemorative plaque honoring Alexander Parkes

1857 >

Gold Colloids

● **IN USE**

short lived. It was expensive to produce, and when Parkes used cheaper material, the end product was not sturdy. Parkesine was also highly flammable. As a result, Parkes closed his manufacturing facility within three years of its opening.

Gold colloids, very fine particles of gold suspended in a liquid, have been around for centuries. The ancient Romans used gold colloids to color glass, and later they were used to create stained-glass windows. Paracelsus, a 16th-century alchemist, created a gold colloid that he claimed held healing and medicinal powers.

The first scientist to become fascinated with colloidal gold and create a pure solution was Michael Faraday. A self-taught researcher, Faraday was experimenting with the effects of electricity on metals in 1857 when he created a ruby-red gold colloid. He was convinced that the solution's color was due to particles of gold that were too small to be viewed with the microscopes of the time. With the invention of much improved microscopes, Faraday's theory was proved right, and his gold colloid is now recognized as an important predecessor to nanotechnology.

Today, nano-size gold in colloid form is being investigated for many potentially significant applications. Colloidal gold, for example, is used as a contrast agent with electron microscopes and is being investigated as a therapy for rheumatoid arthritis. Some scientists are investigating its use in combination with radiation to combat Alzheimer's disease. Researchers are discovering that gold colloids may be used as part of an effective drug delivery system, and could have potential for targeting tumors.

▼ Polyethylene (p. 166)

▼ Electron Microscope (p. 172)

◤ Radioactivity (p. 130)

Michael Faraday

Considered to be one of the most important scientists of his time, Englishman Michael Faraday (1791–1867) was born the son of a blacksmith. Since his family did not have the financial resources to pay for his education, he apprenticed with a bookbinder. This job enabled him to read books and learn about the scientific discoveries of the time.

After listening to a lecture at the Royal Institution of Great Britain by chemist Humphry Davy in 1812, Faraday volunteered to become Davy's assistant. When Davy fired his then assistant for brawling, he hired Faraday in 1813. By 1820 Faraday's work was overshadowing Davy's. He is best known for discovering electrical induction and gold colloids.

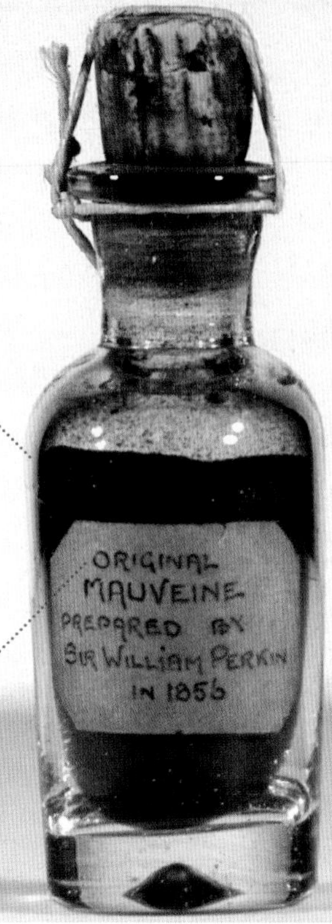

Synthetic Dye
Sir William Perkin's original bottle of mauve-colored dye is labeled "Original Mauveine prepared by Sir William Perkin in 1856." Perkin accidentally discovered the formula for producing synthetic mauve dye while trying to synthesize quinine.

1856 >

Synthetic Dye

● IN USE

A young English chemist, William Henry Perkin, was working at the Royal College of Chemistry in London under August Wilhelm von Hofmann in 1856. Hofmann had assigned Perkin the task of creating artificial quinine, which was in high demand for the treatment of malaria. Instead Perkin, then just 18 years old, created a purple—or mauve, as he called it—synthetic dye by oxidizing the chemical compound allytoluidine.

An avid photographer and painter, Perkin recognized the value of the synthetic dye and applied for a patent. The following year he opened his own factory to produce it. Purple was a highly desirable color because it was associated with royalty. Other companies, such as the German chemical company Badische Anilin- und Soda-Fabrik, soon launched their own dye products, and the manufacturing of synthetic dyes was established.

Bessemer Process
Steel workers on the job in Pittsburgh, Pennsylvania, use a Bessemer converter, a container where molten iron is converted to steel.

Steel hardware

1855 >

Bessemer Process

● IN USE

Sir Henry Bessemer, an English metallurgist, was trying to improve the strength of metals for guns when he discovered a process that converted pig iron (a product of smelting iron ore) to steel. In 1855 he realized that when he oxidized pig iron—a result of blowing air through the molten iron—it created steel. The process also removed impurities and kept the metal molten. It established a much lower cost method for producing steel in large quantities: Prior to the discovery of the Bessemer process, steel was made by heating bars of wrought iron, which was expensive and labor intensive.

With the reduction in cost and labor, the large-scale steel production process was a key catalyst of the Industrial Revolution of the 19th and 20th centuries. Steel replaced wrought iron in the construction of railroads, skyscrapers, and ships, and new products such as steel cable, steel rod, and sheet steel had tremendous effect on the development of many industries. In the field of munitions, steel enabled more durable engines for tanks and ships, as well as more powerful guns. Engineering too was revitalized with the advent of industrial steel, as turbines and generators of previously unobtainable size could now be built. These made it possible to fully harness the power of water and steam.

➡← CONNECTION

When Sir Henry Bessemer discovered a process that converted pig iron to steel, he revolutionized the construction industry—which, prior to the Bessemer process, used wrought iron. The Bessemer process made steel a low-cost option that also took less labor to produce. It soon became the choice of material for many construction projects. Because of the Bessemer process, builders were able to use steel to make bridges, railroads, and eventually skyscrapers.

▼ Stainless Steel (p. 176)
▼ Railway (p. 282)

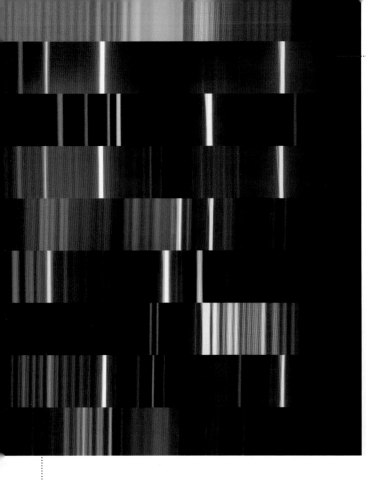

Atomic Spectra
A spectrum displays a number of gases. Atomic spectra is a method devised in the mid-19th century for studying chemicals, including gases.

Lord Kelvin

1850 >

1848 >

Atomic Spectra

▲ IN THEORY

After meeting physicist Gustav Kirchhoff, fellow German Robert Bunsen was able to get Kirchhoff a transfer to the University of Heidelberg so the two could work together. Both were involved in the study of organic chemistry. Together, Kirchhoff and Bunsen created new methods for studying chemical elements, including gases. Bunsen improved a burner—subsequently called the Bunsen burner—that allowed researchers to heat a gas without the burner's flame interfering with the color of the light emitted by the gas. Kirchhoff and Bunsen also invented a spectroscope, an instrument that allowed them to view the wavelengths of the emitted light. They discovered that when light was passed through a gas, characteristic dark lines appeared in the light's spectrum. Since these atomic absorption spectra are unique to each chemical element, the discovery allowed scientists to identify new chemical elements. Kirchhoff and Bunsen, for example, discovered cesium and rubidium this way.

Absolute Zero

▲ IN THEORY

Even though Irishman John Boyle had first proposed the idea of an absolute coldest temperature in 1665, it was not until Lord Kelvin actually devised a scale based on the idea in 1848 that the concept of absolute zero became significant. As an object cools, the molecules that make up the object move more slowly. At absolute zero, this movement is the slowest possible— some scientists argue that motion stops altogether. This temperature is zero on the kelvin scale, which corresponds to minus 273.15° on the Celsius scale and minus 459.67° on the Fahrenheit scale.

►← CONNECTION

Since the early 20th century, physicists and chemists have discovered that some materials develop amazing properties—such as superconductivity (when a material attains zero resistance to electricity) and superfluidity (when a fluid attains zero resistance to pressure)—when their temperatures approach absolute zero. Technologies based on these discoveries include superconducting magnets, used in magnetic resonance imaging; digital circuits, which use superconductors; and radio frequency and microwave filters for cellular phone operations.

Building On >   ▌ Periodic Table (p. 185)   ▌ Superfluid (p. 168)

▌ Superconductivity (p. 190)

−273.15°C

Absolute Zero
A thermometer shows the Celsius equivalent to absolute zero on the kelvin scale. Lord Kelvin devised this scale in 1848. It uses the kelvin as its unit of measurement.

German stamp honoring chemist Friedrich Wöhler

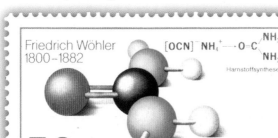

Portrait of Friedrich Wöhler

1828 >

Synthesis of Organic Material

● **IN USE**

A model of the compound urea

Into the 19th century, the educated community held certain assumptions about the nature of organic compounds—the building blocks of all living things, chemical compounds tht we now understand to have carbon atoms at their core. But when German chemist Friedrich Wöhler accidentally synthesized urea, an organic compound that appears in urine, those assumptions had to be revised.

One of Wöhler's areas of research was isolating elements and studying their properties. Prior to 1828 he was working with a group of compounds called cyanates, attempting to create ammonium cyanate by adding ammonium chloride. The result was a white powder that, he discovered upon further investigation, had the same composition and properties as urea.

Showing that he could make a substance identical to urea without human or animal kidneys, Wöhler presented a counter to the long-held assumptions of vitalism, which held that a vital force, ultimately unknowable and uncontrollable by humans, differentiated all life and living material from anything inorganic.

Wöhler's discovery that organic compounds could be synthesized in a laboratory is considered a turning point in the field and the starting point of organic chemistry. He went on four years later to synthesize oxalic acid from similar inorganic components. His synthesis of organic compounds inspired many significant developments in chemistry, including the creation of synthetic organic chemicals for a variety of purposes, from agricultural fertilizer to therapeutic pharmaceuticals and medical diagnostic tests.

Experimental Medicine *(p. 103)*

Portland cement is a basic ingredient of concrete (in background).

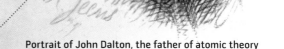

Portrait of John Dalton, the father of atomic theory

1824 >

1808 >

Portland Cement

● IN USE

British bricklayer Joseph Aspdin was canny enough to recognize that a process used by one of his employees to produce cement was worthy of patenting. In 1824 he was awarded the patent for Portland cement, so named because the resulting powder was the same color as stone on the Isle of Portland in England. His son later refined the process.

Portland cement used cement clinker, lumps of cinders created after stone is heated to high temperatures. By using local stone, the cement was easy and cheap to produce. It also hardened faster than previous types and was water resistant. Portland cement is still in worldwide use today in roads, stucco, and mortar.

Atomic Theory

▲ IN THEORY

The idea that matter is made up of atoms was not a new one when English chemist and physicist John Dalton published his atomic theory in the book *New System of Chemical Philosophy*. Even the Greek philosopher Democritus, who lived in the fifth century B.C., had proposed that matter was made up of tiny component particles. What was different about Dalton's theory, however, was that it was the result of careful measurements and observations rather than philosophical debate. Although not all scientists agreed with him, by the mid-1800s his atomic theory was widely accepted. Today, he is known as the father of atomic theory.

Dalton formed his theory after years of observing the atmosphere and taking notes on how gases and liquids are formed and react to varying weather conditions. This led him to the first principle of his theory, that matter is composed of atoms that cannot be divided or destroyed. His second principle was that al l atoms of a specific element have the same mass and properties. He also proposed that chemical compounds are formed

Building On >

ELEMENTS

⊙	Hydrogen	1	⊕	Strontian	46
⊖	Azote	5	✳	Barytes	68
●	Carbon	54	Ⓘ	Iron	50
○	Oxygen	7	Ⓩ	Zinc	56
☮	Phosphorus	9	Ⓒ	Copper	56
⊕	Sulphur	13	Ⓛ	Lead	90
◐	Magnesia	20	Ⓢ	Silver	190
∿	Lime	24	Ⓖ	Gold	190
⦀	Soda	28	Ⓟ	Platina	190
⦀	Potash	42	⊛	Mercury	167

Electrolysis

Electrolysis is the process of applying an electrical charge to a material to create a chemical reaction. Here, a power supply is connected to carbon electrodes in a beaker of copper sulphate solution. Passing an electric current through the sulphate creates a reaction, separating the copper from the sulphur and oxygen.

Atomic Theory

A reproduction of one of a series of four charts by John Dalton shows a list of elements he created, with their atomic weights. This information was based on Dalton's measurements and observations over the course of several years.

1807 >

Breakthroughs continue on page 196

Electrolysis

→← CONNECTION

● IN USE

when two or more different atoms combine and that atoms are rearranged as a result of chemical reactions. In *New System of Chemical Philosophy*, Dalton also created a list of elements along with their atomic weights, again based on his measurements and observations.

When John Dalton's atomic theory was published in 1808, scientists who accepted it were able to make new predictions about the structure of atoms. For example, in the 1880s German physicist Eugen Goldstein concluded that there were positively charged particles in an atom—protons— and British physicist J. J. Thomson discovered the electron. This led to Ernest Rutherford's discovery of an atom's nucleus in 1911. By the 1930s theories of quantum mechanics spurred the development of modern atomic theory.

A handsome, dynamic public figure, Englishman Humphry Davy also was one of the leading scientists of his day. A popular lecturer at the Royal Institution of Great Britain, he was known for performing daring chemical experiments during his talks. In 1807 he used electrolysis— applying an electrical charge to a material to create a chemical reaction—to discover the elements potassium, sodium, barium, strontium, calcium, and magnesium.

It was Davy's assistant Michael Faraday who described the first

laws of electrolysis in 1833. Faraday's two laws were as follows: (1) The amount of chemical change to a material is directly related to the amount of electrical charge applied. (2) When two different objects receive the same amount of electricity, the differing amounts of chemical reaction are related to the differences in their mass.

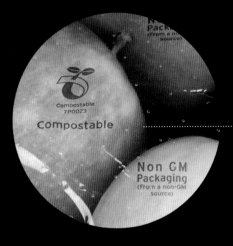

It's a Wrap
Clear wrapping material made from non-genetically modified (non-GM) starch can be composted; after disposal, microbial activity will consume the material as thoroughly as it consumes the apple cores.

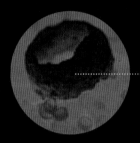

Green Beads
Mater-Bi (shown here in its granular form, highlighted with color) is a bio-polymer manufactured by Italian company Novamont. It emulates plastic in its many uses, but products made of it are completely biodegradable.

Green Chemistry

Green chemistry, the science of developing products that do not use chemicals that harm people or the environment, could have far-reaching and important effects on everyday life. For example, using energy derived from plants and animals would significantly decrease humankind's carbon footprint and the dependency on fossil fuels, and increase the use of sustainable, renewable resources.

The idea of green chemistry is relatively new, originating in response to the U.S. Pollution Prevention Act of 1990. The goals of the act were to reduce pollution and conserve energy; since its passage, researchers have been seeking ways to cut back or eliminate the chemicals used in many everyday products that could have detrimental effects on humans and the environment.

Paul T. Anastas and Tracy C. Williamson, both of the U.S. Environmental Protection Agency, defined green chemistry in their 1996 book *Green Chemistry: Designing Chemistry for the Environment*, which set the standard for researchers who sought to create green products and reduce pollution. The authors put forward 12 principles to guide future research, including reducing waste, creating biodegradable products, and striving for sustainability.

In the first decade of the 21st century scientists and chemists at universities and private companies made progress toward some of green chemistry's goals, a notable example of which is the work of Jason P. Rolland, R. Michael van Dam, Derek A. Schorzman, Stephen R. Quake, and Joseph M. DeSimone, all of the University of North Carolina at Chapel Hill. In 2004 they reported the discovery of a solvent-resistant, liquid Teflon material that can be used to manufacture nonstick cookware as well as other products. This material could replace the use of perfluorooctanoic acid—a suspected carcinogen that is considered toxic to animals and may, according to the EPA, accumulate in humans. It is also nonbiodegradable.

Many large manufacturing companies have embraced green chemistry because using sustainable materials as part of their processes can save them a great deal of money: The materials cost less to produce, and disposing of their waste products costs less as well.

1962

Rachel Carson's *Silent Spring* was a major force in bringing environmental issues to the popular consciousness. *See page 220*

1953

The backlash against polyethylene and other nonbiodegradable materials is a precursor to the search for sustainable materials. *See page 166*

1896

The idea that climate change could be caused by humans was an early theory about how industry could have negative effects on the environment. *See page 232*

Kernels in Our Future
Mater-Bi, a non-polluting plastic-type material, is made from a mixture of starch extracted from non-GM corn plus synthetic polymers that also break down due to microorganisms naturally occurring in soil.

On Beyond Plastic
Green chemistry responds to our consumer habits with materials more sustainable than petroleum-based plastic, including products manufactured from the pellets shown here, which will decompose as readily as a corncob.

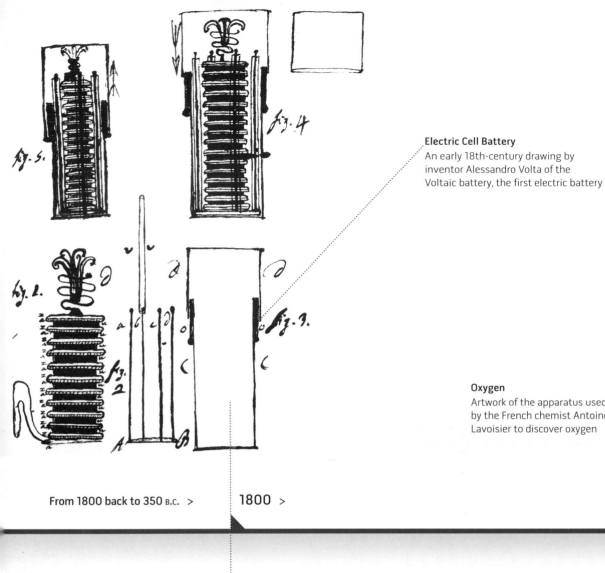

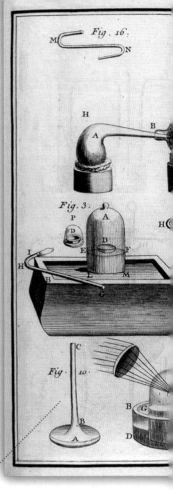

Electric Cell Battery
An early 18th-century drawing by inventor Alessandro Volta of the Voltaic battery, the first electric battery

Oxygen
Artwork of the apparatus used by the French chemist Antoine Lavoisier to discover oxygen

From 1800 back to 350 B.C. >

1800 >

1777 >

Electric Cell Battery

● IN USE

When Italian physicist Alessandro Volta read about the experiments of Italian professor Luigi Galvani, he was inspired. Galvani had discovered that if he touched the nerve of a frog with an electrostatically charged plate, it caused a muscle contraction. He theorized that the frog contained a certain amount of electricity. Volta set out to prove Galvani wrong. Volta felt it was the combination of the metal and water that created the charge.

To test his hypothesis, in 1800 Volta created what is now known as a voltaic pile. The pile consisted of two stacks of metal. The metals he used were alternating copper and zinc; cardboard soaked in salt water was sandwiched between each metal piece. The piles created an electrical charge; when Volta connected the two piles with wires, they sustained that charge for a period of time. It was the first battery.

An alkaline battery

Oxygen

▲ IN THEORY

Oxygen was first discovered in 1772 by Carl Wilhelm Scheele, a Swedish chemist. Two years later chemist Joseph Priestley, working independently in England, published his discovery of oxygen. But it was Antoine Lavoisier, a French chemist, who recognized that oxygen was an element and gave it its name. He called the new element "oxygen" because he believed it caused an acidic chemical reaction in some materials.

Lavoisier's work with oxygen did not end there. He was determined to disprove the phlogiston

Building On >

▼ Electricity *(p. 65)*

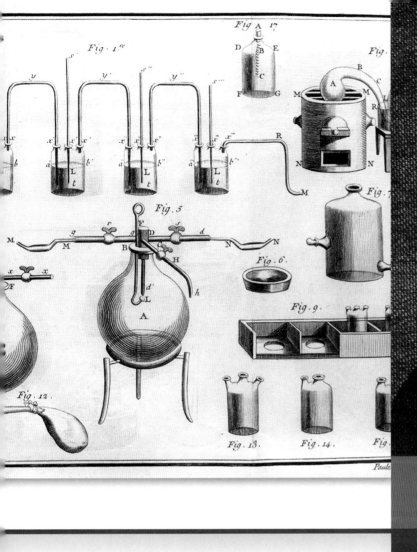

theory, which was commonly accepted by scientists of his day. The phlogiston theory said that fire and other materials would burn because they were rich in a near-weightless substance called phlogiston. When the phlogiston burned off from the item on fire, the remains weighed less than they had because the phlogiston was gone. However, some metals—tin, for example—weighed more when burned. And so chemists of the day explained this problem by saying that some materials had negative quantities of phlogiston to begin with.

Lavoisier showed that materials burned in the presence of oxygen and that when oxygen was removed, the fire would dissipate. One of his first experiments took place in 1777, when he heated mercury in a jar for 12 days. The result was two substances: One he called "red mercury" (now known as mercury oxide), and the other he termed "atmospheric mofette" (today called nitrogen). Lavoisier then reheated the red mercury at a higher temperature, and it reverted to mercury—something that would have been impossible in the phlogiston theory.

Oxygen and Carbon Dioxide (p. 245)

Antoine Lavoisier

[PROFILE]

Antoine Lavoisier (1743-1794), called the father of modern chemistry, was the son of a wealthy attorney in France. He studied law, but turned to his passion, science, upon getting his degree.

Lavoisier's significant contributions include his recognition of oxygen and hydrogen as separate elements, both of which he named. He was the first to theorize that all matter is composed of individual base components—chemical elements—that are unable to be broken down any further. He is also known for his law of conservation of mass. This law says that total mass of the materials that take part in a chemical reaction is conserved—that is, the total mass before the reaction is equal to the total mass after the reaction.

Latent Heat

A 1918 book about Scottish physician Joseph Black. Black developed the theory of latent heat: when a substance transitions from one phase to another—from a solid to a liquid or liquid to gas—it requires energy to do so.

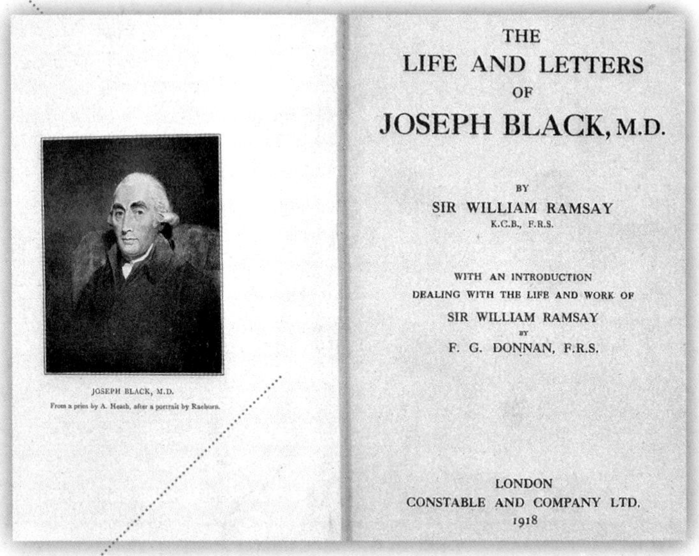

THE
LIFE AND LETTERS
OF
JOSEPH BLACK, M.D.

BY
SIR WILLIAM RAMSAY
K.C.B., F.R.S.

WITH AN INTRODUCTION
DEALING WITH THE LIFE AND WORK OF
SIR WILLIAM RAMSAY
BY
F. G. DONNAN, F.R.S.

LONDON
CONSTABLE AND COMPANY LTD.
1918

JOSEPH BLACK, M.D.
From a print by A. Heath, after a portrait by Raeburn.

Boyle's Law

English natural philosopher Robert Boyle used the apparatus illustrated here for an experiment on air. Boyle's experiments on gas and pressure were the first to show a relationship between the two.

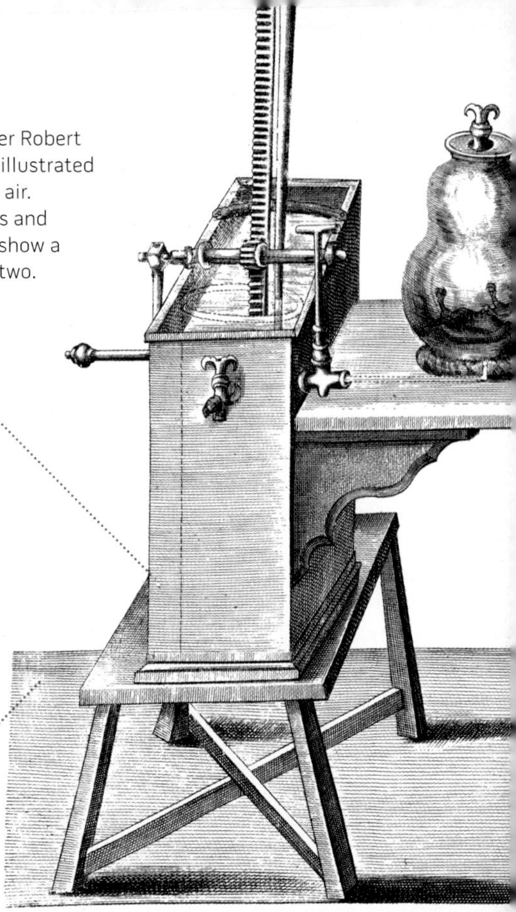

1757 >

1662 >

Latent Heat

▲ IN THEORY

Before formulation of the laws of thermodynamics, Scottish physician and chemist Joseph Black was puzzled by some phenomena he observed. For example, he noticed that when water was boiling, raising its temperature even further did not make the water hotter, it just produced more steam.

He developed his theory of latent heat to explain this and other observations. His theory was that when a material transitioned from one phase to another, like water to steam or ice to water, it required a certain amount of energy that did not contribute to a rise in temperature of the substance—this is the so-called latent heat, or "hidden heat."

Boyle's Law

▲ IN THEORY

Robert Boyle, a pioneering Irish chemist, was an early advocate for the idea that science should be based on the results of careful experimentation rather than theory alone. To affirm this approach, Boyle conducted his own experiment on gas and pressure. While other scientists had already developed theories about the connection between the two, Boyle was the first to prove the relationship through experimentation. And in 1662 he was the first to publish his findings so others could repeat the experiment.

Using a glass tube that was rounded at the bottom and sealed, Boyle trapped air in the tube and added mercury to it to apply pressure. He was careful to keep the temperature of the air constant. He recorded the volumes of the air and mercury, and repeated the experiment several times. At its conclusion, he was able to see an inverse mathematical relationship between volume and pressure. Boyle's law is encapsulated in the equation $pV=K$: pressure (p) multiplied by volume (V) equals a constant (K).

Building On >   Laws of Thermodynamics (p. 131)   Algebra (p. 157)

Robert Boyle

Irish philosopher and chemist Robert Boyle (1627-1691) instigated many changes in the scientific community. The youngest of 14 children, he studied at Eton, and with an unusual broadmindedness embraced the roles of both scientist and theologian.

His most significant contribution to the field of chemistry was his introduction of the idea that chemistry should be considered as important a scientific field as medicine, and that theories should be based on the results of careful experimentation. Boyle also argued that Aristotle's theory of elements was limiting research, and he is well known for Boyle's law, which describes the inverse relationship between the pressure and volume of gases.

1668 edition of Robert Boyle's *Sceptical Chymist*

1661 >

The Sceptical Chymist

▲ IN THEORY

When Robert Boyle's book *The Sceptical Chymist* was published in 1661, it contained what were then considered revolutionary ideas. Most researchers who performed chemical experiments were called alchemists; they practiced a kind of pseudoscience whose central goals were the transformation of base metals into gold, the discovery of a life-extending elixir, and the development of a substance capable of dissolving anything. Though Irish philosopher and chemist Boyle retained a lifelong interest in alchemy, his legacy to chemistry was a more empirical approach to the subject.

For example, Boyle argued that elements were not the basic ones that Aristotle and subsequent philosophers had proposed, such as fire, water, or air. While his book did not propose a theory of what the elements were, it did encourage research in the area. Its most groundbreaking aspect was Boyle's argument that science should be based on experiments rather than philosophy. His book was the first to detail all of his own experiments so that others could replicate them and learn from them.

Theory of Five Elements *(p. 201)*

Glass Lenses

An illustration of a microscope probably designed by Dutch lens maker Zacharias Janssen. Janssen worked with his son Hans to discover the world's first compound microscope.

Porcelain

A mortar and pestle are made of porcelain, a clay-powder mixture that is fired in a kiln at very high temperatures. Porcelain is sturdy and is often brightly painted.

1590 >

550 >

Glass Lenses

● IN USE

Even though glass had been used for bottles and containers for some 4,000 years, it was not until about 1000 when someone noticed that objects appeared larger when looking at them through glass that was thicker in the middle than on the edges,

Around 1590 two Dutch lens makers made another startling discovery. Zacharias and Hans Janssen, a son and his father, inserted two glass lenses in a tube and looked at objects through it. They realized that the object was much larger than it was when looking at it through a single lens: the world's first compound microscope. Less than 20 years later another Dutch glasses maker, Hans Lippershey, conducted a similar experiment with two lenses and produced a telescope. Lippershey was not the first to make a telescope, but he was instrumental in its widespread adoption.

First compound microscope, which used two glass lenses to enlarge an object

Porcelain

● IN USE

Porcelain has been created for centuries, beginning around 550. It was first developed by Chinese artisans, who sought to make beautiful containers for flowers and other objects.

Porcelain starts out as a paste—a combination of clay and powders (bone ash, quartz, or others) that usually contains a large amount of kaolin, a type of clay first discovered on the Gaoling Mountain in China. The potter shapes the clay-powder mixture with water and fires it in a kiln at very high temperatures, usually between 1200°C and 1300°C. The result is a high-gloss, glass-like container that is usually white. It can be easily painted, and is very strong and resistant to weather conditions and chemicals.

Building On >

Telescope (p. 139)

Microscope (p. 101)

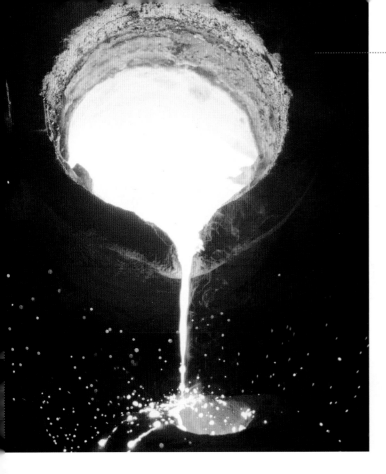

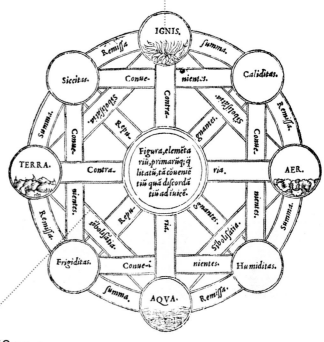

Steel
Molten steel, a combination of iron and carbon, is poured into a mold. The development of steel occurred over centuries, with several cultures contributing to the discovery.

Theory of Five Elements
A 16th-century diagram depicts the four classical Greek elements: fire, air, water, and earth. There was also a fifth element—the heavenly aether, or ether.

200 >

350 B.C. >

Steel

● IN USE

Steel, a combination of iron and carbon, is a material many centuries in the making. Some recently discovered artifacts suggest that people of ancient India and Africa created a carbon steel before the Common Era, or the time of Christ. The Chinese, however, perfected the steel-making process around the year 200. It is thought they created this early version of steel by combining cast iron (iron with high carbon content) and wrought iron (iron with low carbon content), and melting them together at a very high temperature. Steel is much stronger and more rust-resistant than iron, and so was a more desirable material for making swords and farming implements.

Theory of Five Elements

▲ IN THEORY

Greek philosopher Aristotle is considered one of the most important thinkers of his era for many reasons. Born in 384 B.C., he developed what he called the science of logic, a way to pose and solve problems systematically that is still taught today in schools and universities across the world. He also was the first teacher of his day to study the natural sciences in a methodical, three-step process: (1) He defined the subject; (2) he looked at what other philosophers and teachers had written on the subject; and (3) he presented his own theories on the subject.

He also subscribed to an earlier school of thought that everything is composed of four elements: earth, water, air, and fire. Although Aristotle was a student of Plato's, he did not agree with Plato's theory of the elements, which argued that each element was composed of smaller triangles of these elements.

Aristotle took a broader view and said that there were actually five elements, and that all matter consisted of them in pure form or in combination. In addition to the basic four elements, Aristotle added "aether," today called ether, which is what he felt composed the heavens.

▼ Stainless Steel (p. 176)
▼ Railway (p. 282)

▼ Periodic Table (p. 185)
▼ The Sceptical Chymist (p. 199)

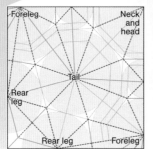

Foreleg. Neck and head. Tail. Rear leg. Rear leg. Foreleg.

The Art of Engineering
Origami folds can be plotted as lines on a flat piece of paper; similar designs drive projects at the macro, micro, and even nano scale. Self-folding DNA may one day deliver drugs to cells in need.

Programmable Matter

Programmable matter, which was first introduced by Massachusetts Institute of Technology researchers Tommaso Toffoli and Norman Margolus in a 1991 paper, is quickly becoming a reality, even if on a relatively small scale.

Programmable matter is matter that can simulate or form different objects as a result of either user input or its own computations. Some programmable matter is designed to create different shapes, while other matter, like synthetic biological cells, is programmed to work as a genetic "toggle" switch that signals other cells to change properties such as color or shape. The potential benefits and applications of programmable matter—in particular, the possibility of using it to perform information processing and other forms of computing—has created a lot of excitement in the research world.

Since the publication of Toffoli and Margolus's paper, much work has been done to fulfill the potential they predicted. In 2008, for example, the Intel Corporation announced that its researchers had developed early prototypes at the centimeter and millimeter scale of a cell phone device using programmable matter. In 2009 the Defense Advanced Research Projects Agency of the U.S. Department of Defense reported that five different teams of researchers from Harvard University, MIT, and Cornell University were making progress in programmable matter research. One of these teams, led by Daniela Rus of MIT, announced in 2010 that it was successful in creating self-folding sheets of origami. The Defense Advanced Research Projects Agency harbors hopes for futuristic applications of the concept—envisioning, for example, a soldier equipped with a lightweight bucket of programmable material that could be fashioned, on the spot, into just about anything he or she needed.

1999

Nanolithography has been used to create nano-size circuits, which could be used in programmable matter. *See page 160*

1988

Quantum dots are nanomaterial semiconductors, and thus could play an important role in programmable matter. *See page 162*

1974

Molecular electronics, in which single molecules are used as components of computers, could play a role in programmable matter. *See page 165*

In a Tight Place

When folded, the prototype Eyeglass telescope measures no more than 15 feet wide and fits as a tidy payload in the bay of a delivery rocket.

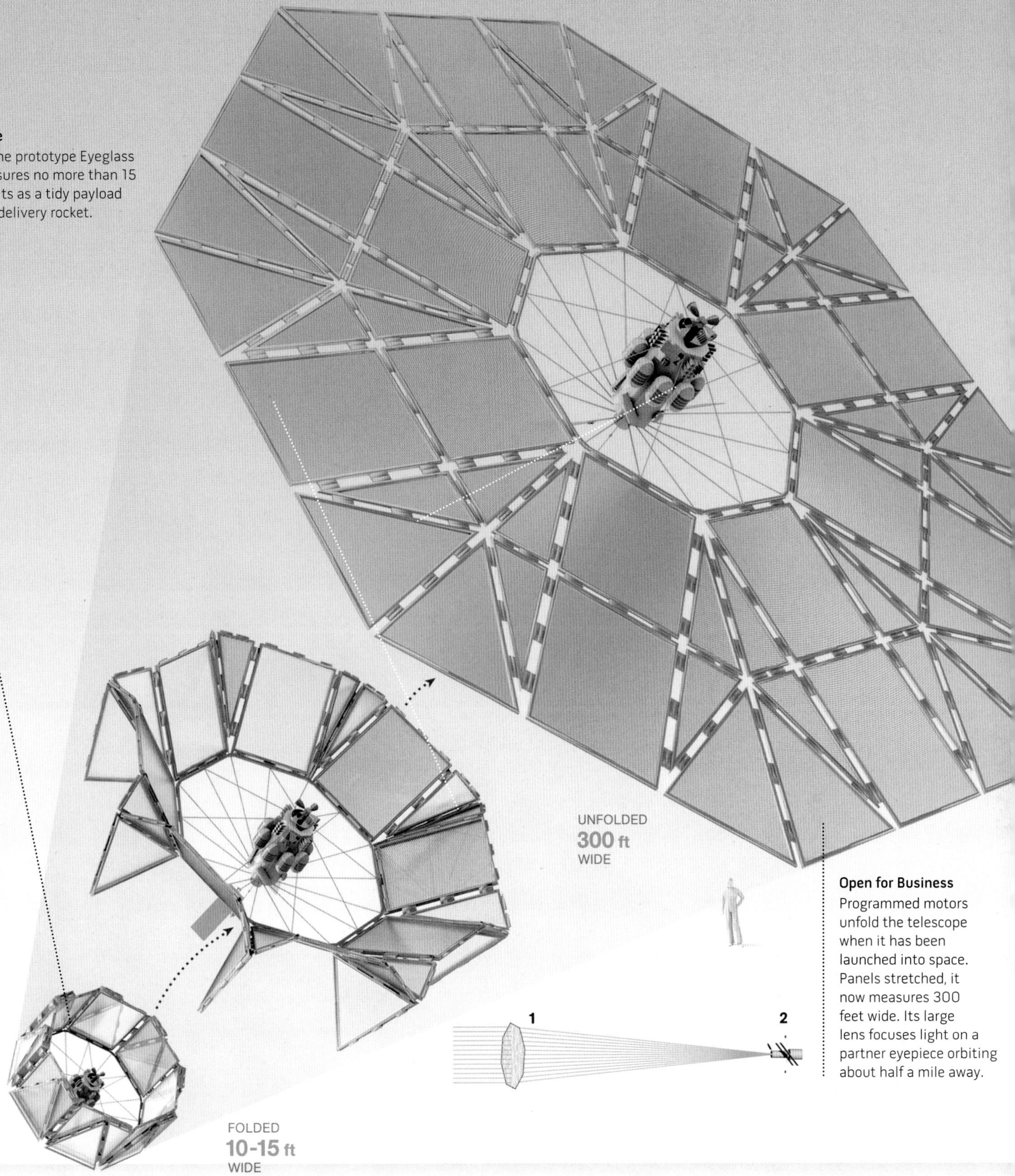

UNFOLDED
300 ft
WIDE

Open for Business

Programmed motors unfold the telescope when it has been launched into space. Panels stretched, it now measures 300 feet wide. Its large lens focuses light on a partner eyepiece orbiting about half a mile away.

1
2

FOLDED
10-15 ft
WIDE

1959

Physicist Richard Feynman predicted in 1959 the possibility of nanotechnology, which will play a crucial role in the creation of programmable matter. *See page 165*

CHAPTER

05

Biology & the Environment

BIG IDEAS

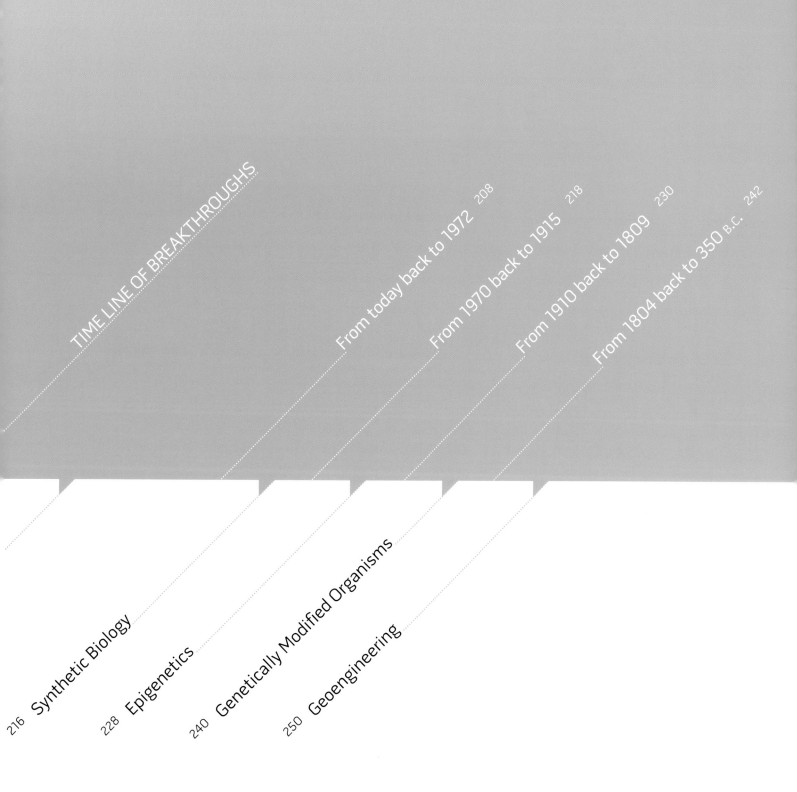

INTRODUCTION

The World Around Us

Scientists have come a long way in their understanding of the planet—both the forces that shape it and the life it nurtures—since Aristotle first took a stab at organizing and classifying animals in the fourth century B.C. Although his classification system proved sufficient for hundreds of years, Carl Linnaeus's 18th-century taxonomy was a clear improvement, both in its consistency and its clarity. Later, men like Arthur Tansley began to unravel the links between organisms and the environments in which they live, introducing concepts like biogeography and ecosystems.

English polymath Robert Hooke first looked through a microscope and observed the strange structures he called cells in the 1600s. By the end of the 20th century researchers had uncovered the structure and function of DNA and completed a map of the human genome. Today, scientists are creating genetically modified organisms and exploring the field of epigenetics, which aims to understand hereditary changes in gene expression without changes to the DNA itself. Innovators in the field of synthetic biology are also harnessing knowledge of microbiology, biochemistry, and other fields to create completely new forms of life.

Early views of the Earth as a static, unchanging rock have given way to knowledge of plate tectonics, continental drift, and climate change. Scientists know that change on this planet happens in fits and starts and that these fits and starts tend to occur consistently over long periods of time. Swedish scientist Svante Arrhenius warned as early as 1896 that human activity was having an effect on the climate of the Earth. In the future, geoengineering may allow science to counteract the effects of climate change.

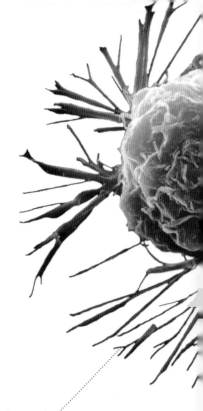

Colored scanning electron micrograph of a breast cancer cell

From today back to 1972 >

2000 >

Human Genome Project

● IN USE

The aim of the Human Genome Project, which began in 1990, was to determine the sequence of the base pairs that make up human DNA and to identify and map the approximately 20,000 to 25,000 genes of the human genome. Most of the government-sponsored sequencing was performed in universities and research centers throughout the world—including the United States, the United Kingdom, Japan, France, Germany, and China.

The project cost three billion dollars and was founded formally by the U.S. Department of Energy

and the National Institutes of Health. It was expected to take 15 years. Widespread international cooperation and advances in the field of genomics (especially in sequence analysis), as well as major advances in computing technology, led to a "rough draft" of the genome being finished in 2000. Work continued, and in April 2003—two years earlier than planned—the announcement was made that the project was complete. In May 2006 the sequence of the last chromosome was published in the journal *Nature*. Whether the project

is truly finished is still open to debate, as some regions remain unsequenced because they contain highly repetitive groups of genes that are expressed in a similar fashion.

Although the project has led to significant advances in science and technology, all humans have unique gene sequences. Therefore data published by the Human Genome Project, which is available on the Internet, does not represent the exact sequence of any one person's genome. It is instead a combined "reference" of a small number of anonymous donors.

An image of DNA

Building On >

Genome Sequencing (p. 212)

DNA Sequencing (p. 212)

Genetic Code (p. 221)

Structure of DNA (p. 223)

Mammal Cloning
Five piglets were cloned recently at a Virginia Tech University research facility. The first litter of cloned pigs follows similar cloning of cattle, mice, and sheep.

1996 >

Mammal Cloning

➤◄ CONNECTION

The Human Genome Project has led to amazing breakthroughs in science, technology, and medicine. Although work on interpreting the results of the project is still in the early stages, clear benefits became apparent from the beginning. For example, genetics companies have started offering simple tests that can show a person's genetic predisposition to a variety of illnesses. In addition, researchers are hopeful that the Human Genome Project will lead to significant advances in the understanding of conditions like Alzheimer's disease and cancer.

● IN USE

In 1996 scientists announced the birth of Dolly the sheep, the world's first cloned mammal. Scottish biologist Ian Wilmut created Dolly by using a process called nuclear transfer: The cell nucleus from an adult cell (in this case, a mammary cell) was transferred into an unfertilized egg cell that had its nucleus removed. The hybrid cell was then electrically stimulated to divide. When the cell developed into a blastocyst, it was implanted into a surrogate mother sheep that carried the embryo to term. Dolly proved that a cell could be taken from any part of the body and used to re-create the entire individual. Since Dolly, other large mammals have been cloned, including horses and beef and dairy cattle. The process is highly inefficient; many embryos, even healthy ones, still have notable abnormalities.

⊃ BACKLASH

Dolly the sheep showed that scientists could clone mammals. This achievement has sparked a fierce backlash from those who believe the practice leads down a slippery slope to the cloning of humans. Reproductive cloning has its risks: More than 90 percent of cloning attempts fail to produce offspring that survive; the immune systems of cloned animals are weaker and more prone to infection, tumors, and other disorders; and cloned animals generally do not live long enough to provide good data about how clones age.

Cloning (p. 219)

Cell Theory (p. 237)

A fossil reveals the earlier presence of ammonites, marine invertebrates that first appeared around 400 million years ago; they became extinct at the end of the Cretaceous period, about 65 million years ago.

Horn-faced dinosaur Zuniceratops

A package of synthetic insulin

1980 >

1978 >

Mass Extinction

▲ IN THEORY

In 1980 Luis Alvarez, an American experimental physicist and inventor, along with his son, geologist Walter Alvarez, uncovered a major discovery about the history of life on the Earth. The two men were studying a 65-million-year-old layer of clay that was deposited during the transition from the Cretaceous period to the Tertiary period. The clay contained an unusually high amount of iridium. Alvarez reasoned that the most plausible source of this element had to be extraterrestrial—in particular, a comet or an asteroid—as iridium is exceedingly rare in the Earth's crust. The Alvarezes put forward what became known as the impact theory: the conjecture that the extinction of the dinosaurs was a result of a comet or asteroid directly hitting the Earth.

In a 1982 paper Jack Sepkoski and David M. Raup described the "Big Five" mass extinctions: End Cretaceous (the one Alvarez studied), End Triassic, End Permian, Late Devonian, and End Ordovician. These are not, however, the only mass extinction events that have occurred in the Earth's history.

Synthetic Insulin

● IN USE

In 1978 biotechnology corporation Genentech, Inc. made history with its introduction of synthetic human insulin. Founded in 1976, the stated goal of the company was "to use recombinant DNA technology in bacterial cells to produce human proteins such as insulin and growth hormone." Scientists can synthetically reproduce the sequence of DNA that codes for insulin because they know the sequence of amino acids in human insulin as well as its chemical structure.

In 1982 the Food and Drug Administration approved synthetic insulin for use in humans. The product Humulin was licensed to and manufactured by Eli Lilly, and was the first approved genetically engineered human therapeutic.

Building On >

Insulin Therapy for Diabetes (p. 82)

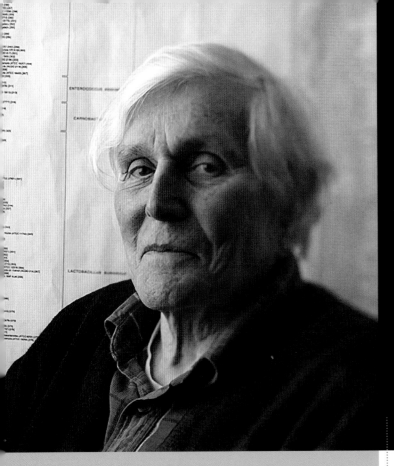

Carl Woese

Archaea
Archaea, similar to bacteria, are single-celled organisms that have no nucleus. Scientists initially thought Archaea were only found in the Earth's harshest environments; the organisms have since been discovered in a wide variety of habitats.

1977 >

[PROFILE]

American microbiologist and physicist Carl Woese (1928-) is perhaps most famous for defining Archaea—a group of single-celled microorganisms that have no cell nucleus—based upon genetic relationships rather than obvious physical similarities. Woese's definition of the taxonomic "tree" divided life into 23 main divisions, all incorporated within three separate domains: Archaea, Eukarya, and bacteria.

Woese's system is noteworthy because it provides significant evidence that an incredibly rich variety of single-celled organisms gave rise to the equally diverse and specialized varieties of life on Earth today.

Archaea

▲ IN THEORY

In 1977 Carl Woese introduced Archaea to the world—his name for a group of single-celled microorganisms that have no cell nucleus or any other membrane-bound organelles within their cells. Scientists had once believed these were simply an anomalous group of bacteria; however, they have a proven independent evolutionary history and show many differences from bacteria. In particular, Archaea possess genes and several metabolic pathways and enzymes that are more closely related to those of eukaryotes—organisms whose cells contain complex structures enclosed within membranes.

Archaea were initially considered extremophiles, suitable only to live in the harshest environments such as hot springs and salt lakes. They have since been discovered in a wide variety of habitats ranging from dirt to deep oceans. In fact, they are especially abundant in the oceans. Archaea in plankton may be one of the most abundant organisms known to humankind.

▼ Microbiology (p. 246)
▼ Microscope (p. 101)

Genome Sequencing

The process of genome sequencing analyzes a nucleotide sequence of DNA base pairs in a genome—that is, the order of the base pairs A, C, G, and T that make up an organism's DNA.

DNA Sequencing

Harvard scientist Walter Gilbert studies a DNA sequencing autoradiogram made during the course of research on the human genome project. The term genome describes the full set of genes expressed by an organism's chromosomes.

1977 >

1976 >

Genome Sequencing

● IN USE

Genome sequencing is a process that "reads" the order of DNA nucleotides in a genome—that is, the order of the base pairs A, C, G, and T that make up an organism's DNA. The 1977 genome sequencing work of Frederick Sanger, one of the most famous scientists in the history of genetics, led to the basic research that made the Human Genome Project possible. (Sanger is also known for methods of amino acid sequencing that he developed, which enabled him to determine the complete amino acid sequence of insulin before anyone else in 1951.)

The system used to determine the sequence of DNA, called Sanger sequencing, involves separating fluorescent-labeled DNA fragments based on the length of a polyacrylamide gel. The base at the end of each fragment is identified by how it reacts to a specific kind of dye.

Sanger used this technique to sequence the DNA of bacteriophage fX174, a viral genome with 5,368 base pairs. He discovered that there was overlap among the genes in some areas with respect to coding, a finding that enabled geneticists

to analyze longer strands of DNA more rapidly and with greater accuracy than before. Sanger was awarded a second Nobel Prize in chemistry in 1980 for this achievement, which he shared with Walter Gilbert and Paul Berg. Sanger received his first Nobel Prize in 1958 for work on the structure of proteins.

DNA Sequencing

● IN USE

In 1976 Allan Maxam and Walter Gilbert, pioneers of molecular genetics, developed a DNA sequencing method that involved the chemical modification of DNA, separating it at specific bases. Frederick Sanger's method actually preceded Maxam and Gilbert's technique by about two years, although he did not complete the work until 1977. The Maxam-Gilbert method was more popular for a time because it required fewer steps in preparing the DNA sequence to be read. Eventually, however, Maxam-Gilbert sequencing was usurped

Building On >

Human Genome Project *(p. 208)*

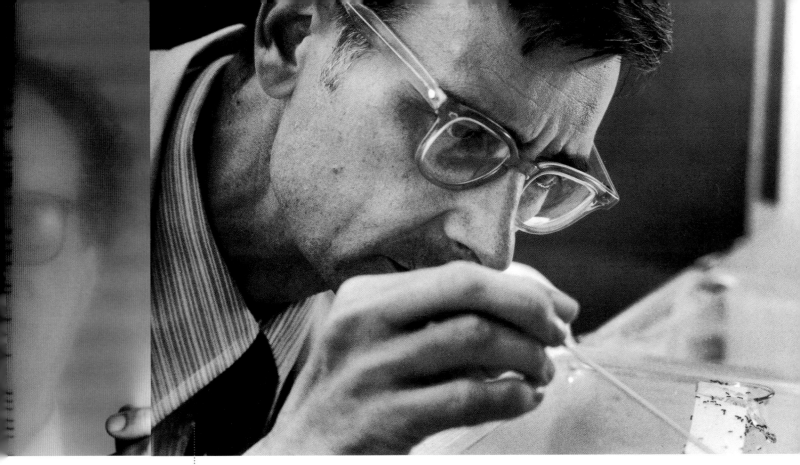

Sociobiology
Sociobiologist Edward O. Wilson studies the behavior of ants as part of his research on social behavior and how it stems from evolution.

1975 >

Sociobiology

▲ IN THEORY

by Sanger's method, which was much more efficient and helped scientists avoid exposure to the toxic chemicals and radioactivity utilized in Maxam-Gilbert. It was also less technically complex and could be used in a wider variety of labs, thus leading to simplified processes of scale-up and increased sequencing speeds.

In 1975 E. O. Wilson published *Sociobiology*, a book that led to one of the greatest scientific controversies of the 20th century. Wilson argued that evolutionary theory could help explain not only animal behavior but also human behavior. He was interested in explaining the evolutionary reasons behind social behaviors in humans such as altruism, aggression, mating patterns, territoriality, and pack behavior. According to sociobiology, natural selection caused animals to evolve ways of interacting with the physical environment that led to their survival and ensured the species' success.

The controversy was immediate—at least when it was applied to humans—with critics claiming that the theory was not scientifically sound and sociobiology could be used to rationalize the status quo, keep the ruling elite class in place, and otherwise maintain certain political agendas. Wilson and his supporters refuted this, claiming that sociobiology does not necessarily lead to any political ideology.

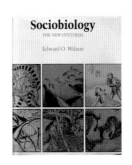

Sociobiology: The New Synthesis, first published in 1975

DNA as Genetic Material *(p. 224)*

Structure of DNA *(p. 223)*

Theory of Evolution *(p. 236)*

Genetic Engineering

The genetic material of a tomato and kiwi has been modified to produce a hybrid fruit. A hybrid is the offspring that results from crossbreeding between the same genus or different species.

1973 >

1972 >

Genetic Engineering

Punctuated Equilibrium

● IN USE

⊃ BACKLASH

▲ IN THEORY

Genetic engineering, also called genetic modification, involves directly manipulating an organism's genetic material. It uses recombinant DNA, in which two or more genetic sequences are combined in a way that would not ordinarily occur in nature. The origin of this field is attributed to American biochemists Herbert Boyer and Stanley Cohen, who invented the technique of DNA cloning. The first genetically engineered organisms were bacteria in 1973, followed by mice in 1974. Since then, genetic engineering techniques have been used in research, biotechnology, medicine, and other fields.

In this process, desired genetic material is isolated and copied with care to ensure that the genes will express themselves correctly. The new genetic material is placed into a host genome. This is the most common form of genetic engineering. Other forms include techniques that are used to target and remove specific genes.

Little evidence exists that genetically engineered foods pose any harm to human health or the environment. In fact, several benefits have been widely accepted. Yet the concern that genetically modified organisms could get into the wild is not unfounded. A 2010 study found transgenes, non-native segments of DNA, in 80 percent of wild plant varieties in North Dakota, meaning that 80 percent of the established plants in the area were genetically engineered. Researchers stated that this "could make it more difficult to manage these plants using herbicides."

According to the theory of punctuated equilibrium, which paleontologists Stephen Jay Gould and Niles Eldredge developed in 1972, evolution consists of long periods of equilibrium—in which not much occurs with regard to the development of new species— punctuated by instances where a species branches off into two distinct formations. In their 1972 paper Eldredge and Gould claimed that the Darwinian model of evolution, with its adherence to the idea of a smooth, continuous change in the development of

Building On >

DNA as Genetic Material *(p. 224)*

Structure of DNA *(p. 223)*

American paleontologist Niles Eldredge

Breakthroughs continue on page 218

Stephen Jay Gould

[PROFILE]

species, is not reflected in the fossil record and that equilibrium is the status quo.

Punctuated equilibrium is often mistaken for a theory of "sudden" evolution. But punctuated equilibrium does not contradict Darwin's model of gradual evolution, per se. Rather, Gould and Eldredge stated that their theory is just a form of gradualism. Evolutionary change may appear "instantaneous" when looking at the fossil record; however, Gould said that one had to think in terms of geological time scales to understand the theory properly. Evolutionary changes are rapid, but not as rapid as humans conceive of them.

Although Stephen Jay Gould (1941-2002) was a paleontologist by profession, he is perhaps better known for his contributions to evolutionary theory and the philosophy and history of science. Highly influential and widely read, Gould was among the most popular scientific writers of the 20th century. He was a strong critic of creationism, believing instead that science and religion should be considered two distinct fields, or "magisteria," that should not overlap. With the accolades came criticism. Some thought Gould downplayed the role of adaptation in biology and the importance of gene selection in evolution.

Theory of Evolution (p. 236)

Building Blocks
Using Lego blocks to convey the possibilities, an artist proposes how biologists may soon be able to detach and reconfigure pieces of a bacterium, thus reengineering the smallest components of life through genetic modifications.

Synthetic Biology

Synthetic biology is a new field of study in which biological entities or systems that are not found in nature are created. It is not the same as genetic engineering, which involves modifying known organisms. Synthetic biology has as its goals the design and construction of new biological parts, devices, and systems, as well as the redesign of existing biological systems for useful purposes. Although this field stands on the cutting edge of the study of biology, the term is actually not new. Polish geneticist Waclaw Szybalski coined the term "synthetic biology" in a paper published in 1974.

There are essentially two sub-branches in this field. The first uses synthetic molecules to mimic natural molecules with the goal of creating artificial life. The second uses natural molecules and assembles them into a system that acts in a way not found in nature. For example, Christopher Voigt, a biologist, molecular biophysicist, and engineer, has been successful in engineering a two-component bacterial system to regulate gene expression in response to red light. He successfully engineered bacteria to sense their environment and invade cancer cells only when the concentration of bacteria is large enough, when the environment has little oxygen, or when a specific chemical is present.

Voigt also constructed a digital logic gate inside bacteria, essentially turning a living organism into a mini-processor of sorts. These life-forms and the ways in which they have been created to behave are not, and likely could not, be found in nature. They are truly synthetic—artificial organisms created with an express, human purpose in mind.

Synthetic biology has its obvious hazards. For instance, what if a potentially harmful organism was either purposefully or accidentally released? Scientists and engineers are taking careful steps to prevent this by working only with organisms and components that are classified as Biosafety Level 1—that is, those that pose minimal risk to humans and the environment—in approved research facilities.

1976
▶
DNA sequencing has enabled scientists to understand how the components of DNA come together in

1953
▶
Understanding the structure of DNA is essential to constructing pieces of DNA for a synthetic organism.

1833
▶
The discovery of the cell nucleus was a crucial step along the way to locating the genetic material for all organisms.

Microscopic Tinkering
When scientists can confirm what an artist visualizes here—the inner mechanics of a single bacterium—they may hold the keys to altering its genetic makeup and thus influencing its ability to cause or cure disease.

1674

Without microbiology, scientists would have no direct knowledge of microorganisms, which are used extensively in synthetic biology. *See page 246*

Gaia Hypothesis
Professor James Lovelock, 1980,
at work in his lab in England.
Lovelock is the originator of the
Gaia hypothesis, which considers
the biosphere to be a self-regulating
system like an organism.

From 1970 back to 1915 >

1970 >

1967 >

Gaia Hypothesis

▲ IN THEORY

In 1965 James Lovelock published the first scientific paper suggesting the Gaia hypothesis, a theory that he continued to develop in the late 1960s and early 1970s. Lovelock defined Gaia as "a complex entity involving the Earth's biosphere, atmosphere, oceans, and soil; the totality constituting a feedback or cybernetic system which seeks an optimal physical and chemical environment for life on this planet." To buttress his theory, Lovelock pointed to the fact that the Earth's surface temperature has remained constant even though the energy provided by the sun has increased. And the composition of the atmosphere has remained constant, as has the salinity of the ocean. If these changes are caused by extraterrestrial, biological, geological, or other disturbances, life responds to them, modifying and regulating the state of the Earth's environment in its favor. In this way the Earth, together with all life on the planet, can be viewed as something like a single organism that maintains equilibrium among its various parts.

An illustration of a dissection of the Earth, revealing its core

Endosymbiotic Theory

▲ IN THEORY

In 1967 American biologist Lynn Margulis, who was trying to explain how mitochondria evolved, first proposed the endosymbiotic theory. Mitochondria are the "power stations" of cells, providing energy. According to Margulis's theory, large anaerobic bacteria (bacteria that do not need oxygen to survive) engulfed aerobic bacteria (bacteria that do need oxygen) in a process called endocytosis. These independent organisms came together in a symbiotic relationship, each helping to ensure the survival of the other. Over time, the

Building On >

Endosymbiotic Theory

The endosymbiotic theory proposes that independent organisms come together in a symbiotic relationship. Here, endosymbiotic cyanophyte is surrounded by colorless chlorophyta.

Cloning
The leopard frog was the first animal to be cloned.

1962 >

Cloning

● IN USE

bacteria that were taken up through endocytosis evolved into mitochondria and possibly other cell organelles. The theory also proposed that chloroplasts, the cell organelles responsible for photosynthesis in plants, originated by way of the same process.

Margulis felt that endosymbiosis provided the best explanation as to why prokaryotes (cells without a nucleus) and the organelles of eukaryotic cells (those with a nucleus) are so similar and appear together in the fossil record.

The quest to clone organisms began in the 1880s when scientists experimented with embryos, trying to discover how genetic material inside cells worked. There were some minor successes in the 1940s, but it was not until 1952 that the first animals—northern leopard frogs—were successfully cloned. American scientists Thomas J. King and Robert Briggs cloned 35 frog embryos from which 27 tadpoles hatched. Based on their results, King and Briggs thought that young cells were necessary for successful cloning. In their

experiments, cells taken from adults resulted in abnormally developed tadpoles.

In 1962 British biologist John Gurdon cloned South African frogs using adult cells, disproving King and Briggs's theory that young cells were necessary for success. Gurdon's work was also significant in that he used intact nuclei from somatic cells, which are any cells in the body aside from those involved in reproduction. In fact, the tools and techniques Gurdon developed for nuclear transfer are still used today.

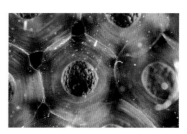

Leopard frog eggs at an early stage of development

Oxygen and Carbon Dioxide (p. 245)

Oxygen (p. 196)

Mammal Cloning (p. 209)

Cell Nucleus (p. 238)

Molecular Clock

A phylogenetic tree of life shows the connection between species whose relationships to common evolutionary ancestors have been calculated by a molecular clock.

Gram-positives
Chlamydiae
Green nonsulfur bacteria
Actinobacteria
Planctomycetes
Spirochaetes
Fusobacteria
Cyanobacteria (blue-green algae)
Thermophilic sulfate-reducers
Acidobacteria
Protoeobacteria

1962 >

Silent Spring ....

A plane sprays alfalfa fields with DDT in California's Imperial Valley in 1947. Rachel Carson, in her groundbreaking book *Silent Spring*, documented the detrimental effects of pesticides on the environment. As a result, DDT was banned in 1972.

1962 >

Molecular Clock

● IN USE

It is unlike any clock most people have seen, yet the molecular clock developed by American chemist Linus Pauling and Austrian-American biologist Emile Zuckerkandl in 1962 does tell time—albeit on an epoch scale. Pauling and Zuckerkandl looked at the fossil record and noted differences in proteins like amino acids over time and across lineages. From this, they hypothesized that the rate of evolutionary change of any given protein was more or less constant.

Thus a molecular clock can be used to determine the point in geologic time when two species diverged. In other words, by tracing the differences in amino acids back to the point where they are the same, scientists can tell how much time has passed since the amino acids first diverged.

Silent Spring

▲ IN THEORY

In 1962 Rachel Carson's book *Silent Spring* was published. It quickly became the impetus for the environmental movement. The book continues to be read widely today, and is considered one of the greatest nonfiction works of the 20th century. In it, Carson documented the detrimental effects of pesticides on the environment, particularly on birds. She argued that DDT, one of the most well-known synthetic pesticides, had caused birds to lay eggs with thinner shells, thus resulting in reproductive problems in the birds and even death. Carson accused the chemical industry of disseminating lies and disinformation deliberately, and public officials of blindly accepting industry claims as to the safety of pesticides without question. As a result the United States banned DDT in 1972.

Building On >   Fossils (p. 247)   Ecosystem (p. 227)

Polarized light micrograph shows crystals of phenylalanine—an amino acid that is the building block of protein. In the 1960s scientists at the National Institutes of Health were able to produce this amino acid from bacteria by adding an artificial form of ribonucleic acid, or RNA, to the bacteria's cells.

1961 >

Genetic Code

➤◄ CONNECTION

The roots of the environmental movement in the United States emerged in the late 19th and early 20th centuries. From the 1950s to the 1970s, several events demonstrated just how badly humans were damaging the environment, including the exposure of the crew of a Japanese fishing vessel to radioactive fallout; publication of *Silent Spring* by Rachel Carson; two oil spills; and a lawsuit in Japan that focused the world's attention on the effects of decades of mercury poisoning.

▲ IN THEORY

Genes are composed of DNA, which is in turn composed of molecules called nucleotides. The nucleotides are arranged in a specific order. This order carries a set of encoded instructions that tells other components of a cell how to make proteins, which are involved in almost every process in the body of a living organism.

After the structure of DNA was discovered by James Watson and Francis Crick in 1953, some in the scientific community sought to understand how genetic material instructs the cell to produce particular proteins. On May 15, 1961, at a National Institutes of Health laboratory in Maryland, J. Heinrich Matthaei and Marshall Warren Nirenberg conducted an experiment in which they caused bacteria cells to produce a protein by adding an artificial form of RNA called poly-U to the cells. This induced the bacteria to make an amino acid (amino acids are the building blocks of protein) called phenylalanine. The finding led to the discovery of the three-nucleotide sequence of DNA, which instructs the components of a cell to make phenylalanine. There are 20 amino acids in total. The code for each is a sequence of three nucleotides called a codon.

Between 1964 and 1965 Nirenberg and Philip Leder developed a filtration machine that enabled them to "read" the order of nucleotides in codons. There are 64 different possible codons because there are four different nucleotides. By 1966 the codons for all 20 amino acids had been deciphered. (Many amino acids have more than one codon.)

DNA as Genetic Material *(p. 224)*

Structure of DNA *(p. 223)*

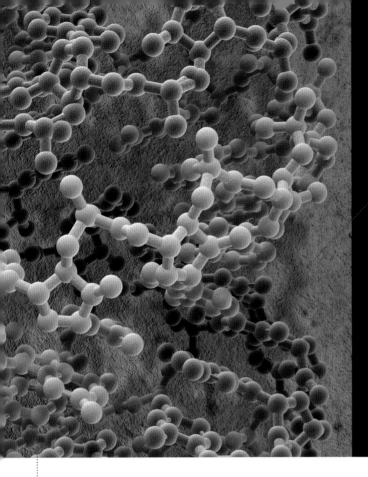

Re-creation of Earth's Early Atmosphere
Dr. Stanley Miller in his laboratory in 1983. Miller tried to mimic the Earth's early atmosphere by combining hydrogen, water, methane, and ammonia.

RNA
RNA, or ribonucleic acid, is made up of a long chain of nucleotides, whose sequence allows RNA to encode genetic information.

1956 >

1953 >

RNA

△ IN THEORY

In 1956 MIT biophysicist Alexander Rich and colleague David R. Davies stunned the scientific community with the announcement that RNA molecules could act just like DNA molecules. That is, two single strands of RNA, or ribonucleic acid, could spontaneously align in the classic double-helix shape of DNA. Many thought the claim highly implausible. And yet when two different strands of RNA were combined, that is exactly what happened. Interestingly, Rich had not set out to discover this; rather, he stumbled upon it while attempting to uncover the structure of RNA and its role in the development of life.

→← CONNECTION

Because of the discovery about RNA, scientists can now identify, isolate, manipulate, and replace genetic material nearly as easily as they can change a flat tire. An understanding of RNA also led to the Human Genome Project and is causing a fundamental shift in the belief of how life works. Proponents of the RNA world theory believe that prior to life-forms based on DNA and proteins, the world was filled with life based on RNA. Because RNA can store information like DNA and act as an enzyme like proteins, this theory does make sense.

Re-creation of Early Atmosphere

● IN USE

A 1953 experiment in which chemist Stanley Miller combined hydrogen, water, methane, and ammonia provided compelling evidence for how life might have formed on Earth. Miller combined these elements in a flask to simulate the Earth's early atmosphere. He sent an electric charge through the flask, which was designed to simulate ultraviolet radiation from the sun. The heat from the charge caused the water in the enclosed microenvironment to be recycled, just like the planet's atmosphere recycles rainwater, oceans, lakes,

Building On >

Human Genome Project (p. 208)

Chemical Structure (p. 186)

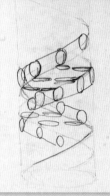

Structure of DNA
James Watson, left, and Francis Crick, who discovered the structure of DNA, pose with their model of part of a DNA molecule in 1953.

Crick's original sketch of DNA

1953 >

Structure of DNA

▲ IN THEORY

and other forms of surface water. Miller left the apparatus to operate for a week. When he returned to the flask, he discovered that a scum containing organic compounds, including amino acids, had built up on the surface of the liquid. Around this time, some scientists were speculating that the origins of life could have come from comet dust, which is known to carry amino acids.

Miller was not the first to come up with this theory. In 1922 Russian biochemist Aleksandr Oparin first suggested that the Earth's early atmosphere

contained hydrogen, methane, water, and ammonia. Oparin believed that life originated in the atmosphere and continued to develop in a prebiotic form in the oceans. His theory was slightly different in that he believed life formed rather spontaneously, whereas Miller acknowledged that the true spark of life had yet to be determined.

Perhaps there is no symbol of science more iconic than the DNA double helix. The discovery of this structure in 1953 by scientists James Watson and Francis Crick at Cambridge University was nothing short of monumental. DNA, or deoxyribonucleic acid, is the substance that contains the genetic instructions for all living things, whether human, horse, housefly, or bacteria. Prior to Watson and Crick, the existence of DNA was known—although some were skeptical that it contained genetic material. What remained to be determined was what DNA

actually looked like. Watson and Crick created models out of sticks and balls similar to Tinker Toys. They originally operated under the erroneous assumption that DNA was a triple helix.

Although Watson and Crick are credited with the discovery of the structure of DNA, they built on the work of others—particularly British biophysicist Rosalind Franklin, who in 1952 made a famous three-dimensional image of DNA using a painstaking technique called x-ray diffraction; she was among the first to speculate on DNA's physical structure.

DNA as Genetic Material

Streptococcus pneumoniae played a key role in the discovery that genetic material consists of DNA. The bacteria, carried by many without causing infection, can cause pneumonia in people with weak immune systems. Oswald Avery conducted experiments to isolate the substance, causing the bacteria to change from a nonvirulent to virulent form. His results indicated DNA was the culprit.

1944 >

Hans Krebs

DNA as Genetic Material

 IN THEORY

No single individual can be credited with the discovery of DNA as the carrier of genetic material. It was the result of the work of a number of people who built on the ideas of one another. In 1944, for example, Oswald Avery conducted experiments on pneumococcus bacteria in which he successfully isolated the substance that caused the bacteria to transform from a nonvirulent to virulent form. His results strongly leaned toward DNA as being the cause of this transformation.

In 1948 Erwin Chargaff studied the individual components, or base pairs, of DNA. He noticed that the amount of adenine was always equal to the amount of thymine, the amount of cytosine always equal to that of guanine.

In 1952 Alfred Hershey and Martha Chase conducted experiments on radioactive bacteriophage viruses. When these viruses infected an organism, they attached to it and injected their DNA into the host cell. Hershey and Chase's experiments proved that DNA, not protein, is the carrier of genetic material from one generation to the next.

Hans Krebs (1900-1981) was well known as a researcher and scientist. But it was his study of metabolism that gained him the most fame. He began his medical career as a practitioner, but soon realized he would rather conduct research than treat patients. Medicine's loss was science's gain: Krebs's work led to important discoveries, most notably the Krebs cycle, which shed light on some of the vital chemical reactions that occur in the body. In 1953 Krebs was awarded the Nobel Prize in medicine for this discovery.

Building On >

Genetic Engineering *(p. 214)*

Genetic Code *(p. 221)*

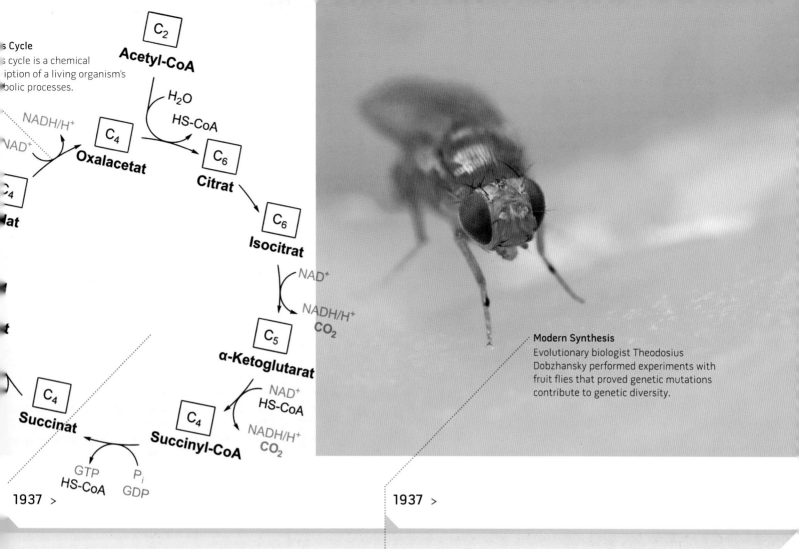

s Cycle
s cycle is a chemical
iption of a living organism's
bolic processes.

C_2
Acetyl-CoA

H_2O
HS-CoA

NADH/H$^+$
NAD$^+$

C_4
Oxalacetat

C_4
at

C_6
Citrat

C_6
Isocitrat

NAD$^+$

NADH/H$^+$
CO_2

C_5
α-Ketoglutarat

NAD$^+$
HS-CoA

NADH/H$^+$
CO_2

C_4
Succinat

C_4
Succinyl-CoA

GTP
P_i
HS-CoA
GDP

1937 >

Modern Synthesis
Evolutionary biologist Theodosius
Dobzhansky performed experiments with
fruit flies that proved genetic mutations
contribute to genetic diversity.

1937 >

Krebs Cycle

▲ IN THEORY

The discovery of the Krebs
cycle, named for German
physician and biochemist Hans
Krebs, significantly increased
the understanding of a living
organism's metabolic processes.
These are chemical reactions that
are essential for life. In 1932 Krebs
discovered that ammonia, which is
toxic to most organisms, undergoes
crucial reactions and is converted
to urea, which is excreted. This is
called the urea cycle.

Building on this work, Krebs
studied the chemical reactions
that take place in an organism
when oxygen is used to break

down fats, sugars, and protein,
giving off carbon dioxide and other
waste products. By 1937 he was
able to accurately describe this
process to a scientific audience.

Modern Synthesis

▲ IN THEORY

Charles Darwin's theory of natural
selection postulated that all
animals have inherent traits, and
the most successful ones are
passed on to future generations.
What Darwin could not explain
was how these traits were passed
on. His critics argued that it was
the environment that shaped
how creatures evolved, and that
mutations were entirely random.

Then scientist Gregor Mendel
performed his famous sweet pea
experiments and showed that
chromosomes were responsible
for the inheritance of traits.
The modern synthesis theory

of evolution combines natural
selection with Mendelian
inheritance to present a novel way
of looking at how evolution works.

In 1937 evolutionary biologist
Theodosius Dobzhansky published
Genetics and the Origin of Species,
which combined Darwin's theory
with what was beginning to
be understood about genetics.
Dobzhansky explained the results
of his experiments with fruit flies,
proving that genetic mutations
led to genetic diversity, which was
what natural selection acted upon,
and can show up in just a single
generation.

Oxygen and Carbon Dioxide *(p. 245)*

Chromosomes Carry Genes *(p. 230)*

Mendelian Genetics *(p. 236)*

Theory of Evolution *(p. 236)*

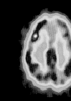

Functional Mapping of the Human Brain
Computed tomography scans reveal the brain of a two-year-old child in the midst of an epileptic seizure. Before the advent of such technology, neurosurgeon Wilder Penfield developed a procedure in which patients would remain awake and describe their reactions as he stimulated areas of the brain. He used the procedure to surgically treat epilepsy.

Canadian neurosurgeon Wilder Penfield

1937 >

Functional Mapping of the Human Brain

▲ IN THEORY

Brain mapping deals with matching the parts of the brain with the functions and abilities of humans. Scientists know that certain parts of the brain are responsible for memory, for example, and other parts are responsible for vision. But what enables humans to discern the difference between specific colors or sounds or tastes? A complete functional map of the brain is still not complete, though efforts to produce one began almost 75 years ago with an American-born Canadian scientist named Wilder Penfield.

In 1937 epilepsy was considered a disease without a cure. Penfield was not satisfied with this answer and set about to disprove this claim. Under local anesthetic, he probed the brain tissues of his patients and used their responses to help determine the areas in the brain affected by epilepsy. One patient, for example, smelled burning toast just prior to a seizure. Penfield was able to probe her brain until she reported that same smell again. Brain mapping has also enabled the scientific community to understand how factors like aging and neurological disease affect the brain.

→← CONNECTION

The functional mapping of the human brain has provided scientists with some amazing insights about how the brain works. As a result of Wilder Penfield's groundbreaking work, they have a better understanding of hard-to-quantify functions like memory, dreams, and sensations. The eventual goal is to have a complete "road map" of the human brain, from the lobes, regions, and centers, all the way down to the networks and pathways between neurons—and perhaps even within a single neuron.

Building On >

Anesthesia *(p. 92)*

Localization of Brain Function *(p. 248)*

Ecosystem
Red mangrove roots penetrate the underwater soil in Florida.

Continental Drift
An illustration of Earth during the Cretaceous period, 100 million years ago

1935 >

1915 >

Breakthroughs continue on page 230

Ecosystem

▲ IN THEORY

However unremarkable it may seem today, the word "ecosystem" represents an insight crucial to the understanding of life on Earth. It was coined in 1935 by British ecologist and botanist Arthur Tansley as a derivation of the phrase "ecological system." Tansley thought the word encapsulated the link between living and nonliving things. Prior to its introduction, animals and plants were believed to interact with each other, but the important role of soil, water, and air as components of the environment had been ignored, or overlooked.

With Tansley's ecosystem, scientists acknowledge that the whole may very well be greater than the sum of the parts.

Continental Drift

▲ IN THEORY

In geology, as with other areas of science, some theories are accepted readily and others are not. The latter was the case with continental drift and plate tectonics, which were first introduced by German scientist Alfred Wegener in 1915 in his book *The Origins of Continents and Oceans*. In his studies Wegener realized that identical fossils of plants and animals were found on opposite sides of the Atlantic Ocean. The common understanding at that time was that land bridges had connected the continents. Wegener, however, noticed the ways in which the continents appeared to have once fit together like puzzle pieces; he speculated that they must have once formed a giant landmass, which he called Pangaea (a Greek term meaning "all the earth").

The scientific community heaped scorn on Wegener for his theory in the beginning. As geologists continued to learn more about Earth's geology, however, Wegener's theory of continental drift did not look so silly anymore. The study of plate tectonics has shown that the continents "float" on a layer of underlying rock.

Ecological Succession Theory *(p. 231)*

Biogeography *(p. 242)*

Messenger of All Traits
Chromosomes, present in every cell of every living thing, carry the information expressed as the individual grows, its organs and features unfolding according to specific rules encoded in the chromosomes.

Epigenetics

Epigenetics is a field of study that attempts to answer the age-old question: nature or nurture? Biologist, paleontologist, geneticist, embryologist, and philosopher Conrad Waddington defined the term in 1942 as "the branch of biology which studies the causal interactions between genes and their products, which bring the phenotype [i.e., the physical characteristics of an organism] into being." More recently, the Epigenome Network of Excellence, which brings together 26 European groups doing research in the field, defined epigenetics as "the study of heritable changes in genome function that occur without a change in DNA sequence." That is, epigenetics is the study of how the expression of genes changes from generation to generation, without a change to the DNA itself.

One way to understand the basic idea behind epigenetics is by looking at how cells undergo differentiation when they multiply and divide. During this process the cells become more and more specialized because some genes activate and others remain dormant. In essence, there are biochemical "switches" that turn genes on and off, therefore influencing how the genetic material of an organism is expressed. For example, a single fertilized egg cell—the zygote—changes into the various cell types, including neurons, muscle cells, epithelia, and blood vessels, as it continues to divide. Each of these cells contains the same DNA, yet they are very different from one another because epigenetic mechanisms activate some genes while inhibiting others.

The study of epigenetics has important implications for humans, allowing scientists to understand better how physical traits and diseases are inherited. For instance, some researchers argue that obesity may be more a result of epigenetics than of genetics or environmental factors like lifestyle. Although this idea requires more study, epigenetic "programming" in the womb may have an effect on the later health of a child, especially with regard to Western countries where diabetes, heart disease, and other obesity-related medical conditions are on the rise.

Epigenetics is also increasing the knowledge of not only how cancer develops and grows but also how to treat it more successfully.

2000

The sequencing of the human genome is crucial to understanding both the genetic and epigenetic aspects of inheritance. *See page 208*

1977

Genome sequencing technology is the basis for sequencing the entire genome of an organism. *See page 212*

1910

The discovery that chromosomes carry genes was a crucial step in understanding the biological basis of inheritance. *See page 230*

Turning Off the Message

Environmental extremes and lifestyle choices can impact an individual's chromosomes, influencing the genetic messages passed on to children. Geneticists are finding that some factors turn off the expression of certain genes.

1865

The ideas of Mendelian genetics were an essential step toward the modern understanding of trait inheritance.
See page 236

Chromosomes Carry Genes

Breeding experiments with fruit flies, whose chromosomes are shown here, revealed that specific genes are carried on specific chromosomes and explained how mutations occur.

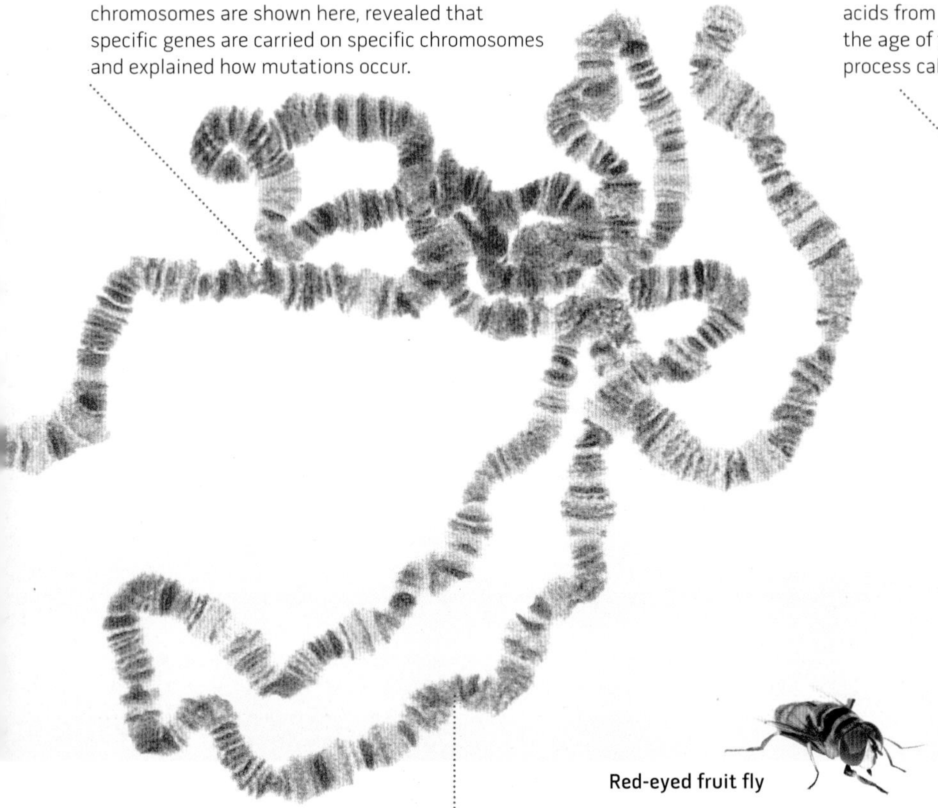

Radioactive Dating

Scientists use a tiny sample of amino acids from a bone to determine the age of the substance through a process called radiocarbon dating.

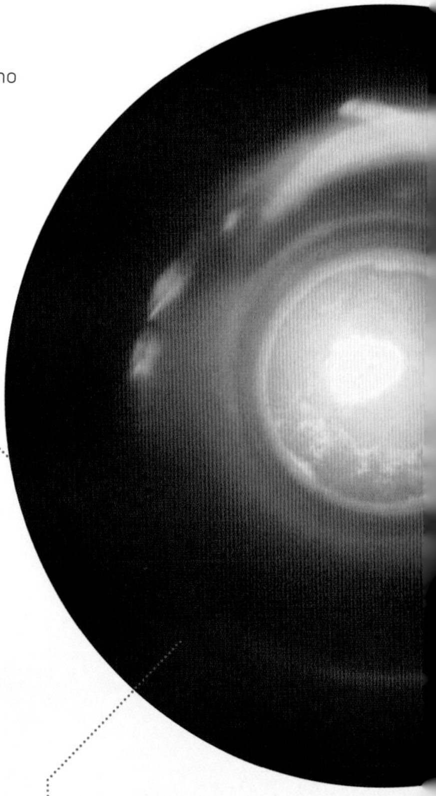

Red-eyed fruit fly

From 1910 back to 1809 >

1910 >

1902 >

Chromosomes Carry Genes

▲ IN THEORY

Perhaps no early scientist spent more time peering at fruit flies through microscopes than American biologist Thomas Hunt Morgan. In 1910 Morgan noticed a single red-eyed fly among his white-eyed specimens. He conducted a series of breeding experiments to study how this mutation would be inherited. He found that the white-eyed trait was recessive—a single red-eyed parent invariably meant red-eyed offspring. He also speculated that it was located on the X chromosome, since only males (with no second X chromosome to counteract the white-eyed form of the gene) displayed the characteristic. Morgan had discovered that specific genes are carried on specific chromosomes. He was building on work pioneered by American geneticist Walter Sutton and German biologist Theodor Boveri, who in 1902 independently came to the conclusion that chromosomes carry genetic material. These were important milestones in the understanding of inheritance and genetics.

Thomas Hunt Morgan

Radioactive Dating

● IN USE

Radioactive dating, which was first conceived in 1902 and demonstrated by English chemists Ernest Rutherford and Frederick Soddy, is a technique that uses the half-life of a radioactive element to determine the age of something, whether that be the Earth or any type of organic material. The technique depends on knowledge of the rate at which certain radioactive elements decompose in matter. By measuring the amount of a radioactive element and the element into which it decomposes, and comparing those

Building On >

Meiosis (p. 233)

Modern Synthesis (p. 225)

Ecological Succession Theory
Floral growth returns after a fire in Yellowstone National Park.

1899 >

Ecological Succession Theory

▲ IN THEORY

proportions to a standard time line, a researcher can estimate the age of an artifact, a fossil, or some other ancient material. The technique that most people are familiar with is carbon dating. Others include potassium-argon and uranium-lead dating. These techniques are considered quite reliable because the nucleus of a radioactive element is only affected by the decay of particles within its nucleus, not by external environmental factors such as temperature.

Henry Chandler Cowles's theory of ecological succession, which the American botanist presented in a paper in 1899 titled *The Ecological Relations of the Vegetation on the Sand Dunes of Lake Michigan,* stated that the composition of an ecological community changes over time. According to this theory, these changes occur in an orderly fashion and can be predicted to some degree. Primary succession occurs when a significant dramatic event changes the environment, such as a volcanic eruption creating an island where one had not

previously existed. Secondary succession occurs when an existing environment is severely disturbed by an event such as a forest fire.

Cowles was not the first to come up with this theory. French naturalist Adolphe Dureau de la Malle coined the term "succession" in the early 19th century to describe the rehabitation of plants after a forest was cleared. Author Henry David Thoreau wrote "The Succession of Forest Trees" in 1859 in which he described his observations of succession in a forest of oak and pine trees.

Frederic Clements, an American plant ecologist, was at the forefront of this field for quite some time during the early 20th century. His succession taxonomy was more complex than Cowles's, but not as complex as that presented by American botanist Henry Allan Gleason, a contemporary of Cowles. Gleason's succession framework incorporated the relationships not only among species but also among the individual members, their physical environments, and other factors that differentiated one organism from another.

Radioactivity *(p. 130)*

Age of the Earth *(p. 238)*

Ecosystem *(p. 227)*

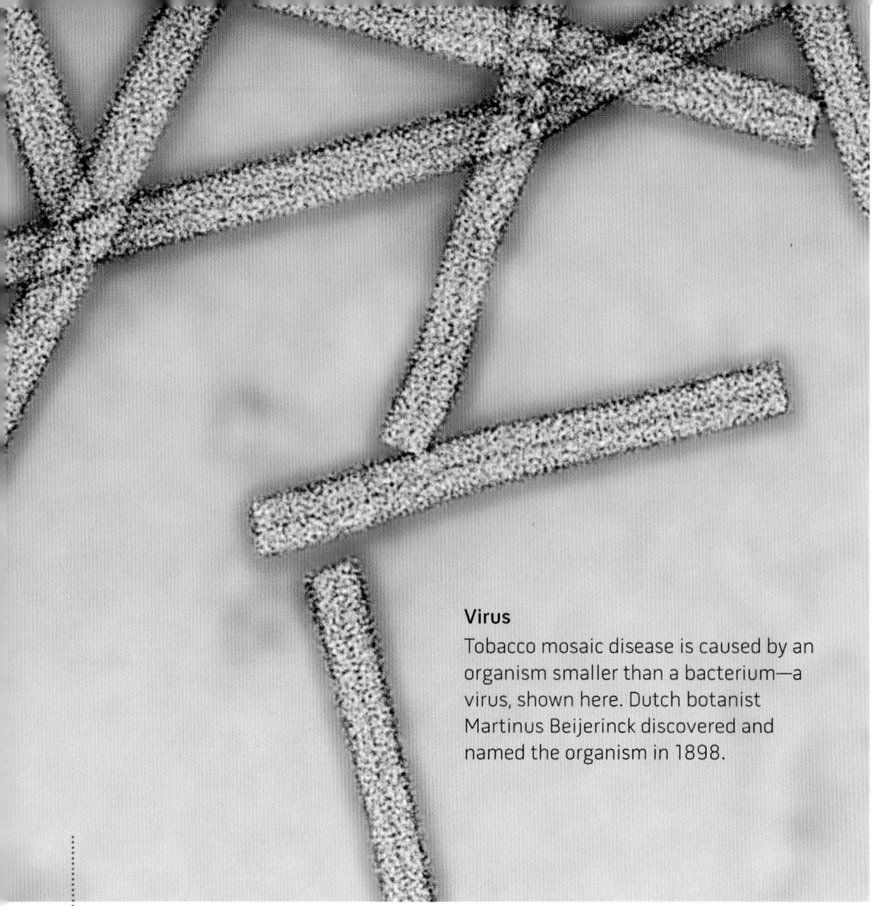

Virus

Tobacco mosaic disease is caused by an organism smaller than a bacterium—a virus, shown here. Dutch botanist Martinus Beijerinck discovered and named the organism in 1898.

1898 >

1896 >

Virus

▲ IN THEORY

In 1898 Martinus Beijerinck was trying to determine the cause of tobacco mosaic disease. What he found was so much more. Through filtration experiments the Dutch microbiologist and botanist showed that the disease—which results in a characteristic mottling pattern on the leaves of tobacco and similar plants—was caused by an organism even smaller than a bacterium. This organism Beijerinck called a virus. Beijerinck believed that viruses were liquid in nature, though American biochemist Wendell Stanley would later prove this assumption to be incorrect. Since Beijerinck's initial discovery, about 5,000 viruses have been located and officially classified. Still millions of different types are known to exist.

Climate Change

▲ IN THEORY

In 1896 Swedish scientist Svante Arrhenius calculated that the temperature of the Earth would increase as the amount of carbon dioxide in the atmosphere increased. Arrhenius did not know it, but he had laid the foundation for a theory that would engender fierce debate a century later. He attributed this increase in carbon dioxide directly to human activity—namely, the burning of fossil fuels—and he calculated that every time the increase in carbon dioxide levels doubled, the temperature would go up by 5°C.

Although Arrhenius was the first to publish this idea formally and support it with scientific evidence, the idea that humans could have a significant and potentially detrimental effect on the planet was not new. The ancient Greeks, for example, speculated on the relationship between rainfall and the cutting down of a forest, and early farmers were well acquainted with the practice of slash-and-burn agriculture. But could humans really affect things on such a global scale? Although many in Arrhenius's time disagreed with

Building On >   ▼ Viruses *(p. 87)*

Climate Change

A computer simulation of global patterns in climate. Research in the late 19th century showed that human activity could have a significant and potentially negative impact on the Earth's environment.

Meiosis

A SEM scan of chromosomes during meiosis. Meiosis is the process during which sex cells divide, a critical component of the reproductive cycle.

1890 >

Meiosis

him, the answer, he affirmed, was a resounding "yes."

As temperatures in the North Atlantic region warmed by the 1930s, most were still reluctant to attribute the cause to humans. English engineer G. S. Callendar, however, refined Arrhenius's calculations using improved techniques in 1938 and sounded the alarm that greenhouse global warming is indeed taking place and should not be ignored. Detailed measurements in the 1960s showed that global warming was not a theory but a fact.

→ ← CONNECTION

Scientists' knowledge about the phenomenon of climate change has increased dramatically since Svante Arrhenius's theory was first published. Today, computers can create climate models. In addition, they can show that as humans have become more technologically advanced the planet has suffered. Advances in meteorology allow meteorologists not only to predict the weather more accurately but also to predict the climate. Warming may not be the only problem. Human activity can release aerosols into the atmosphere, which can have a cooling effect.

▲ IN THEORY

Meiosis is the process by which sex cells—that is, eggs and sperm—divide. It is a critical component of sexual reproduction because it leads to the number of chromosomes in each cell being halved. It is these chromosomes that, when combined in sexual reproduction, determine the unique characteristics of the offspring. German embryologist Oscar Hertwig was the first to discover meiosis in 1876 when studying the eggs of sea urchins. However, German biologist August Weismann realized in 1890 why this process was so important.

Every organism must have a certain number of chromosomes. In humans, for example, every cell has 46 chromosomes. Meiosis ensures that the number stays the same as the cells divide.

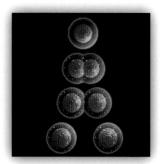

Cell division by meiosis

Chromosomes Carry Genes (p. 230)

Santiago Ramón y Cajal

Spaniard Santiago Ramón y Cajal (1852-1934) is considered the father of neuroscience because of his pioneering work in the study of the central nervous system. Ramón y Cajal proposed that distinct cells called neurons were responsible for the functioning of the nervous system and that these cells communicated in a network-like fashion, sending messages through electrical impulses. This idea was in contrast to the prevailing theory at the time, which held that the nervous system was a tissue-like structure containing interconnected fibers. Ramón y Cajal used Camillo Golgi's staining method to study embryonic cells. Along with Golgi, he won the 1906 Nobel Prize in medicine or physiology.

Neuron Doctrine

Computer artwork depicts a nerve cell, also called a neuron. Neurons are responsible for passing information around the central nervous system and to the rest of the body.

1890 >

Neuron Doctrine

▲ IN THEORY

In the mid to late 19th century, there were two competing ideas about the structure of the nervous system. On one side were those who believed the nervous system was composed of sheaths of fused nerve cell tissue. On the other side were those who believed that the nervous system was a vast network of discrete cells. In 1838 botanist Matthias Schleiden and physiologist Theodor Schwann, both of Germany, had put forth the fundamental tenet of cell theory—that all living things are composed of cells. Microscopes were not very powerful at the time, so the structure of the nervous system could not be seen in much detail. Thus the debate continued.

In the last years of the 19th century, Santiago Ramón y Cajal attempted to resolve the issue by proposing that cells that he called neurons were responsible for the structure and functioning of the nervous system. In his studies he stained cells taken from the brain of a chick and described them as follows: "They are small, globular, and irregular . . . [and] supplied with numerous protoplasmic

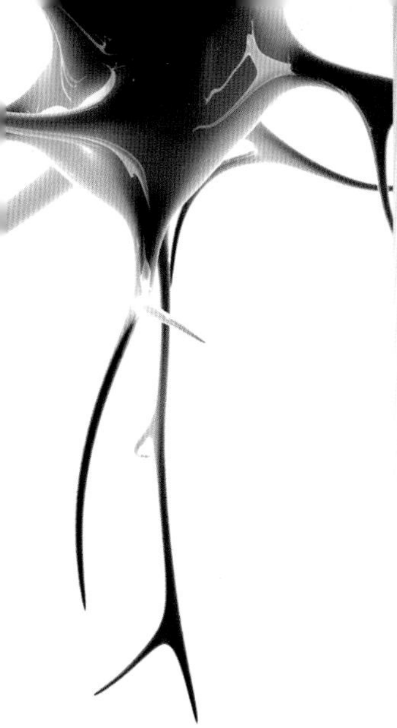

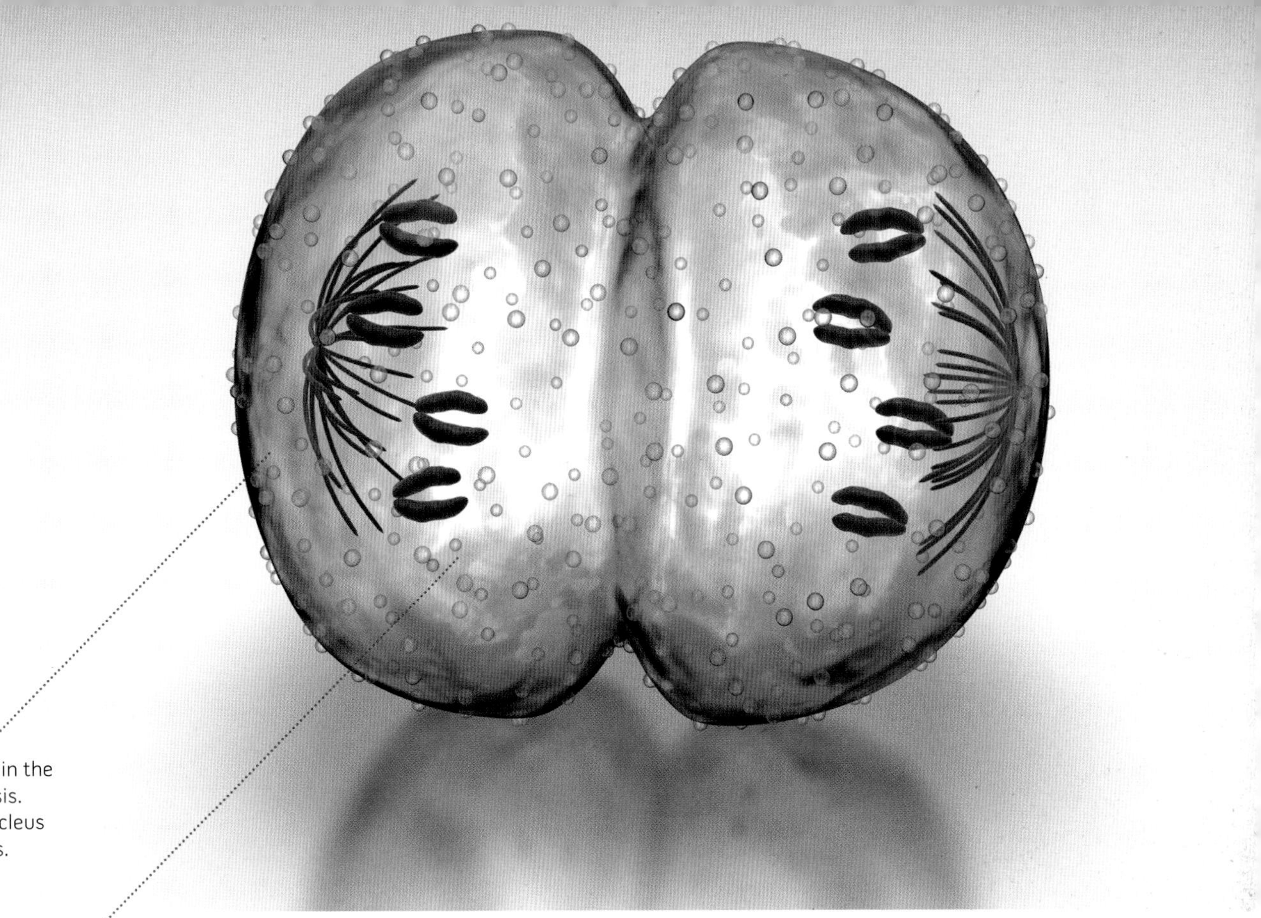

Mitosis ....
A conceptual illustration of a cell in the process of dividing through mitosis. The chromosomes in the cell's nucleus are divided into two identical sets.

1879 >

Mitosis

▲ IN THEORY

prolongations [dendrites]. The special character of these cells is the striking arrangement of their nerve filament [axon], which arises from the cell body but also very often from any thick, protoplasmic expansion [dendrite]. It immediately adopts a horizontal position, runs for a considerable distance through the molecular layer, and is supplied with numerous branches, some ascending and others descending."

Ramón y Cajal showed how information flows through neurons and that neurons are, without a doubt, autonomous units.

At first glance, mitosis and meiosis might sound like the same thing—and to an extent they are, in that both terms describe cell division. The difference, however, lies in why the cells are dividing. Meiosis is concerned only with sex cells. All other cells—those responsible for growth, development, and cellular repair, for example—divide by mitosis.

German cytologist Walther Flemming is credited with the discovery of mitosis in 1879. Flemming had developed a new staining technique that allowed him to identify and observe

chromosomes in greater detail than before. As a result he was able to observe cell division, considered one of the great scientific discoveries of all time.

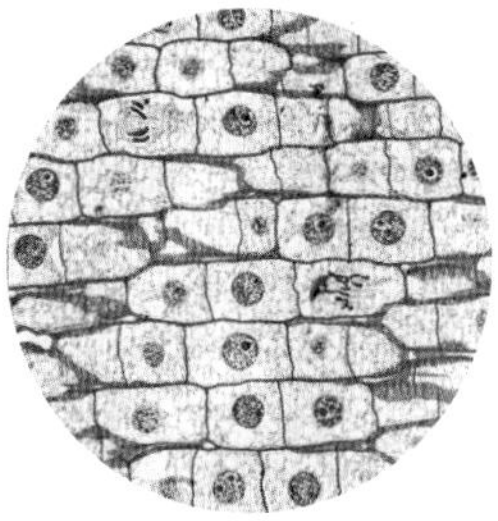

Diagram showing cellular mitosis

▼ Microscope *(p. 101)*

Mendelian Genetics
Research with pea plants, similar to the peas and pods shown here, led Gregor Mendel to develop seminal research that furthered the understanding of trait inheritance.

THE

ORIGIN OF SPECIES

BY MEANS OF NATURAL SELECTION,

OR THE

PRESERVATION OF FAVOURED RACES IN THE STRUGGLE
FOR LIFE.

BY CHARLES DARWIN, M.A., LL.D., F.R.S.

SIXTH EDITION, WITH ADDITIONS AND CORRECTIONS TO 1872.

(TWENTY-FOURTH THOUSAND.)

LONDON:
JOHN MURRAY, ALBEMARLE STREET.
1882.

The right of Translation is reserved.

The Origin of Species by Charles Darwin

1865 >

1859 >

Mendelian Genetics

▲ IN THEORY

Although the study of genetics began before Gregor Mendel, it is his innovative work with pea plants in the 1860s, published in his 1865 seminal paper "Experiments in Plant Hybridization," that furthered the understanding of inheritance. Mendel's work led to three principles that can be called rules for trait inheritance: (1) An organism's phenotype (what it looks like) cannot be used as a basis for determining genotype (its genetic structure). (2) The law of segregation states that genes retain their individuality and do not combine to form a new, blended trait. For example, breeding a black and white dog with a brown and white dog will produce some dogs that are black and white, and some that are brown and white—not brown, black, and white dogs. (3) And the law of independent assortment states that every gene has both dominant and recessive forms, which is why traits can skip generations.

Theory of Evolution

▲ IN THEORY

Perhaps no other scientific theory has sparked such debate and controversy as Charles Darwin's theory of evolution. Prior to Darwin, the long-standing belief was that the Earth was no more than about 6,000 years old and that species had no relationship to one another. Humans were considered distinct and superior to all other organisms.

In 1831 the British naturalist embarked on his now famous voyage on the H.M.S. *Beagle,* which took him around the world and allowed him to study a wide variety of flora and fauna. He returned to England in 1836 and began compiling his observations into his book *On the Origin of Species,* which was published in 1859. In this book Darwin presented his theory of natural selection, whereby organisms that are able to adapt successfully to their environment have more offspring than those who are less successful at adaptation. The traits of those better-adapted individuals will increase in the population, and over time the species will evolve in response to environmental factors. He had studied orchids, finches, and tortoises, and came to the sudden realization that "it is

Building On >

Chromosomes Carry Genes *(p. 230)*

Sociobiology *(p. 213)*

Punctuated Equilibrium *(p. 214)*

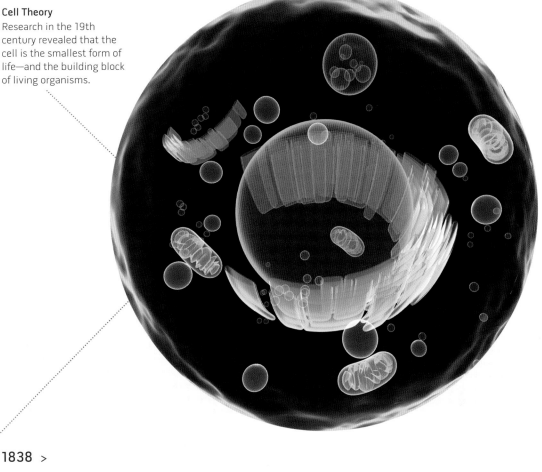

Cell Theory

Research in the 19th century revealed that the cell is the smallest form of life—and the building block of living organisms.

Theory of Evolution

Images of three elephants—two modern-day species at top and center, and an extinct species—reflect Darwin's theory of evolution, which posits that life is related and descended from common ancestors.

1838 >

Cell Theory

▲ IN THEORY

absurd to talk of one animal being higher than another." This flew in the face of religious doctrine whereby humankind was created in the image of God. And so the debate began.

Darwin and natural selection may be inextricably linked in the history books, but he was not the only one to propose a theory of evolution. British naturalist Alfred Russel Wallace was a colleague of Darwin's. Wallace presented his findings in a paper titled "On the Tendency of Varieties to Depart Indefinitely from the Original Type."

The observations of several scientists in the late 19th century led to what is called cell theory—the idea that cells are the building blocks of all life. When Germans Matthias Schleiden and Theodor Schwann presented their findings in 1838, it changed the study of biology forever. According to cell theory, the cell is the smallest form of life and all living things are composed of them. Furthermore, only preexisting cells can create cells; they do not arise spontaneously or come from some other source.

Schleiden based his research on the work of Scottish botanist Robert Brown, who had discovered the cell nucleus. It was Schleiden, however, who understood the true importance of the nucleus and its role in the development of the complete cell. At the same time, Schwann was studying animal cells, trying to work out a puzzle: Why did certain structures in animal and plant cells look so similar? It was Schleiden's observations of the nucleus that gave him the answer. Because both plant and animal cells contain this structure, Schleiden proposed that cells must be the building block of life. The primary difference lay in the fact that plant cells have rigid walls and animal cells do not. This is significant because it gives animal cells the malleability to take on various shapes. In addition, the chloroplasts in plant cells enable them to use sunlight for food in a process called photosynthesis. Animal cells do not have this ability and need to absorb nutrients from other cells in a process called phagocytosis.

Cell Nucleus

Conceptual artwork of a generic human cell. In the 1830s Scottish botanist Robert Brown noticed opaque spots within the cells of plants and sensed their significance. Research proved him right, and he is credited with the discovery of the nucleus.

Age of Earth

Ammonites were marine invertebrates that became extinct 65 million years ago. With this information, the rock layer in which evidence of the ammonites appears can be dated to a specific geological time period. Scientists have used information such as this to estimate the Earth's age at 4.5 billion years.

1833 >

1830 >

Cell Nucleus

▲ IN THEORY

While other scientists had observed the cell nucleus before Robert Brown, the Scottish botanist retains the honor of discovering this important cell structure since he made his findings public in 1833. He was studying the cells of plants—in particular, orchids—and noticed that they all contained an opaque spot within them. Brown sensed that this structure was more important than perhaps other scientists had believed. Further research would prove him right. Although Brown is credited with this discovery, he repeatedly stressed that the honor should be shared with fellow botanist Franz Bauer, who had noted observations similar to Brown's.

→← CONNECTION

Although the discovery of the cell nucleus was significant, the discoveries of other cell components are worthy of mention. Italian physician Camillo Golgi discovered organelles, which are subunits within a cell that have specialized functions. Scientists Albert von Kölliker, Richard Altmann, Otto Warburg, and Carl Benda discovered mitochondria, which are the "powerhouses" of cells. Discovery of cytoplasm—the fluid that supports the structure of cells—is credited to scientists Albert Claude, Christian de Duve, and George E. Palade.

Age of the Earth

▲ IN THEORY

When people first started to speculate about the age of the Earth, they looked to the Bible for an answer. Based on the account given in the Book of Genesis, the Earth was believed to be about 6,000 years old. This remained the prevailing belief until the 19th century, when the field of geology was becoming more accepted as a valid branch of science. Geologists were exploring the planet and making some astounding discoveries: That the Earth's strata showed that the land and the oceans and seas had literally traded places at times;

Building On >

Mammal Cloning (p. 209)

Cloning (p. 219)

French Naturalist
Jean-Baptiste Lamarck

PHILOSOPHIE ZOOLOGIQUE,

ou

EXPOSITION

es Considérations relatives à l'histoire naturelle des Animaux ; à la diversité de leur organisation et des facultés qu'ils en obtiennent ; aux causes physiques qui maintiennent en eux la vie et donnent lieu aux mouvemens qu'ils exécutent ; enfin , à celles qui produisent , les unes le senti-ment , et les autres l'intelligence de ceux qui en sont doués ;

PAR J.-B.-P.-A. LAMARCK,

Professeur de Zoologie au Muséum d'Histoire Naturelle , Membre de l'Institut de France et de la Légion d'Honneur , de la Société Phi-lomatique de Paris , de celle des Naturalistes de Moscou , Membre correspondant de l'Académie Royale des Sciences de Munich , de la Société des Amis de la Nature de Berlin , de la Société Médicale d'Emulation de Bordeaux , de celle d'Agriculture, Sciences et Arts de Strasbourg , de celle d'Agriculture du département de l'Oise , de celle d'Agriculture de Lyon , Associé libre de la Société des Pharmaciens de Paris , etc.

Lamarck's 1809 *Philosophie Zoologique*, later disproved.

1809 >

Breakthroughs continue on page 242

Lamarckian Inheritance

▲ IN THEORY

that the surface of the Earth could be transformed by geologic events like earthquakes and volcanoes; and that forces such as water erosion, for example, could change the Earth as well, just more slowly. The age of the Earth clearly needed to be looked at again in light of such observations.

Scientists like James Ussher and Baron Georges Cuvier attempted to use empiricism to reason their way to an answer. The problem was that they still based their reasoning on a biblical framework. In 1830 geologists Charles Lyell and James Hutton

were among the first to take a different track. Rather than attributing evidence for major geological changes to onetime cataclysmic events in the Bible (like Noah's Flood), Lyell and Hutton reasoned that changes on the face of the Earth were the result of naturally occurring processes that were present throughout the history of the planet. Thus the age of the Earth had to be greater than 6,000 years. Scientists today estimate the age of the Earth to be around 4.5 billion years.

In 1809 French naturalist Jean-Baptiste Lamarck published a book, *Philosophie Zoologique*, in which he outlined his theories of evolution. According to Lamarckian inheritance, characteristics that an organism inherits during its lifetime could be passed on to its offspring. Lamarck pointed to the giraffe as a prime example of his theory. According to Lamarck, early giraffes stretched their necks in order to reach leaves high up in trees. Successive generations of giraffes continued to stretch their necks, resulting in the long-

necked creatures of today. German biologist August Weismann successfully disproved this theory in an experiment where he chopped off the tails of 20 generations of mice. Not one gave birth to tailless offspring.

Radioactive Dating *(p. 230)*

Genetically Modified Organisms

Although genetically modified organisms have been around for a while (the first experiments were conducted in 1978), scientists are just now gaining a better understanding of how these organisms may affect peoples' lives. A genetically engineered organism is created using recombinant DNA technology, in which DNA molecules from different sources are combined into one molecule to create a new set of genes. This modified DNA is inserted into an organism, giving it genes that nature did not.

Genetically modified organisms are used in biological and medical research, the production of pharmaceutical drugs, gene therapy, and agriculture. The general public is perhaps most familiar with genetically modified organisms in the form of crops such as corn that are altered to be "naturally" resistant to pests and herbicides while producing the highest yield possible. However, bacteria were the first organisms to be genetically modified due to their simple structure. These bacteria are now used for several purposes: to produce insulin protein to treat diabetes, as clotting factors to treat hemophilia, and as human growth hormones to treat various forms of dwarfism, to cite three examples.

It comes as no surprise that the use of genetically modified organisms has sparked significant controversy. Some see the technology as unacceptable meddling with biological states or processes that have naturally evolved over long periods, while others are concerned about the limitations of modern science to grasp fully all of the potential negative ramifications of genetic manipulation. To date, no studies have shown a documented link between adverse health effects and the consumption of genetically modified foods; yet environmental groups in many countries, especially those of the European Union, still discourage consumption of genetically modified foods by claiming these foods are unnatural and unsafe. Clearly more research is needed before it is known for certain whether the benefits of this technology outweigh the risks.

1977

With genome sequencing technologies, scientists can glimpse the entire genomes of the organisms they wish to modify. *See page 212*

1973

Genetic engineering forms the foundation for the genetic modification of organisms. *See page 214*

1961, 1953

Genetically modified organisms would not be possible without the cracking of the genetic code and the discovery of the structure of DNA. *See pages 221, 223*

Borrowing a Glow

Researchers imported the gene for fluorescence from a jellyfish into a virus, then introduced the virus into a mouse egg, thus infusing the gene into mouse DNA. The result: a mouse that glows in the dark.

What's the Use?

Glowing mice may interest cats, but this experiment has more profound implications. Using the same technique, doctors may soon tag cancer cells in a patient's body, then track their growth and movement as never before.

1944, 1910

The discoveries of DNA as genetic material and chromosomes as gene carriers were crucial early steps in the science of genetics. *See pages 224, 230*

From 1804 back to 350 B.C. >

Alexander von Humboldt

1804 >

[PROFILE]

Alexander von Humboldt (1769-1859), considered the father of modern geology, was called "the greatest scientific traveler who ever lived" by Charles Darwin. Von Humboldt traversed the globe with men like Abraham Gottlob Werner, a famous geologist, and Georg Forster, Captain James Cook's scientific illustrator. Von Humboldt wrote 30 volumes about his field studies, *Voyages de Humboldt et Bonpland*. In addition to his idea that biology and geology are interconnected, von Humboldt is known for describing the connection between volcanoes and earthquakes; for naming the Jurassic period; and for advancing the understanding of stratigraphy, geology, and geomorphology.

Biogeography

▲ IN THEORY

The field of biogeography, the study of the connections between where species are located and how they are distributed, got its start with an extensive 1804 work by scientific traveler Alexander von Humboldt. The goal of biogeography is to understand why species live where they do, what makes a species thrive better in some areas rather than others, and why some species are restricted to very specific geographic ranges. Von Humboldt came up with this theory while studying plants in Central and South

Building On >

Biogeography

An antique map of the world with the hemispheres laid flat. Biogeography established for the first time a link between a hemisphere or region's geography and its plants and animals.

Photosynthesis

The spherical structures inside the magnified green alga are chloroplasts, the site of photosynthesis, which turns sunlight into energy.

1804 >

Photosynthesis

▲ IN THEORY

America. He recorded conditions surrounding the plants—including temperature, barometric pressure, geomagnetism, and latitude and longitude. Based on this work, von Humboldt was able to document a clear link between a region's geography and its plants and animals.

Swiss chemist and plant physiologist Nicolas-Théodore de Saussure is credited with discovering photosynthesis, although he was not the first, nor the last, to explore the phenomenon of how plants get their food. In the 1600s Flemish scientist Jan Baptista van Helmont proposed that water was the source of life for plants. English naturalist John Woodward refuted van Helmont's hypothesis, showing that plants took in water but released most of it back into the atmosphere. He grew a willow tree inside a glass case and found that while the tree gained mass, the soil lost very little, an observation he explained by suggesting that water made up the difference.

English chemist and theologian Joseph Priestley devised an experiment that showed that gases, namely oxygen and hydrogen, are important to photosynthesis as well. He showed that while a candle inside a glass case eventually extinguished itself, it continued burning if accompanied by a growing mint plant.

Dutch scientist Jan Ingenhousz showed that light was essential for a plant to make its own food. De Saussure repeated van Helmont's experiments in 1804 and showed that the carbon in plants comes from carbon dioxide and the hydrogen from water. The full dimensions of the chemical exchange were eventually understood as photosynthesis, but it would be 40 more years before scientist Julius Robert von Mayer could prove that energy from the sun, captured by plants, played an essential role in the process.

Continental Drift *(p. 227)*

Cell Theory *(p. 237)*

Oxygen and Carbon Dioxide *(p. 245)*

Extinction

The dodo bird became extinct in the 17th century. Human activity played a role in the bird's fate. People destroyed the forests where the birds lived, and introduced dogs, cats, and pigs, which preyed on the flightless creatures.

1796 >

1785 >

Extinction

▲ IN THEORY

French nationalist and geologist Baron Georges Cuvier is credited with hypothesizing and proving that extinction not only could have happened but also had to have happened. He wrote: "Why has not anyone seen that fossils alone gave birth to a theory about the formation of the earth, that without them, no one would have ever dreamed that there were successive epochs in the formation of the globe?"

In 1796 some believed fossils to be the bones of animals that no longer existed. Others claimed that God, having created the Earth and all its creatures, would never cause any of them to vanish from the face of the Earth. Instead fossils were the bones of living species, and the similarities between woolly mammoths and African elephants, for example, were the result of the beasts moving from a colder climate to a warmer one.

Cuvier disproved both viewpoints by showing that the bones of ancient elephants and cats were essentially no different from their modern counterparts, yet there were enough sufficient differences in anatomy that these creatures had to be distinct species. The giant ground sloth, for example, was not just an older version of the South American sloth; it was a different species of sloth that no longer existed. Cuvier proposed that the Earth was much older than was thought at the time, that it had been relatively stable throughout much of its history, and that periodic "revolutions" caused some species to die out and become extinct.

Uniformitarianism

▲ IN THEORY

In his 1785 work, *Theory of the Earth,* Scottish naturalist James Hutton put forth a hypothesis that came to be known as uniformitarianism. It can be summed up in eight words: "The present is the key to the past." It assumes that the geological processes observed today are the same processes, occurring at the same rate, as processes in the Earth's distant past—and these will be the same processes occurring in the Earth's future. Thus geological events in the Earth's past can be explained by looking at the current state

Building On >

Fossils *(p. 247)*

Uniformitarianism

A vertical rock stratum fails to conform with younger, overlying horizontal layers—thus forming a structure known as an unconformity, or a discontinuity in the geological record. This observation, first made in 1787 by geologist James Hutton, was an important step in understanding the history of the Earth.

Oxygen and Carbon Dioxide

Joseph Priestley used a mouse, jar, and mint to discover the lifesaving link between the gases people and plants take in and release.

Scottish geologist James Hutton, circa 1776

1772 >

Oxygen and Carbon Dioxide

of the planet and deriving an explanation based on observation. Uniformitarianism has since been combined with catastrophism in order to explain fossils that occur in multiple strata, missing and misplaced layers in the Earth's crust, and "misplaced" fossils—imprints located in strata out of sync with the defined geologic timetable.

→← CONNECTION

Although uniformitarianism has since been disproved as the sole theory of explaining the Earth's landscape (scientists now know geological events can be both sudden and gradual), it influenced not only the present-day understanding of geology and geography but also other disciplines including paleontology, plate tectonics, and biology. Scholars in these and other fields have incorporated James Hutton's work into their theories. In fact, Hutton's work influenced Charles Lyell, who in turn influenced Charles Darwin.

▲ IN THEORY

In 1774 English chemist and theologian Joseph Priestley conducted a famous experiment in which he proved that plants take in a gas that animals give off (carbon dioxide) and that plants give off a gas that animals take in (oxygen).

Priestley took a mouse and placed it in an enclosed glass container until the mouse collapsed. When he put a plant in the container with the mouse, the mouse survived, thereby proving that the plant was producing something that enabled the mouse to live. Priestley did not know that the substances were oxygen and carbon dioxide, per se, but, in fact, they were the substances that he had discovered.

Theory of Evolution *(p. 236)*

Endosymbiotic Theory *(p. 218)*

Krebs Cycle *(p. 224)*

Photosynthesis *(p. 243)*

Oxygen *(p. 196)*

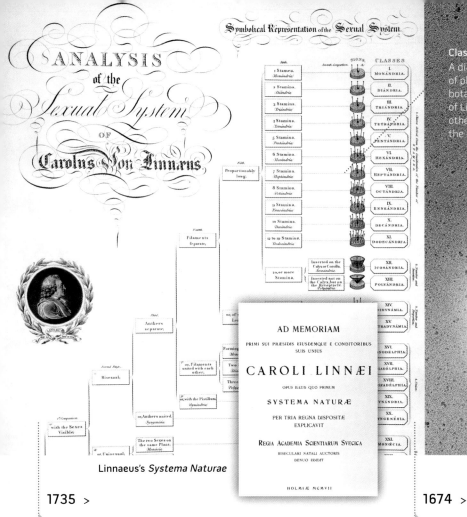

Linnaeus's *Systema Naturae*

Classification of Species
A diagram lists the classification of plants as devised by Swedish botanist Carl Linnaeus. A portrait of Linnaeus is at left. This, and other works by Linnaeus, founded the modern science of taxonomy.

1735 >

1674 >

Classification of Species

▲ IN THEORY

Carl Linnaeus, the father of taxonomy, created a system in 1735 of ranking, classifying, and ordering all living things. Scientists still use the system nearly 300 years later, albeit with modifications. Linnaeus published his system in a work titled *Systema Naturae*, which was based on years of traveling, gathering and studying plants, and refining his system. He classified plants based on the number and arrangement of reproductive organs, which was a highly controversial stance in his day (and, as it turns out, not entirely accurate). His system is especially noteworthy for the consistent way in which it applied scientific names to organisms. Prior to Linnaeus, scientific naming was inconsistent, almost haphazard, and the same organism could have more than one name. Linnaeus simplified the approach by designating a Latin name for an organism's genus and a second "shorthand" name for the species. Linnaeus was so consistent in his application of this naming scheme that organisms named prior to his *Systema Naturae* are considered invalid.

Microbiology

▲ IN THEORY

Known as the father of microscopy because of his advances in the design of microscopes, Anton van Leeuwenhoek is noted for his observations of protozoa and bacteria. The Dutch naturalist was the first to observe and document these organisms in 1674, and his findings paved the way for the field of microbiology and opened a whole new world to the scientists of his day. In addition to protozoa and bacteria, Leeuwenhoek observed yeast cells, blood cells, sperm cells, and more. A man possessing an innate, insatiable curiosity, he wrote in 1716, "[M]y work . . . was not pursued in order to gain the praise I now enjoy, but chiefly from a craving after knowledge . . . whenever I found out anything remarkable, I have thought it my duty to put down my discovery on paper, so that all ingenious people might be informed thereof."

Building On > Classification of Animals (p. 249)

Archaea (p. 211)

Microscope (p. 101)

Microbiology

Anton van Leeuwenhoek observed the presence of human sperm cells as well as yeast and blood cells through microscopes he had devised and was later recognized as the father of microscopy.

Cells

Cork seen under a microscope reveals rectangular-shaped cells, named by Robert Hooke because they reminded him of monks' quarters. Hooke prepared the cork specimen by making thin slices with a razor blade, thus inventing the technique of sectioning.

A fossil of a tiger shark tooth

1669 >

1665 >

Fossils

▲ IN THEORY

Nicholas Steno is noted for his theory of fossil formation in rock layers, which he put forth in his 1669 work *Prodromus*. Steno's theory was crucial to the development of modern geology, and his ideas are still very much in use today. When examining a shark's teeth, the Danish pioneer in geology was struck by how similar they looked to objects found in rocks known as "tongue stones." He correctly assumed that the objects that looked like rocks were not rocks after all, but actual sharks' teeth that had somehow become embedded in rock. But how? He surmised that what was solid rock had once been liquid. When an item such as a shark's tooth is deposited in the liquid and that liquid hardens, it takes the shape of the item and produces a fossil.

Cells

▲ IN THEORY

In 1665, while looking at thin slivers of cork through a microscope, Robert Hooke noticed small holes, or what he coined "cells." The Englishman later said that the cavities reminded him of monks' quarters; hence the name. He believed these cells had once been containers for "noble juices" or "fibrous threads" necessary for the cork tree's survival. In addition, Hooke speculated—as did many of his colleagues at the time—that only plants possessed cells. Apparently it had not yet occurred to anyone to look at animal cells through a microscope. Hooke included drawings of the cells he observed in his book *Micrographia*. He also included instructions for constructing a microscope like the one he used, presumably so that readers could make the same observations. Not content to just observe cells, Hooke calculated how many might be contained in a cubic inch. His result: 1,259,712,000 squared.

Robert Hooke

[PROFILE]

English polymath Robert Hooke (1635-1703) is best known for coining the term "cell." He was widely read and well versed in an array of fields, including physics, astronomy, biology, geology, architecture, and naval technology. He knew Anton van Leeuwenhoek, Isaac Newton, Christopher Wren, and Robert Boyle. Hooke's most enduring work is perhaps *Micrographia*, published in 1665, in which he described his findings using a microscope and illumination system that he had devised. While some mocked Hooke for the lavish detail he paid to documenting his microscopic observations, one reader called *Micrographia* "the most ingenious book that I ever read in my life."

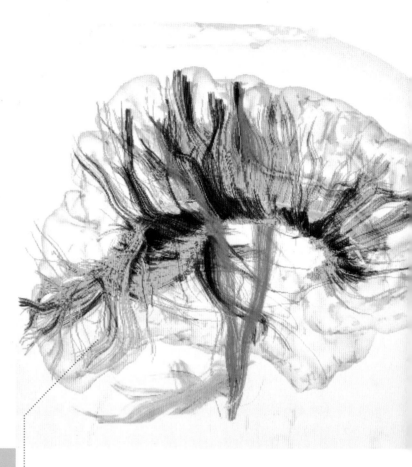

1664 >

Localization of Brain Function

▲ IN THEORY

Today, scientists know that different parts of the brain are responsible for different functions—this is called localization of brain function. The man responsible for initiating study in this field is Thomas Willis, considered the father of neurology. The English doctor's work greatly aided the understanding of anatomy, neurology, physiology, and psychiatry. Several different anatomical parts are named after him, the most well known of which is the Circle of Willis, a ring of arteries at the base of the brain that acts as a communication network.

In his 1664 work *Cerebri Anatome*, Willis described in elaborate, detailed fashion the anatomy of the brain and the nervous system. Others had attempted this prior to Willis, though none had done it in such a meticulous fashion and none had attempted to match function with form. Among the structures Willis identified and named in the brain are the vagus nerve, the cranial nerves, the corpus striatum, and the optic thalamus. Brain pathologies that Willis identified

Localization of Brain Functions

A MRI scan reveals a normal human head and brain. Before today's high-powered scanning machines, other methods were employed to decipher the brain. Thomas Willis used dissections—both human autopsies and animal necroscopies—in combination with observations of living patients.

Classification of Animals

Historical drawing of a classification of animal species as devised by French naturalist Georges Cuvier in the early 19th century. Hundreds of years earlier, Aristotle had introduced a classification system in which he categorized organisms by those with red blood and those without.

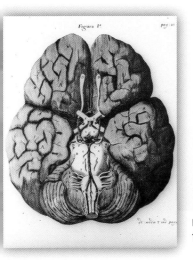

Drawing of a human cranium from *Cerebri Anatome*

350 B.C. **>**

Classification of Animals

→← CONNECTION　　▲ IN THEORY

include diabetes mellitus (called Willis's disease for a long time), myasthenia gravis, akathisia (restless legs syndrome), and paracusis Willisii (a condition in which a deaf person's hearing improves when subjected to noise).

Willis had performed countless dissections in his pursuit of this work—both human autopsies and animal necroscopies—which he combined with his observations of living patients. In the end, he was searching for proof of the soul; *Cerebri Anatome* can be looked at as a philosophical work just as much as a medical treatise.

Scientists who used Thomas Willis's groundbreaking work *Cerebri Anatome* as a jumping-off point gained a better understanding of the brain. In the early 19th century German Franz Joseph Gall put forth his theory of phrenology, which linked mental characteristics to skull shape. In 1861 Paul Broca, of France, proved a link between speech and the left frontal lobe. Less than a decade later German anatomist Gustav Fritsch and associate J. L. Hitzig conducted experiments in which specific parts of the brain were stimulated with electricity.

Around 350 B.C. Aristotle introduced a classification system in which he divided organisms into those with red blood and those without red blood, which essentially boiled down to vertebrates and invertebrates. Aristotle included mammals, birds, reptiles and amphibians, fishes, and whales in the vertebrate group. He put cephalopods (octopus, squid), crustaceans, insects (which included spiders, scorpions, and centipedes), shelled animals (mollusks and echinoderms), and zoophytes (animals that have plantlike

forms) in the invertebrate group. From there, animals with similar characteristics were grouped into genera and from there into species based on distinguishing characteristics.

Aristotle's system reflected his hierarchical view of life. He believed that humans sat at the top of the hierarchy and all other creatures occupied the lower echelons. This system also made use of binomial definition, with one name for an organism's genus and another for its species. This system was not applied as a consistent methodology until the 1700s.

Functional Mapping of the Brain (p. 226)

Classification of Species (p. 246)

Geoengineering

Counteracting the effects of global climate change by large-scale engineering of the Earth's environment may sound like the plot of a Hollywood movie, but scientists are taking this idea quite seriously. Some geoengineering techniques are based on carbon sequestration, including the reduction of greenhouse gases in the atmosphere by capturing carbon dioxide in the air or deliberately depositing iron in the oceans to lock up carbon dioxide in the seabed.

Other proposed projects include solar radiation management, which is designed to reduce the amount of sunlight hitting the Earth. This could be done any number of ways: Using pale-colored roofing and paving materials (called cool roofs), using fine seawater spray to whiten clouds and increase cloud reflectivity, obstructing solar radiation with space-based mirrors or other structures, or cloud seeding. The use of vertical ocean pipes to mix cooler deep water and warmer surface water is another idea on the horizon. Some proponents—including Bill Gates,

chairman of Microsoft—believe this technology could also be used to disrupt hurricanes. Efforts are also under way to counteract climate change by preventing further loss of Arctic sea ice. Many believe that this project is vital, given the role of Arctic sea ice in maintaining the Earth's reflectivity and in keeping methane, a greenhouse gas like carbon dioxide, locked up in permafrost.

Several of these techniques have side effects, and so far no large-scale geoengineering projects are in progress. Some limited tree planting and cool roof projects are under way, and ocean iron fertilization is at an advanced stage of research. Scientists have started field research into sulfur aerosols, which when shot into the stratosphere by volcanic eruptions cause the planet to cool temporarily. Reviews of geoengineering techniques emphasize that geoengineering is not a substitute for emission control. Scientists must continue to develop ways to reduce greenhouse emissions in general.

Cool Shades

One geoengineering proposal to combat global warming is to devise a sun shield for Earth. It might consist of one vast sunshade or a huge array of reflective particles; the shield would emulate the global cooling experienced after a major volcano eruption.

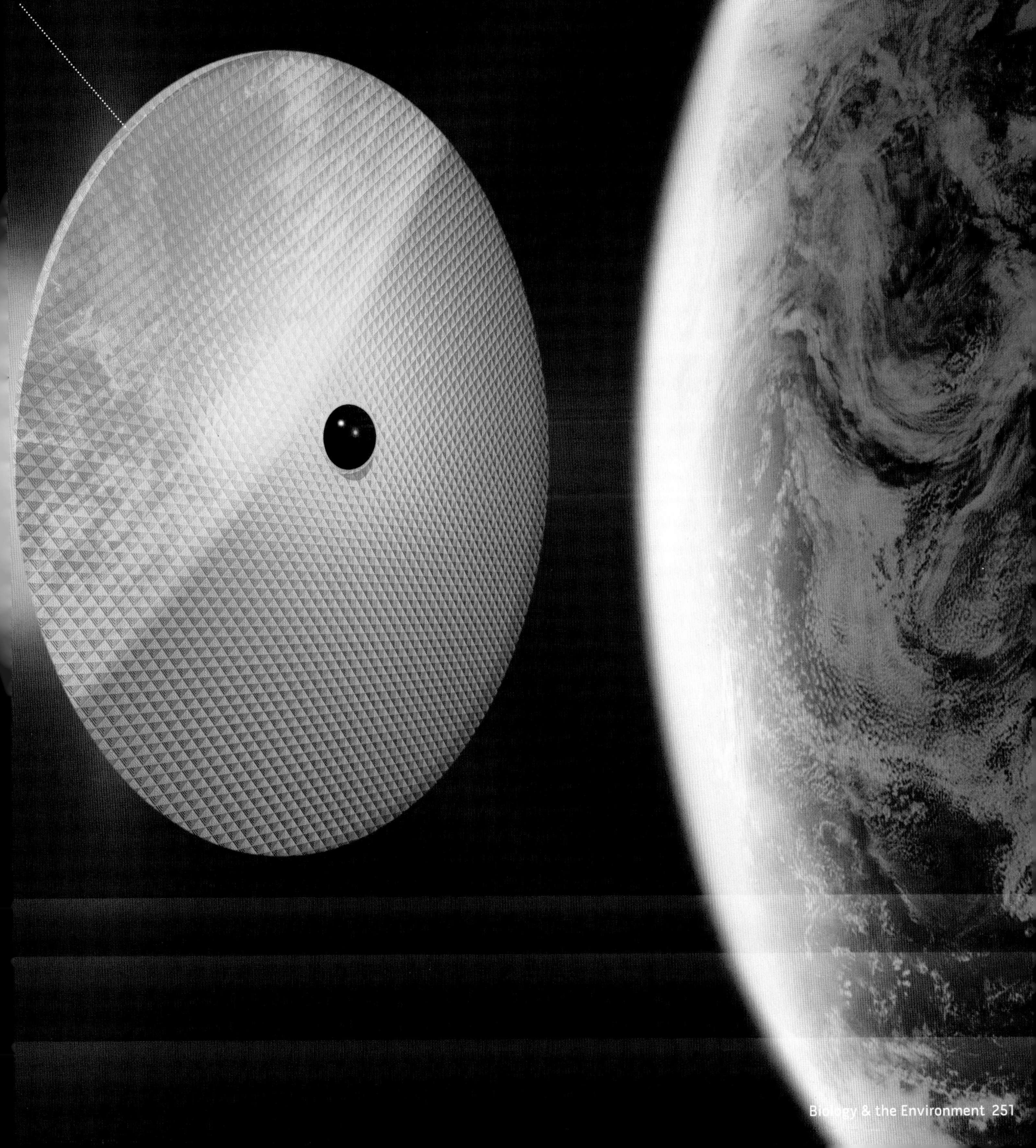

06

Transportation & Space Exploration

BIG IDEAS

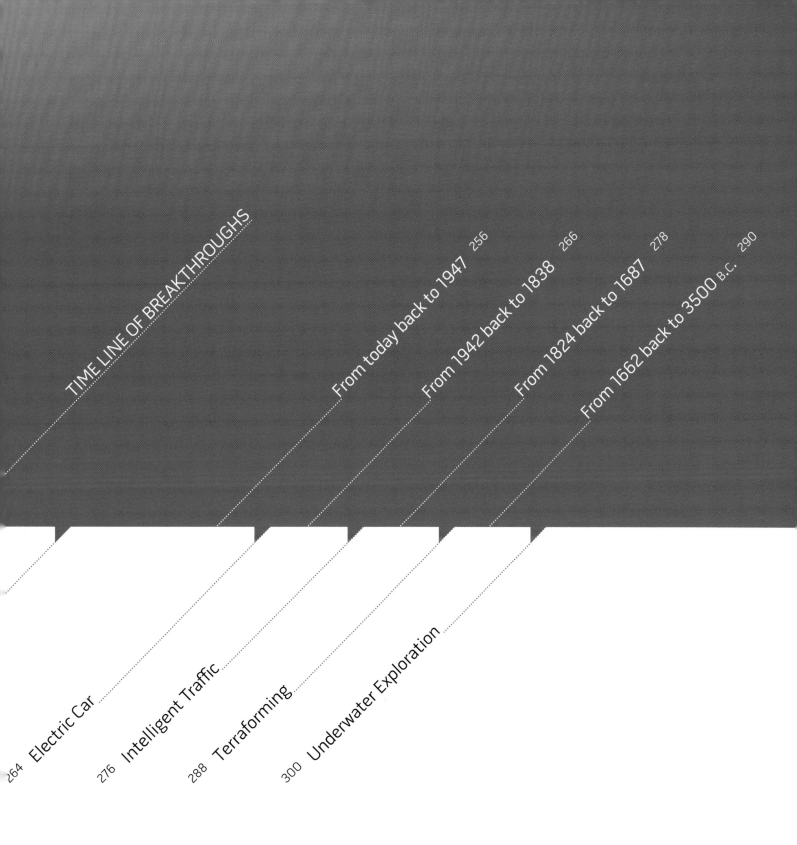

TIME LINE OF BREAKTHROUGHS

INTRODUCTION

Beyond the Wheel

In about 5,500 years—a relatively short period of time in the history of humankind—human beings have gone from inventing the wheel to devising innovative methods of transportation to exploring space with both manned and unmanned vehicles. What were the driving forces behind the development of transportation technologies? What were the big ideas that allowed people to travel by road, by sea, and by air? What technologies are on the horizon?

The wheel and the ship are among the oldest transportation technologies still in use. Of course, how wheels are used in vehicles has changed over the course of thousands of years. No longer are chariots used for getting around, or in warfare for that matter. The bicycle, however, is nearly 200 years old, and the gasoline-powered automobile, patented toward the end of the 19th century by Karl Benz, remains a dominant mode of transportation. The hybrid car was invented nearly four decades ago, and the electric car is a significant technology on the horizon. Researchers are also beginning to create intelligent transportation systems by integrating information and communication technologies into vehicles, roadways, and traffic control systems.

Ships have been around since the ancient world, but they had to rely on manpower or wind for propulsion until Scottish engineer William Symington invented the first practical steamboat, the *Charlotte Dundas*, in the early 19th century. The first submarine—a watertight submersible vehicle powered by men who rowed from its inside—was built in 1620; more than three centuries later the United States launched the *Nautilus*, the world's first nuclear-powered submarine. Researchers are still creating new submersible vehicles to explore the final frontier on the Earth: the depths of the oceans.

Mathematicians and scientists like Archimedes, Robert Boyle, Isaac Newton, Daniel Bernoulli, George Cayley, and Nicolas Léonard Sadi Carnot helped advance transportation technology through their contributions to physics, fluid mechanics, aerodynamics, thermodynamics, and other fields. As a result of their discoveries, scientists can create efficient engines, understand the principles of heavier-than-air flight, and compute the trajectories of rockets and the orbits of satellites.

More than 1,000 years ago Muslim polymath Abbas Ibn Firnas achieved heavier-than-air flight with a glider, but it was not until the 20th century that flight really took off. The Wright brothers successfully tested their powered aircraft in 1903. In 1926 Robert Goddard's liquid-fuel rocket made spaceflight a possibility. By mid-20th century jet engines had been invented and pilot Chuck Yeager in 1947 broke the sound barrier in the Bell X-1 aircraft. Then in the span of about 12 years—from 1957 to 1969—the Soviet Union launched Sputnik and put the first man into space, and the U.S. answered by landing men on the moon during the Apollo 11 missions. The first reusable spacecraft, the space shuttle *Columbia*, was launched in the 1980s; in 2004 *SpaceShipOne* completed the first privately manned spaceflight. There is a long way to go, but far on the horizon is the possibility of "terraforming" a neighboring planet—perhaps Mars—with the goal of making it habitable for humans.

Private Manned Spacecraft

SpaceShipOne, designed as the first commercial spacecraft, glides after being released at high altitude from the underside of its carrier craft. After release it fires its rocket to ascend into space.

From today back to 1947 >

2004 >

1981 >

Private Manned Spacecraft

● IN USE

Space travel is no longer confined to the realm of government entities with huge budgets. In 2004 *SpaceShipOne* became the first privately manned craft to go into space, garnering the $10,000,000 Ansari X PRIZE. Launched by the X PRIZE Foundation, the prize was to be awarded to a private company or person who could successfully launch a manned space mission twice in two weeks, placing three occupants at least 100 kilometers (about 62 miles) above the surface of the Earth. In addition, the spacecraft had to be reusable—or at least the design had to be. The X PRIZE competition was modeled on contests that took place during the early days of flight. The flight of *SpaceShipOne* echoed Charles Lindbergh's famous 1927 flight from New York to Paris, for which he won the $25,000 Orteig Prize and ushered in the modern era of commercial air travel.

So how soon will it be before people can book a trip to space? Sir Richard Branson's Virgin Galactic is taking reservations now (tickets cost $200,000), although an exact date has not been set for the first flight.

Shuttle Program

● IN USE

Prior to the launch of the space shuttle *Columbia* in 1981—the first space shuttle to successfully enter Earth's orbit—spacecraft were not reusable. Previous forays into manned spaceflight, which were carried out by various ships from the Apollo fleet, involved abandoning large sections of the spacecraft. In many cases the nose cone, which carried the astronauts, was the only part that made it back to Earth. The rest was left behind to float in space as junk. With *Columbia*, only the fuel tank did not return with the ship.

Building On >

Human Spaceflight (p. 260)

Space Shuttle *Columbia*

Viking Program
Mosaic of images made by the
Viking Orbiter centers on the Valles
Marineris canyons on Mars. A lander,
part of the same space vehicle,
explored the planet's surface.

1975 >

Viking Program

● IN USE

→← CONNECTION

In addition to conducting experiments, *Columbia* and its sister shuttles *Atlantis*, *Challenger*, *Discovery*, and *Endeavour* were designed to deliver payloads into space. (There were originally five ships, with two still remaining— *Challenger* exploded shortly after leaving the launchpad on January 28, 1986, and *Columbia* broke up on reentry on January 16, 2003.) Payloads consisted of necessary materials and supplies for the International Space Station satellites that were released into orbit around the Earth.

On August 20, 1975, Viking 1 was launched into space; ten months later, it became the first spacecraft to land successfully on Mars. The launch of Viking 2 followed on September 9, 1975. These missions enabled scientists to explore the Martian surface, allowing them to collect samples, gather data on the composition of the Martian atmosphere, and analyze evidence in a search for signs of past and present life. Based on evidence from the missions, scientists concluded that although life may have existed on Mars in the past (water

certainly did, and it is one of the essential requirements for life) Mars today is an icy desert planet with long-dormant volcanoes.

Technologies used in the Viking program had proved so successful they were implemented in missions that followed. Viking technology has been used to send unmanned missions to explore planets other than Mars: Magellan was sent to Venus, and Galileo was sent to Jupiter. The Cassini-Huygens probe is currently in orbit around Saturn. Until scientists figure out a way to overcome the distances necessary to send humans to these planets, these unmanned explorers are the next best thing.

◥ **Apollo 11** *(p. 259)*

◥ **Human Spaceflight** *(p. 260)*

◥ **Telescope** *(p. 139)*

Victor Wouk

Known as the father of the hybrid car, Victor Wouk (1919-2005) was instrumental in the development of the hybrid—although his work has nearly been forgotten by history. After receiving a doctorate in electrical engineering from the California Institute of Technology, the American scientist went on to work for prestigious companies like Westinghouse, where he was involved in designing centrifuges that were used in the uranium-purification process by the Manhattan Project. His brother, novelist Herman Wouk, supposedly based the character Palmer Kirby on Victor in *War and Remembrance*; in the book Kirby was involved in the development of the atom bomb.

1972 >

Hybrid Vehicle

● IN USE

Some people may think the Toyota Prius was the first hybrid vehicle to run on both gas and electricity. Not so. That honor belongs to the hybrid Buick Skylark, which was conceived of by Victor Wouk in 1972. The Environmental Protection Agency refused to approve the vehicle even though it met the clean air emissions standards of the time.

Wouk began his work on this venture in 1962, when Russell Feldman, one of the founders of Motorola, asked him to explore the possibilities presented by a solely electric car. After many studies and tests, Wouk concluded that purely electric cars were not a viable commercial venture. (In the 1970s that was likely true.) Instead Wouk proposed a hybrid vehicle that combined the advantages of an electric vehicle—namely, low emissions—with the power of a gasoline-driven vehicle.

◤ Automobile (p. 270)

◤ Large-scale Electrical Supply Network (p. 46)

◤ Electricity (p. 55)

◤ Wheel (p. 299)

Hybrid Vehicle
Victor Wouk stands beside his 1972 hybrid Buick Skylark at the EPA test site in 1974.

Apollo 11
Buzz Aldrin walks on the moon in 1969, as fellow astronaut Neil Armstrong and the Apollo 11 lunar module are reflected in his visor. The two were the first humans to reach the lunar surface.

1969 >

Apollo II

● IN USE

On July 20, 1969, humans successfully landed on the moon. Astronaut Neil Armstrong, the first to set foot on the celestial body, uttered his famous phrase, "That's one small step for [a] man, one giant leap for mankind." During their time on the moon, Neil Armstrong and fellow crew member Buzz Aldrin collected 47 pounds of material for analysis.

There were six lunar missions in the Apollo program. Aside from Apollo 11, the one that most people remember is the ill-fated Apollo 13 mission, during which a malfunction on the ship nearly caused the crew to be stranded in space. Apollo 1 never made it off the launchpad when a fire broke out in the command module, killing the three astronauts on board. Apollo missions 7 through 10 were never supposed to land on the moon; instead they orbited it, testing the command and lunar modules used by the other missions.

The missions that did make it to the moon conducted experiments on solar wind, soil, meteoroids, seismic activity, and heat flow. These missions were significant not only for their historical importance but also for the data they gathered, which enabled scientists to speculate about the moon's formation and its composition.

Liftoff of Apollo 11, Kennedy Space Center

Human Spaceflight (p. 260)

Magnetic Levitation Transportation
A magnetic levitation train travels on its elevated track. Proposed in 1966 the fuel-less transportation system was first installed at Birmingham, England, in 1984.

Commemorative s[...]
honoring Ga[...]

1966 >

1961 >

Magnetic Levitation Transportation

Human Spaceflight

● IN USE

● IN USE

Magnetic levitation transportation might make some think of a high-tech science-fiction concept. However, patents for these devices were issued as early as 1907, with further developments in the 1940s and 1950s. In 1966 James Powell and Gordon Danby proposed the first formal modern system. Called "maglev" for short, these incredibly energy-efficient vehicles work using the principle of magnetic repulsion: All magnets have positive and negative poles, which repel each other, and the force this creates is used to support the vehicle. Other

magnets propel it along a track.

The advantages of maglev transportation, according to Powell and Danby, are numerous: "It moves passengers and freight at much higher speed and lower cost, using less energy. . . . The vehicles do not physically contact the guideway, do not need engines, and do not burn fuel." In addition, there are safety advantages when compared to automobile highway systems. Speed and the intervals between maglev vehicles are automatically controlled; thus crashes are practically impossible. Also, unlike

a traditional railway crossing, maglev tracks are elevated. Hence there is no chance of a car or truck colliding with one of the trains.

The idea has yet to take off in the United States. Japan, China, and Germany, however, have eagerly embraced the concept. The first commercial application of magnetic levitation occurred in Birmingham, England, in 1984. In fact, this maglev ran between the Birmingham railway and airport until 1995. Another system with which many people are familiar is the Shanghai Maglev Train in China.

The United States may have been the first to put a man on the moon, but it was not the first to put a man into space. That distinction goes to the Soviet Union. On April 12, 1961, Yuri Gagarin made a 108-minute orbital flight at a height of 188 miles as part of the Vostok 1 mission. Although this was considered a significant political victory for the Soviet Union, the United States followed with a manned foray into space a month later. On May 5, 1961, Alan Shepard became the first American to go into space.

Building On >

▼ **Superconductivity** (p. 176)

Human Spaceflight
Yuri Gagarin, first man to travel in space, prepares for launch on Soviet Vostok 1. His craft operated automatically because of uncertainties about human functions beyond the atmosphere.

Sputnik I
Sputnik I, the first artificial satellite placed in orbit around the earth, was 23 inches in diameter and was launched by the Soviet Union.

1957 >

Sputnik I

● IN USE

Although Gagarin could have controlled his spacecraft manually, it was operated automatically. He was given an envelope with the override code in case of emergency, but psychologists had advised against giving him total control from the beginning of the trip because no one really knew what the psychological effects would be once Gagarin was in space.

The space age officially began on October 4, 1957, with the launch of Sputnik 1 by the Soviet Union. This event marked the first time a man-made object was launched into space and placed into orbit around the Earth. It also marked the beginning of the space race between the United States and the Soviet Union, which was heightened by the Cold War. Sputnik 1, a satellite, was no larger than a beach ball. It weighed about 183 pounds and took about 98 minutes to orbit the Earth. About a month later Sputnik 2 followed with its canine cosmonaut aboard,

a dog named Laika. The word "sputnik" originally meant "fellow traveler" in Russian; the term has since become synonymous with the word "satellite."

The goal of the Sputnik mission was not only to place an artificial object into space. The Soviet Union was also hoping to discover information about the density of the Earth's atmosphere, to test both radio and optical methods of measuring the object's orbit, to measure the effects of atmospheric pressure on the satellite, and to record how radio waves moved through space.

Commemorative stamp honoring 25th anniversary of Sputnik

▼ **Private Manned Spacecraft** *(p. 256)*

▼ **Apollo 11** *(p. 259)*

▼ **Hubble Telescope** *(p. 114)*

Highway
Route 66, one of the first U.S. highways—dating back to the 1920s—originally ran from Chicago, Illinois, to California.

Nuclear Powered Submarine
U.S.S *Nautilus*, the first operational nuclear-powered submarine, undergoes sea trials in 1955. Capable of carrying a crew of 105, it completed the first underwater transit of the North Pole.

ROUTE US 66

1956 >

1954 >

Interstate Highway System

Nuclear-powered Subm

→← CONNECTION

The launch of Sputnik 1 proved to be the impetus for other developments in space exploration—many of which were fueled by the United States' fear that the successful Soviet launch of the first man-made object into space meant that the Soviets also surpassed the United States in weapons technology like ballistic missiles. As a result the U.S. Defense Department swung into high gear and the National Aeronautics and Space Administration was created on October 1, 1958.

● IN USE

Considered one of the greatest public works projects in history, the Interstate Highway System—also called the National Interstate and Defense Highways Act of 1956—was created in 1956 when President Dwight Eisenhower signed the Federal-Aid Highway Act. It changed forever how Americans and people throughout the world moved around their countries. The highway system was constructed at a fantastic pace and had to follow strict guidelines. The American Association of State Highway and Transportation Officials, formerly the American Association of State Highway Officials, published a set of standards for interstate highways that dictated "lanes had to be 12 feet wide and shoulders 10 feet wide, the bridges had to have 14 feet of clearance, grades had to be less than 30 percent, and the highway had to be designed for travel at 70 miles an hour."

● IN USE

In 1954 the United States launched the *Nautilus*, the world's first nuclear-powered submarine. The *Nautilus* was not only large (323 feet long and able to accommodate a crew of 104) but also fast—capable of reaching speeds up to 22 knots on the surface of the water and 23 knots submerged (about 41 and 42 miles an hour, respectively).

As the name implies, the sub was powered by a small nuclear reactor. In addition to its method of propulsion, the *Nautilus* was unique in that unlike traditional subs it was designed to stay

Building On >

Automobile *(p. 270)*

Macadam *(p. 281)*

Supersonic Flight
The bullet-shaped Bell X-IA, piloted by Charles "Chuck" Yeager, broke the sound barrier on October 14, 1947.

A 1950s advertisement of the U.S.S. *Nautilus*

1947 >

Breakthroughs continue on page 266

Supersonic Flight

↩ BACKLASH

● IN USE

underwater for extended periods and only surface occasionally. This meant the sub was extremely maneuverable and could be used in a stealth capacity. Subs were no longer confined to the coastlines and could be deployed throughout the waters of the globe.

The Soviet Union launched its first nuclear-powered submarine in 1958. In their quest to overtake and surpass the United States in nuclear technology, and in their eagerness to possess the naval advantages that nuclear subs offered, the Soviets were too hasty. Their nuclear submarine program was rife with problems, which led to many fatal accidents. One of the early Soviet subs, the *K-19*, was called the "Widowmaker." The ship ran into disaster on its first mission when the cooling system malfunctioned, nearly leading to a nuclear meltdown.

On October 14, 1947, pilot Chuck Yeager became the first person to break the sound barrier by flying the experimental aircraft Bell X-1 faster than the speed of sound. The problems some had feared—violent buffeting of the craft, loss of control, choppy flight—did not come to pass.

Aeronautical scientist Theodore von Kármán was the man largely responsible for developing the theory that made this historic flight possible. He distilled 260 years of research in the dynamics of high-speed flight down to the concepts—such as fluid flow, airfoil, laminar flow, and turbulence—that were essential for supersonic flight.

Charge It
The Tesla Roadster's microprocessor-controlled lithium-ion battery has a three-and-a-half-hour charge time—with an expected lifespan of seven years or 100,000 miles.

Power Up
The Roadster electric car can travel 245 miles per charge. It can accelerate from zero to 60 miles per hour in 3.7 seconds.

Electric Car

Many might think of the electric car as a new innovation in transportation. However, electric cars were quite popular between the mid-19th and early 20th centuries because they offered a level of comfort and ease of operation that gasoline cars of the time could not provide. Although electric cars do have the potential to reduce pollution significantly by way of zero tailpipe emissions, they are not necessarily pollution-free. Electricity is required to run these vehicles, and carbon dioxide is still released if the electricity comes from fossil fuels. How much carbon dioxide is released depends on the power source used to charge the vehicle (the stronger the power, the greater the emissions), how efficient the vehicle is, and how much energy is given off as "waste" when the car is charging.

There are currently two types of electric cars: one powered by a gasoline generator (called a hybrid) and one powered by an on-board battery pack (considered a true electric car). Today, there is no shortage of prototype, preproduction, and concept electric cars out there; however, only a few highway-capable models are on the market. The rest are vehicles capable only of low speeds and limited ranges.

What is keeping the electric car from being widely adopted as a mode of transportation? Factors include the costs of developing, producing, and operating electric vehicles compared to those of internal combustion engine vehicles, and the fact that electric cars are generally more expensive than gasoline cars—the batteries, in particular, are pricey. Another factor is what experts dubbed "range anxiety." Manufacturers have marketed these vehicles as ideal for short trips (around 40 miles); longer trips would require some sort of switching technology or rapid recharge system, both of which are being investigated.

1972

The invention of the hybrid vehicle is an important event in the history of the electric car. *See page 258*

1883

The induction motor is a key technology for many electric car models. *See page 271*

1885, 1845

The inventions of the automobile and pneumatic tire are significant steps on the way to the electric car. *See pages 270, 274*

Plug In

The zero-emissions electric vehicle plugs into conventional 110-volt or 220-volt power outlets for charging.

Dashboard Deluxe

A touch screen with GPS, a backup camera, satellite radio, and a wireless control system—many technologies combine in one automobile.

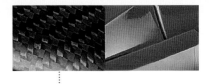

Modern Materials

The chassis of the car is constructed of resin-bonded aluminum, which adds strength and rigidity.

1800

▶

The creation of the first electric cell battery was an important step on the way to the battery-powered electric car. *See page 196*

V2 Rocket

Nazi Germany's V2 rockets were the first ballistic missiles and the first to achieve suborbital flight. Some 3,000 rained on the allies in World War II, each carrying nearly a ton of explosives.

From 1942 back to 1838 >

1942 >

V2 Rocket

● IN USE

The V2 rocket, which was developed by Wernher von Braun during World War II for Nazi Germany, ushered in the modern age of rocket technology. It was a single-stage craft—that is, no parts were jettisoned during flight—fueled by a mixture of alcohol and liquid oxygen. The rocket was a first in two ways: the first ballistic missile and the first craft to reach the edges of space (the V2 climbed to an altitude of 60 miles and broke the sound barrier on its 1942 flight). The warhead was in the nose of the rocket, with the control and

guidance system behind it.

After World War I a defeated Germany was desperate to regain its stature. The country was looking for a weapon that would not violate the terms of the Treaty of Versailles, in which Germany had agreed to reduce its military significantly, to neither import nor export weapons, and to restrict the production of machine guns and rifles. The treaty, however, still allowed Germany to defend itself. Rockets seemed to be the answer, and von Braun proved his skills as an engineer were worthy of this monumental task.

He began work on the rocket in 1932, and despite setbacks and challenges the V2 was launched on October 3, 1942. On September 6, 1944, it was used in an attack against Paris. World War II had been going on since 1939, so the terms of the Treaty of Versailles had long since been disregarded.

Building On >

Apollo 11 (p. 259)

Rocket (p. 293)

Engine

his cutaway of a turbofan jet engine, air accelerated by the
e fan (lower left) and powered by the engine behind it pushes
plane forward. Air enters the engine through the fan, passes
ugh compressors (center), and enters the combustion chamber
, upper right), where it is combined with fuel and ignited.

1939 >

Liquid-fueled Rocket
An early rocket soars skyward,
launched by the civilian American
Rocket Society in 1932. The society,
formed by a group of science fiction
writers, paved the way for the U.S.
space program of the 1960s.

1926 >

Jet Engine

● IN USE

The invention of the jet engine
is credited to Dr. Hans von Ohain
and Sir Frank Whittle, who worked
on the jet engine independently—
so independently that neither
man, one in Germany (von Ohain)
and one in England (Whittle),
was aware of the other's work.
Whittle was the first to register
a patent for his design in 1930;
von Ohain was the first to fly a
jet engine plane in 1939. The
impetus for both men was likely
the same: During the 1930s World
War II was looming on the horizon
and the militaries of the United
States, England, and Germany,
among others, were willing to
fund projects that supported
development of the jet engine.

Jet propulsion works on the
same principles as a turbine
engine. A fan at the front of the
engine sucks air in toward a
compressor, which is composed
of many spinning blades. As the
blades spin, they compress the
air, raising its pressure. At the
same time, the compressed air
is mixed with fuel and ignited
using a spark. This causes a mini-
explosion, the force of which
shoots out the back of the engine
and propels the plane forward.

Liquid-fueled Rocket

● IN USE

On March 16, 1926, American
physicist Robert Goddard moved
space travel from the realm of
theory to the realm of possibility
with the first successful launch
of a liquid-fueled rocket. Charles
Mansfield, a British chemist,
first conceived of liquid-fueled
rocket propulsion in the mid-
1800s while working with coal
tar. Goddard's work on the project
started when he was granted a
patent for a liquid-fueled rocket
in 1914. His rocket was also
noteworthy because it introduced
the design principles—particularly
the steering and control
mechanisms—that were later used
to build the V2 rocket.

British chemist Charles Mansfield,
founder of coal tar chemistry

▼ **Diesel Engine** (p. 270)
▼ **Induction Motor** (p. 271)
▼ **Rocket** (p. 293)

Robert Goddard

[PROFILE]

Considered the father of modern rocket propulsion, Robert Goddard (1882-1945) was an American physicist who played a pivotal role in rocket science by launching the first liquid-fueled rocket. Although this seems like a task the government and military would have jumped on, Goddard struggled his entire career to obtain funding for his work, eventually gaining support in the form of grants from institutions like the Smithsonian and the Guggenheim Foundation. In fact, it was not until the dawn of the space age that Goddard's work received the recognition it deserved. On May 1, 1959, NASA named the Goddard Space Flight Center in Greenbelt, Maryland, in his honor.

Assembly Line

● IN USE

Although Henry Ford did not invent the automobile, he was the first to make it available to the average person—something that was made possible by the assembly line. Ford did not invent the assembly line, but he was the first to capitalize on it. Rather than having a team of people working on one car at a time, a slow and expensive process, Ford reversed the concept in 1908. Instead each person would work on more than one car but would only be responsible for a single task. This process was so much more efficient that Ford was able to cut the time it took to manufacture an automobile from more than 12 hours to less than 6 hours.

Automobile (p. 270)

Assembly Line
The assembly line used by the Ford Motor Company in Detroit in the early 20th century lowered the cost of manufacturing.

Helicopter
The Ka-8 helicopter, designed by Soviet aviation engineer Nikolai Kamov, first flew in 1947. The craft was a single-seater powered by an alcohol-fueled engine.

First powered flight

1907 >

1903 >

Helicopter

● IN USE

The first helicopter made its debut flight in 1907. Invented by Frenchmen Louis and Jacques Breguet, the craft known as Gyroplane No. 1 had to be supported by men who steadied the four arms on which its rotators were affixed. Although Gyroplane No. 1 may not have made the first successful helicopter flight, it was noteworthy for being the first to lift itself off the ground using a rotating wing system that is the hallmark of the helicopter.

21st-century helicopter

First Motor-powered Aircraft

● IN USE

In December 17, 1903, Orville and Wilbur Wright proved not once but four times that sustained, motor-driven air flight was possible. Orville made the first flight, which covered a distance of 120 feet and lasted 12 seconds. Wilbur made the last one, which covered an impressive 852 feet and lasted 59 seconds.

They had prepared for this moment for a long time, using gliders to perfect their technique and gaining a better understanding of how to control the craft, called *The Wright Flyer*. They had also spent a lot of time watching birds in flight. Their observations showed them that it was the curve of the birds' wings that gave them lift. In addition, birds maneuvered by changing the shape of their wings. Thus Orville and Wilbur knew that they would need to employ this same technique, known as wing warping. Wing warping enables a pilot to keep a craft steady by arching the wingtips slightly.

When they realized that an automobile engine was going to be too heavy for the craft, the brothers designed and built their own.

◣ Supersonic Flight (p. 263)

◣ Glider (p. 273)

Diesel Engine

Diesel engines, such as this marine engine, ignite fuel by the heat of compression instead of spark plugs.

Automobile

The driver of this 1898 Packard directs it with a tiller instead of a steering wheel. Self-powered vehicles were developed earlier, but Karl Benz is generally accredited with inventing the automobile in 1885.

1897 >

1885 >

Diesel Engine

● IN USE

In 1893 German engineer Rudolph Diesel published a paper describing an engine in which the fuel is ignited without a spark. He was nearly killed by his experiment when it exploded in one of his tests. In 1897, however, Diesel successfully proved that his engine worked. Whereas a gas-powered combustion engine mixes fuel with air, which is compressed and ignited using a spark plug, a diesel engine compresses the air first and then the fuel is added. When air is compressed it heats up, which causes the fuel to ignite without a spark. Compared to a gas-powered combustion engine, the advantages of a diesel engine are its greater efficiency, decreased fuel consumption, and longer performance life. These engines are used today in everything from cars to submarines to generating plants.

Automobile

● IN USE

In 1885 German engineer Karl Benz introduced the first gasoline-powered automobile, forever changing the world of transportation. Others had worked on the same idea independently, but Benz was the first to patent it. The automobile used an internal combustion engine, had three wheels—Benz built a four-wheeled car in 1891—and was steered using a tiller, much like a boat is steered. The engine had a four-stroke design in which the first stroke draws in an air-fuel mixture, the second stroke compresses it, the third stroke ignites it, and the fourth stroke exhausts the combustive force.

The vehicle had its shortcomings, to be sure: It was somewhat hard to control and it had no gears, so it could not climb hills on its own power. Gasoline was only available in small quantities from pharmacists; in those days it was used as a cleaning product. Benz had a hard time getting anyone to pay significant attention to his invention. It was not until his wife and children took the car one morning and drove it on a 65-mile trip from Mannheim to Pforzheim as a publicity stunt that people

Building On >

Jet Engine (p. 267)

Otto Engine (p. 272)

Hybrid Vehicle (p. 258)

Assembly Line (p. 268)

Pneumatic Tire (p. 274)

Chariot (p. 298)

Induction Motor

Depending on the spin caused by two or more alternating currents, the induction motor was a major factor in the adoption of AC electrical supplies.

1883 >

Induction Motor

● IN USE

started to take an interest. Benz and Company became the largest manufacturer of automobiles by 1900, and around this time merged with Gottlieb Daimler's company, which was producing four-wheeled vehicles. Known today as Mercedes-Benz, the "Mercedes" part of the name comes from one of Daimler's business partners, Emil Jellinek, who would only invest capital in the company if the car was named after his daughter.

The induction motor, a type of electric motor, derives its name from the way in which it generates power. Two alternating currents produce a rotating magnetic field, which provides the force that drives the motor. Induction motors are made of copper, aluminum, and steel, which means they are more expensive to produce than internal combustion engines. The cost is offset by high durability. Induction motors are usually also quieter. In 1883 inventor Nikola Tesla was the first to apply for a patent for an induction motor (the patent was

actually granted in 1887), which he created to support some of his other experiments. He sold the manufacturing rights to George Westinghouse for a reported $65,000 in 1888. Today, induction motors are used in table saws, many home appliances, furnaces, and other industrial applications.

The original Tesla induction motor

Wheel *(p. 299)*

Alternating Current *(p. 45)*

Otto Engine

The four-stroke internal combustion engine devised by German engineer Nicolaus Otto underwent improvements that made it suitable for the motorcar.

Alligator (Submarine)

The U.S. Navy's first successful submarine was the *Alligator,* used during the Civil War. Propelled by a screw, it could submerge completely with a chemical system that could produce oxygen and a bellows that purified air by forcing it through lime.

1876 >

1862 >

Otto Engine

● IN USE

Invented in 1876 by German Nicolaus Otto, the Otto engine still looks much the same today; it is used to power everything from cars to boats. The engine employs a process in which a mixture of fuel and air is drawn into a cylinder, compressed, ignited, and released. Otto's design provided for a slow, safe release of combustion without compromising the engine's effectiveness and power. Together with his partner Eugen Langen, Otto formed the company N. A. Otto & Cie, which was the world's first manufacturer of internal combustion engines; the company is still in existence today as Deutz AG.

Otto was not the first to come up with the internal combustion engine. The design was simple, so it was not too difficult for others to reach the same conclusions. As a result Otto had trouble securing a patent, especially when it became known that French engineer Alphonse Eugène Beau de Rochas had designed a similar engine in 1861. While Otto struggled to get a patent, a fierce competition among engine manufacturers resulted in swift improvements in capacity, speed, and horsepower, and the addition of pistons, valves, and carburetors.

Nicolaus Otto

Alligator (Submarine)

● IN USE

Think submarines are a recent naval invention? Not so. The U.S. Navy's first submarine, called the *Alligator,* was used during the American Civil War. Commissioned by the Navy in 1862, the 47-foot-long craft seemed doomed to failure. It was propelled by an oar system and could not completely submerge beneath the waters in which it was intended for use. It was also difficult to maneuver and had limited power. Its success came when the oar system was replaced with a screw propeller and other modifications were made to the ventilation system

Building On >

Diesel Engine *(p. 270)*

Internal Combustion Engine *(p. 279)*

Bessemer Process *(p. 189)*

Glider
Design for a man-powered flying
machine by Sir George Cayley, 1853

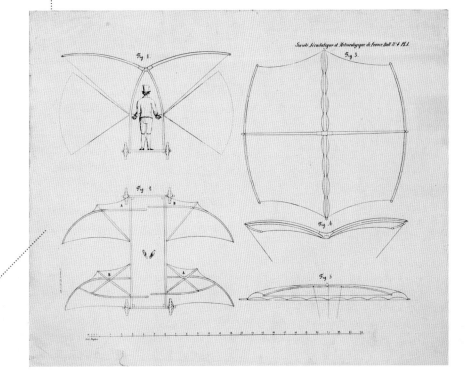

1853 >

Glider

● **IN USE**

and the hull—modifications
that were further refined as
submarines came into their own.

Prior to Sir George Cayley's glider,
early aviators created what are
called ornithopters in an attempt
to achieve heavier-than-air flight.
(The word "ornithopter" refers to
an object that is supported by
air in order to fly.) These early
flying machines had flapping
wings because scientists at the
time believed that both lift and
forward motion were required
to become airborne. Cayley, an
English engineer, realized the
problem of heavier-than-air
flight had to be looked at from a
different perspective, rather than
attempting to imitate the motion
of birds in flight. Propulsion was
certainly necessary, but the wings
did not need to flap—they just
had to be constructed in such a
way that they achieved lift. In the
late 18th century Cayley began
experimenting with different
designs, temporarily reconsidering
flapping wings before discarding
them yet again. His experiments
gave him a greater understanding
of aerodynamics. In 1799 he
designed a fixed-wing aircraft
that, although crude, has a
modern plane's components: a
fuselage, a rudder, elevators, and
"flappers" for thrust.

His 1804 glider is considered
the first true airplane. In 1849 he
built the first glider large enough
to carry a person—a ten-year-
old boy who was the son of one
of his servants. In 1853 Cayley
carried his coachman about 900
feet in a triplane glider. Although
this was an amazing success,
he recognized that sustained
flight would not be possible
until someone created an engine
powerful enough to create
sufficient lift and thrust, yet
light enough not to weigh the
aircraft down.

Nuclear-powered Submarine *(p. 262)*

Submarine *(p. 292)*

First Motor-powered Aircraft *(p. 269)*

George Cayley

[PROFILE]

It is quite possible that without Sir George Cayley (1773-1857) scientists would not be where they are today in terms of aviation science. Known as the father of aviation, Cayley was the first to identify and describe the forces involved in heavier-than-air flight: weight (the downward force exerted by gravity), lift (the force necessary to overcome gravity), drag (the resistance of air to the airplane's motion), and thrust (the force necessary to overcome the resistance of air).

Cayley conducted meticulous experiments in which he studied these forces both individually and in combination, and the principles he outlined are still in use by pilots today.

Pneumatic Tire
Modern tires have their origins in Scotland in the late 1840s, when Robert William Thomson developed an air-filled belt that made the ride less bumpy for drivers and passengers.

1845 >

Pneumatic Tire

● IN USE

Scottish inventor Robert William Thomson invented many things, including the fountain pen, the steam traction engine, and elastic belts. The invention for which the world is perhaps most grateful, however, is the pneumatic tire, which he completed in 1845. Although the pneumatic tire is often attributed to John Boyd Dunlop, Thomson patented his "aerial wheel," a hollow belt inflated with air, 43 years before Dunlop's design. The pneumatic tire reduced the noise of vehicles and made the ride more comfortable for the driver and passengers. The car and the bicycle had not yet emerged as popular modes of transportation, perhaps causing Thomson's aerial wheel to fall off the pages of history, only to be reemerge in the 1880s as a bicycle tire.

▼ **Automobile** (p. 270)

▼ **Bicycle** (p. 280)

Transatlantic Steamship
The *Great Western* steamship with side paddle wheels and masts for auxiliary sails was the first steamship purposely built for transatlantic voyages in 1843. It was the largest steamship for one year—until the *British Queen* was built.

1838 >

Breakthroughs continue on page 278

Transatlantic Steamship

● IN USE

The S.S. *Great Western*, commissioned in 1838, was the first ship built for the express purpose of traversing the Atlantic Ocean. Considered the first ocean liner, the vessel was designed by Isambard Kingdom Brunel. The British engineer envisioned the ship as an extension of his Great Western railway service that connected London to Bristol, thus creating a "line" that ran from London to New York. On April 23, 1838, the S.S. *Great Western* set a record for the fastest transatlantic crossing, making the trip in only 15 days.

The ship had a conventional design with a wooden hull and paddle wheels. Although the S.S. *Great Western* was a steamship, it had masts with sails for times when extra bursts of speed were needed. The ship made 45 round-trips as a passenger ship, then was put into service as a mail carrier for ten years before being decommissioned in 1856.

Model detail of the paddle wheels and funnels of the S.S. *Great Western*

➡◀ CONNECTION

There was nothing unusual about the fact that the S.S. *Great Western* still used sails even though it was a steamship. When powered by steam alone, vessels were somewhat slow. The addition of sail power made up for lost time and helped conserve fuel. As nautical technology continued to improve, ships' hulls were no longer constructed out of wood but instead out of iron. Bulkheads were double-lined and watertight, and paddles were replaced with screw propellers.

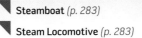

Steamboat *(p. 283)*

Steam Locomotive *(p. 283)*

Beaming Up and Back
Many innovations depend on the satellites now in place that support GPS, the global positioning system, which uses a signal transmitted by a vehicle to locate its position in a traffic grid.

Intelligent Traffic

The goal behind an intelligent transportation system is to combine information and communications technology with transportation systems and vehicles—including devices that control traffic signals, navigation systems, message signs, bridge deicing systems, and systems that monitor traffic flows and weather. Intelligent transportation systems, in theory, will help make roads safer, add more life to cars, reduce the amount of fuel consumed, and make trips shorter. Traffic congestion, which has become a significant problem worldwide, has been the primary impetus for this area of research. Congestion reduces the efficiency of transportation infrastructures and increases travel time, air pollution, and fuel consumption. In the United States, homeland security and safety are also motivating factors. As part of their traffic monitoring and navigation systems, for example, many proposed intelligent transportation systems include roadway surveillance and plans to use highways and major thoroughfares as mass evacuation routes after a significant disaster.

Basic intelligent transportation systems are already in action. Electronic toll collection systems, for example, allow drivers to move through toll gates at standard speeds; as a result congestion is reduced at tollbooths and traffic keeps moving smoothly. OnStar, an onboard emergency response system found in many vehicles, is another example. An emergency call is generated either manually or automatically after an accident. The device establishes an emergency call carrying data about the accident to the nearest emergency point, and help is sent.

1978

GPS will be a crucial component of many intelligent transportation systems. *See page 21*

1958, 1936

Computers and the integrated circuits from which they are built are essential to any intelligent transportation system. *See pages 22, 23*

1945

Without communication satellites, integrating information technologies with transportation systems would be very limited. *See page 38*

Stop and Go

Intelligent traffic signaling uses laser cameras and microchips to sense vehicle flux and adjust stoplight timing accordingly. The system can also switch into emergency mode, reconfiguring traffic controls immediately so ambulances and firetrucks can pass through safely.

Where in the World

Personal GPS systems provide drivers with a host of information, from driving conditions to the nearest coffee shop. Intelligent systems use information sent from individual autos to shape and interpret traffic patterns on the spot.

1956, 1903, 1885, 1814

The automobile, highways, aircraft, and railways are the foundations for any transportation system.
See pages 262, 269, 270, 282

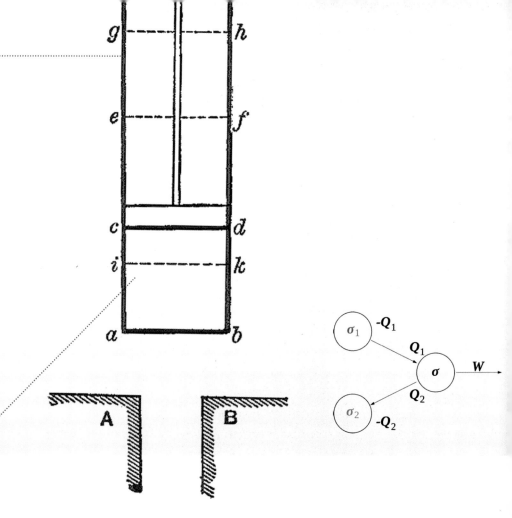

An 1824 diagram illustrates the theoretical heat engine designed by and named for Nicolas Léonard Sadi Carnot. The working principle of Carnot's heat engine, which expanded the understanding of thermodynamics, is depicted here.

From 1824 back to 1687 >

1824 >

Carnot Heat Engine

▲ IN THEORY

Prior to the ideas of French engineer and physicist Nicolas Léonard Sadi Carnot, water was the primary means of power (as in a waterwheel, for example). When the steam engine replaced the waterwheel, a natural question arose: Just how efficient can such an engine be? The Carnot heat engine—which is a theoretical construct, not a physical object—attempted to answer that question and at the same time greatly expanded the understanding of thermodynamics. Water is a fluid, and Carnot reasoned that

heat must be a type of fluid too. This was actually a popular misconception at the time, although it did not invalidate Carnot's theory.

As water moves from a position at the top of a waterwheel to a lower one, it causes a release of energy that allows a machine to do work. Analogously, as heat is transferred from a higher temperature area to a lower temperature area, it releases energy, which too can be used to do mechanical work. To make the most efficient engine possible, Carnot theorized that the amount

of friction in this system had to be reduced to a minimum. He also theorized that his heat engine would be reversible—that is, energy applied from outside of a system could cause heat to move from a lower temperature area to a higher temperature area.

A French postage stamp depicting Nicolas Léonard Sadi Carnot

Nicolas Léonard Sadi Carnot

[PROFILE]

Called the father of thermodynamics, French engineer and physicist Nicolas Léonard Sadi Carnot (1796-1832) is perhaps most well known for the theoretical heat engine that bears his name. He was a brilliant theorist, showing promise at an early age and getting accepted into the École Polytechnique in Paris at age 16. He died in 1832 at age 36, one day after contracting cholera.

Internal Combustion Engine
Samuel Brown's gas vacuum engine, shown in this illustration, used a flame to generate power. Brown later designed an engine that used hydrogen as fuel.

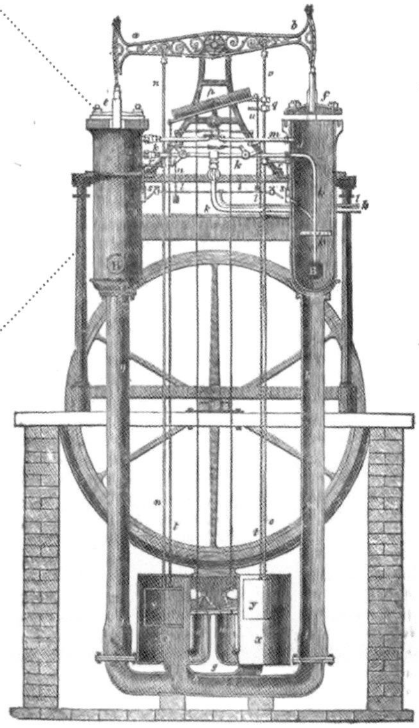

(*Brown's Gas Vacuum Engine. 1823.*)

1823 >

Internal Combustion Engine

● IN USE

In 1823 English inventor and engineer Samuel Brown developed an internal combustion engine based on an earlier steam engine model. While not the first of its kind, the engine was the first to be used in an industrial capacity to pump water and propel boats and barges on rivers. It was a modified version of the Newcomen steam engine. Brown's engine used hydrogen for fuel instead of steam, and had separate compartments for combustion and cooling. The engine also employed the use of cylinders. Earlier internal combustion engines, such as those designed by French inventor François Isaac de Rivaz and Dutch scientist Christiaan Huygens, used different fuels and slightly different designs, but none had the same degree of effectiveness and success as Brown's combustion engine.

◣ Diesel Engine (*p. 270*)

◤ Otto Engine (*p. 272*)

Navier Stokes Equations
A formula depicts one of the Navier-Stokes equations, which as a group describe the motion of fluids. These equations are particularly useful in modeling the weather, ocean currents, and airflow around a wing

1822 >

Bicycle
An early bicycle, Denis Johnson's Hobby Horse of 1819, was a refinement of the Draisienne, invented by Karl von Drais two years earlier. The rider straddled a frame supported by two in-line wheels and pushed the vehicle along with feet on the ground.

1817 >

Navier-Stokes Equations

▲ IN THEORY

The Navier-Stokes equations describe the motion of fluids, which include both compressible and incompressible fluids. They were the combined work of two men who never met: the French engineer Claude-Louis Navier, who originated them, and the English mathematicians George Gabriel Stokes, who perfected them.

The Navier-Stokes equations express the changing physical state of fluids. Compressible fluids change volume as pressure is applied; incompressible fluids do not, and their density remains constant. These equations have become the foundation for fluid dynamics, central to all engineering analyses of moving vehicles, whether in air, water, or outer space. What makes these equations, first formulated by Navier in 1822, so useful is that they can still be used in the design of aircraft wings, car bodies, and even rocket fuselages in order to make them as aerodynamic as possible.

Bicycle

● IN USE

An early version of the bicycle invented in 1817 by German inventor Karl von Drais had some familiar components: two wheels, a seat, and handlebars. What it did not have were pedals. Called the Laufmaschine, German for "running machine," riders moved the wooden vehicle by pushing against the ground with their feet. Drais's design needed a few modifications to turn it into the modern bicycle of today, although he would not be the one to make them. Drais had a patent for his two-wheeled vehicle, but it did not apply throughout all of Germany and France, and the design was quickly copied. In 1818 Nicéphore Niépce coined the term "velocipede" (Latin for "fast foot") to describe his improvements on the Drais model, which included a fully adjustable seat. In the 1860s the French inventors Pierre Michaux and Pierre Lallement developed the first pedal-powered crank drive for the velocipede; they quickly formed a company to mass-produce their product, and it quickly emerged as a popular means of transport. Using these advances, Scottish inventor Thomas McCall began

Building On > ▼ Bernoulli's Principle *(p. 284)*

▼ Pneumatic Tire *(p. 274)*
▼ Wheel *(p. 299)*

Macadam. The old stone foundation beneath roughed macadam is visible prior to resurfacing in the modern day. Paved roads in 1832, developed by Scot John Loudon Macadam, were built by placing crushed stone mixed with water atop larger stones, creating a smooth surface.

1815 >

Macadam

● IN USE

experimenting with rear-wheel drive and introduced a rod-driven model in 1869. In the 1870s the first all-metal velocipedes appeared, as well as the first sets of rubber tires.

A modern bicycle

Macadam, which takes its name directly from its inventor, Scottish engineer John Loudon McAdam, was a milestone in roadbuilding. Roads in the early 1800s were not only expensive to build, but also expensive to maintain. McAdam was made trustee of Scotland's Ayrshire Turnpike in 1783; the title led him to become more involved with the processes and methods of road construction. Following a move to Bristol, England, in 1812 he worked with the Bristol Corporation on various road-engineering projects. Between 1816 and 1819 he wrote

and published two treatises on the subject, arguing through his empirical findings that the best material for roads consisted of crushed stone mixed with water and covered with a layer of small stones to create a uniform surface. Upon his promotion to surveyor of the Bristol Turnpike Trust in 1816, he began to rebuild roads in this fashion, layering the mixture over a base of large stones. He also introduced the practice of shaping roads with a slight "crown" to aid in the drainage of rainwater, thus preserving the life expectancy

of the foundation. Others built on his designs, experimenting with binding agents to hold the crushed rock together. The result: Water was replaced with bitumen to create the familiar asphalt blacktop roads of today.

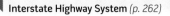

Interstate Highway System *(p. 262)*

Railway

Volunteer Matthew Jackson works on a replica of an 1830 steam locomotive at the Museum of Science and Industry in Manchester, England.

1814 >

Railway

● IN USE

Considered the father of railways, English engineer George Stephenson built the first steam engine locomotive to run on rails—no small feat, given that each piece of the locomotive had to be fashioned by hand out of iron and hammered into shape. It took Stephenson ten months to build Blücher, his name for the locomotive, which was successfully tested on July 25, 1814. The engine was not fast—the top speed was around four miles an hour—but it was strong. Blücher's twin vertical boilers allowed it to pull eight coal cars uphill for 450 feet, with each car weighing 30 tons. Stephenson went on to build 16 different engines, and continued to modify locomotive design by using connecting rods to drive the wheels instead of a pinion system.

After Blücher, Stephenson built both the Stockton-Darlington railway and the Liverpool-Manchester railway, considered the world's first public railways. He kept a hand in their operation, acting as chief engineer for several of the lines.

English engineer George Stephenson

➡️⬅️ CONNECTION

With the advent of George Stephenson's railway system came the realization that goods as well as people could be transported over long distances in less time than it took with wagons. For a time, some railways served as a toll road of sorts for locomotives and horse-drawn carriages. The system was confusing and was eventually replaced with trains that ran on a timetable. At the same time, locomotive engines continued to be improved upon in terms of speed, stability, and size.

Building On >

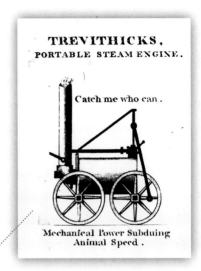

Advertisement for Trevithick's
steam engine, 1808

Steamboat
This drawing accompanied a patent issued to British
inventor Jonathon Hulls in 1736. The steam engine
drove a paddle wheel, but the boat was never built
because the engine was considered too cumbersome.

1803 >

1801 >

Steamboat

● IN USE

Considered the world's first
practical steamboat, the *Charlotte
Dundas* was designed in 1802
by William Symington, built by
John Allan (both men worked
for the Carron Company), and
launched in 1803. Symington
had long believed that the steam
engine, introduced by Thomas
Newcomen in 1712, could be
used to power a boat without
the vessel catching fire. (Boats
were constructed primarily of
wood at the time.) Symington's
first boat to use steam power
did not catch fire, but the paddle
wheel was too weak for the job
and fell apart. He had proved his
point, however, and continued his
work. He combined the designs
of Newcomen and James Watt to
create something that was simple
yet efficient. On March 28, 1803,
the *Charlotte Dundas* towed two
fully loaded river barges 18.5
miles in just over nine hours,
demonstrating the steamship's
potential not only as a vehicle for
passengers, but also as a vehicle
that could be widely used for
commercial purposes.

Steam Locomotive

● IN USE

One of British engineer Richard
Trevithick's most notable
inventions is the steam
locomotive, which he built in
1801. Although perhaps not a true
locomotive in modern terms, in
that it ran on roads rather than
rails, his vehicle did pave the way
for those that came later, such as
George Stephenson's Blücher.

Known as the Puffing Devil,
Trevithick's locomotive made use
of a simple design consisting of
a single boiler connected to a
single cylinder. Steam from the
boiler caused a piston to move,
which operated a crankshaft that
moved a flywheel (a flywheel
makes use of inertia to create
motion). Throughout his life,
Trevithick continued to modify his
design and conduct experiments;
unfortunately, none of his
endeavors garnered him much
money and he died a pauper.

Transatlantic Steamship *(p. 275)*

Newcomen Steam Engine *(p. 286)*

Hot-air Balloon

On November 21, 1783, the first manned hot-air balloon ascended the Bois de Bologne in Paris. The balloon, made of paper-covered cloth, was built by the Montgolfier brothers, Joseph-Michel and Jacques-Étienne.

Joseph-Michel de Montgolfier

Bernoulli's Principle

An F-22 Raptor flies according to the principle stated by Daniel Bernoulli in 1738—that the internal pressure of a gas (air) is lower the faster it travels. A wing more curvaceous on the top than on the bottom creates lift because air under the wing travels more slowly.

1783 >

1738 >

Hot-air Balloon

● IN USE

On June 4, 1783, brothers Joseph-Michel and Jacques-Étienne Montgolfier demonstrated the first hot-air balloon flight in a marketplace in Annonay, France. The balloon rose 6,562 feet. The two men had discovered that when a flame was held near the bottom of a fabric and paper bag, the hot air filled the bag and caused it to expand and float. The hot-air balloon proved to be a viable method of transportation just a few months later when French aviation pioneers Jean-François Pilâtre de Rozier and François Laurent,

Marquis d'Arlandes, became the first passengers to man a hot-air balloon flight. Two years later, in 1785, another milestone in the history of the hot-air balloon was achieved when French inventor Jean-Pierre Blanchard and American physician John Jeffries successfully crossed the English Channel in a hot-air balloon.

The English Channel is 21 miles wide at its narrowest point and 112 miles wide at the widest point. History does not indicate exactly where Blanchard and Jeffries made their journey. In any case, they demonstrated the viability of

the hot-air balloon as a means of long-distance transportation.

In 1999 balloonists Bertrand Piccard and Brian Jones were the first to travel around the world in a hot-air balloon, making the trip in 19 days, 21 hours, and 55 minutes.

Bernoulli's Principle

▲ IN THEORY

Bernoulli's principle describes the relationship between the pressure and velocity of a moving fluid. As velocity increases, pressure decreases, and as pressure increases, velocity decreases. Swiss mathematician Daniel Bernoulli published this pivotal concept in the study of fluid mechanics in his 1738 book *Hydrodynamica*. Air is considered a fluid, a term that is used to describe both liquids and gases, and Bernoulli's principle reveals how an airplane is able to get lift and thus fly.

Consider the wing of an airplane. As the craft moves along the

Building On >

Latent Heat (p. 198)

Daniel Bernoulli

[PROFILE]

Born into a family of prominent mathematicians, it is no surprise that Daniel Bernoulli (1700-1782) achieved greatness in this field—although his father tried to push his son into a career in business or medicine, claiming there was no money to be had in mathematics. Bernoulli found his passion, however, and was persistent, so his father finally relented. Bernoulli's study of blood pressure and flow caused him to speculate about fluid flow in general. This work ultimately led him to Bernoulli's principle, which plays a critical role in flight.

ground and picks up speed, the air flowing along the top of the wing, which is slightly curved, creates a decrease in pressure because it is moving faster than the air flowing beneath the wing. The increased pressure below the wing produces lift, which causes the aircraft to rise into the air. The aircraft stays aloft partly because the pressure differences remain in place above and below the airplane's wings.

Mathematician Bernoulli discovered this principle when he was conducting experiments on one of the primary laws of physics: the conservation of energy. He was trying to understand why water flows faster through a pipe with a smaller diameter than it does through one with a larger diameter, yet the total volume of water does not change. He speculated that a force (pressure) must be acting on the water, causing the water to move faster in the smaller pipe.

A wind tunnel demonstrating Bernoulli's principle

Navier-Stokes Equations (p. 280)

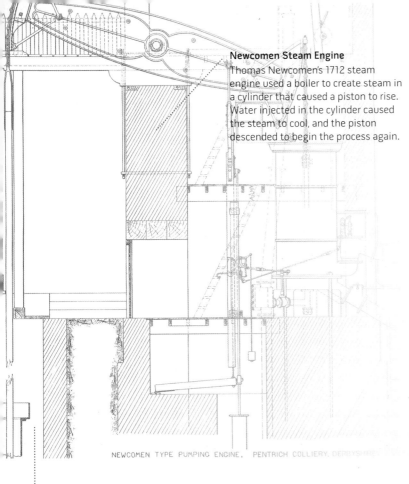

Newcomen Steam Engine
Thomas Newcomen's 1712 steam engine used a boiler to create steam in a cylinder that caused a piston to rise. Water injected in the cylinder caused the steam to cool, and the piston descended to begin the process again.

NEWCOMEN TYPE PUMPING ENGINE, PENTRICH COLLIERY, DERBYSHIRE

1712 >

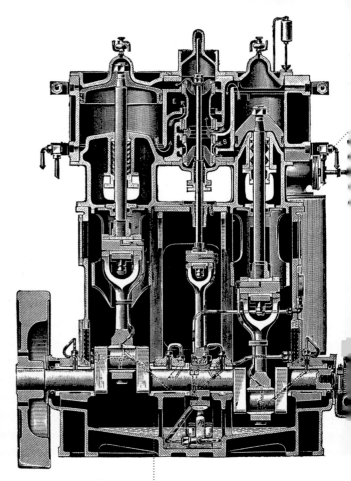

1690 >

Newcomen Steam Engine

● IN USE

Thomas Newcomen's steam engine, invented in 1712, was dubbed the "atmospheric steam engine" because it worked primarily through the use of atmospheric pressure. Newcomen and his partner, John Calley, were not exactly mechanically inclined—neither knew much about mechanical engineering—yet they did understand how Denis Papin's steam engine worked and wanted to adapt his design. Their model, like Papin's, employed a boiler, pumps, a piston, and surface condensation. It worked as follows: A boiler at the bottom of the engine turned water into steam, which moved into a cylinder. The pressure from the steam caused a piston contained in the cylinder to rise. When the piston was at the top of its motion, water was injected into the cylinder, which caused the steam to cool and thus decreased the pressure in the cylinder. The piston then returned to its original position and the water drained from the cylinder, allowing the process to start again.

→← CONNECTION

Steam engines were not just used for transportation purposes. Another use was as a pump to remove water from mines and wells. They were also used to operate machinery in textile mills and other factories, such as looms and spinning mules. Other names in the history of the steam engine include Benjamin Franklin Tibbets, who invented the first steam engine for marine use in the 1820s; and George Herman Babcock and Stephen Wilcox, who jointly invented the first steam boiler that employed water tubes in 1867. The Babcock & Wilcox Company is still in existence today.

Steam Engine

● IN USE

The steam engine was not the invention of one man in particular. Rather, it was the end result of the work of several men who built on each other's ideas. The French inventor Denis Papin, however, is the one person who is generally credited with being the first to explore the power of steam.

Papin understood the link between steam and pressure, and in 1679 he developed the world's first steam cooker. In 1690 he built a steam-powered device that moved water. He called this first steam-powered piston engine a "steam digester." For it, Papin

Building On >   Steam Locomotive (p. 283)

taway artwork shows a
o-piston steam engine
:ached to a drive shaft and
wheel developed by two
tish engineers in the 1890s.
e engine used an oil pump
force lubrication into the
inder so the pistons would
: seize up from the heat.

Newton's Laws

The falling of an apple may have inspired the laws of gravitation by English physicist Isaac Newton. His *Principia*, published in 1687, was the foundation for the study of the motion of bodies under a system of forces.

Denis Papin

1687 >

Breakthroughs continue on page 290

Newton's Laws of Motion and Universal Gravitation

▲ IN THEORY

assembled a three-inch-long glass tube with water at the bottom and the top sealed by a piston. When the water was heated so that it gave off steam, the resulting pressure moved the piston. When the steam cooled and evaporated, atmospheric pressure caused the piston to return to its original position. The constantly moving piston drove a screw or crankshaft. Devices along these lines were put to use, for example, to move water between canals or to draw water up onto a rooftop so that gravity fed it downward into nearby fountains. Papin

was also the first to construct a steam-powered vehicle when he linked his engine to a system of mechanical paddles to power a riverboat.

Isaac Newton's three laws of motion, published for the first time in his monumental *Principia Mathematica Philosophiae Naturalis*, are: (1) An object at rest will stay at rest, or stay in motion, unless affected by an external force. (2) Force is equal to mass times acceleration. (3) For every action, there is an opposite and equal reaction.

Newton's law of universal gravitation states that all bodies in the universe—that is, anything that has mass—attract one another with a force that is proportional to their masses

and inversely proportional to the square of the distance between them. These laws are still used today to calculate the trajectories of rockets, satellites, and spacecraft.

Crankshaft (p. 294)

General Theory of Relativity (p. 126)

Newton's Laws of Motion and Universal Gravitation (p. 136)

03

03

01

02

Terraforming

Anyone who has read Kim Stanley Robinson's *Mars* trilogy knows all about "terraforming," a term that was coined by Jack Williamson in the science-fiction story "Collision Orbit" in 1942. But the idea is not just in the realm of science fiction. In fact, for several reasons, Mars is a likely candidate for terraforming—modifying the planet's atmosphere so that it is habitable for humans.

Recently NASA probes have discovered hints that water might have flowed on Mars. This is an indicator that life may have existed in the planet's distant past. The water might still be there, trapped in ice caps at the poles, which means life could exist there again—provided scientists can transform the currently cold, dry Martian atmosphere into one like Earth's. In addition to water, Mars holds other elements that are needed for life to exist, including carbon, oxygen, and nitrogen.

So how would scientists manage to make Mars suitable for humans? And more important, if they figure out a way to do it, should they do so? The first question might be easier to answer than the second. Three

terraforming methods that have been proposed include installing large mirrors in orbit around Mars that will reflect sunlight and heat the planet's surface; constructing greenhouse gas–producing "factories" to trap solar radiation; and smashing asteroids laden with ammonia into the planet, which would also cause a greenhouse-like effect.

Regardless of the method used, this is not a process that could be completed in decades—and maybe not even in centuries. Some scientists believe that such a project could take millennia to become a reality. In addition, although the technological capacities to pull off a project of this magnitude are potentially within grasp, the economic capacity is not.

1975

The Viking program put the first human spacecraft on Mars—a candidate for the first potential terraforming efforts. *See page 257*

1969

The accomplishment of the Apollo 11 mission, landing humans on the moon, is a direct precursor to landing humans on other planets. *See page 259*

1961

Human spaceflight makes the idea of terraforming possible, at least in theory. *See page 260*

01
Not in Our Lifetime
Terraforming Mars will be a thousand-year project, starting with a number of exploratory missions that gradually build an infrastructure. Flight to Mars will take six months; a mission might last eighteen months.

02
Pioneer Village
Each new mission will construct more habitation modules, extending the stay time, expanding the living space, and increasing our knowledge of life on the surface of Mars.

03
Global Warming
To create a water cycle and make an atmosphere conducive to life, we will need to increase its carbon dioxide level. Space mirrors will melt Mars's ice; factories will be designed to spew greenhouse gases.

04
Life Under Domes
Geodesic domes will provide climate-controlled living spaces, first for plants and later for humans. Nourishing the desert rock into a life-supporting substrate will take centuries after introducing microbes and oxygen.

05
Power to the Planet
Nuclear power and wind turbines are two current technologies that could be carried to Mars. Better yet, we will perfect nuclear fission power plants and export them to the red planet for electricity.

06
Don't Forget Your Mask
Even after a millennium of development, Mars's atmosphere will not provide enough oxygen for humans to breathe without equipment akin to scuba gear.

1935, 1804, 1774

Ecosystems, biogeography, and the role of oxygen and carbon dioxide in Earth-based life is crucial to contemplating terraforming. *See pages 227, 242, 245*

Blaise Pascal

1662 >

[PROFILE]

French mathematician Blaise Pascal (1623-1772) was an intense man who saw divine intervention in many events in his life. He also suffered throughout his life from fragile health, dying at age 39 from a brain hemorrhage. Although Pascal played a role in transportation systems, he is primarily known for his theoretical and applied mathematical work, including the creation of a mechanical adding machine that can be considered to be a precursor to the computer. In 1654, after a mystical experience, Pascal retired from the study of mathematics and devoted what remained of his short life to studying religion. It was during this time that he wrote his *Pensées*, in which he outlined a rational defense of Christianity.

Public Bus

● IN USE

Imagine waiting for a bus, only to have a horse-drawn carriage pull up to the curb. That is exactly what one of the first early public transportation systems was like in 1662. Passengers paid a fare for the service, and the carriages had regular timetables and routes, just like the public bus system today. The 1662 system was the invention of French philosopher and mathematician Blaise Pascal, who sought to provide an affordable means of transportation for Parisians. Concerned with the plight of the poor, he donated the profits his system earned to charity.

▼ Automobile *(p. 270)*

▼ Chariot *(p. 298)*

▼ Wheel *(p. 299)*

Building On >

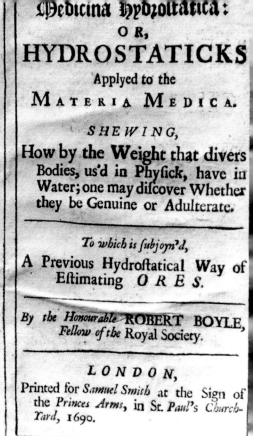

1662 >

Boyle's Law

● IN USE

According to Boyle's law (also called the Boyle-Mariotte law), there is a precise mathematical relationship among the pressure, temperature, and volume of a gas. When the temperature of a gas is constant, its volume is inversely proportional to its pressure. That is, as pressure goes up, volume goes down, and vice versa. Irish-born Robert Boyle published this law in 1662 in an appendix to the second edition of his 1660 book, *New Experiments Physico-Mechanical, Touching the Spring of the Air and Its Effects,* and used it to describe the behavior of an "ideal gas"—a theoretical concept that is used to model the behavior of real gases. While most gases do behave like ideal gases at average pressures and temperatures, the limitations of 17th-century scientific methods made it difficult to create high pressures or low temperatures in experimental environments. Developments in technology enabled scientists after Boyle to detect nuances in the behavior of ideal gases, including the relationship between pressure and volume. Still, Boyle's law remains crucial in understanding the physical principles on which many engines operate. Some historians refer to the law as the Boyle-Mariotte law, acknowledging the fact that French physicist Edme Mariotte made a similar discovery in 1676 without prior awareness of Boyle's publication.

A modern double-decker bus

Cornelius Drebbel

[PROFILE]

Cornelius Jacobszoon Drebbel (1572-1633) did not just invent the world's first submarine. Drebbel is also credited with inventing a scarlet dye that produced such a vivid hue that it became the rage throughout Europe, a microscope with not just one but two lenses, a perpetual-motion machine and perpetual-motion clock, a chimney, and a thermostat for a self-regulating oven. Given the diversity of Drebbel's creations, perhaps it is no surprise that some thought he was a sorcerer.

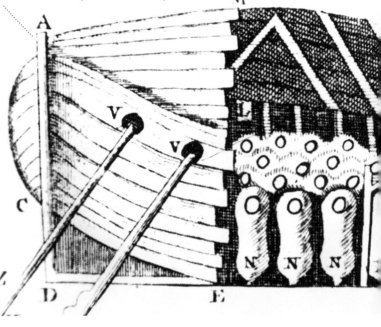

Submarine
Inventor Cornelius Drebbel solved the problem of supplying air to a boat submerged underwater with several tubes that extended beyond the water's surface. Oarsmen powered his 1620 craft. Submarines would not play a significant role in the military for another 200 years.

1620 >

Submarine

● IN USE

The submarine is not as recent an invention as one might think. Invented in 1620 by Dutch inventor Cornelius Jacobszoon Drebbel, what made the craft a success was how it addressed the problem of being watertight while maintaining a continuous air supply. Made out of wood and covered with leather, Drebbel's submersible was powered by several men who rowed from inside its body. Tubes, which reached the surface of the water and were supported by floats, supplied the air, allowing the craft to stay submerged for several hours. Drebbel built two other vessels, each larger that the one before. He tested his craft several times on the Thames River, reaching depths of 12 to 15 feet. It would be nearly 200 years before the submarine's true potential would be recognized and harnessed.

In 1775 American inventor David Bushnell designed the first military submarine, *Turtle*. The hand-powered craft could only hold one person at a time. It was the first vessel capable of underwater movement, and the first to use screws (or propellers)

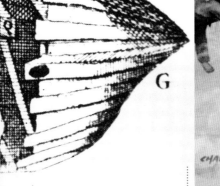

Rocket

Rockets bombard Mongols attacking the Chinese city of Kai-fung-fu in this painting of the 1232 conflict. An arrow stuck in the front of a tube of gunpowder produced a deadly missile of flying fire.

1232 >

Rocket

● IN USE

as a form of propulsion. Its use of water as a ballast for raising and lowering is still standard today. Bushnell intended *Turtle* as a means of secretly attaching explosives to the undersides of ships during warfare. On September 7, 1776, Sgt. Ezra Lee, operating the craft, tried unsuccessfully to sink the British warship H.M.S. *Eagle* in New York Harbor.

Who made the first rocket? The answer depends on the definition of the term. Various cultures have experimented with rocket-like devices, and the concept dates as far back in recorded history as 400 B.C., when a Greek inventor heated a hollow ball full of water and escaping steam propelled it.

Sources indicate the first documented use of rockets was in China. The Chinese had invented gunpowder made of charcoal dust, sulfur, and saltpeter (potassium nitrate); they discovered that when this substance was packed into hollow bamboo tubes and

thrown into a fire, some of the tubes exploded. They attached arrows to such tubes to stabilize their path, and thus the first military rockets were born. Their first recorded use was in the battle of Kai-feng-fu, in 1232, when "fire arrows" helped villagers defend against invading Mongols.

Small bottle rocket

Crankshaft

Offset connections to eight pistons (not shown) turn this central shaft, powering a machine. Crankshafts, used in water wheels by the 13th century, would be significant in the later development of the automobile.

1206 >

1050 >

Crankshaft

● IN USE

Attributed to Islamic inventor Al-Jazari, the crankshaft was significant in the later development of the engine. Al-Jazari created the device in 1206 for use in a waterwheel. This primitive engine consisted of a "chain" of buckets strung together between two large wheels. As the wheels were turned, the chain moved, driven primarily by a crankshaft connected to a piston that drove the motion of the buckets. The buckets constantly scooped up water to the top of an arc and then dropped it down again, which provided a ready source of power. These and other devices were described in depth in Al-Jazari's treatise *The Book of Knowledge of Ingenious Mechanical Devices.*

Engine cutaway showing a crankshaft and pistons

Flywheel

● IN USE

Andalusian Ibn Bassal was experimenting with the design of waterwheels before Ismail Al-Jazari, but his device is particularly noted for its flywheel. He first described the device in the mid-11th century in his work *Kitab al-Filaha.* The purpose of a flywheel is to even out the motion of the driving force of an engine by absorbing the excess rotational energy and releasing it when needed. These devices date back as far as the Bronze Age (3300 to 1200 B.C.).

Ancient Egyptians used flywheels in pottery wheels and

Building On >

Diesel Engine *(p. 270)*

Otto Engine *(p. 272)*

Flywheel

Andalusian inventor Ibn Bassal realized power from an engine can be irregular. To smooth it out he applied a heavy flywheel to a water wheel in 1150. This flywheel attached to a 19th-century steam engine includes a centrifugal governor with two balls to control the speed of the engine.

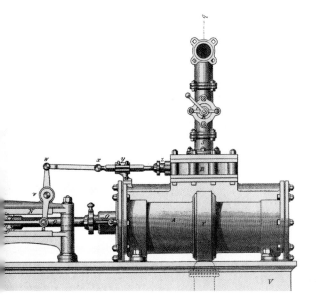

Glider

The Wright Brothers fly a glider as a kite in 1901. Centuries earlier, astronomer Abbas Ibn Firnas built a glider, based on his observations of birds' wings. The takeoff was a success, but he struggled with his landing.

875 >

drilling devices, but it was Ibn Bassal who paved the way for its later use in modern-day engines. Flywheels are still used today in the designs of spacecraft and satellites, as they can direct the movements of satellites without having to employ thruster rockets, and have been used in some types of electric cars as a means of storing energy for later use. With internal combustion engines, flywheels are mounted on crankshafts to keep angular velocity at a constant level. Some designs have proved to lengthen the operation time of electric cars and increase their speed. Flywheels are also used in punching and riveting machines, capturing energy from the motor and releasing it over the course of the punching and riveting cycle.

Glider

● IN USE

Astronomer Abbas Ibn Firnas wanted to fly, and he achieved his goal in 875 at age 65. Having watched birds fly, he thought he understood the physical principles involved. He built himself a glider, which served as his "wings," and had a successful flight. It was the landing that was the problem. Ibn Firnas had not accounted for how birds pull up into a land and he crashed upon landing, sustaining an injury to his back. A crater on the moon was named in his honor in recognition of his achievement. Some aviation historians suggest that Ibn Firnas's flight inspired Eilmer of Malmesbury, an English Benedictine monk, to attempt the same feat around the year 1000. Eilmer's flight ended in tragedy: he was disabled for life after breaking both legs upon landing.

▶ Jet Engine (p. 267)

▶ Wheel (p. 299)

▶ Glider (p. 273)

▶ First Motor-powered Aircraft (p. 269)

Abbas Ibn Firnas

Muslim polymath Abbas Ibn Firnas (810-887) was a man with a lot of interests, studying physics, chemistry, astronomy, and even poetry. He figured out how to make glass from sand. Ibn Firnas is perhaps most well known for being the first human to achieve heavier-than-air flight with his glider; he was the Islamic world's answer to the Wright brothers a thousand years before they would make their historic flight.

Archimedes' Principles

A rubber duck in water illustrates a principal of buoyancy explained by Greek mathematician and inventor Archimedes: An object's ability to float depends on the weight of water it displaces. His military inventions helped defend his home city of Syracuse.

250 B.C. >

Archimedes' Principles

▲ IN THEORY

Archimedes put forth his law of buoyancy in the third century B.C. in his work *On Floating Bodies*. It states that when an object is placed in a fluid, the weight of the fluid that the object displaces determines the amount of force necessary to support the object. It does not matter how much the object itself weighs or even what shape it is. The critical element is the weight of the fluid being displaced. It is said that Archimedes discovered this law when the king, Heron, believed his crown was not gold but gilded silver. He asked Archimedes to prove or disprove his presumption.

Archimedes had an epiphany while stepping into a full bath: he realized he could figure out the volume of the crown by submerging it in water and measuring the amount displaced. By multiplying this volume by the crown's weight and comparing the result to the already known masses of gold and silver, he could arrive at a conclusion.

The law of buoyancy helps scientists understand why ships float rather than sink. If the fluid's density is less than that of the object, the object will sink. If the fluid's density is greater than that of the object, the object will float. The

Appian Way
Squared stones of one of the first paved roads can still be seen today even though the Appian Way was built around 300 B.C. Romans constructed thousands of miles of hard-surface roads to quickly deploy troops to far frontiers.

312 B.C. >

Appian Way

→← CONNECTION

● IN USE

hull of a ship has less density than that of the water it is displacing; thus the ship floats.

Archimedes

Greek mathematician Archimedes is noted for many discoveries: the screw propeller, the lever, and the compound pulley. Legend has it that when Romans attacked Syracuse in Sicily, he suggested using mirrors from a distance to set the Roman ships on fire. His law of buoyancy had a major influence on hydrostatics, which is the scientific study of fluids at rest. This principle has been essential in the understanding of transportation in the air, on the land, and on the sea. It is what enables a ship to float, a submarine to sink, and a hot-air balloon to rise.

Constructed in circa 312 B.C., the Appian Way, or Via Appia, is one of the earliest paved roads. Vital for the expansion and defense of the Roman Empire, it was constructed at the behest of Appius Claudius Caecus, for whom it is named. Appius was a censor—one of a pair of officials who took the census and served as a figurehead of moral guidance and judgment in ancient Rome.

Eventually reaching 350 miles long, the Appian Way ran from Rome south to Capua and later to Beneventum (Benevento) and the coastal cities of Tarentum (Taranto) and Brundisium (Brindisi), on the heel of the Italian peninsula. The road was so well constructed that it is still in existence today. Its tightly cemented, square stone blocks bring to mind the footsteps of legions of Roman soldiers, and its path still carries one past a first-century aqueduct, a second-century villa, and the third-century Baths of Caracalla.

Interstate Highway System (p. 262)

Chariot

Model of a chariot from Ur during the Babylonian period around 2000 B.C. The solid wheel preceded the improved, spoked wheel. Initially a means of transportation only, chariots were later used in the military as well.

Ship

Ancient Egyptians may have built wooden craft such as this one around 2000 B.C. Egyptians also used sails, relying on the wind to propel their ships, the oldest form of transportation still around.

2000 B.C. >

3000 B.C. >

Chariot

● IN USE

It is difficult to determine when the chariot was invented or who invented it—as with many discoveries in ancient history. The iconic wheeled vehicle was used in many ancient civilizations—and, in fact, both the chariot and the wheel stand as important sculptural symbols in many ancient sites.

Sources generally agree that the Egyptians probably created the first chariots around 2000 B.C. Chariots were probably used initially for transportation; later in war; and ultimately in sport, for races. The first use of chariots in battle is documented as occurring among the Hittites around 1600 B.C. Evidence of chariots has also been found in ancient India from around 1500 b.c., and a bronze statue of a horse pulling the sun in a chariot was found in a Danish site and dated to 1400 or 1300 B.C.

What made chariots unique was the spoked design of their wheels, which was an improvement over solid wheels: Lighter and larger wheels allowed horses to pull the chariots faster.

Ship

● IN USE

The ship may well be the oldest mode of transportation still around today. While many ancient cultures had their own designs, the Egyptians were among the first to incorporate sails. At first, these were simply sheets of cloth designed to catch the wind and push the boat along faster. Eventually the Egyptians realized that sails could be used to harness the power of crosswinds or side winds as well, which meant boats could move against the wind and not just with it.

The hull of the boat was constructed first. This was done with wooden planks joined together in a mortise fashion employing tongues and grooves. Caulking made out of plant materials was applied between the joints. Ropes woven through holes in the planks helped ensure everything stayed together. The entire boat was reinforced with crossbeams and girders. Because wood was not in rich supply in Egypt in 3000 B.C., early Egyptian boats did not have keels (these add stability and keep the boat from drifting sideways). Instead a thick sturdy rope was extended along the length of the boat's

Building On >

Automobile (p. 270)

Bicycle (p. 280)

Wheel

Stone wheel dates from a time when ancients found they could move heavy objects by placing beneath them a round device attached to an axle. Wheels were used to ground grain and make pottery before they were used in transportation.

3500 B.C. >

Wheel

➜← CONNECTION

● IN USE

underside, from stern to bow, and lashed tight. Paintings on the walls of tombs and temples show three different types of ancient Egyptian boats: one with straight, cut-off ends; one where the ends of the boat are rounded; and one where one end is rounded and the other is cut off.

Ancient Egyptian boats were also noteworthy for their rudders. The rudder is used to steer a boat, and quarter rudders were well known in ancient times. These were positioned on the sides of boats.

Today, the framework of a ship is built first and then the outer layers are applied. Early ships, however, were typically built starting from the outer surface and working in. Among the simplest early ships were dugout canoes and rafts. In the medieval world, ships were often constructed with both ends rounded and a system of oars along the sides.

Shipbuilding in the early modern era—from the 16th to the early 19th century—was marked by the increasing sophistication of sails.

Among the most significant ideas known to humankind, the wheel may have been invented in Mesopotamia around 3500 B.C. The wheel's potential was recognized in areas of manufacturing and industry such as pottery before it was applied to transportation. Eventually wheels appeared on chariots, carts, wagons, and anything else a person might want to move. Despite the wheel's usefulness, it was not found as a means of transportation in ancient cultures in the Americas. Nor did the wheel evolve much beyond its original form until the 19th century and the advent of the industrial revolution.

Steamboat (p. 283)

Transatlantic Steamship (p. 275)

Hybrid Vehicle (p. 258)

Automobile (p. 270)

Pneumatic Tire (p. 274)

Bicycle (p. 280)

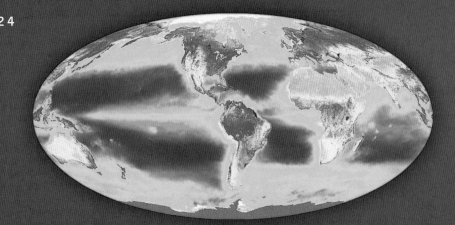

Measuring Ocean Life From Space
NASA's SeaWiFS—a Sea-viewing Wide Field-of-view Sensor—orbited Earth and beamed back information on phytoplankton and algae density, variables in climate change. Dark blue regions are chlorophyll free; dark red areas are dangerously high in nutrients.

Underwater Exploration

After exploring for hundreds of years, it seems as if humans have reached every corner of the Earth. What is left to learn about the planet? It turns out that scientists know more about the solar system than they do about the deepest parts of the world's oceans. In fact, less than one percent of the seafloor has been explored.

Underwater exploration is difficult. Oceans are huge, mostly empty places; the deepest parts of the oceans are perpetually dark; and even though the temperatures of deep oceans are around 30° to 35°F, cold water can remove heat from a person's body 25 times faster than when exposed to the same temperature in air. To explore the depths of the oceans, explorers need to be able to stay in deep water for a long time, protected against the cold, able to see—with a good idea of where to look to find something interesting. To pinpoint a location to explore, scientists use sonar to create overview maps of the ocean floor. Then a transponder signaling system is used to make a more detailed map, along with photographs taken at regular intervals. Another emerging technology in the form of satellites with special sensors is being used to create "maps" based on the amount of plankton, sediment, or organic chemicals on the ocean floor. This system has the added benefit of giving scientists a picture of the health and vitality of the oceans by allowing them to see an overview of plankton blooms, for example, or areas of ocean desert that were once teeming with life.

Once scientists have determined where to look, the next question is how to get there. Detailed observation of the oceans' depths relies on submersible vehicles: remotely operated vehicles and automatic underwater vehicles, as well as submersibles carrying humans. Human-occupied submersibles have played an important part in underwater exploration, allowing researchers to discover hydrothermal vents and the unusual tube worms, microbes, and other creatures that thrive in extreme deep ocean environments. Submersibles also have explored mid-ocean ridges, the bridge between volcanoes and mountains where the Earth's crust is created.

1978, 1945

Communication technologies such as GPS and communications satellites are essential for the exploration of the world's oceans. *See pages 21, 38*

1862

The *Alligator* submarine was a major development in underwater vehicle technology. *See page 272*

1620

The oar-propelled 17th-century submarine is one of the first examples of submersible transportation technologies. *See page 292*

Personal Submersibles
One-person underwater vehicles allow oceanographers and eager citizen scientists to take their explorations to new depths—literally.

Deep Breaths
Humans can maneuver underwater only inside a pressurized vehicle, invented in the 17th century. The deepest submersible dive took place in 1960, when Don Walsh and Jacques Piccard dove to the bottom of the Mariana Trench, 10,920 meters down.

250 B.C., **3000** B.C.

The formulation of Archimedes' principle and the building of the first ships began the exploration of the Earth's oceans. *See pages 296, 298*

Big Ideas Through Time

From today back to 3500 B.C.

Understanding takes analysis—breaking down into categories, time spans, areas of interest—and synthesis—putting it all back together. So far, this book delved into the analysis of how big ideas of today and tomorrow link back to the big ideas of centuries past. So far, this book also depended on an analytical division of the realms of science and technology into six categories, which became our chapter divisions. Now it is time to put it all back together. In real time, big ideas interact. They bounce off each other, they borrow from each other, they influence and build upon each other. Seeing world history as a stream of big ideas through time helps us understand those relationships.

In the next eight pages, come with us on a visual journey. Once again, we start in the recent past and move backward in time. Once again, we use the six categories, designated by color, to distinguish the six realms of science and technology. But placing these streams of big ideas one on top of another gives us a way to see how they interact. Every breakthrough from all the time lines appears on the next eight pages, keyed to its realm of science and technology and to its year.

Where are the 24 big ideas of today? If we were to plot them on this reverse chronology, they would all cluster at the beginning. Think instead of this eight-page, full-book time line as a picture of all the ideas as they stream together, building to the big ideas of today—and to the big ideas we cannot even imagine, in store for us tomorrow.

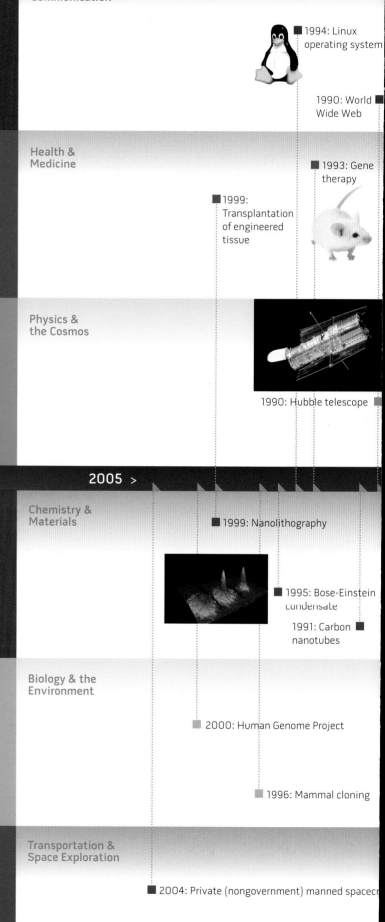

Information & Communication

1994: Linux operating system

1990: World Wide Web

Health & Medicine

1993: Gene therapy

1999: Transplantation of engineered tissue

Physics & the Cosmos

1990: Hubble telescope

2005 >

Chemistry & Materials

1999: Nanolithography

1995: Bose-Einstein condensate

1991: Carbon nanotubes

Biology & the Environment

2000: Human Genome Project

1996: Mammal cloning

Transportation & Space Exploration

2004: Private (nongovernment) manned spacecr

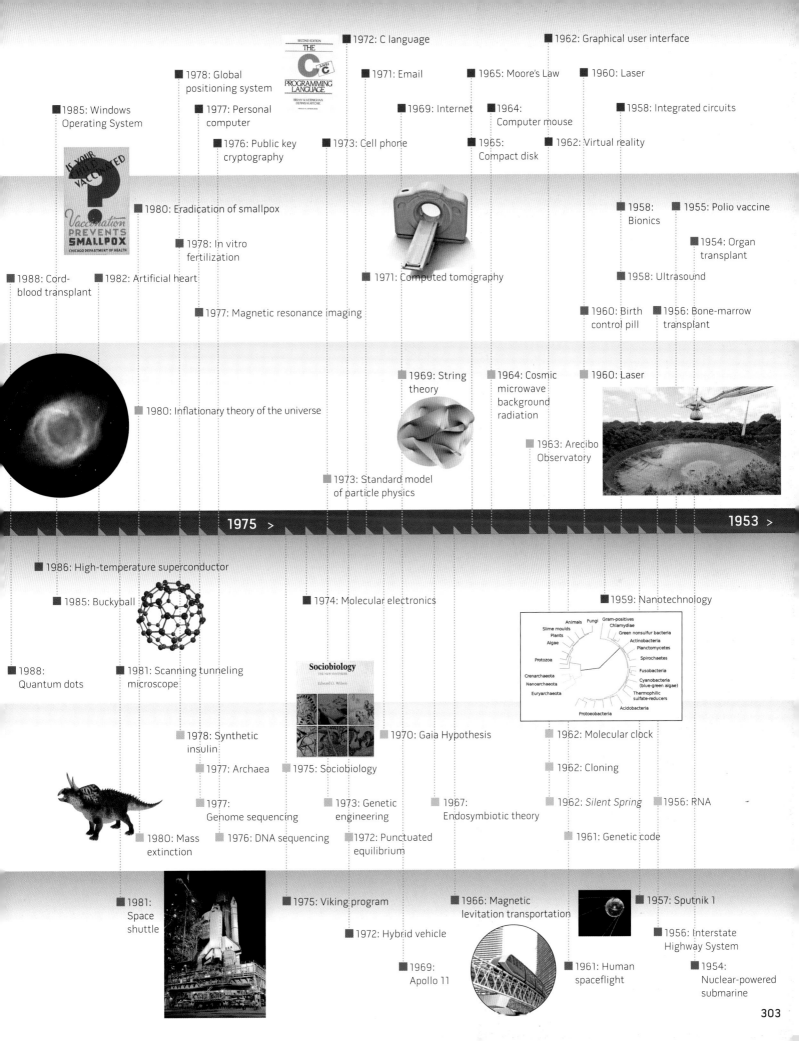

1972: C language

1962: Graphical user interface

1978: Global positioning system

1971: Email

1965: Moore's Law

1960: Laser

1977: Personal computer

1969: Internet

1964: Computer mouse

1958: Integrated circuits

1985: Windows Operating System

1976: Public key cryptography

1973: Cell phone

1965: Compact disk

1962: Virtual reality

1980: Eradication of smallpox

1958: Bionics

1955: Polio vaccine

1978: In vitro fertilization

1954: Organ transplant

1988: Cord-blood transplant

1982: Artificial heart

1971: Computed tomography

1958: Ultrasound

1977: Magnetic resonance imaging

1960: Birth control pill

1956: Bone-marrow transplant

1969: String theory

1964: Cosmic microwave background radiation

1960: Laser

1980: Inflationary theory of the universe

1963: Arecibo Observatory

1973: Standard model of particle physics

1975 >

1953 >

1986: High-temperature superconductor

1985: Buckyball

1974: Molecular electronics

1959: Nanotechnology

1988: Quantum dots

1981: Scanning tunneling microscope

1978: Synthetic insulin

1970: Gaia Hypothesis

1962: Molecular clock

1977: Archaea

1975: Sociobiology

1962: Cloning

1977: Genome sequencing

1973: Genetic engineering

1967: Endosymbiotic theory

1962: Silent Spring

1956: RNA

1980: Mass extinction

1976: DNA sequencing

1972: Punctuated equilibrium

1961: Genetic code

1981: Space shuttle

1975: Viking program

1966: Magnetic levitation transportation

1957: Sputnik 1

1972: Hybrid vehicle

1956: Interstate Highway System

1969: Apollo 11

1961: Human spaceflight

1954: Nuclear-powered submarine

303

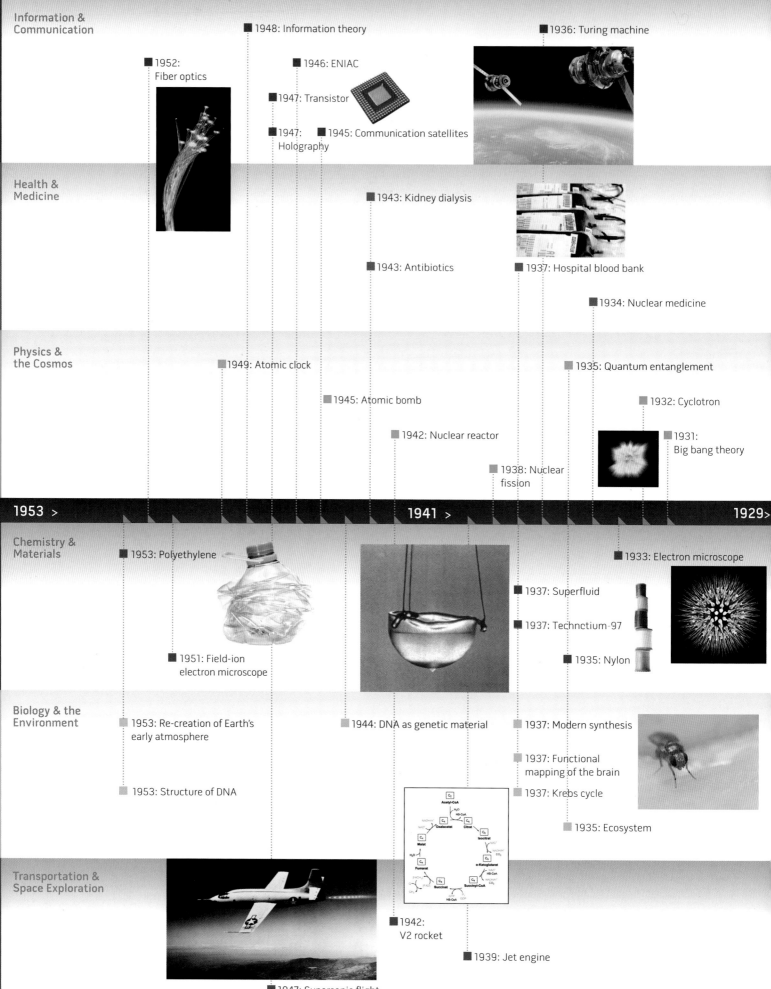

Information & Communication

1948: Information theory

1936: Turing machine

1952: Fiber optics

1946: ENIAC

1947: Transistor

1947: Holography

1945: Communication satellites

Health & Medicine

1943: Kidney dialysis

1943: Antibiotics

1937: Hospital blood bank

1934: Nuclear medicine

Physics & the Cosmos

1949: Atomic clock

1935: Quantum entanglement

1945: Atomic bomb

1932: Cyclotron

1942: Nuclear reactor

1931: Big bang theory

1938: Nuclear fission

1953 >   **1941 >**   **1929 >**

Chemistry & Materials

1953: Polyethylene

1933: Electron microscope

1937: Superfluid

1937: Technctium-97

1951: Field-ion electron microscope

1935: Nylon

Biology & the Environment

1953: Re-creation of Earth's early atmosphere

1944: DNA as genetic material

1937: Modern synthesis

1937: Functional mapping of the brain

1937: Krebs cycle

1953: Structure of DNA

1935: Ecosystem

Transportation & Space Exploration

1942: V2 rocket

1939: Jet engine

1947: Supersonic flight

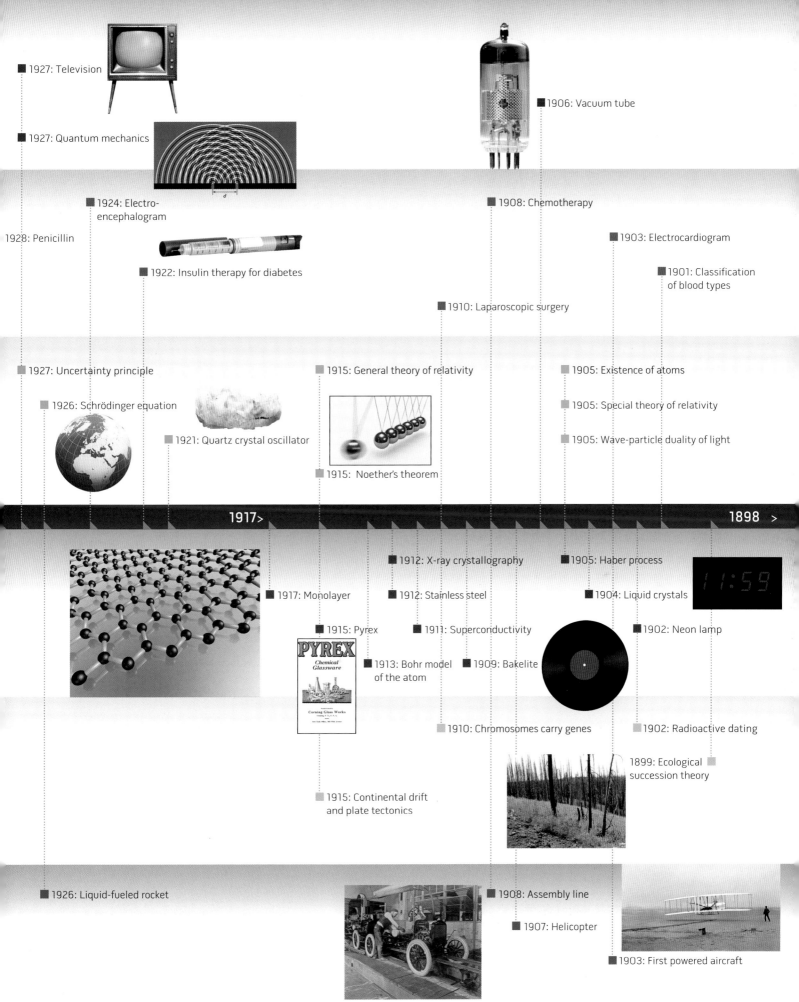

■ 1927: Television

■ 1927: Quantum mechanics

■ 1906: Vacuum tube

■ 1924: Electro-
encephalogram

■ 1908: Chemotherapy

1928: Penicillin

■ 1903: Electrocardiogram

■ 1922: Insulin therapy for diabetes

■ 1901: Classification
of blood types

■ 1910: Laparoscopic surgery

■ 1927: Uncertainty principle

■ 1915: General theory of relativity

■ 1905: Existence of atoms

■ 1926: Schrödinger equation

■ 1905: Special theory of relativity

■ 1921: Quartz crystal oscillator

■ 1905: Wave-particle duality of light

■ 1915: Noether's theorem

1917>

1898 >

■ 1912: X-ray crystallography

■ 1905: Haber process

■ 1917: Monolayer

■ 1912: Stainless steel

■ 1904: Liquid crystals

11:59

■ 1915: Pyrex

■ 1911: Superconductivity

■ 1902: Neon lamp

PYREX
Chemical
Glassware

Manufactured by the
Corning Glass Works
Corning, N. Y., U. S. A.

New York Office: 165 Fifth Avenue

■ 1913: Bohr model
of the atom

■ 1909: Bakelite

■ 1910: Chromosomes carry genes

■ 1902: Radioactive dating

1899: Ecological
succession theory

■ 1915: Continental drift
and plate tectonics

■ 1926: Liquid-fueled rocket

■ 1908: Assembly line

■ 1907: Helicopter

■ 1903: First powered aircraft

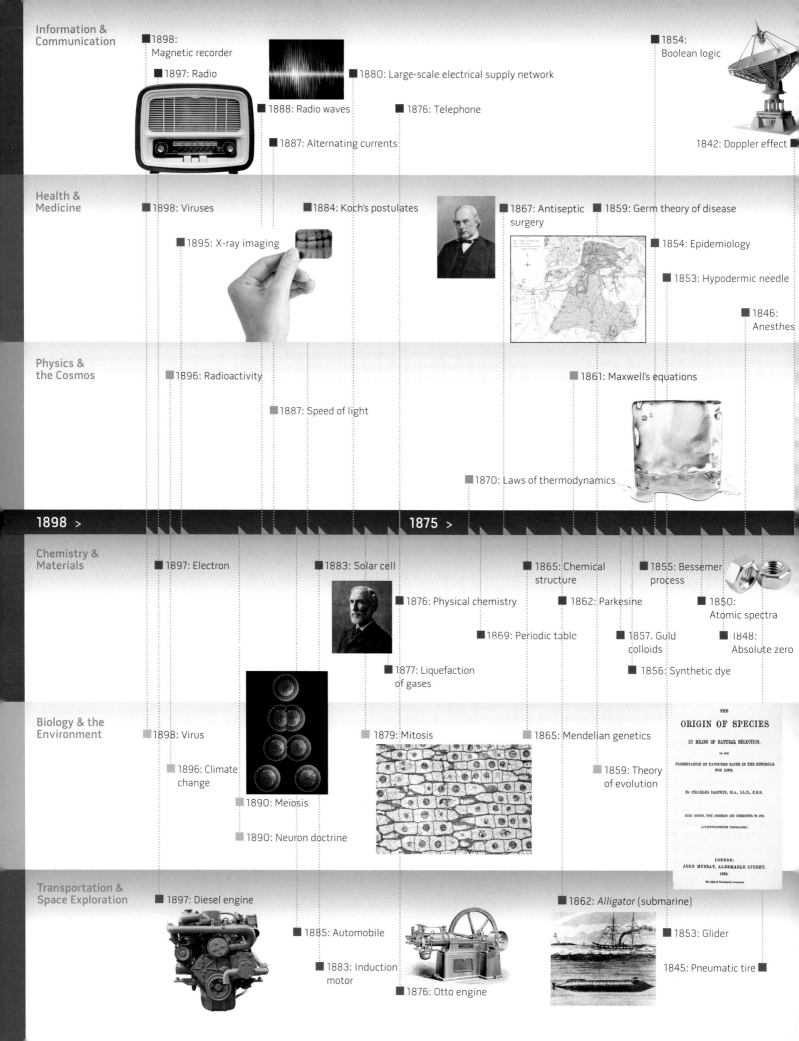

Information & Communication

1898: Magnetic recorder

1897: Radio

1880: Large-scale electrical supply network

1888: Radio waves

1876: Telephone

1887: Alternating currents

1854: Boolean logic

1842: Doppler effect

Health & Medicine

1898: Viruses

1884: Koch's postulates

1867: Antiseptic surgery

1859: Germ theory of disease

1895: X-ray imaging

1854: Epidemiology

1853: Hypodermic needle

1846: Anesthes

Physics & the Cosmos

1896: Radioactivity

1861: Maxwell's equations

1887: Speed of light

1870: Laws of thermodynamics

1898 >

1875 >

Chemistry & Materials

1897: Electron

1883: Solar cell

1865: Chemical structure

1855: Bessemer process

1876: Physical chemistry

1862: Parkesine

1850: Atomic spectra

1869: Periodic table

1857. Gold colloids

1848: Absolute zero

1877: Liquefaction of gases

1856: Synthetic dye

Biology & the Environment

1898: Virus

1879: Mitosis

1865: Mendelian genetics

1896: Climate change

1890: Meiosis

1859: Theory of evolution

1890: Neuron doctrine

THE
ORIGIN OF SPECIES
BY MEANS OF NATURAL SELECTION,
OR THE
PRESERVATION OF FAVOURED RACES IN THE STRUGGLE
FOR LIFE.
BY CHARLES DARWIN, M.A., LL.D., F.R.S.

SIXTH EDITION, WITH ADDITIONS AND CORRECTIONS TO 1872.
(TWENTY-FOURTH THOUSAND.)

LONDON:
JOHN MURRAY, ALBEMARLE STREET.
1882.

Transportation & Space Exploration

1897: Diesel engine

1862: *Alligator* (submarine)

1885: Automobile

1853: Glider

1883: Induction motor

1845: Pneumatic tire

1876: Otto engine

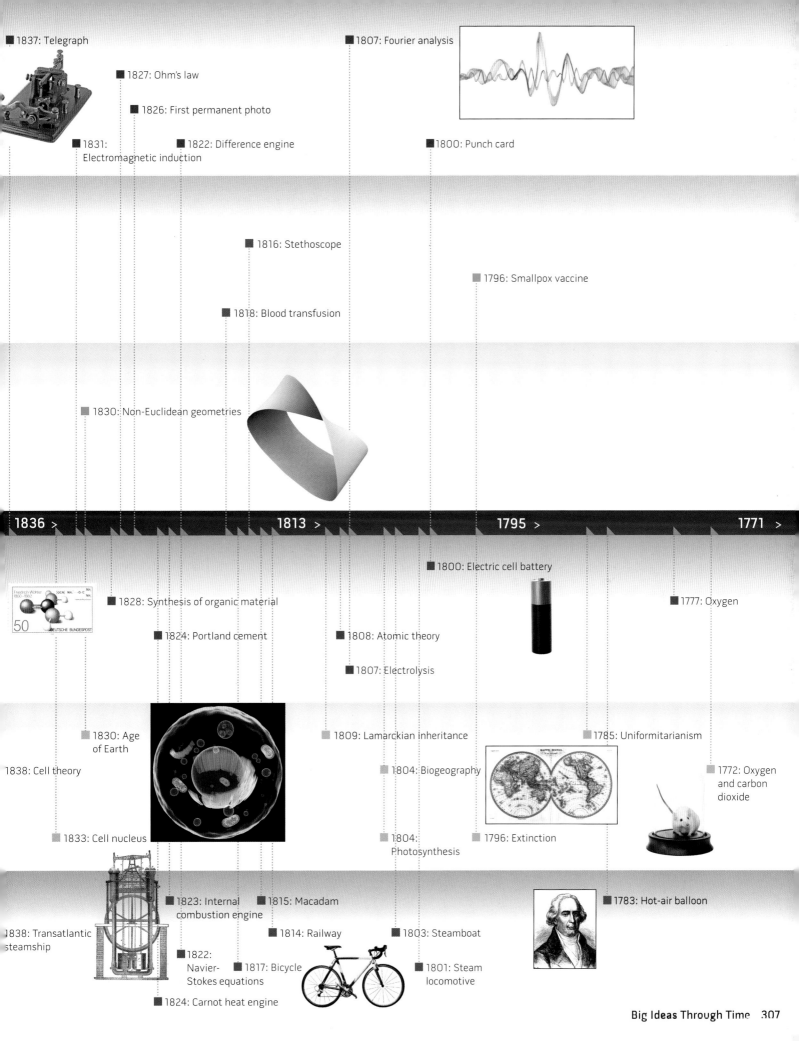

■ 1837: Telegraph

■ 1827: Ohm's law

■ 1826: First permanent photo

■ 1831: Electromagnetic induction

■ 1822: Difference engine

■ 1807: Fourier analysis

■ 1800: Punch card

■ 1816: Stethoscope

■ 1796: Smallpox vaccine

■ 1818: Blood transfusion

■ 1830: Non-Euclidean geometries

1836 > **1813 >** **1795 >** **1771 >**

■ 1828: Synthesis of organic material

■ 1800: Electric cell battery

■ 1777: Oxygen

■ 1824: Portland cement

■ 1808: Atomic theory

■ 1807: Electrolysis

■ 1830: Age of Earth

■ 1809: Lamarckian inheritance

■ 1785: Uniformitarianism

1838: Cell theory

■ 1804: Biogeography

■ 1772: Oxygen and carbon dioxide

■ 1833: Cell nucleus

■ 1804: Photosynthesis

■ 1796: Extinction

■ 1823: Internal combustion engine

■ 1815: Macadam

■ 1783: Hot-air balloon

1838: Transatlantic steamship

■ 1814: Railway

■ 1803: Steamboat

■ 1822: Navier-Stokes equations

■ 1817: Bicycle

■ 1801: Steam locomotive

■ 1824: Carnot heat engine

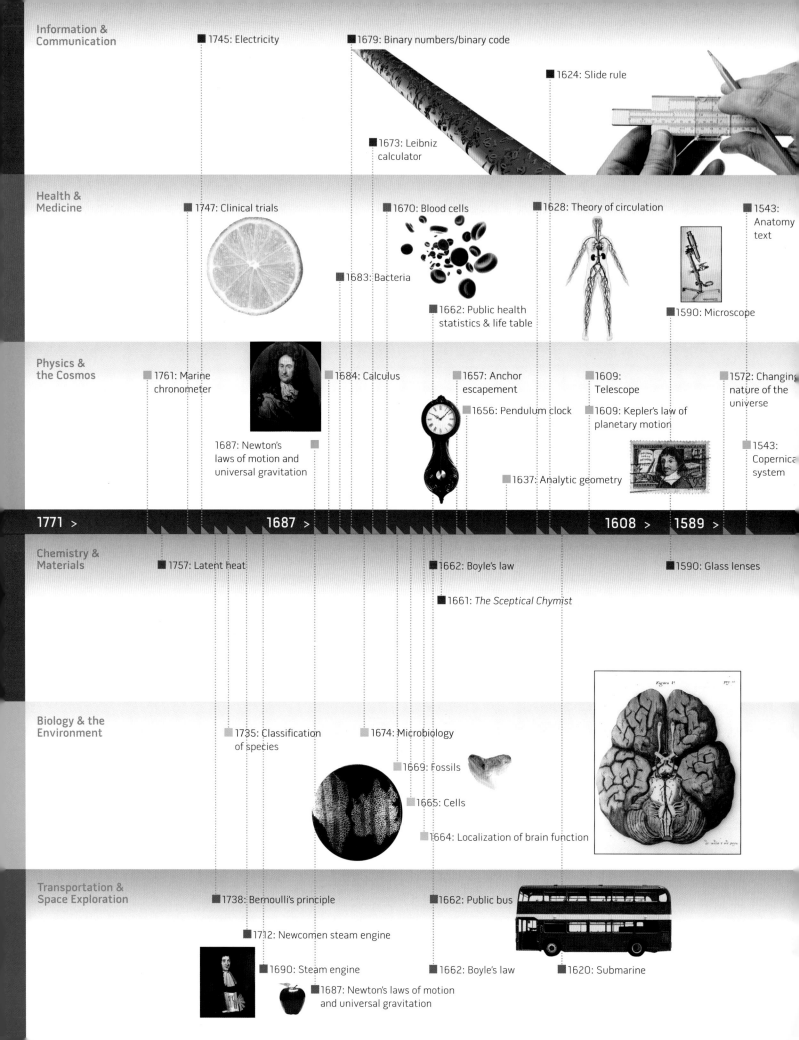

Information & Communication

- 1745: Electricity
- 1679: Binary numbers/binary code
- 1624: Slide rule
- 1673: Leibniz calculator

Health & Medicine

- 1747: Clinical trials
- 1670: Blood cells
- 1628: Theory of circulation
- 1543: Anatomy text
- 1683: Bacteria
- 1662: Public health statistics & life table
- 1590: Microscope

Physics & the Cosmos

- 1761: Marine chronometer
- 1684: Calculus
- 1657: Anchor escapement
- 1609: Telescope
- 1572: Changing nature of the universe
- 1656: Pendulum clock
- 1609: Kepler's law of planetary motion
- 1687: Newton's laws of motion and universal gravitation
- 1637: Analytic geometry
- 1543: Copernican system

1771 >   **1687 >**   **1608 >**   **1589 >**

Chemistry & Materials

- 1757: Latent heat
- 1662: Boyle's law
- 1590: Glass lenses
- 1661: *The Sceptical Chymist*

Biology & the Environment

- 1735: Classification of species
- 1674: Microbiology
- 1669: Fossils
- 1665: Cells
- 1664: Localization of brain function

Transportation & Space Exploration

- 1738: Bernoulli's principle
- 1662: Public bus
- 1712: Newcomen steam engine
- 1690: Steam engine
- 1662: Boyle's law
- 1620: Submarine
- 1687: Newton's laws of motion and universal gravitation

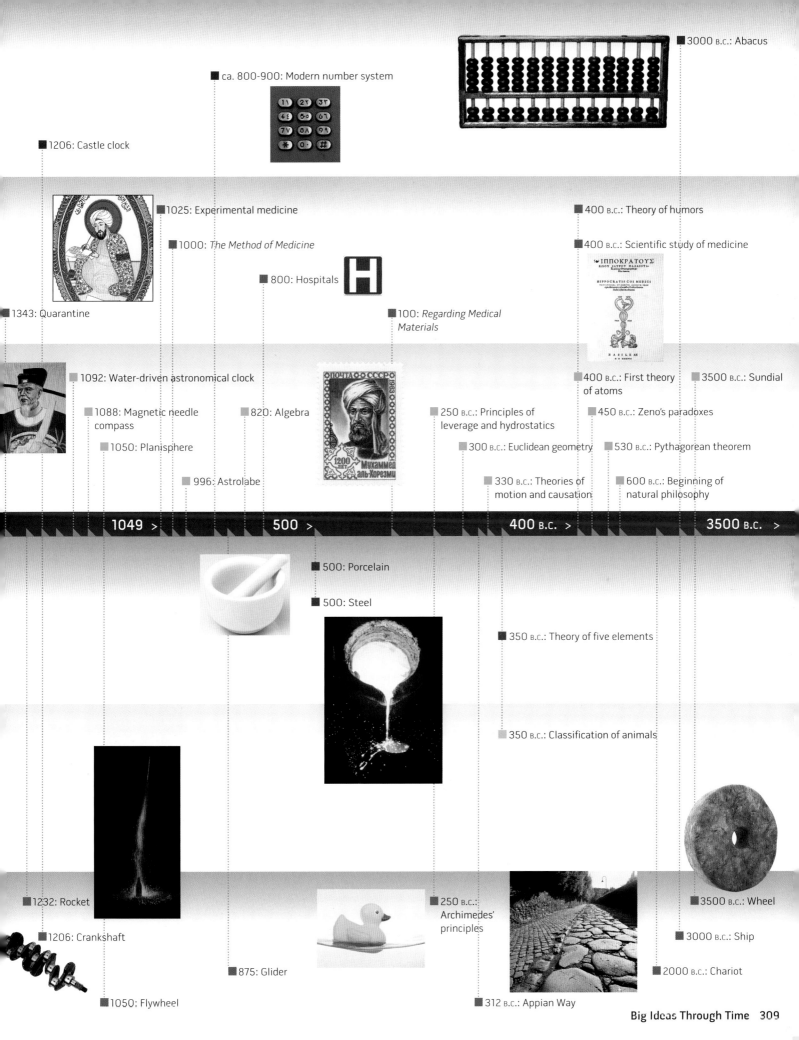

■ 3000 B.C.: Abacus

■ ca. 800-900: Modern number system

■ 1206: Castle clock

■ 1025: Experimental medicine

■ 400 B.C.: Theory of humors

■ 1000: *The Method of Medicine*

■ 400 B.C.: Scientific study of medicine

■ 800: Hospitals

■ 1343: Quarantine

■ 100: *Regarding Medical Materials*

■ 1092: Water-driven astronomical clock

■ 400 B.C.: First theory of atoms

■ 3500 B.C.: Sundial

■ 1088: Magnetic needle compass

■ 820: Algebra

■ 250 B.C.: Principles of leverage and hydrostatics

■ 450 B.C.: Zeno's paradoxes

■ 1050: Planisphere

■ 300 B.C.: Euclidean geometry

■ 530 B.C.: Pythagorean theorem

■ 996: Astrolabe

■ 330 B.C.: Theories of motion and causation

■ 600 B.C.: Beginning of natural philosophy

1049 > **500 >** **400 B.C. >** **3500 B.C. >**

■ 500: Porcelain

■ 500: Steel

■ 350 B.C.: Theory of five elements

■ 350 B.C.: Classification of animals

■ 1232: Rocket

■ 250 B.C.: Archimedes' principles

■ 3500 B.C.: Wheel

■ 1206: Crankshaft

■ 3000 B.C.: Ship

■ 875: Glider

■ 2000 B.C.: Chariot

■ 1050: Flywheel

■ 312 B.C.: Appian Way

FOREWORD

Author Timothy Ferris, called "the best popular science writer in the English language" by the *Christian Science Monitor*, has written a dozen books, including *Seeing in the Dark*, *The Whole Shebang*, and *Coming of Age in the Milky Way*. His books have been nominated for the Pulitzer Prize and the National Book Award. Ferris also notably created the Voyager phonograph record, a relic of human civilization depicting life on Earth that was launched aboard the twin Voyager spacecraft.

Ferris is a former newspaper reporter and editor of *Rolling Stone*. He contributed to such publications as the *New Yorker*, *National Geographic*, the *New York Review of Books*, *Forbes*, *Harper's*, *Life*, *Nature*, *Time*, *Newsweek*, *Readers' Digest*, *Scientific American*, the *Nation*, *New Republic*, and the *New York Times*. Ferris, a fellow of the American Association for the Advancement of Science, is currently professor emeritus at the University of California, Berkeley.

INFORMATION & COMMUNICATION, BIOLOGY & THE ENVIRONMENT, PHYSICS & THE COSMOS, TRANSPORTATION & SPACE EXPLORATION

Lisa McCoy has been a freelance writer and editor for more than 12 years. Her work covers a wide range of industries but is focused primarily on technology and medicine. She co-authored the book *Microsoft Office Word 2003 QuickSteps* and was the editor of *Microsoft Flight Simulator 2002*. Titles she has edited include *ASP.NET at Work*, *Migrating to Visual Basic.NET*, and *Secrets of Rock Star Programmers*. A recent short story by McCoy was awarded Honorable Mention in the L. Ron Hubbard Writers of the Future contest.

HEALTH & MEDICINE

Katharine Greider is a freelance writer and author living in New York City. She began in journalism at a national alternative newsweekly and then worked for a small-town daily newspaper. As a freelancer for more than 15 years, Greider has written for numerous local and national magazines, newspapers, and nonprofits, including the *New York Times* and the *AARP Bulletin*. She is the author, most recently, of *The Archaeology of Home: An Epic Set on a Thousand Square Feet of the Lower East Side* (PublicAffairs 2011).

CHEMISTRY & MATERIALS

Kelly Kagamas Tomkies is a freelance writer and editor. She is the author or co-author of four books and has served as editor of publications such as *Smart Business* and *Midwest Food Service News*. She has written hundreds of articles for publications and websites on subjects ranging from children and pets to careers, business, finance, and biotechnology, and she has edited articles, blogs, and book manuscripts for publishers, publications, and authors.

Illustrations Credits

18 (LO LE), Larry Ewing; 18 (UP), ianwhite.com/CORBIS Outline; 19, Matt Britt; 20 (UP LE), Ed Quinn/CORBIS; 20 (UP), Courtesy Microsoft; 20 (UP RT), Courtesy Microsoft; 20 (LO), Deborah Feingold/CORBIS; 21, iStockphoto.com; 22 (LE), Science Source/Photo Researchers, Inc.; 22 (RT), Wikipedia; 23 (LE), Courtesy Apple; 23 (RT), alengoalengo/iStockphoto.com; 24 (LE), Saleeee/Shutterstock; 24 (CTR), iStockphoto.com; 24 (RT), Wikipedia; 24-25 (CTR), Ashby Design; 25 (LO), z576/Shutterstock; 25 (UP), Viorika/iStockphoto.com; 26-27, BigStock, Jose Fuste Raga/CORBIS, Andrea Pistolesi/Getty Images, Trent Nelson, Wikipedia; 28, Chris Harrison; 29 (UP LE), kydna/iStockphoto.com; 29 (UP RT), drfelice/Shutterstock; 29 (LO), Vadim Subbotin/Shutterstock; 30 (LE), kaarsten/Shutterstock; 30 (UP RT), Wikipedia; 30 (LO RT), Skocko/Shutterstock; 31 (LE), TonisPan/iStockphoto.com; 31 (RT), Fippzor/Shutterstock; 32, Pgiam/iStockphoto.com; 33 (LE), Paul Orr/Shutterstock; 33 (RT), Time & Life Pictures/Getty Images; 34 (LE), djgis/Shutterstock; 34 (RT), Tony Kwan/iStockphoto.com; 35, TRINACRIA PHOTO/Shutterstock; 36-37, Stefan Kuhr & Immanuel Bloch, MPQ; 38, Time & Life Pictures/Getty Images; 38-39, Petrovich9/iStockphoto.com; 39, The Art Archive/Alamy; 40 (LE), Alessia Pierdomenico/Reuters/CORBIS; 40 (RT), shaunl/iStockphoto.com; 41 (LO), John Springer Collection/CORBIS; 41 (UP), Michael Taylor/Shutterstock; 42 (LE), Jozsef Szasz-Fabian/Shutterstock; 42 (RT), 3DStock/iStockphoto.com; 43 (LE), Zhukov Oleg/Shutterstock; 43 (RT), gallofoto/Shutterstock; 44 (LE), Photosani/Shutterstock; 44 (RT), Iaroslav Neliubov/Shutterstock; 45 (UP LE), U.S. Library of Congress/Photo Researchers, Inc.; 45 (UP RT), Wikipedia; 45 (LO), Wikipedia; 46 (LE), Library of Congress; 46 (RT), SSPL/Getty Images; 47, spaxiax/Shutterstock; 48-49, iStockphoto.com, Shutterstock.com, Melissa Brandts/National Geographic My Shot, Satyaki Basu, Glennis Siverson; 50 (LE), SSPL/Getty Images; 50 (RT), Elerium/iStockphoto.com; 51, Adrio Communications Ltd/Shutterstock; 52 (LE), DK Limited/CORBIS; 52 (RT), Stephen Oliver/Getty Images; 53 (LE), SPL/Photo Researchers, Inc.; 53 (RT), Bettmann/CORBIS; 54 (LE), Mikhail/Shutterstock; 54 (RT), c./Shutterstock; 55 (LE), MPI/Getty Images; 55 (RT), Dalibor/Shutterstock; 56 (LE), Universal History Archive/Getty Images; 56 (RT), Wikipedia; 57 (LE), Granite/Shutterstock; 57 (RT), Museum of Fine Arts, Boston; 57 (LO), Paul Paladin/Shutterstock; 58 (LE), The Art Archive/Alamy; 58 (RT), Bas Photo/Shutterstock; 59, happystock/Shutterstock; 60-61, Vika Valter/iStockphoto.com; 66 (LE), AP Photo/Lynn Hey; 66 (RT), George Steinmetz/CORBIS; 67 (LE), zmeelzmeel/iStockphoto.com; 67 (CTR), dra schwartz/iStockphoto.com; 67 (RT), MedicalRF.com/Visuals Unlimited, Inc.; 68 (UP LE), SPL/Photo Researchers, Inc.; 68 (UP RT), Bettmann/CORBIS; 68 (LO), Eugene Sim/Shutterstock; 69 (UP LE), Bettmann/CORBIS; 69 (UP RT), 3D4Medical/Photo Researchers, Inc.; 69 (LO), Library of Congress; 70 (LE), AJ Photos/Photo Researchers, Inc.; 70 (RT), SPL/Photo Researchers, Inc.; 71 (LE), Mary Rice/Shutterstock; 71 (RT), patrimonio designs limited/Shutterstock; 72-73, Rebecca Hale; 74 (UP LE), Ryan J. Lane/iStockphoto.com; 74 (UP RT), Lusoimages/Shutterstock; 74 (LO), pixeljuice/iStockphoto.com; 75 (LE), Haywiremedia/Shutterstock; 75 (RT), Mark Thiessen; 76 (LE), Dr. Keith Wheeler/Photo Researchers, Inc.; 76 (RT), BSIP/Photo Researchers, Inc.; 77 (LE), Sven Torfinn/Panos Pictures; 77 (RT), Paul Popper/Popperfoto/Getty Images; 78 (LE), Kevin Curtis/Photo Researchers, Inc.; 78 (RT), Photo Researchers, Inc.; 79 (LE), Time & Life Pictures/Getty Images; 79 (RT), BSIP/Photo Researchers, Inc.; 80 (UP LE), Bettmann/CORBIS; 80 (UP RT), Ted Kinsman/Photo Researchers, Inc.; 80 (LO), vladm/Shutterstock; 81 (UP LE), James King-Holmes/Photo Researchers, Inc.; 81 (UP RT), Dr. Fred Hossler/Visuals Unlimited, Inc.; 81 (LO), Geoff Kidd/Photo Researchers, Inc.; 82 (UP LE), Library of Congress; 82 (UP RT), BSIP/Photo Researchers, Inc.; 82 (LO), Brian A Jackson/Shutterstock; 83 (LE), Science Source/Photo Researchers, Inc.; 83 (CTR), Dr. P. Marazzi/Photo Researchers, Inc.; 83 (RT), BIODISC/Visuals Unlimited; 84-85, Zephyr/Photo Researchers, Inc., Shutterstock.com, ISM/Phototake; 86, freelion/Shutterstock; 86-87, Jean Claude Revy/ISM/Phototake; 87, MedicalRF.com/Visuals Unlimited, Inc.; 88 (LE), Jeremys78/Shutterstock; 88 (RT), Ted Kinsman/Photo Researchers, Inc.; 89 (UP LE), akva/Shutterstock; 89 (UP RT), Bettmann/CORBIS; 89 (LO), Wikipedia; 90 (LE), Smithsonian Institution Libraries; 90 (RT), George Mattei/Photo Researchers, Inc.; 91 (LE), Wikipedia; 91 (RT), John Snow; 92 (LE), Bettmann/CORBIS; 92 (RT), CC Studio/Photo Researchers, Inc.; 93 (LE), Wellcome Library, London; 93 (RT), Wellcome Library, London; 93 (LO), BSIP/Photo Researchers, Inc.; 94 (UP LE), Getty Images; 94 (UP RT), CDC/Photo Researchers, Inc.; 94 (LO), Wellcome Library, London; 95 (LE), tatniz/Shutterstock; 95 (RT), Wellcome Library, London; 96-97, Matthias Kulka/CORBIS; 98 (LE), Bettmann/CORBIS; 98 (RT), Tim Vernon, LTH NHS Trust/Photo Researchers, Inc.; 99 (UP LE), Wellcome Library, London; 99 (UP RT), Shutterstock; 99 (LO), Wellcome Library, London; 100, Wikipedia; 100-101, Sebastian Kaulitzki/Shutterstock; 101 (UP), National Library of Medicine/NIH; 101 (LO), Wellcome Library, London; 102 (LE), National Library of Medicine/NIH; 102 (RT), ISM/Phototake; 103 (UP LE), Wellcome Library, London; 103 (UP RT), New York Public Library/Photo Researchers, Inc.; 103 (LO), Wikipedia; 104 (LE), The Art Archive/Pharaonic Village Cairo/Gianni Dagli Orti; 104 (RT), French School/Getty Images; 105 (LE), Wikipedia; 105 (RT), AFP/Getty Images ; 106 (LE), Wikipedia; 106 (RT), New York Public Library/Photo Researchers, Inc.; 107 (UP LE), Hulton Archive/Getty Images; 107 (UP RT), Wikipedia; 107 (LO), Thank You/Shutterstock; 108-109, Pasieka/Photo Researchers, Inc., SPL/Photo Researchers, Inc., Sheila Terry/Photo Researchers, Inc.; 114 (UP LE), NASA; 114-115, NASA; 114 (LO), Hale Observatories/Photo Researchers, Inc.; 115, Michael Taylor/Shutterstock; 116 (UP LE), Wikipedia; 116 (UP RT), David Nunuk/Photo Researchers, Inc.; 116 (LO), NASA/WMAP Science Team/Photo Researchers, Inc.; 116-117, TexPhoto/iStockphoto.com; 117 (RT), evirgen/iStockphoto.com; 118 (UP LE), Royal Greenwich Observatory/Photo Researchers, Inc.; 118 (UP RT), U.S. National Archives/Photo Researchers, Inc.; 118 (LO), Brian Brake/Photo Researchers, Inc.; 119 (LE), SPL/Photo Researchers, Inc.; 119 (RT), Moncherie/Shutterstock; 120 (LE), Pascal Goetgheluck/Photo Researchers, Inc; 120 (RT), Corbin O'Grady Studio/Photo Researchers, Inc.; 121 (LE), Lawrence Berkeley Laboratory/Photo Researchers, Inc.; 121 (RT), Risto Viita/Shutterstock; 122-123, BigStock, Shutterstock; 124 (UP LE), Ashby Design; 124 (UP RT), W. F. Meggers Collection/AIP/Photo Researchers, Inc.; 124 (LO), Ashby Design; 125 (UP LE), sbayramsbayram/iStockphoto.com; 125 (UP RT), GIPhotoStock/Photo Researchers, Inc.; 125 (LO), optimarc/Shutterstock; 126 (LE), Royal Astronomical Society/Photo Researchers, Inc.; 126 (RT), NASA/ESA/STSCI/G. Bower & R. Green, NOAO/Photo Researchers, Inc.; 127 (LE), FreshPaint/Shutterstock; 127 (RT), Universitäts-Archiv Göttingen/Archives of the Mathematisches Forschungsinstitut Oberwolfach; 128 (LE), SPL/Photo Researchers, Inc.; 128 (RT), SPL/Photo Researchers, Inc.; 128-129, Detlev van Ravenswaay/Photo Researchers, Inc.; 129 (LE), Arnd Wiegmann/Reuters/CORBIS; 129 (RT), E. R. Degginger/Photo Researchers, Inc.; 130 (LE), GIPhotoStock/Photo Researchers, Inc.; 130 (CTR), Omikron/Photo Researchers, Inc.; 130 (LO), pashapixel/Shutterstock; 130-131, Royal Astronomical Society/Photo Researchers, Inc.; 131 (LE),

Inc.; 239 (CTR), National Library of Medicine/NIH; 239 (RT), Wellcome Library, London; 240-241, Eye of Science/Photo Researchers, Inc.; 242, Library of Congress; 242-243, Steven Wright/Shutterstock; 243, Gerd Guenther/Photo Researchers, Inc.; 244 (LE), Photo Researchers Inc.; 244 (RT), Royal Institution of Great Britain/Photo Researchers, Inc.; 245 (LE), Hulton Archive/Getty Images; 245 (RT), James Brey/iStockphoto.com; 246 (LE), Humanities and Social Sciences Library/NYPL/Photo Researchers, Inc.; 246 (CTR), Wellcome Library, London; 246-247, SPL/Photo Researchers, Inc.; 247 (LE), Photon75/Shutterstock; 247 (RT), National Library of Medicine/NIH; 248 (LE), Rita Greer; 248 (RT), Philippe Psaila/Photo Researchers, Inc.; 249 (LE), Wikipedia; 249 (RT), Sheila Terry/Photo Researchers, Inc.; 250-251, Victor Habbick Visions/Photo Researchers, Inc., Mike Agliolo/Photo Researchers, Inc.; 256 (LE), Scaled Composites/Photo Researchers, Inc.; 256 (RT), NASA; 257, NASA; 258 (LE), Caltech Archives; 258 (RT), Caltech Archives; 259 (UP), NASA; 259 (LO), NASA; 260 (LE), Kameleon007/iStockphoto.com; 260-261, NASA; 261 (UP LE), Wikipedia; 261 (UP RT), Mark Thiessen; 261 (LO), nadi555/Shutterstock; 262 (LE), hartcreations/iStockphoto.com; 262-263, U.S. National Archives and Records Administration/Photo Researchers, Inc.; 263 (LE), Swim Ink 2/CORBIS; 263 (RT), NASA; 264-265, Tesla Motors; 266, Detlev van Ravenswaay/Photo Researchers, Inc.; 267 (UP LE), Paul Wootton/Photo Researchers, Inc.; 267 (UP RT), Detlev van Ravenswaay/Photo Researchers, Inc.; 267 (LO), SPL/Photo Researchers, Inc.; 268 (LE), NASA; 268 (RT), Library of Congress; 269 (LE), RIA Novosti/Photo Researchers, Inc.; 269 (RT), Wikipedia; 269 (LO), Mr. Twister/iStockphoto.com; 270 (LE), stocksnapp/Shutterstock; 270-271, Miriam & Ira Wallach Division of Arts, Prints and Photographs/NYPL/Photo Researchers, Inc.; 271 (UP), SSPL/Getty Images; 271 (LO), Wikipedia; 272 (UP), Wikipedia; 272 (LO), SPL/Photo Researchers, Inc.; 272-273, Wikipedia; 273, Library of Congress; 274 (LE), SPL/Photo Researchers, Inc.; 274 (RT), Péter Gudella/Shutterstock; 275 (UP), SPL/Photo Researchers, Inc.; 275 (LO), Burwell Photography/iStockphoto.com; 275 (LO), SSPL/Getty Images; 276-277, Shutterstock; 278 (RT), Wikipedia; 278 (LO), Wikipedia; 278 (LE), Wikipedia; 279 (LE), SPL/Photo Researchers, Inc.; 279 (RT), Wikipedia; 280 (LE), Okea/iStockphoto.com; 280 (RT), SPL/Photo Researchers, Inc.; 281 (UP), G. H. Steele/Alamy; 281 (LO), Reinhold Foeger/Shutterstock; 282 (UP), Christopher Furlong/Getty Images; 282 (LO), Wikipedia; 283 (LE), Sheila Terry/Photo Researchers, Inc.; 283 (RT), Hulton Archive/Getty Images; 284 (LE), SPL/Photo Researchers, Inc.; 284 (RT), Wikipedia; 284-285, Ed Darack/Science Faction/CORBIS; 285 (UP), Wikipedia; 285 (LO), Omikron/Photo Researchers, Inc.; 286 (LE), SSPL/Getty Images; 286 (RT), Mark Sykes/Photo Researchers, Inc.; 287 (LE), Wikipedia; 287 (RT), Alex Staroseltsev/Shutterstock; 288-289, Stephen Morrell; 290 (LE), Wikipedia; 290-291, Gianni Dagli Orti/CORBIS; 291 (UP), SPL/Photo Researchers, Inc.; 291 (LO), James Steidl/Shutterstock; 292 (LE), Wellcome Library, London; 292 (RT), Henry Guttmann/Hulton Archive/Getty Images; 293 (UP), Wikipedia; 293 (LO), dtimiraos/iStockphoto.com; 294 (LE), Sergey Goruppa/Shutterstock; 294-295, Sheila Terry/Photo Researchers, Inc.; 294 (LO), Stephen Dorey ABIPP/Alamy; 295, U.S. Library of Congress/Photo Researchers, Inc.; 296 (LE), AP Images; 296 (RT), Gewitterkind/iStockphoto.com; 297 (UP), imagestalk/Shutterstock; 297 (LO), SPL/Photo Researchers, Inc.; 298 (LE), The Art Archive/Archaeological Museum Baghdad/Gianni Dagli Orti; 298-299, The Art Archive/Egyptian Museum Turin/Gianni Dagli Orti; 299, ZargonDesign/iStockphoto.com; 300-301, Stephen Frink/CORBIS, SeaWiFS/NASA.

The Big Idea

Published by the National Geographic Society

John M. Fahey, Jr., *Chairman of the Board and Chief Executive Officer*
Timothy T. Kelly, *President*
Declan Moore, *Executive Vice President; President, Publishing*
Melina Gerosa Bellows, *Executive Vice President; Chief Creative Officer, Books, Kids, and Family*

Prepared by the Book Division

Barbara Brownell Grogan, *Vice President and Editor in Chief*
Jonathan Halling, *Design Director, Books and Children's Publishing*
Marianne R. Koszorus, *Design Director, Books*
Susan Tyler Hitchcock, *Senior Editor*
Carl Mehler, *Director of Maps*
R. Gary Colbert, *Production Director*
Jennifer A. Thornton, *Managing Editor*
Meredith C. Wilcox, *Administrative Director, Illustrations*

Staff for This Book

Bridget A. English, *Editor*
Barbara Payne, *Text Editor*
Neal Ashby, *Art Director*
Miriam Stein, *Illustrations Editor*
Patrick Donahue, *Designer*
Judith Klein, *Production Editor*
Lisa A. Walker, *Production Manager*
Robert Waymouth, *Illustrations Specialist*
Jodie Morris, *Design Assistant*

Developed by Print Matters Inc. (www.printmattersinc.com)

Manufacturing and Quality Management

Christopher A. Liedel, *Chief Financial Officer*
Phillip L. Schlosser, *Senior Vice President*
Chris Brown, *Technical Director*
Nicole Elliott, *Manager*
Rachel Faulise, *Manager*
Robert L. Barr, *Manager*

The National Geographic Society is one of the world's largest nonprofit scientific and educational organizations. Founded in 1888 to "increase and diffuse geographic knowledge," the Society works to inspire people to care about the planet. National Geographic reflects the world through its magazines, television programs, films, music and radio, books, DVDs, maps, exhibitions, live events, school publishing programs, interactive media and merchandise. *National Geographic* magazine, the Society's official journal, published in English and 33 local-language editions, is read by more than 40 million people each month. The National Geographic Channel reaches 370 million households in 34 languages in 168 countries. National Geographic Digital Media receives more than 15 million visitors a month. National Geographic has funded more than 9,600 scientific research, conservation and exploration projects and supports an education program promoting geography literacy. For more information, visit www.nationalgeographic.com.

For more information, please call 1-800-NGS LINE (647-5463) or write to the following address:

National Geographic Society
1145 17th Street N.W.
Washington, D.C. 20036-4688 U.S.A.

For information about special discounts for bulk purchases, please contact National Geographic Books Special Sales: ngspecsales@ngs.org

For rights or permissions inquiries, please contact National Geographic Books Subsidiary Rights: ngbookrights@ngs.org

This 2014 edition printed for Barnes & Noble, Inc. by the National Geographic Society.

ISBN: 978-1-4262-0810-2
ISBN: 978-1-4351-5406-3 (B&N ed.)

Printed in Hong Kong

14/THK/2